World Languag Critical Pedagogy

Accessible and cutting-edge, this text is a pivotal update to the field and offers a much-needed critical perspective on world language education. Building off their classic 2002 book, *The Foreign Language Educator in Society*, Timothy G. Reagan and Terry A. Osborn address major issues facing the world language educator today, including language myths, advocacy, the perceived and real benefits of language learning, linguistic human rights, constructivism, learning theories, language standards, monolingualism, bilingualism and multiculturalism.

Organized into three parts – "Knowing Language," "Learning Language," and "Teaching Language" – this book applies a critical take on conventional wisdom on language education, and evaluates social and political realities, assumptions, and controversies in the field. Each chapter includes questions for reflection and discussion to support students and educators in developing their own perspectives on teaching and learning languages. With a critical pedagogy and social justice lens, this book is ideal for scholars and students in foreign/world language education, social justice education, and language teaching methodology courses, as well as pre- and in-service teachers.

Timothy G. Reagan is Professor at the University of Maine and Research Fellow at the University of the Free State in Bloemfontein, South Africa.

Terry A. Osborn is Professor at the University of South Florida, USA.

World Language Education as Critical Pedagogy

The Promise of Social Justice

Timothy G. Reagan and
Terry A. Osborn

NEW YORK AND LONDON

First published 2021
by Routledge
52 Vanderbilt Avenue, New York, NY 10017

and by Routledge
2 Park Square, Milton Park, Abingdon, Oxon OX14 4RN

Routledge is an imprint of the Taylor & Francis Group, an informa business

Library of Congress Cataloging-in-Publication Data
Names: Reagan, Timothy G., author. | Osborn, Terry A., 1966- author.
Title: World language education as critical pedagogy : the promise of social justice / Timothy G. Reagan, Terry A. Osborn.
Description: New York : Routledge, 2020. | Includes bibliographical references and index. |
Identifiers: LCCN 2020014233 (print) | LCCN 2020014234 (ebook) | ISBN 9780367465216 (hardback) | ISBN 9780367465209 (paperback) | ISBN 9781003029267 (ebook)
Subjects: LCSH: Language and languages--Study and teaching--United States. | Language teachers--Training of--United States. | Social justice.
Classification: LCC P51 .R43 2020 (print) | LCC P51 (ebook) | DDC 418.0071--dc23
LC record available at https://lccn.loc.gov/2020014233
LC ebook record available at https://lccn.loc.gov/2020014234

ISBN: 978-0-367-46521-6 (hbk)
ISBN: 978-0-367-46520-9 (pbk)
ISBN: 978-1-003-02926-7 (ebk)

Typeset in Goudy
by Taylor & Francis Books

Contents

Illustrations

Figures

Tables

Author Biographies

Timothy G. Reagan is Professor of Applied Linguistics and Foreign Language Education in the School of Learning and Teaching in the College of Education and Human Development at the University of Maine. He also holds the post of Research Fellow in the Department of South African Sign Language and Deaf Studies in the Faculty of Humanities at the University of the Free State in Bloemfontein, South Africa. Previously, he served as the Dean of the College of Education and Human Development at the University of Maine, as the Founding Dean of the Graduate School of Education at Nazarbayev University in Nur-Sultan (Astana), Kazakhstan, as the Executive Dean of the Faculty of Humanities at the University of the Witwatersrand in Johannesburg, South Africa, as the Dean of the School of Education at Roger Williams University in Bristol, Rhode Island, as the Executive Associate Dean of the Neag School of Education and Chair of the Department of Educational Leadership at the University of Connecticut, and as Chair of the Department of Teacher Education and 'CSU Professor' at Central Connecticut State University in New Britain, Connecticut. His primary areas of research are applied and educational linguistics, foreign language education, sign language and Deaf culture, and language in educational policy.

Terry A. Osborn is Professor of Education at the University of South Florida. He served twice as Interim Chancellor and as Vice Chancellor of Academic and Student Affairs at the University of South Florida Sarasota-Manatee. Osborn taught German in public schools for six years and was previously Dean of the College of Education at University of South Florida Sarasota-Manatee. He was on the faculties of Fordham University, Queens College of City University of New York and the University of Connecticut. As Dean, he led in the formation of the Center for Partnerships for Arts-Integrated Teaching (PAInT), and led the Center to receive a legislatively mandated statewide mission He was a founding officer of the International Society for Language Studies and founding co-editor of *Critical Inquiry in Language Studies: An International Journal* currently published by Routledge. He is

Executive Director of the Florida Association of Colleges for Teacher Education and editor of several academic book series in education. He also served on the Professional Learning Committee of the American Council on the Teaching of Foreign Languages. Osborn's research has received a number of awards, including the American Educational Studies Association's Critic's Choice Award for his book, *Critical Reflection and the Foreign Language Classroom*, published by Bergin & Garvey in Henry Giroux's series, Critical Studies in Education and Culture. Osborn was awarded the Stephen Freeman Award by NECTFL for the best published article on foreign language teaching techniques.

List of Abbreviations

AAE	African American English
AATSP	American Associate of Teachers of Spanish and Portuguese
ACTFL	American Council on the Teaching of Foreign Languages
ALM	Audiolingual Method
ASL	American Sign Language
BCE	Before the Common Era (i.e., B.C.)
CARLA	Center for Applied Research on Language Acquisition
CE	Common Era (i.e., A.D.)
CIA	Central Intelligence Agency
CLS	Critical Language Scholarship Program
CLT	Communicative Language Teaching
FBI	Federal Bureau of Investigation
ILR	Interagency Language Roundtable
ISN	Idioma de Señas de Nicaragua (Nicaraguan Sign Language)
LCTLs	Less Commonly Taught Languages
LOTEs	Languages Other Than English
LSA	Linguistic Society of America
LTC	Language Training Center
LWC	Language of Wider Communication
MBA	Masters of Business Administration
NABE	National Association for Bilingual Education
NAD	National Association of the Deaf
NDEA	National Defense Education Act
NEA	National Education Association
NSA	National Security Agency
NSEP	National Security Education Program
SAE	Standard American English
SAP	Systeme, Anwendungen und Produkte in der Datenverarbeitung [Systems, Applications and Products in Data Processing]
SES	Socioeconomic Status
SIG	Special Interest Group

SIL	Summer Institute of Linguistics
STEM	Science, Technology, Engineering and Mathematics
TESOL	Teachers of English to Speakers of Other Languages
TPR	Total Physical Response
VOA	Voice of America

Acknowledgements

In writing *World Language Education as Critical Pedagogy: The Promise of Social Justice*, we have benefitted from the love and support of our families. We are also grateful to our many friends and colleagues at the University of Connecticut, Central Connecticut State University, Fordham University, Nazarbayev University (Nur-Sultan [Astana], Kazakhstan), Queens College of the City University of New York, the University of Florida, the University of the Free State (Bloemfontein, South Africa), the University of Maine, the University of South Florida, and the University of the Witwatersrand (Johannesburg, South Africa) for their critical insights and suggestions.

1 Introduction

World Language Educators *Still* Need Critical Pedagogy

Almost twenty years ago, in our book *The Foreign Language Educator in Society: Toward a Critical Pedagogy*, we wrote that:

> Critical reflection ... thus becomes prerequisite to the critical pedagogy that we are advocating here. Teachers who cannot reflect critically possess little hope of providing their students meaningful opportunities to reflect on the issues of language diversity and critical language awareness ... criticisms that critical pedagogy is not applicable to the real world of the classroom teacher, go far beyond a simple lack of understanding about critical pedagogy. Those who doubt the practicality of using critical pedagogy in teaching are also extremely likely to have an overly constrained understanding of the profession of teaching. Simply put, teaching is much more than the conveyance of material to be memorized and regurgitated. It is ... an art and science of engaging students intellectually and emotionally in their understanding of the world.
>
> (Reagan & Osborn, 2002, p. 84)

When we wrote these words, we did not know that the journey on which we had begun, and which we were encouraging others to undertake, would prove to be as difficult and challenging as it has been. At the same time, we did not have any sense of how successful world language educators across the United States, and indeed around the world, would be in devising and implementing creative, innovative and effective ways to incorporate critical pedagogy in world language education. There is a great deal for those committed to critical pedagogy in world language education to celebrate, and much for which we can be grateful. If the journey is well under way, though, it is not a journey with any end in sight, and many barriers remain – some of them much greater than any we expected or foresaw twenty years ago. The very concerns that first led many of us to critical pedagogy are still present, and while we have been successful in challenging many of these, others continue to dominate much of public education. We still need critical pedagogy, arguably more now than ever.

Language is at the core and heart of the human experience. It is not only what makes us unique among our fellow beings on our planet, but it is arguably the single most important tool that we use in creating and maintaining human societies and civilizations. It is the glue that holds virtually everything else that we value together. Without language, there could be only fairly rudimentary human relationships, little technology, and at best incredibly limited political, economic, social, religious and cultural systems. To be sure, one can imagine communication without language – a dog is certainly capable of conveying feelings, needs, desires, affections, and so on, and many species have evolved fairly complex systems for communicating both within their own species and between themselves and other species. Such communication, though, is far more limited and restricted in nature than is human language.

We have spent our lives studying, learning, teaching, and thinking about languages; the love of language runs deep in us both. As world language educators, we have not only an affection for the languages that we study and teach, but also a desire to share that affection with our students, colleagues and friends. We have found, however, that outside of a fairly small circle of bilingual and multilingual individuals we know in our own society, apathy (and even sometimes antipathy) are by far the more common responses among our fellow citizens toward foreign languages and foreign language study. A recent poll conducted by the Pew Research Center, for instance, found that 47% of white Republicans in the United States indicated that "it would bother them some or a lot to hear people speak a language other than English in a public place" (VOA News, 2019). It would be easy to minimize the importance of this finding by pointing out that this resistance to foreign languages was mitigated by age, education and ethnicity, and further, that while Democrats were far more open to hearing foreign languages spoken around them, it was still the case that some 18% of Democrats – that is, nearly one-fifth of Democrats – also found such situations to be uncomfortable. This hostility to the language use and choices of other people strikes us as remarkable – and as remarkably worrying, as well. It reflects not only the growing anti-immigrant sentiments in many parts of the U.S. population, but also the continuing failure of the public schools to teach English native speakers languages other than English.

There is another aspect of the resistance to languages other than English in the United States, and that is an ideological division first identified by Jeannie Haubert and Elizabeth Fussell. They argued that our society is characterized by two very different ideological groupings, which they label the "cosmopolitan" and the "parochial" (Haubert & Fussell, 2006). The fundamental difference between these two groups is that "parochials, are more likely to identify with the nation and take an ethnocentric stance on public issues … [while] cosmopolitans are more open to the virtues of other nations and to criticism of their own" (Bean, 1995, p. 32). Not surprisingly, cosmopolitans tend to be better educated, hold white-collar jobs, reject ethnocentrism and racism, hold liberal political views, and to some extent are likely to have lived in other countries (see Haubert & Fussell, 2006). As Emanuel Alvarado has noted:

> Individuals in America with a higher level of proficiency in a foreign language may hold more positive views toward immigrants because they are more familiar than individuals who only speak English about the socio-historical and socio-economic circumstances that drive people away from their home countries into the U.S. In essence, the more fluent individuals become in a language other than English, the more likely they are to acquire knowledge of foreign cultures and societies and perhaps also the more likely they are to conceptualize the entrance of immigrants to the U.S. as an opportunity rather than an economic or cultural threat.
>
> (Alvarado, 2009)

The overwhelming majority of native speakers of English in the U.S. have never learned another language; indeed, most have never even tried, and of those who studied a language in school, most have had unsuccessful experiences at doing so. Not only has the study of foreign languages not been a terribly successful or rewarding experience for many, but further, the lessons that seem to have been learned *about* language are problematic. Many, perhaps even most, people in our society have fundamental misconceptions about the nature of language, the attributes and characteristics of language, the social and cultural functions of languages, and the role of language in human society. All too often these misconceptions and misunderstandings are found not only among those whose language learning experiences have been unsuccessful, but also, ironically, among the smaller group of people who have met with some degree of success in language learning. As Humphrey Tonkin (personal communication) once observed, linguistic chauvinism is by no means necessarily counteracted by bilingualism or even by multilingualism. A further point that should be raised here, since our primary audience is an American one,[1] is that monolingualism is not, in fact, "normal," but is profoundly unusual. As John Edwards noted:

> To be bilingual or multilingual is not the aberration supposed by many (particularly, perhaps, by people in Europe and North America who speak a "big" language); it is, rather, a normal and unremarkable necessity for the majority in the world today. A monolingual perspective is often, unfortunately, a consequence of possession of a "language of wider communication," as English, French, German, Spanish and other such languages are sometimes styled. This linguistic myopia is sometimes accompanied by a narrow cultural awareness

> and is reinforced by state policies which, in the main, elevate only one language to official status.
>
> (Edwards, 1994, p. 1)

This book seeks to address the social context of language, language teaching and language learning in the United States. Its emphasis is on what pre- and in-service teachers of world languages in this country ought to know and understand about language, language attitudes, language practices, language rights, language policy, and so on. More to the point, however, we are committed to advocating not simply for the teaching and learning of foreign languages in our society, but also for critical perspectives and approaches in the teaching of such languages. We hope that *World Language Education as Critical Pedagogy: The Promise of Social Justice* will encourage world language educators to broaden their conception of our discipline, and to do so in ways that will make language study both more relevant for students and more critical with respect to its value in the development of the "educated person" in a democratic society.

A Word about Terminology

The use of the phrase *foreign language* to refer to any language other than English in the United States has a long and well-established history, but in recent years it has also come to be seen as not only dated, but also potentially misleading. By labeling a language like Spanish *foreign*, one suggests that it is alien to the United States. This is, of course, clearly untrue. Spanish has been spoken in North America longer than has English, and large numbers of individuals in the United States speak it as their native language. This latter point is true as well for French, German, Russian, Japanese, Chinese, and virtually any other language that is likely to be taught in a public school. It is also obviously true for American Sign Language (ASL), not to mention, in an even stronger sense, for Native American languages such as Navajo and Mohawk. By using the term "foreign," one can credibly argue that we are establishing a false bifurcation between "Us" and "Them," and further, that we are suggesting that languages other than English are not part of our society or history. Both of these points are valid ones.

The alternative terminology to "foreign language" that has gained widespread acceptance in the United States has been to speak of "world languages" and of "world language education." In dealing with the problem of what to call such languages, in Canada the choice has been to talk about "second languages" and "second language education," while in Australia the more common terminology is "Languages Other Than English" (or LOTEs). We welcome the recognition that such terminological debates suggest, and agree that speakers of the various languages that are commonly (and less commonly) taught in U.S. schools do indeed have local speaker communities; indeed, we have advocated connecting with those communities as a means of both increasing language awareness and making the target language more topical and relevant for students (see, e.g., Osborn, 2006).

When we wrote our book *The Foreign Language Educator in Society: Toward a Critical Pedagogy* (Reagan & Osborn, 2002), the phrase "foreign language" as the marker of the kinds of languages being taught had already become uncomfortable for some in the profession. Yet, by consciously choosing to continue to use the term "foreign language," we decided to make use of that discomfort to serve as a reminder of the work still before us as a field. In other words, we deliberately chose a term that, though widely accepted in the past, was on its way to becoming less so – and so it served, in the tradition of critical pedagogies, to disrupt that which had become comfortable to the field despite being demonstrably misleading at the least, and prejudicial at worst. Political correctness and word games with nomenclature changes could not solve the challenges before us, we believed. That hasn't changed.

We also believed then, and continue to believe, that the meaning of "foreign language" was that the language being learned was *foreign to the learner*. This way of talking about "foreign languages" and "foreign language education" works very well, of course, until one considers the case of English Language Learners (ELLs) learning English as a second language in the U.S. context. For such students, *English* is the "foreign language" being studied, and yet there is virtually no tradition of including this use of the term in our discourse. Indeed, this is a distinction that is made not only in our everyday language, but in terms of teacher preparation, professional organizations (e.g., ACTFL versus NABE versus TESOL), and a host of other ways. This particular differentiation simply reinforces the fundamental point that we are attempting to make here: there is an ideological component to the use of the phrase "foreign language," but the effect of that usage can be reversed if it is recognized and discussed as problematic. An additional problem with the use of the term "foreign" in this context is that it involves a clear identification of the target language of the classroom as "Other" (see National Standards Collaborative Board, 2015; Osborn, 1998). Recent efforts to change nomenclature, utilizing the term "world languages" in place of "foreign languages" have, we would agree, to some extent addressed such concerns, but only at the level of what might be termed "articulated bias." Regardless of what they are called, in U.S. schools languages other than English are *in fact* perceived, by both adults and students, as "foreign." As we have already noted, this perception is only strengthened by encouraging the use of what is often seen as merely a politically correct label such as "world languages." The risk with such word games (for such they are), as Michael Apple noted, is that "historically outmoded, and socially and politically conservative (and often educationally disastrous) practices are not only continued, but are made to sound as if they were actually more enlightened and ethically responsive ways of dealing with children" (Apple, 1979, p. 144). We accept Apple's point, but have also, after some twenty years, decided that this is a battle that is probably no longer worth fighting. To be sure, our earlier deliberate use of the term "foreign language" was a way of emphasizing rather than hiding the hidden agenda that goes with the concept of "*foreign-ness*" in American society, but in this book, we have decided for the most part to simply accept the common use of "world language education" to refer to our field and profession (though we have kept "foreign language" where it seems most appropriate).

What this Book Is *Not* about

Given the primary audience for which this book has been written – pre- and in-service world language educators – a few words here about what this book is *not* intended to provide or accomplish are probably appropriate. There are many issues that are often covered in both introductory and advanced courses in world language education, including topics such as classroom management, writing lesson plans,[2] different approaches to teaching world languages, designing classroom tests, the effective use of the Internet in world language education, the integration of culture into the world language classroom, and so on. All of these things are important – they are the focus of many existing works (see Brown, 2001; Curtain & Dahlberg, 2004; Horowitz, 2008; Lessow-Hurley, 2009; Omaggio Hadley, 1993; Richard-Amato, 1996; Shrum & Glisan, 2016), but they are not the primary focus of this book. Rather, we are concerned with what philosophers would call the *a priori* questions: that is, questions about the underlying assumptions that all of these matters entail. For example, classroom management is, without any doubt, a serious challenge for many teachers, and there is a great deal that can be learned, both theoretically and experientially, that will assist educators in managing their classrooms more effectively. Our questions would not focus on the "how" of classroom management, though, but rather on what the concept "classroom management" is all about, especially in the context of a critical pedagogical approach to teaching and learning. We would be interested in issues of power, control and domination as these are reflected in the standard discourse on classroom management. This certainly does not mean that we are opposed to well-organized classrooms, nor that we believe that the teacher has no obligation to maintain order in the classroom – just that the "how" questions are not sufficient for the critical and reflective world language educator. We emphasize this at the outset, because readers who expect a traditional world language teaching methods text will be disappointed with much of *World Language Education as Critical Pedagogy: The Promise of Social Justice*.

What this Book *Is* about

If *World Language Education as Critical Pedagogy: The Promise of Social Justice* is not intended to provide a general introduction to world language teaching methodology and related matters, what, then, is its goal? At its heart, this book is about assisting educators to develop critical perspectives on the teaching and learning of languages – critical perspectives that will, in turn, impact both the ways in which they teach world languages and the content that they use in doing so. Even more, though, it is intended to present pre- and in-service world language educators with a set of arguments about what it is, fundamentally, that we are and should be attempting to accomplish in the world language classroom. Our classrooms are certainly places in which students should begin the process of learning the target language and gaining some degree of familiarity with the cultures of the people who speak that language, but as is true with all subjects and content matter, we seek to achieve far more than this. We want our students to become critical and reflective learners, both about the specific subject matter that they are studying (in our case, the target language) and more generally.

The Organization of *World Language Education as Critical Pedagogy*

Apart from this introductory chapter and a concluding chapter, *World Language Education as Critical Pedagogy: The Promise of Social Justice* is divided into three parts, each organized around a central theme. Part I, concerned broadly with the idea of "Knowing Language," begins with a foundational chapter about the nature of human language, as well as a critique of many commonly held but erroneous myths about language (Chapter 2). Some programs designed to prepare world language educators include an introductory course in linguistics, while others (unfortunately, in our view) do not. For students who have had such a course, this chapter will most likely be largely a review of material to which they have already been exposed, while for others, the content may be new. Chapter 3 continues some of the themes raised in the last part of Chapter 2, focusing on the ideology of linguistic legitimacy – the idea that some languages are somehow better than or superior to other languages. This chapter also includes a discussion of linguicism, the kind of prejudice and discrimination about language that parallels racism, sexism, ableism, ageism, and so on. Finally, Chapter 3 includes three case studies to provide illustrations of both the ideology of linguistic legitimacy and linguicism: African American English, Spanglish and ASL.

Part II of *World Language Education as Critical Pedagogy: The Promise of Social Justice* is focused on issues related to "Learning Language." This unit begins with a chapter that seeks to offer a compelling response to the question, "Why study a foreign language?" (Chapter 4). To be sure, this is a question that requires no answer in most parts of the world, where language study – indeed, often the study of multiple languages other than one's own – is simply a given. In the United States, however – and in most other Anglophone countries as well – this is not the case. An important part of every world language educator's career in this country will involve advocacy, and so it is important for the teacher to be able to present clear, cogent and compelling arguments for why world language education is valuable, worthwhile and necessary. Chapter 5 then moves us to a discussion of the underlying epistemology of education, and of what it means to "know" a language. In addition, this chapter explores some of the more common traditional theories of learning as they relate to the learning of languages, and concludes with a detailed discussion of constructivist approaches to world language education.

Part III of *World Language Education as Critical Pedagogy: The Promise of Social Justice*, entitled "Teaching Language," is in many ways the core of the book. It is in this unit that aspects of critical pedagogy and social justice, critical reflective practice, critical teaching methods, national standards and the curriculum, critical pedagogy and the canon that exists in different target languages are all addressed. Part III begins with Chapter 6, which sets the stage for the unit asking us to move beyond the typical focus on methodology in world language teaching and learning. In this chapter, we explore the practical and ideological realities of world language education in contemporary U.S. society, and suggest that our efforts to teach American students foreign languages have been largely unsuccessful – not because of any problem with world language educators, but because of a combination of structural, cultural, and ideological limitations that go far beyond what the classroom world language educator can address.

Chapter 7, which deals with critical reflective practice, includes a discussion of the knowledge base that is required for effective world language teaching, and how this knowledge base is a key part of critical reflective practice as a component of both critical pedagogy and schooling in and for a democratic society. In Chapter 8, we turn our focus to critical pedagogy itself, which has become an increasingly common concern of teacher education programs across the country, and indeed, around the world. This chapter explicitly lays out the core themes, concepts, ideas and commitments associated with critical pedagogy. In so doing, we hope to bring together the embedded discussions of critical pedagogy in the other chapters of the book in a manner that will assist the reader to more fully grasp the need for critical pedagogical approaches to teaching and learning in general, and to the teaching and learning of world languages in particular.

Chapter 9 deals with the nature of the curriculum in world language education, and much of the chapter is given over to a discussion of different aspects of understanding the curriculum from a critical perspective. The complex and highly controversial issue of the literary canon, especially as it relates to content issues in world language education courses and curricula, is also addressed in this chapter. The so-called "Canon Debate" is one that is grounded in radically different perspectives on the nature of knowledge, knowledge construction, and the role of the values and perspectives of both those who have historically been expected to create "public knowledge" and the consumers of knowledge (see Banks, 1993; Kolbas, 2001; McCarthy & Crichlow, 1993; Rhoads, 1995). It is our hope that this section of the chapter will contribute to a discussion about correcting what we take to be a gap in the literature in world language education; although the canon debate has generated powerful discussions in a number of other content areas, including social studies and history education (see Richardson & Blades, 2006; Symcox & Wilschut, 2009), English education (see Applebee, 1992; Greenbaum, 1994; Nicol, 2008; Pike, 2003), music education (Kindall-Smith, McKoy & Mills, 2011), and art (Heise, 2004), it has received relatively little attention in world language education.

In Chapter 10, we turn to one of the most important revolutions in U.S. education in the last quarter of the 20th century: the emergence of the National Standards movement. In this chapter we explore the national standards for world language learning produced by ACTFL, beginning with the *Standards for Foreign Language Learning: Preparing for the 21st Century* (National Standards in Foreign Language Education Project, 1996), and culminating (at least for the present) in the *World-Readiness Standards for Learning Languages* (National Standards Collaborative Board, 2015). A key component of our discussion of the national standards will be a detailed discussion of the "Five C's" (Communication, Cultures, Connections, Comparisons, and Communities) around which the standards are based. Although we believe that the national standards in world language education are among the best that have been produced in any content area, we will nevertheless point out what we take to be some of the underlying (and problematic) assumptions that underlie these standards, and how they may well conflict with the goals of critical pedagogy. In this chapter, we will also examine some of the curricular aspects of critical pedagogy in world language education.

Finally, we conclude *World Language Education as Critical Pedagogy: The Promise of Social Justice* with an epilogue in which we review some of what we take to be the central lessons of the book, and in which we offer some suggestions for the next steps that need to be taken if world language education is to live up to its potential both in promoting critical pedagogy and helping us all to achieve social justice.

Questions for Reflection and Discussion

1 The authors claim that, in their experience, there is a good degree of apathy, and even antipathy, toward both bilingualism (and multilingualism) and speakers of other languages in certain contexts and

settings in U.S. society. Does this match your own experience? If it does not, how might the difference between your experience and that of others be explained?

2 Although they note that "world languages" is the phrase most commonly used today to describe languages such as French, German, Spanish, and so on, the authors appear to prefer the older label, "foreign languages." What is their argument for this preference? What label do you believe is most appropriate, and why?

3 John Edwards is quoted in this chapter suggesting that, "to be bilingual or multilingual is not the aberration supposed by many (particularly, perhaps ... in ... North America)." Why is North America, in particular, different from most other parts of the world with respect to how many people view bilingualism and multilingualism? What are the implications of this view for world language education?

4 The authors explain that *World Language Education as Critical Pedagogy: The Promise of Social Justice* does not, for the most part, address issues like classroom management, writing lesson plans, designing classroom tests, using the Internet in the world language classroom, the integration of culture into the world language classes, and so on, but rather, focuses on what they call *a priori* questions. What do you think that they mean by this? Does such a focus make sense to you? What does this tell you about the authors' concerns about teaching and learning in the world language classroom?

5 In the quotation at the beginning of this chapter, the authors write that, "Those who doubt the practicality of using critical pedagogy in teaching are also extremely likely to have an overly constrained understanding of the profession of teaching." What do you believe that they meant by this? Why do you think that they make this claim?

Notes

1 The term "American" is used here to refer to the United States. We recognize, of course, that this is extremely misleading, and certainly accept the fact that those in other parts of the Americas are every bit as "American" as those in the United States. However, this usage –though as inappropriate as we may believe it to be – is nonetheless the dominant one in the United States, and is widely used in this sense even in other non-U.S. American settings. Finally, the problem that one faces is the lack of a truly appropriate adjective for one from the United States.

2 The ability to create lesson plans is obviously extremely important for any teacher, regardless of her or his subject area. That said, we do not believe that there is any single format or model of lesson plans that would merit universal use. Different classrooms, different schools, different school districts, and so on, may require different kinds of lesson plans, and such plans may include or exclude various kinds of information. For the most part, this is not particularly problematic, although the design and implementation of a strong world language curriculum would make the inclusion of certain kinds of information and planning essential.

References

Alvarado, E. (2009). Attitudes toward immigrants and multiculturalism in contemporary America: The role of foreign language fluency. *Sociation Today*, 7(2). Downloaded from http://ncsociology.org/sociationtoday/v72/attitude.htm on November 11, 2019.

Apple, M. (1979). *Ideology and curriculum*. Boston, MA: Routledge & Kegan Paul.

Applebee, A. (1992). Stability and change in the high school canon. *The English Journal*, 81(5): 27–32.

Banks, J. (1993). The Canon debate, knowledge construction, and multicultural education. *Educational Researcher*, 22(5): 4–14.

Bean, C. (1995). Determinants of attitudes towards questions of border maintenance in Australia. *People and Places*, 3(3): 32–40.

Brown, H. D. (2001). *Teaching by principles: An interactive approach to language pedagogy* (2nd ed.). White Plains, NY: Longman.

Curtain, H. & Dahlberg, C. (2004). *Languages and children, making the match: New languages for young learners, grades K-8* (3rd ed.). Boston, MA: Pearson.

Edwards, J. (1994). *Multilingualism*. New York: Routledge.

Greenbaum, V. (1994). Expanding the canon: Shaping inclusive reading lists. *The English Journal*, 83(8): 36–39.

Haubert, J. & Fussell, E. (2006). Explaining pro-immigrant sentiment in the U.S.: Social class, cosmopolitanism, and perceptions of immigrants. *International Migration Review*, 40(3): 489–507.

Heise, D. (2004). Is visual culture becoming our canon of art? *Art Education*, 57(5): 41–46.

Horowitz, E. (2008). *Becoming a language teacher: A practical guide to second language learning and teaching*. Boston, MA: Pearson.

Kindall-Smith, M., McKoy, C & Mills, S. (2011). Challenging exclusionary paradigms in the traditional music canon: Implications for music education practice. *International Journal of Music Education*, 29(4): 374–386.

Kolbas, E. (2001). *Critical theory and the literary canon*. New York: Routledge.

Lessow-Hurley, J. (2009). *The foundations of dual language instruction* (5th ed.). Boston, MA: Pearson.

McCarthy, C. & Crichlow, W. (Eds.). (1993). *Race, identity, and representation in education*. New York: Routledge.

National Standards Collaborative Board. (2015). *World-readiness standards for learning languages* (4th ed.). Alexandria, VA: Author.

National Standards in Foreign Language Education Project. (1996). *Standards for foreign language learning: Preparing for the 21st century*. Lawrence, KS: Allen Press.

Nicol, J. (2008). Questioning the canon: Issues surrounding the selection of literature for the high school English curriculum. *English Quarterly*, 38(2–3):22–28.

Omaggio Hadley, A. (1993). *Teaching language in context* (2nd ed.). Boston, MA: Heinle & Heinle.

Osborn, T. A. (1998). The concept of "foreignness" in U.S. secondary language curricula: A critical philosophical analysis. Unpublished Ph.D. dissertation, University of Connecticut, Storrs, Connecticut.

Osborn, T. A. (2006). *Teaching world languages for social justice: A sourcebook of principles and practices*. Mahwah, NJ: Lawrence Erlbaum Associates.

Pike, M. (2003). The canon in the classroom: Students' experiences of texts from other times. *Journal of Curriculum Studies*, 35(3): 355–370.

Reagan, T. & Osborn, T. A. (2002). *The foreign language educator in society: Toward a critical pedagogy*. Mahwah, NJ: Lawrence Erlbaum Associates.

Rhoads, R. (1995). Critical multiculturalism, border knowledge, and the canon: Implications for general education and the academy. *The Journal of General Education*, 44(4): 256–273.

Richard-Amato, P. (1996). *Making it happen: Interaction in the second language classroom, from theory to practice* (2nd ed.). White Plains, NY: Longman.

Richardson, G. & Blades, D. (Eds.). (2006). *Troubling the canon of citizenship education*. New York: Peter Lang.

Shrum, J. & Glisan, E. (2016). *Teacher's handbook: Contextualized language instruction* (5th ed.). Boston, MA: Cengage Learning.

Symcox, L. & Wilschut, A. (Eds.). (2009). *National history standards: The problem of the canon and the future of teaching history*. Charlotte, NC: Information Age Publishing.

VOA News. (2019). U.S. survey: Many white Republicans wary around foreign languages. *VOA News* (May 8). Downloaded from www.voanews.com/usa/us-survey-many-white-republicans-wary-around-foreign-languages on January 15, 2020.

Part I

Knowing Language

2 Language and Language Mythology
What We Need to Learn and Unlearn

The linguist Ronald Wardhaugh, writing about the average person's knowledge about language, once observed:

> Language plays an important role in the lives of all of us and is our most distinctive human possession. We might expect, therefore, to be well-informed about it. The truth is we are not. Many statements we believe to be true about language are likely as not false. Many of the questions we concern ourselves with are either unanswerable and therefore not really worth asking or betray a serious misunderstanding of the nature of language. Most of us have learned many things about language from others, but generally the wrong things.
>
> (Wardhaugh, 1999, p. viii)

We believe that he was correct in this observation, but that the situation, especially for critical world language educators, is perhaps even worse than he suggests. In spite of all of the linguistics textbooks that have been and continue to be published, and regardless of the many courses that students take which are devoted to linguistics, the amount of misinformation that continues to characterize both the lay public and a substantial part of the world language education community is hard to minimize. If language were unimportant, if it had few implications for the teaching and learning experience, and if the results of this misinformation did not have any significant impact on children's lives, then perhaps this might not matter quite so much. However, language is incredibly important – it is, indeed, at the core of our being human. As Neil Smith has written:

> Language makes us human … Whatever we do, language is central to our lives, and the use of language underpins the study of every other discipline. Understanding language gives us insight into ourselves and a tool for the investigation of the rest of the universe. Proposing marriage, opposing globalization, composing a speech, all require the use of language; to buy a meal or sell a car involves communication, which is made possible by language; to be without language – as an

> infant, a foreigner or a stroke victim – is to be at a devastating disadvantage. Martians and dolphins, bonobos and bees, may be just as intelligent, cute, adept at social organization and morally worthwhile, but they don't share our language, they don't speak "human."
>
> (Smith, 2002, p. 3)

Language is also at the heart of the teaching and learning experience, not just in the world language classroom but in *every* classroom, since it is the medium through which both teaching and learning take place. Finally, language, coupled with beliefs about and attitudes toward language, have immense consequences not just for student learning, but for the very identity of each student. In short, language *matters*, and it matters a great deal – and what we *believe* to be true about language matters as well. This is true regardless of whether what we believe is true or false, but when what we believe is false, a great deal of lasting harm can be done to children, communities, and to society as a whole.

The purpose of this chapter is two-fold: first, we will examine what language actually is, focusing on the characteristics that are shared by all human languages. Second, we will explore a number of the myths we have faced over the course of our careers that, although very common, are simply not true. In both cases – elements that we take to be true of all languages, and frequent myths about languages – it is not our intention to offer a comprehensive or complete list. Indeed, in both cases there is good reason to believe that such a comprehensive list would be virtually impossible to formulate. Nevertheless, we do believe that in this chapter we can cover the core issues related to the nature and characteristics of language, and many of the more common myths and false beliefs about language, that are found both in general in our society and, even more importantly, in schools.

The Nature and Characteristics of Language

Language, at least as we understand the concept today, has probably been used by human beings for somewhere around 100,000 to 150,000 years, although there is considerable debate about both when and where it first emerged (see Barnard, 2016; Dunbar, Gamble & Gowlett, 2014). Although something like a proto-language was perhaps employed by our closest evolutionary relative *Homo (sapiens) neanderthalis*, what we think of as human language is probably unique to modern *Homo sapiens sapiens* (Dunbar et al., 2014). Among contemporary linguists, there are broadly speaking two different sets of views about the origins of human language: the majority advocate a continuity position (see Fout & Waters, 2001; Gibson, 1994; Hurford, Studdert-Kennedy & Knight, 1998; Pinker, 1997). Basically, this means that the emergence of language was the result of the evolution of pre- and proto-linguistic forms which over time became increasingly complex and which ultimately took the form of human language as it now exists. The alternative perspective, advocated by Noam Chomsky and some others, is that language is so unique that it cannot be explained by any kind of gradual evolution from earlier types of communicative behavior, and so must be the result of a relatively sudden – genetic and cognitive – change (see Hurford, Studdert-Kennedy & Knight, 1998; Lieberman, 1991). Thus, this position argues, the emergence of language must have been the result of an evolutionary discontinuity.

It appears most likely that language first emerged in East Africa, before human beings migrated out of Africa (Botha & Knight, 2009; Klein, 2008). Not only are we unsure of precisely when and where it emerged, though, we also do not know (and will almost certainly never know) whether what we think of as language began once (suggesting that all human languages must have, at some distant point in the past, a common ancestral language) or multiple times (Renfrew, 1991). In fact, the lack of empirical evidence makes the resolution of these questions virtually impossible – after a period of intense debate about the matter, inspired in part by the emergence of Darwinian theory, in 1866 the Société de Linguistique de Paris actually banned any future discussions of the matter. While this ban is no longer universally accepted, it is clear that what we are able to determine about the origins of human language is extremely limited.[1]

When we speak of "language," we are not concerned with any specific or particular language (such as Chinese, English, French, German, Navajo, Russian, Zulu, or whatever), but rather, with human language in general. In other words, what we are actually interested in are the characteristics that are common to *all* human languages. We might suggest, for instance, that "all languages have nouns and verbs" (Hudson, 2000, p. 74), which is a general claim about human language as a singular, unitary construct. On the other hand, we can make observations about features and characteristics of a specific language, as is done in the following passage about a particular feature of Russian:

> In Russian, где is used to inquire about location and куда is used to inquire about destination … Verbs such as жить – *to live*, работать – *to work*, and учиться – *to study, to be a student* refer to location and require the use of где – *where*. Verbs like ходить / идти – *to go*, ездить / ехать – *to go (by vehicle)*, and опаздывать – *to be late* refer to destination and require the use of куда.
>
> (Robin, Evans-Romaine, Shatalina & Robin, 2007, p. 162)

Both of these types of claims are potentially useful, but they require very different kinds of evidence to determine whether or not the claim being made is true. Claims that purport to be *universal* are particularly difficult to defend, since to reject such a claim requires evidence only from a single language – that is, if a claim is true universally, then it must be true of each and every human language, without exception. The claim that "all languages have nouns and verbs," for instance, might be true *as far as we know at the present time*, but to disprove it, all we would need to do is find a single language (out of the 6,500 to 7,000 languages that currently exist in the world) that somehow makes due without anything remotely noun-like or verb-like. In fact, there are many languages in which the noun-verb distinction is, at the very least, quite different from the way in which we normally conceive of it. For instance, in Yup'ik we find *kaipiallrullniuk*, which roughly translates as, "The two of them were apparently really hungry" (Mithun, 1999, p. 38; see also Jacobson, 1995). For a speaker of English (or French, German, Russian or Spanish, for that matter), this is an entire sentence, and to ask what part of speech it constitutes is basically impossible to answer. A similar challenge is presented in the Bantu languages of Africa, as Patrick Bennett has noted,

> There has been debate as to the proper arrangement of the Bantu lexicon, and the question is far from settled. The inflection of nominal and verbals by means of prefixes, and the complex and productive derivational system, both characteristic of Bantu languages, pose difficulties ... If items are alphabetized by prefix ... a verb will be listed far from its nominal derivations, however transparent these may be ... A competing school arranges the lexicon by stem or root; this usefully groups related items, and saves on cross-referencing. Unfortunately, in such a system the user must be able to identify the stem, which given the sometimes complex morphophonemics of Bantu languages may not be easy.
>
> (Bennett, 1986, pp. 3–4)

Although it is extremely difficult to identify specific universal characteristics common to all human languages, there are nevertheless a number of broad principles which do seem to be universal. These principles are not concerned with particular linguistic features, though, as they are with the ways in which human languages – *all* human languages – differ from all of the other kinds of communication with which we are familiar. Some of these principles, taken on their own, may be found in other kinds of communicative behavior – honeybees communicate, dogs and cats communicate, and so on – but taken together, these principles are unique (at least as far as we know) to human language.

Language is Creative

Unlike other kinds of communication, human beings are able to use language to convey ideas, concepts, thoughts, and so on that have never before been communicated (see Azevedo, 1992, pp. 5–6; Fromkin, Rodman & Hyams, 2017, pp. 5–6; Hudson, 2000, p. 10). When we use language, we are not simply putting together elements of the language in ways that we have already heard modelled. Each of us produces and understands sentences that are novel, and which have never been said or understood before. One example of this was provided by the comedian George Carlin, who as part of a stand-up routine demonstrated this point by using the phrase, "Hand me that piano." To be sure, one can imagine two children playing with a dollhouse, for instance, with miniature pieces of furniture in which one child asks the other to hand him the miniature piano – but Carlin's basic point is well taken. Similarly, when Terry was driving home from McDonald's with his two young children in the backseat of the car, there was a disagreement about a toy figure that one of the children had gotten as part of his lunch. Trying to resolve the issue, Terry's wife said to their son, "Joshua, give your sister that alien right now!" This is a perfectly well-formed, proper and correct English sentence, and it is one that made sense in the context in which it was used. It was also understood by the child to whom it was directed. It seems unlikely, though, that that particular sentence had ever before, at any point in the entire history of the English language, been uttered. This is a very different matter from what a dog or cat can communicate – it can indicate hunger, thirst, fear, anger, a desire to go on a walk, and so on, but nothing remotely like the comments about either pianos or aliens.

Language is Arbitrary

Languages are composed of lexical items, although as we have already mentioned what sometimes counts as a lexical item (as well as what part of speech a particular lexical item might be considered to be) can be difficult to define (see Azevedo, 1992, p. 6; Fasold & Connor-Linton, 2014, pp. 5–7; Fromkin, Rodman & Hyams, 2017, pp. 3–5; Hudson, 2000, p. 9; Trask, 1999, pp. 12–14; Yule, 2017, pp. 14–15). What is clear, though, is that there is no natural, inherent or logical relationship between the words of a language and the meanings of those words. Although there are a tiny number of words that may be considered to be onomatopoeic – that is, words whose phonology or sound in some way resembles or copies the thing or idea that they represent – for the vast majority of words, there is no relationship at all between a word and the thing that it represents.[2] The word used for a concept in any particular language is simply arbitrary: the words *table* and *chair* are no more correct, obvious or "right" than the comparable words стол and стул in Russian, *mesa* and *silla* in Spanish, *tafel* and *stoel* in Afrikaans, or *ithebula* and *isihlalo* in Zulu.

Language is Symbolic, Abstract and Conventional

Words in a language are not only arbitrary, but they are also symbolic and abstract – that is, they are symbols of meaning (see Azevedo, 1992, p.

6; Hudson, 2000, pp. 5–7). This means that there must be a conventional acceptance of the meaning of each word by the speakers of the language. Without this general acceptance of meaning, speakers of a language would be unable to understand one another, and could not be said to share a language at all. It is the symbolic nature of human language that makes mutual intelligibility possible. Thus, not only is human language both arbitrary and symbolic, it is also conventional – by which we mean that the elements of a particular language are, in essence, agreed to and shared by its speaker community. Lexical items in a language mean only what speakers of the language generally agree that they mean. Individuals cannot, for the most part, simply decide to use words with meanings that are not recognized or accepted by other speakers of their language. This was the point that Lewis Carroll made in *Through the Looking Glass*, when Alice and Humpty Dumpty engage in the following conversation:

> "There's glory for you."
>
> "I don't know what you mean by 'glory'," Alice said.
>
> Humpty Dumpty smiled contemptuously. "Of course you don't – till I tell you. I meant 'There's a nice knock-down argument for you!'"
>
> "But 'glory' doesn't mean 'a nice knock-down argument'," Alice objected.
>
> "When I use a word," Humpty Dumpty said, in a rather scornful tone, "it means just what I choose it to mean – neither more nor less."
>
> "The question is," said Alice, "whether you can make words mean so many different things."
>
> (Carroll, 1992, p. 163)

Alice is of course quite correct here – although a speech community can determine the meaning of a particular lexical item, no individual in the speech community can simply use words with whatever meaning she or he wishes and still expect to be understood. Words, in short, simply do not mean whatever we wish them to mean. Furthermore, all languages have the ability to create and introduce new symbols (i.e., words) to meet new social, cultural and technological needs. When new words are first introduced in a language, they are called *neologisms*. Examples of some neologisms that have entered the English language in recent years include *laser* (from "light amplification by stimulated emission of radiation"), *PC* (for both "personal computer" and "political correctness"), *to google* (to use an online search engine), and so on. Neologisms are especially common during periods of significant change; in the case of Russian, the fall of the Tsarist regime in 1917 led to the introduction of a whole host of new terms that were needed to accommodate the changed ideological and political system; new terms included **комиссар**, *commissar*, **контрреволюционный**, *counter-revolutionary*, **мандат**, *mandate*, and **пролетариат**, *proletariat* (see Reagan, 2016; Smith, 1998). With the collapse of the

Soviet Union in 1991, a similar phenomenon took place, and a substantial number of new words were either created or borrowed from other languages: гуглить, *to google*, ток-шоу, *talk show*, плей-лист, *playlist*, and, of course, Биг-мак, *Big Mac* (see Reagan, 2016; Ryazanova-Clark & Wade, 1999). The same process takes place in all languages as speakers need new terminology to express new concepts and needs.

Language is Based on Duality of Patterning

One of the interesting features of human languages is that they demonstrate what linguists call "duality of patterning" (see Hudson, 2000, pp. 10–11; Trask, 1999, pp. 2–5; Yule, 2017, p. 17). Basically, what duality of patterning means is that from a finite number of phonemes (i.e., the smallest units of sound used in a language), it is possible to produce an infinite number of meaningful elements (words or morphemes). Although it is not completely clear how many phonemes a human being can produce that could be used in a language, the International Phonetic Alphabet (IPA) includes over 160 symbols that can be used to represent phonemes, and the IPA is used by linguists to describe the phonology of virtually every language. Of course, no single language uses all of these phonemes – each language uses a subset of the total of possible phonemes that a human being could produce. The range of number of phonemes used in different languages is considerable – a few languages (such as Rotakas, spoken in New Guinea) use as few as 11 or 12 phonemes (see Robinson, 2006), while !Xu, a Khoisan language spoken in Southern Africa, uses a total of around 140 phonemes (though there is some disagreement about the exact number) (see Heikkinen, 1986; Snyman, 1973). With respect to languages that are more familiar to most of us, depending on the particular variety of the language one is talking about, English has around 40 phonemes, Arabic has 34, French has 39, Russian has 40, Spanish has 25, and so on.[3] In each of these cases, however, an unlimited number of lexical and morphological forms can be formed from the finite set of phonemes. This duality of patterning is thus one of the senses in which human languages can be said to be infinite.

Language is Systematic

Although language is arbitrary, it is also systematic – systematic with respect to its phonology, its morphology, and its syntax (see Azevedo, 1992, pp. 7–10). In other words, human language is based on a complex set of rules that govern its operation. For example, the phonological rules of English allow us to combine the phonemes /s/, /p/ and /r/ to form a consonant cluster, as in such words as "spring," "spread" and "spray." At the same time, the phonological rules of English would prevent us from combining the phonemes /f/, /l/ and /b/. This is a phonological rule *in English*, however – another language could have a very different set of phonological rules that might very well allow these phonemes to be put together. Morphological rules in English would include rules for indicating singular and plural nouns, for instance. Syntactically, word order would provide an example of different rules in different languages; inflections commonly provide syntactic information in many languages, such as Latin and Russian, allow a fairly high degree of flexibility in word order, because they are highly inflected. Thus, in Latin one can translate the English sentence "The boy loves the girl" as:

Puer amat puellam.
Puellam puer amat.
Amat puer puellam.
Amat puellam puer.
Puer puellam amat.

In this sentence, *puer* can *only* function as the subject of the sentence, and *puellam* can *only* be the object of the verb *amat.* In English, though, any word order except "The boy loves the girl" – "Boy the girl loves," "Girl boy loves the," and so on, would simply not make sense. It is important to note here that when we talk about rules, we are referring to the rules employed by native speakers of a language in using the language – not to prescriptive or artificial rules that native speakers frequently violate (e.g., "do not split an infinitive" or "do not end a sentence with a preposition").

Language is Innate for Human Beings

When we say that language is innate for human beings, it is important to understand that we do not mean that any *particular* language is innate for any particular person. There is no genetic tie between the language of any group of human beings and the offspring of that group – rather, children acquire whatever language or languages they are exposed to. A child of German-speaking parents raised in a Chinese-speaking community will grow up speaking Chinese as her or his native language, and the child's language use will be indistinguishable from that of any other native speaker of Chinese.[4] We see this every day in the United States – almost all of us had parents, grandparents or great-grandparents who spoke a language other than English, but most of us are native speakers of American English, and further, we have no ability to speak the language of our ancestors unless that language was deliberately passed on to us, or we studied it in some formal setting.

If we do not mean that knowledge or acquisition of a *particular* language is innate, then what do we mean? Basically, what this means is that not only do all human beings possess the ability to acquire a human language, but that virtually all human beings *will* do so – indeed, it is only in the most extreme cases that a child does not acquire a human language (see Fromkin, Rodman & Hyams, 2017, p. 14; Hudson, 2000, pp. 120–146; Yule, 2017, p. 7). It would perhaps be more accurate to say that it is necessary to take deliberate and abusive steps to *prevent* a child from acquiring a language.[5] Having said this, there can be variation in the developmental stages of first language acquisition, and sometimes there are barriers (such as profound or severe deafness) which can result in delayed language acquisition – but these are exceptional situations and do not change the basic point that virtually all children can and will acquire a human language.[6]

Language is Universal

The claim that language is universal is related to the claim that a central characteristic of language is that it is innate for human beings. Just as almost every child will acquire the language or languages to which she or he is exposed in childhood, so too does every human community have a language. No matter how remote, how cut off from other human societies, how "primitive" a community might be,[7] no human society has been discovered that does not have a full and complete language – and often a language of considerable complexity. Even in rare cases where the development of a language faces incredible odds, a language will develop. Recently, for instance, there has been considerable research on the emergence of Nicaraguan Sign Language (*Idioma de Señas de Nicaragua*, or ISN) (see Senghas, 1995a, 1995b, 2003; Senghas & Coppola, 2001; Senghas, Kita & Özyürek, 2004; Senghas, Newport & Supalla, 1997). ISN developed largely among deaf children in several schools for the deaf in western Nicaragua in the 1970s and 1980s, although there is some evidence of limited exposure to sign language (and to ASL in particular) as early as the 1940s (see Polich, 2005). Prior to 1977, though, there was not a Nicaraguan Sign Language at least in a strong and robust sense because deaf people in general had very little contact with one another.[8] It was only with the establishment of a school in Managua that deaf children – independently of their teachers – developed ISN. The first children appear to have developed a pidgin-like kind of sign language, which was quickly made more complex by younger children.

Language is Recursive

Another way in which human languages are infinite is that they are recursive in nature (Fasold & Connor-Linton, 2014, pp. 4–5; Hudson, 2000, p. 10). Recursion refers in part to the creative nature of language. In theory, just as there is no limitation to the number of sentences that can be produced in any language, there is also no limit to the length of any given sentence. Consider the sentence, "John saw Mary." This is a fairly simple and straightforward sentence, but we can make it longer by adding other information, such as "Paul said that John saw Mary." This can then be extended to "I believe that Paul said that John saw Mary," and so on. The only limit to the length of a sentence is the amount of information that an individual can remember or keep track of – but as far as the nature of language is concerned, we can keep adding on words and phrases quite literally forever. Recursion is not, incidentally, unique to language – it also exists in mathematics, computer science, and a number of other fields. In mathematics, for instance, a very well-known example of recursion is the "Fibonacci sequence."[9]

Language is Social

The fact that language is conventional leads us to another fundamental characteristic of human language, which is that by its very nature language is *social* (Azevedo, 1992, pp. 3–4; Everett, 2013, pp. 13–30). Languages are used by *groups* of people; they exist in human societies. It is only in the context of a human society that a language can be acquired or learned. In order to fully understand the nature and functions of human language, it is necessary to understand the interaction of language with societies and social groups. Indeed, one very interesting question is when a language should actually be considered to be extinct. So long as a language has at least two speakers, those two speakers are able to use it to communicate – but when one of the two dies, then in what sense is the language still a living language? To be sure, we typically talk about a language being extinct after its last speaker dies, but there is a powerful sense in which it is already extinct when the *next to last* speaker dies.

Language Can Be Used in an Unlimited Number of Domains

Human beings communicate with one another in a variety of different settings or domains. We use language when we are engaged in hunting, in agriculture, in cooking, in buying and selling, in discussions topics of mutual interest and concern, in courting and marriage, in childrearing, in passing on traditional knowledge of different sorts, in religious ceremonies, in travel and transportation, in military actions, in scientific and scholarly activities, and even in space exploration. In fact, in any domain in which we require communication, we are able to use language – although sometimes we need to create new lexical items to do so effectively and efficiently.

Language is Stimulus-Free

One of the key ways in which human language differs from other kinds of animal communication is that it is "stimulus-free" rather than "stimulus-bound" in nature (Trask, 1999, pp. 10–11). Basically, what this means is that language is independent of context – that is, we can use language to communicate about anything in any context. As R. L. Trask has explained this characteristic of human language,

> Non-human signals are not stimulus-free, but rather *stimulus-bound*. That is, a non-human creature produces a particular signal always and only when the appropriate stimulus is present. If Fred the monkey is up a tree, and he sees a dangerous eagle approaching, he automatically produces the cry that means, "Look out – eagle!," and he never does this at any other time. He doesn't, on spotting the eagle, think to himself, "Maybe if I keep quiet the eagle will grab old Charlie down there, and I'll be safe." Nor does a bored Fred suddenly come out with an eagle warning and then guffaw, "Haw, haw, Charlie – gotcha this time!"
>
> (Trask, 1999, p. 11, emphasis in original)

Not only does the fact that language is stimulus free allow us to communicate with others about things that are not present, but it also allows us to communicate about abstract ideas and concepts – things like "democracy," "science," "justice," and even "language"!

Language is Dynamic

Languages are dynamic. In other words, every human language is constantly in a state of change, and this change involves all aspects of the language: the phonology, the morphology and lexicon, and the syntax (see Azevedo, 1992, pp. 16–17, 283–324; Hudson, 2000, pp. 392–405; Labov, 1994, 2001, 2010). The codification of a language – in written languages – can slow this process down to some extent, but change in language is inevitable. As Joan Bybee has suggested:

> Language change is endlessly fascinating, whether it involves change in sounds, morphology, words, syntax, or meaning. When language changes we see that language users are not just passive recipients of the language of their culture, but are active participants in the very dynamic system that is communication with spoken language. Change reveals the nature of the cognitive processes and patterns used in speaking and listening, and shows us what ordinary language users can make out of the material they are given to work with. In fact, I believe that no approach to language is complete unless it deals as much with language change as with language states.
>
> (Bybee, 2015, p. xv)

We have already noted that languages – all human languages – engage in the creation of new lexical items to meet new needs of their speakers, but we also find that the meanings and forms of particular words in a language are subject to change over time.

Change in the lexicon is certainly one important aspect of language dynamism and language change, but it is far from the only one. The morphosyntactic features of a language gradually evolve time as well – in Old French, spoken between the 9th and 14th centuries CE, for example, *ne* functioned as the mandatory negative marker. In Modern French, most of the time *ne … pas* is required, and in some instances the *ne* can be eliminated completely as long as the *pas* is present (Bybee, 2015, p. 4). But language change can go far beyond such specific changes – or, more accurately, can accumulate in ways that produce what is basically a different language.

The English that we speak today is the result of a long series of historical, social and cultural events. In fact, in studying the history of the English language, we typically distinguish among Old English (also called Anglo-Saxon), Middle English, Early Modern English (the language of Shakespeare), and Late Modern English (see Barber, 1993; Baugh & Cable, 2002; Freeborn, 1998). As the language evolved over time from Old English to Late Modern English, huge changes took place in virtually every part of it – so much so that a speaker of Late Modern English finds a text in Old English almost incomprehensible without specialized study. One of the greatest works of Old English literature is the epic poem *Beowulf*, which was written between the middle of the 7th and the end of the 10th centuries CE – only a few centuries ago. *Beowulf* begins as follows:

Hwæt wē Gār-Dena in gear-dagum
þēod-cyninga þrym gefrūnon,
hū ðā æþelingas ellen fremedon.

The chances are fairly good that you did not find this instantly comprehensible, and that is because of the amount of change that has taken place in our language over the past five to six centuries. The best modern translation of this passage, by Seamus Heaney, reads:

So. The Spear-Danes in days gone by
and the kings who ruled them had courage and greatness.
We have heard of those princes' heroic campaigns.
(Heaney, 2000, lines 1–3)

Although there was never a particular point in time when Old English became Middle English, or Middle English became Early Modern English – such changes took place over generations – the end result was that our language is a very different one indeed from that of our ancestors. The same sort of linguistic change led to the emergence of the modern Romance languages (Catalan, French, Italian, Portuguese, Romanian, Spanish, and so on) from the kinds of Latin spoken by soldiers and the common people in the time of the Roman Empire (see Posner, 1996), and that takes place, although at different rates, in all languages.

Language is Diverse

We have already noted that there are around 7,000 languages spoken in the world today, although that number is a very rough estimate – indeed, it is common to say that there are somewhere between 6,500 and 7,000 languages, which provides some idea of how difficult it is to provide a good response to the question of how many languages might actually exist. This difficulty is both created and compounded by a number of issues, not the least of which are our lack of knowledge of communities in many parts of the world (places such as the Amazon and Papua New Guinea – both incredibly linguistically diverse areas – come to mind here), the fact that the distinction between a dialect and a language is often problematic (as in variations in Arabic, Chinese, and so on), and because for political reasons some mutually intelligible language varieties are considered to be distinctive languages (as in Danish, Norwegian and Swedish). The closest thing that exists to a definitive guide to all of the languages in the world is the *Ethnologue*, published by SIL International (previously called the Summer Institute of Linguistics), as of 2019 in its 22nd edition. In that edition, some 7,111 languages are identified.

A further complication is that there are a small number of languages with extremely large numbers of speakers, and a great many languages with relatively small speaker communities. Thus, of the 7.7 billion people on Earth today, 94% speak one of only 400+ languages as their primary or secondary language. If we extend the number of languages to about 1,000+ languages, then some 98% speak one of these as either their primary or secondary language. One way to think about this is to consider the languages with the largest number of speakers. If we consider the numbers of both native speakers and second or additional language users of the language, Table 2.1 provides a list of the most widely spoken languages in the world. Another extremely useful way of thinking about this can be found in considering not merely the raw numbers of speakers of a language, but those languages that reflect the economic, political, diplomatic, social, military, and educational importance of the language's speakers around the world. A relatively small collection of languages, called the "languages of wider communication" (LWCs), are those which are widely used as both first and second languages, and which have widespread power on the international stage (see Maurais & Morris, 2003). The most commonly identified LWCs are English, French, Spanish, Portuguese, Russian, Arabic and German, though the case for some of these languages is stronger than for others. It is worth noting the relationship that exists between the LWCs and the history of colonialism, in large part because the continued reliance on the LWCs is an important aspect of neocolonialism in the modern world (see Calvet, 2005; Heller, 2010).

Table 2.1 Most Commonly Spoken Languages (Primary and Secondary Languages)

Language	*Number of L1 Speakers*	*Number of L2 Speakers*	*Total Number of Speakers*
English	379,000,000	753,300,000	1,132,300,000
Mandarin	918,000,000	198,900,000	1,116,900,000
Hindi	341,000,000	274,200,000	615,200,000
Spanish	460,000,000	74,200,000	534,200,000
French	77,200,000	202,600,000	279,800,000
Arabic	64,600,000[1]	273,900,000	338,600,000
Bengali	228,000,000	36,700,000	264,700,000
Russian	154,000,000	104,400,000	258,400,000
Portuguese	221,000,000	13,400,000	234,400,000
Indonesian	43,300,000	155,300,000	198,600,000
Urdu	68,600,000	101,600,000	170,200,000
German	76,100,000	56,000,000	132,100,000
Japanese	128,000,000	131,000	128,131,000
Swahili	16,000,000	82,300,000	98,300,000

[1]Native speakers of Egyptian Arabic.

Language is Learnable

The fact that virtually all human beings acquire their first language or languages naturally in a social context is clear. What is also clear, though, is that human beings are not limited to knowing the language or languages that they acquire as children. While it is true that there seems to be a critical period for acquisition of a language or languages that ends around the time of puberty (see DeKeyser, 2000; Singleton & Lengyel, 1995), individuals are perfectly able to *learn* languages throughout their lives. Indeed, much of world language education is predicated on the assumption that it is possible not only to acquire a language, but also to learn a language. Our point here is that human beings can and do learn languages other than their own, and do so in many different settings and in many different ways – but a key feature of language is nevertheless that it not only is naturally *acquired* by all human beings, but that it can *also* be *learned*.

Myths about Language

Up to this point, we have attempted to identify some of the key characteristics and features of human language. Because of the ubiquity of language, though, there is a great deal of folk wisdom about language and languages, and unfortunately, much of that folk wisdom – however much it may seem to be commonsense – is in fact wrong, misguided or even dangerous, as Wardhaugh pointed out in the quote with which this chapter begins (see Bauer & Trudgill, 1998). In this part of the chapter, we will explore some of the more common misunderstandings and mistaken beliefs about human language, and attempt to explain why they are erroneous.

Language is Oral

Until the 1960s, it was quite common in linguistics textbooks to find the assertion that human languages use an oral/aural modality – that is, that they are *spoken*, and involve the production and understanding of particular sounds. Such a definition seemed to make perfectly good sense, and fit nicely with the way in which we conceptualized the components of linguistics: the study of phonology, morphology, syntax, semantics, and pragmatics. At the very foundation of this conceptualization was phonology, the study of the sound system of a language. This way of conceptualizing language also had the advantage of stressing the fact that when linguists talk about language, it is not the *written* variety of a language with which we are most concerned – language in a written form is inevitably somewhat artificial (a point that we will further discuss shortly) (see Azevedo, 1992, pp. 4–5). We no longer include speech as a necessary component of language – or, to be more precise, we now make a distinction between speech and language. Most human languages *do* rely on the production and reception of sounds, of course, but we now recognize a very important exception to this claim: the sign languages that are used by deaf people, and which are full and complete human languages in every sense of the term except insofar as they do not utilize an oral/aural modality, but rather a visual/gestural one.[10]

The history of the recognition of sign languages as legitimate human languages is a fascinating one, at least in part because it was such an obvious fact that took so long to recognize. It was not until the publication of William Stokoe's landmark monograph *Sign Language Structure* in 1960 that the idea that sign languages were somehow not "real" languages was challenged (Stokoe, 1993). The status of sign languages is no longer a matter of dispute, at least among linguists, although many non-linguists continue to hold demonstrably false beliefs about sign language, an issue to which we will return in the next chapter.

Written Language is More Important than Spoken Language

Because we live in a society in which literacy is largely taken for granted, and in which we tend to assume that everyone can read and write, we also often think of language in terms of its written forms. Thus, "proper" or "correct" language usage is often believed to be that of the formal, written linguistic norms that we have learned in school. Although such assumptions are understandable, they are profoundly problematic from a linguistic perspective. For most of our existence as a species, and in the cases of the overwhelming number of human languages that have existed over time, and which are spoken today, language is a primarily spoken (or signed) phenomenon. Indeed, written language is a remarkably recent development – although human beings have been using language for between 100,000 and 150,000 years, it has only been in the last 5,000 years or so that any language has had a written form. The first human beings to develop a way of writing their language were probably the Sumerians, who began creating written texts around 3,500 BCE (see Edzard, 2003; Huehnergard, 2011, p. xxvii).[11] Further, although there have been many cultures and civilizations with impressive literary accomplishments and traditions, it has only been in the past few centuries when universal or near-universal literacy has become common – for most of human history, reading and writing were the province of a relatively tiny élite in virtually all societies. As John McWhorter has noted, "spoken language was not 'waiting' for written conventions to come along ... Rather, written language ... [is] an artificial add-on to human language, designed for the specific and highly historically contingent task of transcribing speech effectively into writing" (McWhorter, 2001, p. 239). In linguistics, when we study languages, it is the spoken (or signed) language with which we are concerned and upon which we are focused.

Some People Have Accents and Others Don't

An accent, from a linguistic perspective, can be defined as "a way of pronouncing words that identifies one speaker of a language as speaking differently from another speaker of the same language" (Rowe & Levine, 2018, p. 42).[12] Since each of us pronounces different words in particular ways, this would suggest that each of us must also have an accent – and, in linguistics, this is absolutely the case. And yet, it is very common for individuals to be described (or to describe themselves) as "not having an accent." What this actually means is that the individual does not have an accent that is in some setting considered to be "marked" – that is, an accent that differs from what is socially, educationally, politically, and so on, assumed to be the acceptable standard norm. In many parts of the United States, for instance, two commonly identified accents (or, more accurately, collections of accents) are British accents and Southern accents. As the British linguist Peter Trudgill has noted:

> A number of people have written letters to the [*Eastern Daily Press*] in which they claim, or mention in passing, that they "don't have an accent" ....They are not alone: there are many people in the world who think that only other people have accents. "You have an accent!" people in America exclaim when they meet an English person. They do not mean anything bad by it – they are just being friendly and are intrigued by the way you speak; but they clearly do

> not think they have an accent themselves. Which of course they do – an American accent .... I have not met any of the letter writers "without an accent," but I am happy to say that I am quite sure that, like the Americans, they are not correct in what they say. The fact is that everybody has an accent, including you and me and Her Majesty the Queen. *There are no exceptions.*
>
> (Trudgill, 2016, pp. 125–126, our emphasis)

Nevertheless, it is true that, as Suzanne Romaine has commented, "People have strong views on accents, including the idea that it is always others who have accents and never themselves!" (Romaine, 2000, p. 20). It is also true, of course, that regardless of the fact that we all have accents, one's accent *does* in many ways – socially, culturally, educationally, economically, and so on – make a great deal of difference in how others respond to what we say. As John Honey, in his book *Does Accent Matter?* (1989), has explained, "Children should be warned to expect in the real world their accents may be used as an indicator of their origins, the extent of their educatedness, the system of values with which they identify and whether these are associated with a narrow local group or with the wider society" (quoted in Wardhaugh, 1999, p. 98).

The Quality of Language is Declining

There is a very popular conviction that the quality of our language (whatever that language may be) is in decline (Baron, 1989; Daniels, 1983; Milroy & Milroy, 2012). Typical of this view is the following passage from an article by Allison Burr:

> I remember being rebuked at the age of 13 by a highly educated person for my incessant (and improper) use of the word "like." I was no different than my peers ... The teacher was right to rebuke me because he knew then what I had not yet discovered: Rules of language do exist, and when they are followed, beauty has the potential to emerge. When they are discarded, both the listener and the speaker are impoverished and, in some sense, less human .... The problem is that now, 25 years later, many adults and people of influence continue to eviscerate the English language in such a way that it would be inconceivable for a 13-year-old to be convinced of her own need for an improved and redeemed language.
>
> (Burr, 2017)

Indeed, the idea that our language is getting worse is not only ubiquitous in the modern world, but is one that has been voiced repeatedly over history. With respect to English, one recent story in *The Economist* noted that,

> The English language, we all know, is in decline. The average schoolchild can hardly write, one author has recently warned. Well, not that recently perhaps. It was William Langland, author of *Piers Plowman*, who wrote that "There is not a single modern schoolboy who can compose verses or write a decent letter." He died in 1386.
>
> (R.L.G., 2015)

Nor, is it worth observing, is it only English that is widely believed to be suffering from such a decline in quality. One scholar at Princeton University has written that,

> The earliest language "crisis" … that I have been able to discover occurred in ancient Sumeria …. It seems that among the first of the clay tablets discovered and deciphered by modern scholars was one which recorded the agonized complaints of a Sumerian teacher about the sudden drop-off in students' writing ability.
>
> (Browning, n.d.)

Concerns with the decline of language were also voiced repeatedly in both Greece and Roman during antiquity; the 4th-century CE Greek teacher of rhetoric Libanius blamed the decline in the quality of Greek on the negative influence of Latin, for instance (Rochette, 2011, p. 560). Comparable concerns continue to be raised today, not only about English, but also about French, Spanish, Russian, and virtually every other language.

In point of fact, such concerns – however historically common and widely held they may be – are not well-grounded in an understanding of the nature of language.[13] As we have seen, languages are constantly changing, and the norms of any particular language are also in an ongoing state of flux. Further, in every language there are many varieties and variations, and judgments about "proper" or "better" usage are social rather than linguistic ones (see Daniels, 1983; Milroy & Milroy, 2012).

A Trifecta of Myths about Language Inequality

The final three myths about language that we will discuss in this chapter are variations on what is basically a single, broad and widely believed theme: the idea that some languages or language varieties are in some sense superior to others. This idea has important implications for how we think about standard languages, dialects, and languages spoken by different groups around the world. A key conviction of many, probably most, linguists about human language, as articulated in one of the more widely used introductory college and university linguistics textbooks, however, is that:

> No language or variety of language … is superior or inferior to any other in a linguistic sense. Every [language] is equally complex,

> logical, and capable of producing an infinite set of sentences to express any thought. If something can be expressed in one language … it can be expressed in any other language … It might involve different means and different words, but it can be expressed … All human languages … are fully expressive, complete and logical …
>
> (Fromkin, Rodman & Hyams, 2014, pp. 10–11)

In linguistics, in short, our goal is to study language and languages in a non-judgmental manner (that is, *descriptively* rather than *prescriptively*) – for linguists, it simply makes no sense to talk about a "better" or "superior" language variety.[14] As Ralph Fasold and Jeff Connor-Linton have commented,

> Linguists approach language in the same way that astronomers approach the study of the universe or that anthropologists approach the study of human cultural systems. It would be ridiculous for astronomers to speak about planets orbiting stars "incorrectly" and inappropriate for anthropologists to declare a culture "degenerate" simply because it differs from their own. Similarly, linguists take language as they find it, rather than attempting to regulate it in the direction of preconceived criteria. Linguists are equally curious about *all* the forms of language that they encounter, no matter what the education or social standing of their speakers might be.
>
> (Fasold & Connor-Linton, 2014, p. 9, our emphasis)[15]

Dialects are Inferior to Languages

In everyday speech, people tend to distinguish between "languages" and "dialects"[16] as if there were a meaningful distinction between the two – and, inevitably, the assumption that is made is that "dialects" are in some important and meaningful sense inferior to "languages." From a linguistic perspective, things are far more complicated than this – and, at the same time, far simpler. The problem, in a nutshell, is that the labels "language" and "dialect" are not technical linguistic terms at all (see Azevedo, 1992, pp. 13–15). Rather, they express social and political realities. In essence, the distinction between a language and a dialect is merely where a society wishes to draw it, based on social, political, economic, and even military factors. As Ronelle Alexander has explained, "Each dialect, in fact, is actually a separate language, with its own internally consistent system" (Alexander, 2000, p. 316).

To be sure, this can be a puzzling concept for many people, who assume that there is a difference between, say, French and Chinese that is fundamentally distinct from that between British and American English. The most common way that this distinction is conceptualized is that speakers of British and American English can understand one another, while speakers of French and Chinese cannot. This phenomenon is called "mutual intelligibility": the basic idea is that if two speakers understand each other, they are speaking one language; if they do not understand each other, then they are speaking two different languages. Mutual intelligibility does work effectively to distinguish "languages" from "dialects" in many instances, as the case of British and American English makes clear. At the same time, though, there are many examples in which mutual intelligibility does not seem to be adequate. Danish, Norwegian and Swedish provide an excellent example of where mutual intelligibility is problematic, since speakers of any of these languages can fairly easily understand speakers of the others. At the same time, speakers of Bavarian German would not be easily understandable by speakers of *Hochdeutsch* (Standard German). As a way of avoiding the confusion related to the vague nature of the terms "dialect" and "language," linguists generally prefer to use the term "language variety," which avoids the use (and problems) of this distinction altogether.

The Standard Language is Superior to Other Varieties

Some languages have particular varieties that have gained recognition or status as the "standard" variety of the language for spoken and written purposes. Language standardization, which has often historically been an aspect of the development of a nation-state (and is hence largely a European invention) (Romaine, 2000, p. 88), can involve such things as pronunciation, lexical choices and preferences, generally accepted grammatical norms, orthographic norms, and so on. In some cases, such as Russian, there is a single monocentric standard language, while in others – English, Portuguese, and Spanish, for instance – there are multiple standard language varieties. The standard language is typically the language used by the State in governmental and educational institutions, as well as by the society's élite. In many countries, there are official language academies that are responsible for monitoring language standardization, official or semi-official dictionaries that determine what is and is not acceptable lexical usage, and so on. Language standardization and literacy are, in most cases, tied together quite closely – and literacy, of course, is tied not only to education, but also to economic and social class. Even more relevant here is that it is widely believed that the standard language is in some objective sense superior to other varieties of the language – a belief that is strongly encouraged in educational institutions. Furthermore, it is important to understand that "the process of standardization … is one of the main agents of inequality" in society (Romaine, 2000, p. 87).

Some Languages are Better than Others

Our discussion about languages, dialects and the standard language variety focuses on the situation with respect to a single language community.

A similar phenomenon exists in terms of attitudes and beliefs about different languages. Thus, it is sometimes claimed that one language is more logical than another, that a language is clearer or better organized than some other language, or that a particular language is more suited to discussing certain topics than another language. None of these claims is really defensible from a linguistic perspective, although it is true that at any given point in time a language may not have all of the lexical items necessary for dealing with a particular subject. For example, of the roughly 7,000 languages spoken in the world today, it is likely that a huge number do not have the vocabulary that would be necessary to talk about many technical and scientific fields – but that is, after all, only a temporary problem, since, as we have seen, any language can create new terminology to meet new needs.

Conclusion

In this chapter, we have tried to accomplish two things that are very important for the focus of this book: first, we have discussed what we take to be the key characteristics that, taken together, essentially define human language, and second, we have identified a number of common myths about language, and provided explanations for why these myths are not true. Both of these foci are, we believe, incredibly important. As Thomas Ricento has pointed out:

> What we believe about language and how language functions are often two different things. Sociolinguists show us how language actually functions in society, while most political theorists hold "common sense" views on language as a discrete system used for communication without any appreciation of the complex roles that language(s) play in human interactions and civil society, especially in multilingual contexts. In order to develop inclusive and socially just policies to advance the common good, we need to better understand the ways that language actually works in society and why language diversity is not an obstacle to development but rather a resource to be valued and embraced.
>
> (Ricento, 2019)

Underlying this chapter is the recognition on our part that, as Wardhaugh has argued,

> Linguists have their own beliefs about language. What is remarkable is the gap between these two sets of beliefs, the beliefs that linguists hold about language and the beliefs that most others hold … In the absence of informed opinion, popular views of language abound, assume importance, and have consequences. None of us is free of

> them, for even if we do not share these views we are still subject to them as others act in accordance with them. I suspect that much public discussion of language will continue to be dominated by irrational and emotional arguments presented under the guise of reason, logic, and common sense.
>
> (Wardhaugh, 1999, p. 24)

It is, we believe, in part the job of the world language educator – both in and out of the classroom – to challenge these "irrational and emotional" arguments and claims about language, and it is the overriding purpose of this book to help both pre- and in-service teachers to do just that.

Questions for Reflection and Discussion

1 Early in this chapter, there is a quote from the linguist Neil Smith, who claims that "Language makes us human." There are, though, many things that might be given as examples of how human beings differ from other members of the animal kingdom – we produce incredibly complex and sophisticated art, music, architecture, social systems, literary traditions, and so on. To what extent do you believe that Smith's claim is correct? Why?
2 The authors suggest that one fundamental characteristic of human language is that it is *social*. Thus, there is a sense in which an extinct language is no longer really a human language; rather, it is an artifact. And yet, if you consider Hittite, for example, there are tens of thousands of texts of this language that remain. There are also at least some scholars who are able to read these texts. Does this suggest that Hittite is perhaps more than an artifact? How can you reconcile this with the claims of the authors?
3 The concept of language death is actually a very complex one, and there are different ways in which one might talk about a language becoming extinct. Some languages do disappear entirely, leaving no record and having no daughter languages. But, at the same time, there are cases like Latin. At least one variety of Latin, for instance, never really stopped existing: it changed over time, becoming the modern Romance languages. Similarly, Anglo-Saxon did not disappear – it simply evolved into Middle English, which in turn became Modern English. Is it, then, really useful to talk about a language becoming extinct?
4 Is it useful or valuable for students of a modern language to be familiar with how the target language has historically evolved? Why or why not?
5 If the authors are correct in their claim that there are not "superior" and "inferior" languages, and that all human languages are of fundamentally equal value, what are the implications of this claim for the world language classroom?

Notes

1 The discussion provided here presupposes that one accepts evolutionary theory as the most credible explanation that we have at the present time to explain the origins and evolution of our species. We recognize that for those who reject evolutionary theory, and accept Creationism, Creation Science, New Creationism, Intelligent Design, or some other (generally theistic) model, some of what we say here will conflict with deeply held beliefs. Among linguists, as among other scientists, although there are debates about particular aspects of evolutionary theory, taken as a whole the theory is almost universally accepted, however. With respect to the tension between Creation Science and contemporary linguistics, see Pennock (2002). A radical alternative to traditional explanations of the emergence of human language has recently been offered, incidentally, by Daniel Everett (2017). We find Everett's claims generally unconvincing, though nevertheless intriguing.

2 There is a phenomenon in some languages, including many Bantu languages, called an "ideophone," which is a word that is a "vivid representation of an idea in sound … often onomatopoeic, which describes a predicate, qualificative or adverb in respect to manner, color, sound, smell, action, state or intensity" (Doke, 1935, p. 118).

3 The number of phonemes in each of these languages varies from one variety of the language to another. In English, for instance, there is a range from 36 to about 45 phonemes, depending on which variety of English one is examining.

4 The use of gendered pronouns in English (she and he, her and his, and so on) is a challenge, since historically the male pronoun has been used both in a gender-specific and generic manner. This inevitably leads to sexist assumptions related to language, and in recent years writers have attempted to correct this problem in a number of ways: using *he or she*, *s/he*, *his or her*, *they and their*, or even creating new, gender-neutral pronouns. We have chosen to use both the female and male pronouns whenever this is appropriate, but have also deliberately decided to place the female pronoun first. We do this because it is, for many of us, a bit jarring – which is precisely the point. By emphasizing the issue of gender, we believe that we are reminding ourselves and others of the fundamental problem that we are trying to address.

5 An extreme case of this sort is provided by Genie (a pseudonym), a child in California who was the victim of severe abuse until she was discovered by child welfare authorities in 1970, when she was nearly 14 years old. Because of her isolation from linguistic input, Genie never fully acquired an L1. This case is discussed in detail in Curtiss (1977) and Rymer (1994).

6 Developmental delays, and, indeed, the rate of L1 acquisition, are obviously important, but in no way contradict the basic point that we are making here: human beings in almost all settings acquire the human language which surrounds them, more or less in the first few years of life.

7 The concept of a "primitive" society is a higher contentious and controversial one that has been widely rejected (see Diamond, 2017; Hallpike, 2011; Kuper, 2017). Regardless of one's position about whether there could be such a thing as a "primitive" society, however, with respect to languages there is simply no such thing as a "primitive language" (see also Dixon, 2016, pp. 4–6; Scancarelli, 1994).

8 The initial discovery of Nicaraguan Sign Language was a very exciting event for linguists, since it appeared to provide an example of the spontaneous emergence of a human language among children without external input. However, Laura Polich (2005) has suggested, fairly compellingly in our view, that in fact the emergence of Nicaraguan Sign Language was far more complex

than was initially believed, and further, that there were a number of external linguistic influences that contributed to its development.

9 The Fibonacci Sequence is a sequence in which each number is the sum of the two preceding numbers, starting from 0 and 1. The mathematical formula for this is $F_0 = 0$, $F_1 = 1$, and $F_n = F_{n-1} + F_{n-2}$, for $n > 1$.

10 In recent years a number of scholars have made the case – quite compellingly, in our view – that the first human languages may have been signed rather than spoken languages (see Armstrong, 2002; Armstrong, Stokoe & Wilcox, 1995; Corballis, 2002; Stokoe, 2001).

11 The Sumerians are typically credited with creating the first written script, cuneiform, but the Egyptians began writing using hieroglyphics at around the same time – the earliest Egyptian glyphs have been dated to about 3400 BCE. It is not clear whether these two systems developed independently of each other, or whether there was a process of cultural diffusion at work.

12 It is important to note that we are talking about different accents of native speakers of a language, *not* with the kind of accent that is common in second language learners of a language (i.e., *foreign* accents).

13 It is worth noting here that there is a distinction between the "deterioration" of language with respect to the ability to write an essay following prescribed (and thus artificial) formats, and change in language that is misunderstood and mischaracterized as deterioration. We recognize that there are agreed-upon norms in the formal written varieties of standard languages, and that there are contexts in which such norms do need to be observed – albeit for educational, social, economic, political, and generally non-linguistic reasons rather than for linguistic ones.

14 In fact, although the claims made in the passage quoted from Victoria Fromkin, Robert Rodman and Nina Hyams (2014) are well-intentioned, and given the folk wisdom about and misunderstandings of language held by most students, there are compelling pedagogical arguments for them, the reality is a bit more complicated. Although claims about the fundamental equality of languages may be useful in introducing students to linguistics as an academic discipline, and while such claims may be valuable as a working assumption for linguists in a variety of ways, neither of these advantages makes them *necessarily* true. Given our limited knowledge of many of the roughly 6,500 to 7,000 languages used by human beings around the world, such a claim must, for the time being, remain largely unproven – at best, a working hypothesis.

15 It is important to note here that we are concerned with the language use of native speakers – the situation in the foreign language classroom is obviously quite different, since second language learners can and often do produce errors in the L2, and it is perfectly appropriate to correct such errors. The student who says, "Estoy frío" instead of "Tengo frío," for instance, has made an error that violates that rules of Spanish as these rules are used by native speakers.

16 A related distinction is that between a "dialect" and an "accent." The key difference between these two concepts is that an "accent" is distinguished with respect to phonology, while a dialect is distinguished by its phonology, lexicon, morphology, and syntax.

References

Alexander, R. (2000). *Intensive Bulgarian: A textbook and reference grammar, volume 2*. Madison, WI: University of Wisconsin Press.

Armstrong, D. (2002). *Original signs: Gesture, sign, and the sources of language*. Washington, DC: Gallaudet University Press.

Armstrong, D., Stokoe, W. & Wilcox, S. (1995). *Gesture and the nature of language*. Cambridge: Cambridge University Press.

Azevedo, M. (1992). *Introducción a la lingüística española*. Englewood Cliffs, NJ: Prentice Hall.

Barber, C. (1993). *The English language: A historical introduction*. Cambridge: Cambridge University Press.

Barnard, A. (2016). *Language in prehistory*. Cambridge: Cambridge University Press.

Baron, D. (1989). *Declining grammar, and other essays on the English vocabulary*. Urbana, IL: National Council of Teachers of English.

Bauer, L. & Trudgill, P. (Eds.). (1998). *Language myths*. New York: Penguin.

Baugh, A. & Cable, T. (2002). *A history of the English language* (5th ed.). New York: Routledge.

Bennett, P. R. (1986). Grammar in the lexicon: Two Bantu cases. *Journal of African Languages and Linguistics*, 8(1): 1–30.

Botha, R. & Knight, C. (Eds.). (2009). *The cradle of language*. Oxford: Oxford University Press.

Browning, M. (n.d.). Is English deteriorating? Downloaded from www.princeton.edu/~browning/decline.html on January 15, 2020.

Burr, A. (2017). The decline and fall of the English language. *Circe Institute: Cultivating Wisdom and Virtue*. Downloaded from www.circeinstitute.org/blog/decline-and-fall-english-language on January 15, 2020.

Bybee, J. (2015). *Language change*. Cambridge: Cambridge University Press.

Calvet, L.-J. (2005). *Lingüística y colonialismo: Breve tratado de glotofagia*. Buenos Aires: Fondo de Cultura Económica de Argentina.

Carroll, L. (1992). *Alice's adventures in Wonderland and Through the looking glass*. New York: New American Library. (Original works published 1865 and 1896)

Corballis, M. (2002). *From hand to mouth: The origins of language*. Princeton, NJ: Princeton University Press.

Curtiss, S. (1977). *Genie: A psycholinguistic study of a modern-day "wild child."*New York: Academic Press.

Daniels, D. (1983). *Famous last words: The American language crisis reconsidered*. Carbondale, IL: Southern Illinois University Press.

DeKeyser, R. (2000). The robustness of critical period effects in second language acquisition. *Studies in Second Language Acquisition*, 22(4): 499–533.

Diamond, S. (2017). *In search of the primitive: A critique of civilization*. New York: Routledge.

Dixon, R. (2016). *Are some languages better than others?* Oxford: Oxford University Press.

Doke, C. (1935). *Bantu linguistic terminology*. London: Longmans Green.

Dunbar, R., Gamble, C. & Gowlett, J. (Eds.). (2014). *Lucy to language: The benchmark papers*. Oxford: Oxford University Press.

Edzard, D. (2003). *Sumerian grammar*. Atlanta, GA: Society of Biblical Literature.

Everett, D. (2013). *Language: The cultural tool*. London: Profile Books.

Everett, D. (2017). *How language began: The story of humanity's greatest invention*. New York: Liveright.

Fasold, R. & Connor-Linton, J. (Eds.). (2014). *An introduction to language and linguistics* (2nd ed.). Cambridge: Cambridge University Press.

Fout, R. & Waters, G. (2001). Chimpanzee sign language and Darwinian continuity: Evidence for a neurological continuity for language. *Neurological Research*, 23(8): 787–794.

Freeborn, D. (1998). *From Old English to Standard English* (2nd ed.). New York: Palgrave.

Fromkin, V., Rodman, R. & Hyams, N. (2014). *An introduction to language* (10th ed.). Boston: Wadsworth.

Fromkin, V., Rodman, R. & Hyams, N. (2017). *An introduction to language* (11th ed.). Boston: Cengage.

Gibson, K. (1994). Continuity theories of human language origins versus the Lieberman model. *Language and Communication*, 14(1): 97–114.

Hallpike, C. (2011). *On primitive society: And other forbidden topics*. Bloomington, IN: AuthorHouse.

Heaney, S. (2000). *Beowulf: A new verse translation*. New York: Farrar, Straus & Giroux.

Heikkinen, T. (1986). Phonology of the!Xũ dialect spoken in Ovamboland and western Kavango. *South African Journal of African Languages*, 6(1): 18–28.

Heller, M. (2010). The commodification of language. *Annual Review of Anthropology*, 39: 101–114.

Honey, J. (1989). *Does accent matter? The Pygmalion factor*. London: Faber & Faber.

Hudson, G. (2000). *Essential introductory linguistics*. Malden, MA: Blackwell.

Huehnergard, J. (2011). *A grammar of Akkadian* (3rd ed.). Winona Lake, IN: Eisenbrauns.

Hurford, J., Studdert-Kennedy, M. & Knight, C. (Eds.). (1998). *Evolution of language: Social and cognitive bases*. Cambridge: Cambridge University Press.

Jacobson, S. (1995). *A practical grammar of the Central Alaskan Yup'ik Eskimo language*. Fairbanks, AK: University of Alaska, Alaska Native Language Center and Program.

Klein, R. (2008). Out of Africa and the evolution of human behavior. *Evolutionary Anthropology*, 17(6): 267–281.

Kuper, A. (2017). *The invention of primitive society: Transformations of an illusion* (2nd ed.). New York: Routledge.

Labov, W. (1994). *Principles of linguistic change, volume* 1. Oxford: Basil Blackwell.

Labov, W. (2001). *Principles of linguistic change, volume* 2. Oxford: Basil Blackwell.

Labov, W. (2010). *Principles of linguistic change: Cognitive and culture factors*. Chichester, UK: Wiley-Blackwell.

Lieberman, P. (1991). *Uniquely human: Speech, thought, and selfless behavior*. Cambridge, MA: Harvard University Press.

Maurais, J. & Morris, M. (Eds.). (2003). *Languages in a globalising world*. Cambridge: Cambridge University Press.

McWhorter, J. (2001). *The power of Babel: A natural history of language*. New York: W. H. Freeman.

Milroy, J. & Milroy, L. (2012). *Authority in language: Investigating standard English* (4th ed.). New York: Routledge.

Mithun, M. (1999). *The languages of North America*. Cambridge: Cambridge University Press.

Pennock, R. (2002). *Tower of Babel: The evidence against the new Creationism*. Cambridge, MA: MIT Press.

Pinker, S. (1997). Evolutionary biology and the evolution of language. In M. Gopnik (Ed.), *The inheritance and innateness of grammars* (pp. 181–208). Oxford: Oxford University Press.

Polich, L. (2005). *The emergence of the deaf community in Nicaragua*. Washington, DC: Gallaudet University Press.

Posner, R. (1996). *The Romance languages*. Cambridge: Cambridge University Press.

Reagan, T. (2016). Language engineering in totalitarian régimes: Controlling belief and behavior through language. In P. Miller, B. Rubrecht, E. Mikulec & C. McGivern (Eds.), *Readings in language studies, volume 6: A critical examination of language and community* (pp. 39–56). Laguna Beach, CA: International Society for Language Studies.

Renfrew, C. (1991). Before Babel: Speculation on the origins of linguistic diversity. *Cambridge Archeological Journal*, 1(1): 3–23.

Ricento, T. (2019). *Conceptualizing language: Linguistic theory and language policy*. Keynote address, delivered at "The United Nations at 75: Listening, Talking and Taking Action in a Multilingual World" conference, New York City, May 9–10.

R.L.G. (2015). A long decline: Fears of language decline seem to be a human universal. *The Economist* (February 12). Downloaded from www.economist.com/prospero/2015/02/12/a-long-decline on August 1, 2019.

Robin, R., Evans-Romaine, K., Shatalina, G. & Robin, J. (2007). *Голоса: A basic course in Russian, Book* 1 (4th ed.). Upper Saddle River, NJ: Pearson Prentice Hall.

Robinson, S. (2006). The phoneme inventory of the Aita dialect of Rotokas. *Oceanic Linguistics*, 45(1): 206–209.

Rochette, B. (2011). Language policies in the Roman republic and empire. In J. Clackson (Ed.), *A companion to the Latin language* (pp. 549–563). Oxford: Wiley-Blackwell.

Romaine, S. (2000). *Language in society: An introduction to sociolinguistics* (2nd ed.). Oxford: Oxford University Press.

Rowe, B. & Levine, D. (2018). *A concise introduction to linguistics* (5th ed.). New York: Routledge.

Ryazanova-Clarke, L. & Wade, T. (1999). *The Russian language today*. New York: Routledge.

Rymer, R. (1994). *Genie: A scientific tragedy* (2nd ed.). New York: HarperCollins.

Scancarelli, J. (1994). Another look at a "primitive language." *International Journal of American Linguistics*, 60(2): 149–160.

Senghas, A. (1995a). The development of Nicaraguan Sign Language via the language acquisition process. In D. MacLaughlin & S. McEwen (Eds.), *Proceedings of the 19th annual Boston University Conference on Language Development* (pp. 543–552). Boston, MA: Cascadilla Press.

Senghas, A. (1995b). Children's contribution to the birth of Nicaraguan Sign Language. Unpublished Ph.D. dissertation, Massachusetts Institute of Technology, Cambridge, Massachusetts.

Senghas, A. (2003). Intergenerational influence and ontogenetic development in the emergence of spatial grammar in Nicaraguan Sign Language. *Cognitive Development*, 18(4): 511–531.

Senghas, A. & Coppola, M. (2001). Children creating language: How Nicaraguan Sign Language acquired a spatial grammar. *Psychological Science*, 12(4): 323–328.

Senghas, A., Kita, S. & Özyürek, A. (2004). Children creating core properties of language: Evidence from an emerging sign language in Nicaragua. *Science*, 305(5691): 1779–1782.

Senghas, A., Newport, E. & Supalla, T. (1997). Argument structure in Nicaraguan Sign Language: The emergence of grammatical devices. In E. Hughes & A. Greenhill (Eds.), *Proceedings of the 21st annual Boston University Conference on Language Development* (pp. 550–561). Boston, MA: Cascadilla Press.

Singleton, D. & Lengyel, Z. (Eds.). (1995). *The age factor in second language acquisition: A critical look at the critical period hypothesis*. Clevedon: Multilingual Matters.

Smith, M. (1998). *Language and power in the creation of the U.S.S.R., 1917–1953.* Berlin: Walter de Gruyter.

Smith, N. (2002). *Language, bananas, and bonobos: Linguistic problems, puzzles and polemics*. Oxford: Blackwell.

Snyman, J. (1973). *An introduction to the!Xũ language*. Cape Town: Balkema.

Stokoe, W. (1993). *Sign language structure*. Silver Spring, MD: Linstok Press (Original work published 1960)

Stokoe, W. (2001). *Language in hand: Why sign came before speech*. Washington, DC: Gallaudet University Press.

Trask, R. (1999). *Language: The basics* (2nd ed.). New York: Routledge.

Trudgill, P. (2016). *Dialect matters: Respecting vernacular language*. Cambridge: Cambridge University Press.

Wardhaugh, R. (1999). *Proper English: Myths and misunderstandings about language*. Oxford: Blackwell.

Yule, G. (2017). *The study of language* (6th ed.). Cambridge: Cambridge University Press.

3 Linguistic Legitimacy and the World Language Educator

Whose Language is Real?

Underlying the educational discourse dealing with issues of language are a number of common assumptions about the nature of language, language structure, language difference, and so on, that are shared by both classroom teachers and the general public. As we saw in the preceding chapter, one of the more powerful of these assumptions concerns what counts as a "real" language, and, even more important, what does *not* count as a "real language." What is at issue here is what has been called the ideology of linguistic legitimacy: which language varieties are deemed by the society (or some subset of the society) to be legitimate, and which are not. In this chapter, we will further explore the concept of linguistic legitimacy, and then examine how it applies in three specific cases: African American English (AAE), Spanglish and ASL. After examining these cases, we will discuss the implications of the concept of linguistic legitimacy for the world language educator.

The Concept of Linguistic Legitimacy

The concept of linguistic legitimacy is an important one, entailing issues of social class, ethnicity, and culture, as well as being embedded in relations of dominance, power and control (Fairclough, 2015; Mayr, 2008; Reagan, 2016, 2019; Wodak, 2012). Whether making claims of logical or lexical superiority, about the complexity and sophistication of a language variety, or attempting to ensure that "proper" language use is maintained, one is inevitably engaged in attitudes, beliefs and practices that are firmly grounded in the ideology of linguistic legitimacy. The core idea at the heart of the ideology of linguistic legitimacy is that some languages or language varieties are superior in some fundamental way to others. In turn, some languages are thus inferior to others – indeed, in some cases defective, limited or even "primitive" (see Dixon, 2016, pp. 4–6; Kuper, 2017; Scancarelli, 1994). The criteria for making such judgments are subjective, but they are typically grounded in beliefs and attitudes that are in no way linguistic in nature, although they usually cite phonological, lexical, and syntactic features of a language variety in contrast with some other language or language variety. Given the currency of the idea of linguistic legitimacy, it is hardly surprising that so many examples of this phenomenon abound, both in our own society and elsewhere. From the colonial era, the languages of non-Western indigenous people were believed to be primitive, well into the 20th (and perhaps even into the 21st) century.[1] Furthermore, there continue to be many everyday settings in which claims of linguistic legitimacy occur: in social discourse, in educational institutions, in politics and political discourse, in the workplace, and even in scholarly settings. Such beliefs are not only factually wrong, but they are also potentially destructive and oppressive. As Rosina Lippi-Green has observed, "We do not, cannot under our laws, ask people to change the color of their skin, their religion, their gender, but we regularly demand of people that they suppress or deny the most effective way they have of situating themselves socially in the world" (Lippi-Green, 2012, p. 66). In a similar vein, Leah Zuidema argued that "Linguistic prejudice is one of the few 'acceptable' American prejudices. In polite society, we don't allow jokes that we consider racist or sexist, and we are careful not to disparage a person's religious beliefs. Language is another matter" (Zuidema, 2005, p. 686). Nevertheless, such beliefs and attitudes – which are part of a broader challenge that has been called *linguicism* – remain incredibly common, and have powerful implications.[2]

The ideology of linguistic legitimacy is a key component of what has been called the "standard language ideology" in American society. This standard language ideology supports institutionalized social and educational policies that initiate children into the linguistic biases and prejudices of middle-class American society (see Lippi-Green, 2012, pp. 67–68; Woolard, 1992). In essence,

> Dominant institutions promote the notion of an overarching, homogenous standard language which is primarily Anglo, upper middle-class, and ethnically middle-American. Whether the issues at hand are large-scale sociopolitical in nature or more subtle, whether the approach is coercion or consent, there are two sides to this process: first, devaluation of all that is not (or does not seek to be) politically, culturally or socially marked as belonging to the privileged class, and second, validation of the social (and linguistic) values of the dominant institutions. The process of linguistic assimilation to an abstracted standard is cast as a natural one, necessary and positive for the greater social good.
>
> (Lippi-Green, 2012, p. 68)

The concept of linguistic legitimacy appears in formal and informal discourse in two related ways. The first way in which the concept emerged was in the work of the French sociologist, anthropologist, and philosopher Pierre Bourdieu (see Bourdieu, 1971, 1972, 1975, 1979, 1980, 1982,

1984, 2001; Bourdieu & Passeron, 1970, 1997). Bourdieu identified linguistic capital as the form of the social capital which serves to distinguish and divide different social classes in societies. Linguistic capital, like social capital more generally, rests at the level of the individual. Bourdieu argued that traditional linguists had failed to recognize that language in general, and standard languages in particular, are socially and politically constructed rather than preconstructed objects. On Bourdieu's account, certain language varieties are dominant as a result of their association and identification with the political and economic powers in society (Bourdieu, 2001). Thus, the ability to make use of the prestige language or language variety is simply an extension of the many ways in which particular groups in society are able to dominate, oppress and disempower other groups. This view of linguistic legitimacy emphasizes the complex dynamics of the workings of political and economic power and how these impact social and cultural norms, and, even more important, the ways in which these norms are used to maintain the power and status of socially dominant groups – and, hence, to transfer this power and status cross-generationally to their children.

Although Bourdieu's approach is an extremely insightful and valuable one, it largely overlooks the specific claims that are made in various social, political and educational contexts about *particular* language varieties – claims that essentially delegitimize some language varieties while valorizing others. It is the combination of the processes of delegitimation and legitimation that addresses the question of how *linguistic* domination operates in different settings in the real world, such as classrooms, the workplace, the media, and so on. If we wish to understand the ways in which the process of linguistic delegitimation takes place in society and in educational institutions, let alone to be able to challenge such delegitimation, we believe that a more linguistically-grounded and nuanced conceptualization of linguistic legitimacy is required. In other words, the metalevel analysis provided by Bourdieu and others must also be demonstrated at the microlevel, focusing on the specific beliefs and claims made about dominated and marginalized languages and language varieties.

As has already been suggested, a core belief associated with the ideology of linguistic legitimacy, and one which goes far beyond mere prescriptivism, is the idea that there are inferior or primitive languages. Such claims, from a linguistic perspective, are not just impossible, they are quite literally unintelligible. There is no reasonable doubt that human language is a uniquely complex variety of communication, and that all languages are far more sophisticated than the communication systems of any other species (see McWhorter, 2001, pp. 5–10; Trask, 1999, pp. 1–26). As R. L. Trask has argued,

> Human language is arguably the single most remarkable characteristic that we have, the one that most truly sets our species apart. Our

> faculty of language, which we usually take for granted, exhibits a number of properties which are remarkable, even astonishing. Without language, we could hardly have created the human world we know. Our development of everything from music to warfare could never have come about in the absence of language. More than any other single characteristic, then, language is what makes us human. And human language is unique.
>
> (Trask, 1999, p. 1)

Our point here is that this is true of *all* human languages, and claims to the contrary about the relative simplicity of different languages are problematic for a number of reasons. Let us begin with the assertion, quoted in Chapter 2, that, "Every [language] is equally complex, logical, and capable of producing an infinite set of sentences to express any thought" (Fromkin, Rodman & Hyams, 2014, p. 10). There are in fact several distinct claims here, some that are true, some that are debatable, and some that are simply false. For example, the claim that all languages are equally complex is simply false: with respect to phonology, morphology and syntax, some languages are clearly more complex than others. Guy Deutscher has challenged this idea quite powerfully, arguing that,

> the dogma of equal complexity [of languages] is based on no evidence whatsoever. No one has ever measured the overall complexity of even one single language, not to mention all of them. No one even has an idea *how* to measure the overall complexity of a language … The equal complexity slogan is just a myth, an urban legend that linguists repeat because they have heard other linguists repeat it before them, having in turn heard others repeat it earlier.
>
> (Deutscher, 2010, p. 105, emphasis in original).

It is of course indisputable that languages differ, and that they differ in a variety of ways – but it is *how* these differences are perceived that matters. As John McWhorter has noted, it is perhaps best to recognize that "*all languages are complex to some degree*" (McWhorter, 2001, p. 200, emphasis in original). As Roman Jakobson observed, "languages differ essentially in what they *must* convey and not in what they *may* convey" (quoted in Deutscher, 2010, p. 151, emphasis in original).[3] Further, it is important to understand that linguistic complexity is neither intrinsically a good thing nor a bad thing. The idea that there are primitive languages which are less complex than others, and thus in some manner inferior to more complex ones, is simply false. There are, in fact, languages which have far greater morphological and syntactic complexity than others, but these tend to be not the "big" languages (that is, the languages of wider communication, such as English, French, Portuguese, Russian, Spanish, etc.), but rather, are often smaller and less well-known languages (many of which are endangered in the modern world).[4] Languages like Xhosa, Thai, Estonian, Hopi, and Uzbek, for instance, are in many ways far more complex than are languages such as English, French and Spanish.

If some language varieties are praised, valued and respected, and are the targets of efforts to maintain or restore linguistic "purity," others are held in contempt and disdained by the powers that be. Challenges to the legitimacy of marginalized languages and language varieties typically share a number of common themes. One of the most powerful of these themes is the rejection of the language variety as a "real" language altogether – terms like "slang," "dialect," "jargon," "patois," "argot," and "vernacular" are often used to describe such language varieties. Indeed, even commonly used terminology that appears to be relatively neutral is a problem in this regard. In linguistics, the phrase "non-standard language" is commonly used in contradistinction to that of "standard language." As Lippi-Green has observed, though,

> The persistence of the terms *standard* and *non-standard* among linguists is a testament to the deep roots of language ideology. This is a problem with no easy solution ... I [have] attempted to sidestep the use of standard and non-standard by borrowing *mainstream* as a reference to the varieties of American English which [are] broadly considered to be correct by prescriptivists ... I have come to the conclusion that *mainstream* is just as inaccurate as the term *standard.*
>
> (Lippi-Green, 2012, p. 62, emphasis in original)

Marginalized languages are often criticized for what are claimed to be their phonological, lexical and syntactic inadequacies. In such cases, what takes place is the conflation of linguistic *difference* (which is non-judgmental in nature) with judgments about the relative value, correctness, efficiency, clarity, purity, and logic of a language variety – judgments that are not only inappropriate but linguistically indefensible (see Díaz-Campos, 2014; Dixon, 2016; Hughes, Trudgill & Watt, 2012; Trudgill, 2016; Wardhaugh & Fuller, 2015). Linguistic differences negatively impact on marginalized and dominated groups *not* because of any intrinsic disadvantage that they may pose, but rather, because judgments are made about both individuals and groups based on speech – assumptions are made about education, intelligence, culture, sophistication, and so on. The problem is that although such judgments are not defensible *linguistically*, they *do* influence decisions and evaluations in society that directly impact speakers. They also reflect the power of language on the one hand, and the close ties between language and identity on the other.

One of the more interesting aspects of the phenomenon of linguistic legitimacy is not simply that certain languages and language varieties are preferred over others, or that some language varieties are seen as inferior to others, by socially dominant groups. Rather, what is in some ways perhaps most concerning is that these linguistic judgments are all too often shared by speakers of the marginalized language varieties themselves. It is this part of linguistic delegitimation that is perhaps most dangerous, as well as most puzzling, as Lippi-Green explains:

> What we do not understand clearly, what is mysterious and important, is not so much the way in which the powerful deny others acknowledgement and permission to be heard in their own voices, but more so how and why those groups cooperate. How do the dominant bloc institutions manage to convince whole groups of human beings that they do not fully or adequately possess an appropriate human language? And, more mysteriously, why do those groups hand over this authority? .... When speakers of devalued or stigmatized varieties of English consent to the standard language ideology, they become complicit in its propagation against themselves, their own interests and identities.
>
> (Lippi-Green, 2012, p. 68)

It is the combination of the overwhelming ubiquity of the ideology of linguistic legitimacy and its general invisibility that makes it so dangerous:

> Ideology is most effective when its workings are least visible. If one becomes aware that a particular aspect of common sense is sustaining power inequalities at one's own expense, it ceases to be common sense, and may cease to have the capacity to sustain power inequalities, i.e. to function ideologically ... The more mechanical the functioning of an ideological assumption in the construction of coherent interpretations, the less likely it is to become a focus of conscious awareness, and hence the more secure its ideological status – which means also the more effectively it is reproduced by being drawn upon in discourse.
>
> (Fairclough, 2015, p. 108)

As Lippi-Green has suggested, social élites "exploit linguistic variation ... in order to send complex messages" about the way different groups are placed in society (Lippi-Green, 2012, p. 38). From an educational perspective, the concept of linguistic legitimacy is an especially important (and potentially harmful) one since it entails the delegitimation of the student's home language. Such delegitimation has implications for the child's ability to function effectively in what has been termed "school language" (see Bailey, 2007; Eder, 1995), for language attitudes and beliefs about students and student ability that are based on the language varieties that they speak (see Bowie & Bond, 1994; García-Nevarez, Stafford, & Arias, 2005; Reeves, 2006; Walker, Shafer & Iiams, 2004), on the acquisition of literacy (see Ivanič, 1998; Olson, Torrance & Hildyard, 1985), and on virtually all aspects of academic achievement (see Cummins, 1986,

1996, 2000; Weiher & Tedin, 2006). Finally, the rejection of the child's language constitutes in an important way a rejection of the child's fundamental identity – and, arguably, of the child her or himself. It is also, as we shall see, a violation of the child's linguistic human rights.

Linguistic legitimacy as a construct is also important with respect to the implications that it has for the development and implementation of educational policy, as controversies about AAE, Spanglish and ASL have made abundantly clear in recent years. In all three cases, popular beliefs – largely inaccurate at best, and more often just downright wrong – have led to political, ideological, and most especially educational debates about language and the relationship among language, education, and the academic challenges faced by various linguistic groups.

African American English

One of the most divisive and controversial linguistic issues in contemporary U.S. education has been that surrounding African American English (AAE). The 1979 *Martin Luther King Junior Elementary School Children vs. Ann Arbor School District* court decision led to a vociferous and on-going debate about the nature, status and educational implications of AAE – a debate that reemerged in full force after the Oakland, California, Board of Education passed a resolution recognizing Ebonics (i.e., AAE) as the primary language of a significant proportion of students in the school district in December 1996. Virtually every aspect of AAE has been surrounded by disagreement, discord and dissent: its nature and characteristics, its origins, history and evolution, its implications for student learning and achievement, even the best name by which it should be called. In many ways, AAE is one of the most powerful example of the process of linguistic delegitimation imaginable, because the social, educational and linguistic issues involved all reflect and overlap the deep racial divides and divisions in our society.

The controversy surrounding AAE is particularly interesting from a linguistic perspective because there has been a vast amount of linguistic research conducted about AAE over the past half-century. Indeed, as Walt Wolfram and Erik Thomas commented, "no topic in modern sociolinguistics has engendered more interest than [AAE]" (Wolfram & Thomas, 2002, p. xiii). In spite of this, though, negative perceptions of and attitudes toward AAE are ubiquitous, especially in popular literature in the United States (see Baugh, 2000; Green, 1993, 2002, 2004, 2011; McWhorter, 1998; Rickford, 1998, 1999, 2006; Rickford & Rickford, 2000; Wolfram & Thomas, 2002). Typical of such views is that of Roger Hernandez, who, after the *King* decision, asserted that, "The notion that [AAE] is a language and that black kids are actually bilingual is ludicrous and patronizing. [AAE] is ungrammatical English. What students who speak [AAE] need to learn is that they are speaking substandard English and that substandard English brands them as uneducated" (Hernandez, 1996, p. A-21). In addition, the use of AAE by African American children is often used as an explanation for their low academic performance. Eleanor Wilson Orr, for instance, suggested – based on significant misunderstandings of AAE, the role of language in the learning of both mathematics and science, and of language more generally – that "for students whose first language is [AAE] … language can be a barrier to success in mathematics and science" (Orr, 1987, p. 9).

One of the challenges that faces any educationally sound discussion about AAE is the definition of how the label AAE should best be defined. AAE is, at the most basic level, a collection of varieties of American English[5] falling along a continuum that taken together are "the dialect[s] that the vast majority of black Americans speak, or can speak, to some extent regardless of age group" (McWhorter, 2011, p. 105). Most speakers of AAE are, at least to some degree, bidialectal. The varieties of AAE differ from those of SAE in a number of significant ways, including with respect to phonology, morphology, lexicon, and syntax. They are also very much stigmatized and marginalized varieties of English in our society.[6] At the same time, though, AAE is also deeply valued by many African Americans, as John Baugh has explained:

> Many speakers of [AAE] view this dialect from an entirely different perspective: they value it. Their personal and cultural identities are closely linked to the language of their friends, family, and forebears. And [AAE] symbolizes racial solidarity. As long as the adoption of standard English is perceived to be an abandonment of black culture, an African American vernacular will continue to survive, and it will do so despite perceptions that black speech is ignorant.
>
> (Baugh, 1999, p. 5)

Indeed, many writers, poets and others have pointed out the "vibrancy and vitality of [AAE] as an expressive instrument in American literature, religion, entertainment, and everyday life," calling it "Spoken Soul" (see Rickford & Rickford, 2000, p. 4). What AAE is *not* is in many ways far more important than what it *is*. It is *not* slang, bad English, or illogical, nor are its speakers lazy, ignorant, sloppy, or uneducated.

The label that we use to identify AAE has also been problematic. AAE has called many things over the years. Wolfram and Thomas have noted that the diversity of labels that have been used for AAE is in fact an indication of the controversy that has surrounded virtually all issues related to it:

> The fact that African American Vernacular English has undergone so many name changes over the past four decades speaks symptomatically of the controversy associated with the recognition of this

> variety. Over the last half century this variety has been assigned the following labels, listed here in approximate chronological sequence: *Negro Dialect, Substandard Negro English, Nonstandard Negro English, Black English, Vernacular Black English/Black English Vernacular, Afro-American English, Ebonics, African American Vernacular English, African American Language, Ebonics* (again), and *Spoken Soul.*
>
> (Wolfram & Thomas, 2002, p. iii)[7]

Virtually any choice that might be made to provide a label for this collection of language varieties is certain to be problematic, though some are so dated as to be deeply offensive to modern ears. The fundamental problem with all of these labels is that they conflate race and language to at least some degree. There is, to be sure, a relationship between those who use AAE and who are African American; most African Americans are able to understand and use at least some AAE in at least some contexts, and relatively few non-African Americans are likely to use AAE as their vernacular language. At the same time, though, there are many African Americans who are not able to use AAE at all, and there are individuals who are not themselves African American who use AAE, even as their primary and preferred language variety (see Cutler, 2002). Given these challenges, we have chosen to follow the most common practice used by linguists, both African American and white, and use AAE, even as we recognize its limitations.

The delegitimation of AAE is widespread and pernicious in educational settings, but even more than this, it is extremely common to find examples of misunderstandings and miscommunication between classroom teachers and other educators and AAE-speaking children. A powerful example of why such misunderstandings matter was provided by Baugh, who describes an interaction between himself as a child (and speaker of AAE) and his Standard English-speaking teacher. As he recounts:

> At that time I was relatively small – and quite small in comparison to Carlos. To my physical detriment. Carlos decided it was time to stop talking and start fighting, and he began to give me the "ass whippin'" he and his fellow Latinos and Latinas felt I deserved … I wish I could say that I held my own during the fight, but that would be a lie. Carlos was a far more skilled fighter than I, and – although I kept spewing verbal insults – I beat a fairly hasty retreat to the relative safety of our classroom, where the teacher, a middle-aged white man, overheard me "badmouthing" Carlos.

TEACHER: John: stop it.
JB: Hey man! He's hitting me. I ain't doing nothing.
TEACHER: You're making fun of him.

JB: Yeah, but he's hitting me. I'm just talking.
TEACHER: But you're making fun of the way he talks, so stop it.
JB: (shucking and jiving in my best rendition of exaggerated standard English) I'm very sorry. I didn't realize I was doing anything wrong.
TEACHER: Now John, why don't you speak that way all of the time and improve yourself?

> The teacher failed to realize what my black peers sensed immediately; namely, my rendition of standard English was an overt attempt to mock the teacher and standard English with one blow. He assumed I was being contrite – not sarcastic, and his statement regarding my linguistic self-improvement was intended to reinforce the virtues of speaking standard English, which had little linguistic usefulness or value among the African American peer group I so desperately wanted to impress.
>
> (Baugh, 2000, p. 9)

The mismatch between AAE-speaking students and SAE-speaking teachers is not only extremely common in U.S. schools, but it often has far more important consequences than this example might suggest. Embedded in much of the contemporary educational discourse about AAE are strongly held views of linguistic inferiority – views that a number of practicing classroom teachers have written about in what can only be considered to be, from a linguistic perspective, ill-informed (see, for example, Orr, 1987; Stotsky, 1999). A powerful example of this tendency is Orr's *Twice as Less: Does Black English Stand Between Black Students and Success in Math and Science?* Orr's argument is that a great deal of the failure of African American students is due to language – specifically, the result of "the usage by these students of such function words as prepositions, conjunctions, and relative pronouns, and in their usage of standard English" (Orr, 1987, p. 21). Although we believe that Orr was honestly attempting to address a serious challenge, and that she sincerely cares about the students that she teaches, her ideas about AAE are, in the words of Baugh, "uninformed and somewhat naïve" (Baugh, 1988, p. 395). Further, not only was the information provided about the structure of AAE out of date and inaccurate even when she wrote the book, but the book as a whole, "despite claims to the contrary … merely serves to perpetuate racist myths about the relationship between language and thought" (Baugh, 1988, p. 403).

Another aspect of the delegitimation of AAE worth mentioning here that followed both the *King* decision in 1979 and the Oakland "Resolution" in 1996 was the emergence of substantial bodies of what has been called "Ebonics humor" or "Ebonics satire" of various kinds – cartoons, jokes, stories, and so on seeking to poke fun at AAE and any claim made for its legitimacy (see Baugh, 2000, pp. 87–99; Gayles & Denerville, 2007;

Rickford, 1999; Rickford & Rickford, 2000, pp. 203–218, Ronkin & Karn, 1999; Scott, 1998). As John Rickford and Russell Rickford noted, "long after the media abandoned [AAE], humorists continued to stoke the coals. In fact, [AAE] seemed to have become a national punch line the very instant the Oakland school board released its resolution" (Rickford & Rickford, 2000, p. 203). Not all of this "Ebonics humor" is necessarily racist, at least in intent, but much of it is in fact extremely so. "Ebonics humor" is important both because of what it tells us about the knowledge and understanding of many people about language in general, and because of what it tells us about the nexus of language, race and education in our society. As Baugh has argued:

> Through racial obfuscation, much of Ebonics satire has turned back the clock regarding prospects for greater linguistic tolerance or a better understanding of the dismal educational plight of so many African American students .... These issues go far beyond the realm of Ebonics satire ... It's painfully clear that, in the name of satire, some remain willing, if not eager, to heap salt on tender social wounds that continue to be aggravated by racially motivated church burnings, police brutality, and heinous murders that serve as recent reminders that African Americans, Jews and other minorities, may still fall victim to racist attacks.
>
> (Baugh, 2000, p. 99)

Most educators and applied linguists who have addressed the matter believe that it is important for the teachers of children who are AAE speakers to know something about AAE, and to be familiar with some of its key features. This does not mean that teachers should be required to be able to speak AAE, nor does it mean that we should teach children AAE at school, nor that the teaching of SAE is not an important goal for education. None of these would be considered to be a mainstream linguistic or educational position, although there are individuals who might advocate them. Rather, much of the discussion and debate about AAE in education, as Elliot Diringer and Lori Olszewski have pointed out, is that "the goal is to help black students master standard English" (Diringer & Olszewski, 1996). In his detailed discussion of AAE, McWhorter has compellingly argued that,

> Black English is not "bad grammar" under any logical conception ... My pointing this out is not to be taken as a call for black people to be able to skip learning Standard English. Certainly someone who could only communicate in [AAE] would be unlikely to get an upwardly mobile job, whether or not that way of speaking is "intricate." The proper idea is that many people will be bidialectal, using Black English in casual settings and the standard in formal ones – as a great many do and always have ... This is, in itself, rather unfair and

> illogical ... The reason we find the idea of all Americans speaking their home dialects in public and print so bizarre, then, is not about comprehensibility, even if we convince ourselves otherwise. It's about social evaluation: Black English is read as inappropriate for the formal. And that will not change.
>
> (McWhorter, 2011, p. 131)

What is really at stake educationally is the fact that the "poor scholastic performance of African-American children is due in considerable degree to an alienation from standard English caused by the stigma attached to speaking Black English, and the wariness of mainstream society which many African-American children feel" (McWhorter, 1998, p. 234).

The case of AAE is a very useful one in understanding the ideology of linguistic legitimation, as well as the many ways in which the process of delegitimation takes place – especially, although by no means exclusively, in the classroom context. To be sure, delegitimation occurs with respect to many (probably most) non-standard language varieties:

> Because the standard variety is the vehicle of almost all writing and official discourse, it is natural for us to conceive of it as "the real deal" and nonstandard varieties as "other" and generally lesser, even if pleasantly quaint or familiar ... . But in fact standard dialects were generally only chosen for this role because they happened to be spoken by those who came into power as the nation coalesced into an administratively centralized political entity. What this means is that there is no logical conception of "language" as "proper" speech as distinguished from "quaint," "broken" varieties best kept down on the farm or over on the other side of the tracks.
>
> (McWhorter, 2001, p. 64)

The nexus of language, social class, and race that surrounds AAE, though, makes it both clearer and more complex than is often the case with other non-standard language varieties. Both individual and institutional racism *do* play a large part in common responses to AAE, but racism is not always the only element involved in popular rejections of AAE. As Baugh notes:

> racist reactions to [AAE fall] into two categories: (1) mean-spirited, overtly racist attacks that were akin to any of the worse racist discourse every produced in American history and (2) benign linguistic prejudice toward vernacular African American English, based on combinations of false linguistic stereotypes.
>
> (Baugh, 2000, p. 88)

Even assuming the most benign of intentions (and even benign racism is deeply offensive), McWhorter has argued that:

> we cannot pretend that our social and cultural perceptions do not affect how we perceive and evaluate language. The idea that Black English is somehow illegitimate or broken can be mightily difficult to shake – even with all due understanding of the history of its speakers. That is, one may suppose that Black English is broken language that is the heritage of a people denied education for so long – understandable, but still deformed.
>
> (McWhorter, 2011, p. 119)

Finally, in the case of AAE, as in many others, the most significant aspect of linguistic delegitimation is what takes place in the classroom, most often between teachers who speak the standard variety of the language and children who speak a non-standard variety of the language. The reliance upon deficit theories, models and assumptions about children and their language(s) serves not to help such students (let alone to empower them), but rather to reinforce the existing rules, norms and structures of the dominant society in which they live.

Spanglish

Spanish is the second most commonly language spoken in the United States, where there are over 50 million native speakers of Spanish. What is less recognized is that the United States is also the second largest Spanish-speaking country in the world, following only Mexico in terms of the total number of Spanish speakers. The situation is even more complex than this might suggest, since in the United States there are a number of different national and indigenous varieties of Spanish (see del Valle & García, 2013; Lipski, 2012; López Morales, 2009; López Morales & Domínguez, 2009; Roca & Lipski, 1993). Further complicating this picture is that:

> Studying the demographics of Spanish speakers in the United States is confusing and tortuous, because the population is ever changing, return migration to countries of origin is a frequent occurrence, underrepresentation in census counts is the rule rather than the exception, and undocumented members of the Spanish-speaking population may elude any attempts to study them. Moreover, the data, both official and unofficial, embody apparent paradoxes. On one hand, the total number of Spanish speakers in the United States is steadily growing, particularly in urban areas of the Southwest, in New York City, and in southern Florida. On the other hand, in many communities the retention of Spanish by U.S.-born speakers is at an all-time low, and the shift from Spanish to English is often complete after only two generations.
>
> (Lipski, 2008, p. 5)

The different varieties of both standard and non-standard Spanish present in the United States have been strongly influenced by extensive contact with English, sometimes resulting in a language variety that has been labelled "Spanglish." This is in no way surprising, but it is nevertheless very controversial. As Ilan Stavans has noted:

> The topic of Spanglish generates enormous controversy. Its army of critics uses an array of arguments against it: that it bastardizes standard English and/or Spanish; it delays the process of assimilation of Hispanics into the melting pot; it is proof of the way the American empire dismantles other competing cultures; it confuses children in the age of language acquisition; and it segregates an ethnic minority already ghettoized by economic factors.
>
> (Stavans, 2008, p. ix)

As was the case with AAE, Spanglish is commonly delegitimized by its own speakers. As the Cuban-American actress Eva Mendes commented in discussing the challenges of raising her two daughters bilingually in Spanish and English, "we're trying to teach the kids Spanish, and it's harder than I thought … I speak Spanglish and that's what they're picking up … *it's technically not a language*. It's Spanglish" (quoted in Tailor, 2019, our emphasis). At the same time that such criticisms have been raised, however, many advocates of Spanglish have asserted that, "In response [to the criticisms of Spanglish], the supporters of Spanglish … celebrate this hybrid form of communication for its dynamism, creativity, and political savvy" (Stavans, 2008, p. ix). A humorous, but nonetheless powerful, response to the question of whether Spanglish is really a language was provided by Bill Santiago:

> Is Spanglish a language? … Yes, *por supuesto*. Spanglish is one of the most innovative languages of our time … Why wouldn't you consider it a language? Because it's made up of other languages? *Pero, si no hay ningún idioma natural que se haya creado desde* scratch. *Resultan siempre* from intimate contact *entre otros idiomas*. There's no such thing as immaculate vocabulary.
>
> (Santiago, 2008, p. 16)

Just as was the case with AAE, it is misleading to speak of Spanglish as *a* language variety. The contact between English and Spanish in the United States has led to the emergence not of a single language variety that can be called Spanglish, but rather, a collection of varieties of Spanglish which are commonly (but misleadingly) grouped together under a single label (see Nadeau & Barlow, 2013, p. 331). As Susan Tamasi and Lamont Antieau have explained:

> Long-term contact between Spanish and English speakers in bilingual American communities has given rise to novel means of communication, with emergent language varieties often being used to identify speakers as members of these communities. These perfectly valid varieties have often been scorned by English and Spanish speakers alike as "Tex-Mex" or "Spanglish," although such terms have often merely become fodder for reclamation by the speakers of these varieties.
>
> (Tamasi & Antieau, 2015, pp. 219–220)

In the late 1940s, the Puerto Rican poet and writer Salvador Tió y Montes de Oca first coined the term *espanglish*, [8] which later evolved into the English *Spanglish*. The term was intended to be pejorative, critiquing those who were, in his view, abandoning Spanish as a result of increasing contact with English. As the quotation from Ilan Stavans above suggests, though, the term has become quite controversial, and is often used by *latinos* who wish to indicate that they do not speak Spanish well, or, paradoxically, by those who do not speak English fluently (see Martínez & Petrucci, 2004; Otheguy & Stern, 2011, p. 86). In both of these senses, the term is used to suggest a linguistic deficit, in Spanish, English, or both. As Milton Azevedo has described it, Spanglish is often seen as nothing more than "*una mezcla agramatical de las lenguas*" ("a non-grammatical mixture of the languages") (Azevedo, 1992, p. 394). Even more strongly, Ricardo Otheguy and Nancy Stern have argued that:

> There is no justification for the use of the term *Spanglish* … features that characterize popular varieties of Spanish in the U.S.A. are, for the most part, parallel to those of popular forms of the language in Latin America and Spain. Further … Spanish in the U.S.A. is not of a hybrid character, that is, not centrally characterized by structural mixing with English. We reject the use of the term Spanglish because there is no objective justification for the term, and because it expresses an ideology of exceptionalism and scorn that actually deprives the North American latino community of a major resource in this globalized world: mastery of a world language.
>
> (Otheguy & Stern, 2011, p. 85)

Although a common perspective (see Escobar & Potowski, 2015, pp. 148–149), this is not the view of many linguists and, even more importantly, of many speakers of these language varieties themselves. The term "Spanglish" is widely used in *latino* communities in a positive manner, indicating the complex and mixed linguistic and cultural heritage of these communities, and can be used as a sign of pride of membership (see Stavans, 2000, 2004; Zentella, 2008, p. 6). Finally, the term is used by many linguists in a more neutral way to describe what are a collection of distinctive varieties of contact language. Indeed, as Alfredo Ardila has noted, "Spanglish represents the most important contemporary linguistic phenomenon in the United States that has barely been approached from a linguistic point of view" (Ardila, 2005, p. 60).

Although Spanglish is the result of the contact and interaction of different varieties of Spanish and English,[9] and although it employs both syntactic and lexical markers drawn from both, it is *neither* Spanish *nor* English. Indeed, for the most part Spanglish is not easily (or even at all) intelligible for monolingual native speakers of either Spanish or English, nor does bilingualism in Spanish and English ensure comprehension of Spanglish. It is also important to note that the use of Spanglish is distinct from code switching between the two languages, although sometimes the two linguistic processes may appear to be similar.[10] As Ardila has explained:

> The blend between Spanish and English found in Hispanic or Latino communities in the United States is usually known as "Spanglish." It is suggested that Spanglish represents the most important contemporary linguistic phenomenon in the United States that has barely been approached from a linguistic point of view. Spanglish may be interpreted in different ways: as a pidgin, a Creole language, an interlanguage, or an anglicized Spanish dialect. Regardless that Spanglish is spoken by millions of people, significant variations within the language are observed.
>
> (Ardila, 2005, p. 60)

Miriam Sánchez (2008) and Ana Celia Zentella (2008) have both written about the syntax of Spanglish, though the former has focused on Spanglish in the Southwestern United States and the latter on the Spanglish used by Puerto Ricans on the mainland. Although there are significant differences between these two varieties of Spanglish, there are also important commonalities. For instance, in discussing the grammars of English and Spanish and their relationship to that of Spanglish, Sánchez notes that:

> The grammatical systems of [English and Spanish] are totally different in terms of underlying structures, rules, ordering of rules, and rule transformations. Some rules, however, are somewhat similar at the categorical level. Both languages, for example, form the progressive tenses with an auxiliary verb plus present progressive morpheme. In some cases, as in the formation of questions, the transformational rules differ significantly, with English requiring reordering of categories and the addition of the verb *do*. Shifts seem to occur where there are similarities in structures but not in cases where the surface structures are entirely different.
>
> (Sánchez, 2008, p. 36)

Thus, while in Spanglish one can say, *Lo hizo slowly*, **How lo hizo?*[11] is completely unacceptable and ungrammatical. Similarly, **Con quién Peter go?* cannot be used in place of *¿Con quién va Pedro?*, nor can **Cuándo is Mary coming?* replace *¿Cuándo viene María?* Further, while an English noun may be preceded by a Spanish article (*el wedding, los officials, los munchies, una friend con benefits*, etc.), Spanish nouns cannot be preceded by an English article (**the casa*, **the chica*). English nouns can be modified by Spanish adjectives, and Spanish nouns may be modified by an English adjectival clause.[12] Although the rules are far from completely clear, as Sánchez has observed, since "both English and Spanish have underlying sentences of this type: S → noun phrase + auxiliary + verb + (noun phrases) … sentences initiated in Spanish, with Spanish auxiliaries, [can] be followed by English particles" (Sánchez, 2008, p. 39).

Spanglish differs from different varieties of standard Spanish[13] in a number of important ways: phonologically, morphologically, lexically and syntactically. Although one could provide detailed analyses of the ways in which different varieties of Spanglish are distinct from standard Spanish, for our purposes here such an analysis is not necessary. What is necessary, though, is a brief discussion about the implications of Spanglish in the school context. In school settings, Spanglish is often denigrated as inadequate and inferior to both Spanish and English, and speakers of Spanglish are dismissed as speaking neither language adequately. In her study of second-generation New York City Puerto Ricans, Ana Celia Zentella cites a poem by Sandra María Estéves, "Not neither," in which Estéves writes that she "not really *hablando bien*" (in Zentella, 2008, p. 42) – a common view held by many Spanglish-speaking students, and one that is encouraged by both Spanish-speaking and English-speaking teachers. In fact, the use of Spanglish ranges from what is similar to code switching to extremely complex linguistic behaviors. The former is exemplified in the following conversation, reported by Ramón Martínez, which took place in a sixth-grade English language arts classroom in East Los Angeles:

ZULEMA: Page what?
CAROLINE: Um.
ZULEMA: Twenty-something, *¿no?*
CAROLINE: Wait. This one? *¿Como ésta?*
ZULEMA: *Sí*, circle. *¿Cuál es?*
CAROLINE: *Como ésta, mira. Como ésta. Esta está bien bonita.*
ZULEMA: *Sí, pero ¿qué* page?
CAROLINE: *A ver, ¿qué* page? Twenty-one.

(Martínez, 2010 p. 24)

Although this conversation was identified as an example of Spanglish by the participants, it differs significantly from the following commentary that occurred in a university classroom at the University of Texas, Austin;

> This is the way we speak. *Así hablamos en los barrios en las comunidades.* You know, we have to use English to survive and Spanish to preserve our heritage. Why you use the one or the other *eso tiene mucho que ver con* what kind of impact you give to your words. *Ves, hay palabras en inglés que tienen mucha fuerza emocional, como práctica. El idioma anglosajón es muy práctico.* It's a business language.
>
> (Stewart, 1999, p. 197)

This second example is far more complex and sophisticated linguistically than the first conversation, not least because of the age and education of the speaker, but both are nevertheless instances of Spanglish. Interestingly, all of the individuals involved in this complex linguistic behavior would, in many places, be considered to be "language deficient" in some sense by educators (see Zentella, 2008, p. 60). What is at stake is the fundamental legitimacy of the language that these people are speaking. The case of Spanglish provides us with an excellent example of linguistic exploitation, since not only is Spanglish an instance in which a language variety's very legitimacy as a language is questioned, but it is challenged by speakers of *both* standard English and standard Spanish. Nor is this merely a semantic or theoretical issue: as Peter Sayer has commented,

> educators can put into practice the valorization of the vernacular and its use as a pedagogical resource … [The acceptance of Spanglish] provides a critical sociolinguistic orientation … [and empowers classroom teachers to] consider[] the ways that students' use of English, Spanish, and Spanglish [can] inform how educators see language use in the classroom. Finally, it considers the ramifications of embracing Spanglish as a social language …
>
> (Sayer, 2008, p. 94)

This need not be the end of the story, however. As Ramón Martínez has suggested, studies have shown that:

> students' *language ideologies* with respect to Spanish-English code switching, a language practice that many of the students referred to as "*Spanglish*" … reveals that students articulated and embodied both *dominant* language ideologies that framed *Spanglish* in pejorative terms and *counter-hegemonic* language ideologies that valorized and normalized this bilingual language practice … this ideological variation and contradiction provide fertile ground for transformative dialog that could potentially help students cultivate *critical language awareness* and *critical literacy* more broadly.
>
> (Martínez, 2013, p. 276)

The case of Spanglish, then, offers us yet another example of the power of the ideology of linguistic legitimacy while at the same time suggesting that users of the language varieties deemed "non-legitimate" may both accept and reject this ideology simultaneously – a paradox, to be sure, but one definitely worth further exploration and reflection.

American Sign Language

For most of human history, the visual and gestural systems that deaf people use to communicate were seen, both by most hearing people and by most deaf people,[14] as undoubtedly useful, but by no means fully *linguistic* in nature. In 1960 [1993], William Stokoe, a young Assistant Professor at Gallaudet College in Washington, DC – an institution explicitly designed to serve deaf students – published a short monograph entitled *Sign Language Structure*. This publication, which generated considerable controversy when it first appeared, was the result of what Stokoe observed taking place all around him at Gallaudet. *Sign Language Structure* launched a revolution, as not only ASL but a host of other sign languages were studied as languages by linguists (see, for example, Baker, van den Bogaerde & Crasborn, 2003; Baker, van den Bogaerde, Pfau & Schermer, 2016; Johnston & Schembri, 2007; Meir & Sandler, 2013; Neidle, Kegl, MacLaughlin, Bahan & Lee, 2000; Sutton-Spence & Woll, 1999; Valli, Lucas, Mulrooney & Villanueva, 2011). Word of this exciting and important revolution, though, was slow to reach most of the general public, and a number of myths, misconceptions, and erroneous ideas about sign language remain common. As Harry Markowicz commented as late as 1980, "American Sign Language is often described in the following ways: It is a universal language whose grammar is poor compared to that of spoken language; its vocabulary is concrete and iconic; it consists of gestures accompanied by facial expressions" (Markowicz, 1980, p. 1). Such views, however common they may be, are simply not true, and they are simply no longer at all credible. There is no longer any question that, as Sherman Wilcox has observed, sign languages are "fully developed human languages independent of the languages spoken in the linguistic communities in the same region" (Wilcox, 1990, p. 141).

It is important note that not all kinds of *signing* are *sign language*. This is an incredibly important point, and one that helps to explain many of the common misconceptions and misunderstandings about ASL and other sign languages. There are, broadly speaking, three different kinds of signing: (i) natural sign languages, used by deaf people in *intragroup* communication, (ii) contact signing, which is typically used by deaf and hearing people in *intergroup* communication, and (iii) manual sign codes, which are deliberated constructed artificial systems that are designed to represent spoken languages in a visual-manual modality, and which are used in educational settings. Our focus here is on *natural* sign languages, that is, sign languages which have emerged within deaf communities and which are used primarily by deaf in their contacts with other deaf people. Such sign languages (which include ASL, as well as many others, some of which are identified in Table 3.1), are visual/gestural languages characterized by radically different syntactic and morphological features from those found in spoken languages. Such languages are used primarily by deaf people, and as we have seen, their status has changed significantly in recent years: historically, they were seen by both deaf and hearing people as indicators of lower status, inferior to spoken languages, and characteristic of uneducated, and often illiterate, individuals. In recent decades, these sign languages have become of increasing interest to both deaf and hearing people, as well as becoming a source of considerable pride and a key element of cultural and group identity for many deaf people.

There may be more than half a million users of ASL in the U.S., and some researchers have argued that ASL is, after English and Spanish, the third most widely used language in the country (see Mitchell, Young, Bachleda & Karchmer, 2006, p. 315). The vast majority of U.S. states have granted ASL some sort of official status in the past few decades (see Reagan, 2011).[15] Typically, such recognition involves two elements: the recognition of ASL as a "real" language, and some sort of enabling clause that allows ASL to be taught in public schools (often as a world language, and to meet world language curricular requirements). Although such language policies are symbolically important, and while they do increase the opportunities for hearing students to study ASL, they also send a powerful message about the need to establish, by legislative fiat, the *legitimacy* of ASL (see Reagan, 2011, 2016). Furthermore, the official recognition of ASL almost never includes any explicit recognition of the *rights* of deaf students to education in ASL as a fundamental linguistic human right – which is arguably the single most important issue related to language and language rights for the deaf community (see Grosjean, 2010a, 2010b; Komesaroff, 2008; Ramsey, 2004; Simms & Thumann, 2007; Skutnabb-Kangas, 2008).

The growing recognition of ASL, and especially its acceptance at both the K-12 and tertiary levels to meet world language requirements, has generated significant backlash, especially among world language educators – a great deal of which is embedded in the ideology of linguistic legitimacy. To some extent, the rejection of ASL by professional language educators has been greater than that aimed at either AAE or Spanglish – but that may well be explained by the fact that no one has (thus far) suggested offering either AAE or Spanglish as a world language in a public school setting, while ASL is not only offered, its enrollments are growing. This resistance is, we believe, an unfortunate commentary on our own profession, and is the result of a combination of ignorance of ASL and other sign languages, and a concern with protecting declining student numbers in many traditional languages while enrollments in ASL are

Table 3.1 Selected Sign Languages

American Sign Language (ASL)
Argentine Sign Language (Lengua de Señas Argentina)
Australian Sign Language (AUSLAN)
Austrian Sign Language (Österreichische Gebärdensprache)
Belgian Francophone Sign Language (Langue des Signes de Belgique Francophone)
Brazilian Sign Language (Língua Brasileira de Sinais, or LIBRAS)
British Sign Language (BSL)
Bulgarian Sign Language (Български Жестомимичен Език)
Catalan Sign Language (Llengua de signes catalana)
Chilean Sign Language (Lengua de Señas Chilena)
Chinese Sign Language
Colombian Sign Language (Lengua de Señas Colombiana)
Czech Sign Language (Český Znakový Jazyk)
Danish Sign Language (Dansk Tegnsprog)
Dutch Sign Language (Nederlandse Gebarentaal)
Finnish Sign Language (Suomalainen Viittomakieli)
Flemish Sign Language (Vlaamse Gebarentaal)
French Sign Language (Langue des Signes Française)
German Sign Language (Deutsche Gebärdensprache)
Greek Sign Language (Ελληνική νοηματική γλώσσα)
Hungarian Sign Language (Magyar Jelnyelv)
Icelandic Sign Language (Íslenskt Táknmál)
Japanese Sign Language
Korean Sign Language
Latvian Sign Language (Latviešu Zimju Valoda)
Lithuanian Sign Language (Lietuvių Gestų Kalba)
Mexican Sign Language (Lengua de Señas Mexicana)
Norwegian Sign Language (Norsk Tegnspråk)
New Zealand Sign Language (NZSL)
Polish Sign Language (Polski Język Migowy)
Portuguese Sign Language (Língua Gestual Portuguesa)
Quebec Sign Language (Langue des Signes Québécoise)
Russian Sign Language (Русский Язык Жестов)
South African Sign Language (SASL)
Spanish Sign Language (Lengua de Signos Española)
Swedish Sign Language (Svenskt Teckenspråk)
Modern Thai Sign Language (แบบสะกดนิ้วมือไทย)
Turkish Sign Language (Türk İşaret Dili)

rising. There are typically five broad objections to the inclusion of ASL as a world language in U.S. schools and universities, and we will address each here. It is worth noting, incidentally, that none of these objections actually suggest that ASL is not a full and complete human language – although one might suspect in some cases that that idea remains a powerful, albeit unarticulated, belief. The common objections are as follows:

- Since it is used primarily in the U.S., ASL cannot be considered a *foreign* language – it is, after all, *American* Sign Language. This argument does not address the issue of whether ASL should be considered to be a "real" language at all; its focus is simply that it because it is American, it cannot be a foreign or world language.
- World languages are not studied solely for linguistic purposes; they are studied in order to expose students to other *cultures* and worldviews. Indeed, some advocates of world language education have argued that it is this exposure to another culture, one different from the student's own, that is among the greatest benefits of studying a world language.
- An important component and purpose of world language education has traditionally been that it serves as a way to expose students to *international* or global perspectives. Since ASL is used in the U.S., it is simply not capable of serving this purpose.
- An important component of studying traditional foreign languages has been to expose students to the literature of those languages – that is, to their *written* literatures. ASL is not a written language, and therefore does not have a comparable literature to which students might be exposed.
- Many students will avoid taking traditional world languages because learning ASL will prove to be an *easier* option that learning a spoken language.

Each of these objectives might appear to have what researchers call "face validity" – on the surface, without further examination or evaluation, they look like they are compelling. As we will see, in each case this is profoundly misleading.

There is no question that ASL is used primarily in the U.S. and Anglophone Canada. It is also, in fact, used in some deaf schools and communities in other parts of the world where it has supplanted local sign languages, but this is a trivial point here. The more relevant and important argument, we think, is the idea that any language that is spoken in the U.S. is definitionally not *foreign*. There are huge numbers of Spanish speakers in many parts of the U.S., but it is hard to consider the argument that Spanish should not be considered a foreign language as a serious one. Of course, Spanish is also widely spoken in many other countries, so it is certainly foreign in that sense. This argument would remain problematic, though, if we consider any indigenous language – should students be prevented from studying Navajo, Hopi, Mohawk, or any other Native American language if they wished, on the grounds that it is not foreign? This seems to be a very odd argument given the very real advantages of foreign language study. It would seem to us that the extent to which a particular language is foreign can only have to do with the extent to which it is new or different *to the learner.*

The ties between language and culture are unquestionable, and it is absolutely true that an important aspect of world language teaching and learning is concerned with exposing students to cultures and worldviews other than their own. As we have already seen, though, the DEAF-WORLD (the ASL sign for the idea of the deaf community) is a unique culture and provides students with an opportunity to come to understand a worldview with very different norms and assumptions than those of the hearing world. Some world language educators have argued that when we talk about deaf culture we are employing the term "culture" in a non-literal, metaphorical sense, but even a minimal exposure to the literature on ASL and the DEAF-WORLD makes clear that this is just not the case.

Although there are ways that international and global perspectives are sometimes (actually, quite commonly) incorporated into the teaching of ASL, it cannot be denied that such perspectives are not really at the core of the teaching and learning of ASL. Nor, of course, are they at the core of the teaching or learning of indigenous languages, so we return to the cases of Navajo, Hopi, Mohawk, and so on. To be sure, such languages are overwhelmingly studied as heritage languages, but there is no obvious reason why this should necessarily be so. In short, while an international and global perspective is certainly a good thing, it can and should be the result not merely of world language education, but other parts of the curriculum as well – social studies, literature, art, music, and so on – and to prevent students from studying ASL on such grounds seems rather strange.

The argument that students should not be allowed to take ASL in place of a world language because it is not a *written* language, and hence does not have a literature to which students can be exposed, is in fact two separate claims: first, that ASL is not a written language, and second, that it has no literary tradition. Although it is technically not quite true that ASL is not a written language – there actually are several notational systems that can be used for reducing it to written form that are used by linguists, for instance – it *is* true that ASL is not a *commonly* or *normally* written language. Indeed, the written language of the American deaf community is English, although that English often shows interference from ASL. Having granted, then, this first objection, what of the second – that is, the lack of a literature in ASL? Since ASL is not normally written, it obviously does not have a *written* literature in the way that French, German, Russian, Spanish and English do. Of course, the same might be said of the vast majority of the languages currently spoken around the world. What ASL *does* have, however, is a literary tradition that is *comparable* to the oral traditions found in the majority of languages spoken around the world (see also Bahan, 1992; Peters, 2000). Nancy Frishberg, for instance, has identified three major indigenous literary genres in ASL: oratory, folklore and performance art. She argues that:

> ASL has been excluded from fulfilling foreign or second language requirements in some institutions because of claims that it has no … tradition of literature … [However,] a literary aesthetic can be defined prior to a written literary tradition, as in the case of Greek and Balkan epic poetry. We know that other languages which are socially stigmatized nonetheless adapt literature through translation and develop their own literary institutions. Non-Western cultures without writing traditions convey their traditions of history and philosophy within community-defined forms of expression. And, finally, the presence or absence of writing (systematized orthography) has little relationship to the existence of a traditional verbal art form.
>
> (Frishberg, 1988, pp. 165–166)

Finally, the last objection to students studying ASL in place of a traditional world language is that by doing so, they are taking an "easy out," since learning ASL is presumably much easier to accomplish than learning French, German, Spanish or some other traditional world language. This is, to put it bluntly, a claim that could only be made by a person who has not attempted to learn ASL. There is understandably a considerable literature dealing with the acquisition of ASL by young deaf children, but considerably less empirical work on the study and learning of ASL as a world language. There is, however, nevertheless a body of work that does address this matter, and it is uniformly consistent about the very real difficulties faced by students in learning ASL as a second or world language (see, for example, Armstrong, 1988; Kemp, 1998a, 1998b; McKee & McKee, 1992; McKee, Rosen & McKee, 2014; Snoddon, 2014) – indeed, Rhonda Jacobs (1996) has gone so far as to offer the case for learning ASL as "a truly foreign language." In short, as Edward Dolnick, writing in *The Atlantic*, wrote:

> Lately … the deaf community has begun to speak for itself. To the surprise and bewilderment of outsiders, its message is utterly contrary to the wisdom of centuries: deaf people, far from groaning under a heavy yoke, are not handicapped at all. Deafness is not a disability. Instead, many deaf people now proclaim, they are a subculture like any other. They are simply a linguistic minority (speaking American Sign Language) and are no more in need of a cure than are Haitians or Hispanics.
>
> (Dolnick, 1993, p. 37)

The reality, from a hearing perspective, is even more extreme than Dolnick suggested. Many deaf people not only do not believe that deafness is in any way a handicap or a disability, but view it in very positive terms. Some deaf people hope that they will have deaf, rather than hearing, children – a profoundly puzzling and upsetting thought for most hearing people, but one that arguably makes a great deal of sense from the perspective of the DEAF-WORLD. Our point here is not to convince anyone of this perspective, but rather, to raise an awareness of a very different way to conceptualize deafness, and certainly of sign language. More than one hundred years ago, Robert McGregor, the first president of the National Association of the Deaf (NAD), argued that:

> The utmost extreme to which tyranny can go when its mailed hand descends upon a conquered people is the proscription of their national language ... But all the attempts to suppress signs, wherever tried, have most signally failed. After a hundred years of proscription ... they still flourish, and will continue to flourish to the end of time ... What heinous crime have the deaf been guilty of that their language should be proscribed?
>
> (Quoted in Lane, 1984, p. xvii)

From the vantage point of many deaf people, the rejection of ASL amounts to little more than an example of the tyranny of the majority, and is no different from the rejection of any other language – nor is it any more justifiable.

Linguistic Legitimacy and the World Language Educator

For the world language educator, the implications of our discussion thus far in this chapter are profound. Language educators are very much at the forefront of the education that students receive with respect to the nature of language and language variation. World language educators need to be aware of the issues surrounding the concept of linguistic legitimacy, as do all teachers, but they also need to understand the specific implications of these issues for the world language classroom. Students in the world language classroom need to be exposed not only to the mainstream variety of the target language, but also need to learn about other variations of that language. It is by no means inappropriate for us to focus to some degree on Parisian French in the French classroom, but it is very much a mistake to exclude from our teaching the different varieties of French spoken around the world (see, for instance, Hale, 1999; Natsis, 1999; Valdman, 2000). Further, in at least some instances local varieties of the target language should actually be incorporated into the formal school curriculum. This would, for instance, make sense in Spanish classes located in areas where there are large numbers of native speakers of the language who speak a variety of Spanish, or even a distinctive language variety such as Spanglish. It makes little sense, we would suggest, to teach a variety of the target language that has few local uses, when another variety might prove quite useful to students. Again, this is not to say that students should not learn the standard or mainstream variety of the target language (or, in a case like Spanish, one or more of the standard varieties of the language). However, if our students' second language interactions are most likely to take place with Spanish speakers for whom *troca* rather than *camión* is the recognized term for "truck," then surely both Spanish forms should be learned. What we are advocating here is fairly simple: world language education should be informed by an understanding and sensitivity to the sociolinguistic aspects of the target language (for the case of French, see Ball, 1997, Lodge, Armstrong, Ellis & Shelton, 1997, and Walter, 1988; for the case of Spanish, see Klee, 1998 and Mar-Molinero, 1997, 2000; for the case of German, see Johnson, 1998, and Stevenson, 1997).

Beyond such sociolinguistic understandings, though, the world language classroom is also an ideal place to help students to begin to develop what can be called *critical language awareness*. In other words, the study of language needs to include not only the communicative and cultural aspects of language, but also the often implicit political and ideological issues related to language. Students need to understand the ways in which language is used to convey and protect social status, as well as how it can be used to oppress and denigrate both individuals and groups. The world language classroom can either reinforce negative language attitudes and prejudices, or can be used to empower students to better understand the social roles of language in society (see Lippi-Green, 2012). In the past, world language educators have done both: we have fought many battles against language prejudice and bigotry, but, as the case of ASL makes clear, we have also sometimes denied and denigrated languages for which we ought to have been advocates. The choice remains very much ours to make in our classrooms and in our interactions with our students. This is precisely the point at which world language education can become *critical* world language pedagogy.

Conclusion

The concept of linguistic legitimacy is an incredibly important one for world language educators to understand, since it has the potential to color and impact much of *what* we teach, *how* we teach, and *how* students in the world language classroom are assessed and evaluated. From a purely linguistic perspective, there is no such thing as a legitimate or non-legitimate language – all languages are fundamentally equal, insofar as they are able to meet the needs of their speakers. All languages are not equal, though, in many other, non-linguistic, ways. This is the point made clearly in the lyrics of the 1979 country song "Good Ole Boys Like Me," when Don Williams sings, "But I was smarter than most and I could choose / Learned to talk like the man on the six o'clock news." The way that the news anchor speaks may not, in any objective way, be superior, to how anyone else speaks, but that does not mean that there are not significant social advantages to using a variety of the standard language – advantages that make a huge difference in the life and life-outcomes of the individual. In this chapter, we have explored the nature and implications of the concept of linguistic legitimacy, and have attempted to demonstrate that the concept itself is not only deeply flawed, but that from an educational perspective it is profoundly harmful. We have examined three specific cases in which claims of linguistic non-legitimacy have had, and continue to have, important educational implications: AAE, Spanglish and ASL. In all three of these cases, there is a substantial amount of misinformation and misunderstanding about the language variety itself, coupled with assumptions that are linguicist as well as racist, audist or biased in some other unacceptable manner. One facet of the job of the world language educator, apart from simply teaching a world language, is to challenge and correct such beliefs and the attitudes that undergird them.

Questions for Reflection and Discussion

1 Identify some of the major varieties of the language that you teach (or plan to teach). Which varieties are the socially preferred varieties? Which varieties are socially stigmatized? How do these language attitudes reflect historical and contemporary power relations in society?
2 What, in your view, are the most important implications of the concept of linguistic legitimacy for the teaching of world languages in the U.S. context? In your answer, be sure to include both curricular and methodological implications.
3 How can a world language educator explain the concept of "language variety" to students? Why is this a concept that students of world languages need to understand?
4 The correction of student errors plays an important role in the context of the world language classroom. Under what circumstances can we say that a sentence created by a student is "wrong"? Under what conditions is such a judgment on the part of the teacher inappropriate? Why?
5 Are there native speakers of the target language you teach locally available to you? Do any of these native speakers use different varieties of the target language? What are the implications of this for classroom instruction?

Notes

1 In fact, the notion that other cultures are "primitive" goes back historically at least as far as the ancient Greeks, who referred to those peoples who did not speak Greek as βάρβαροι – "barbarians."

2 The term *linguicism* was coined in the 1980s by Tove Skutnabb-Kangas to refer to both the attitudes and practices of language discrimination that parallel such other "isms" as racism, sexism, classism, ableism and so on. She has defined linguicism specifically as the "ideologies and structures which are used to legitimate, effectuate, and reproduce unequal division of power and resources (both material and non-material) between groups which are defined on the basis of language" (Skutnabb-Kangas & Phillipson, 1989, p. 456).

3 For instance, in English you can say that, "I have a new friend," without specifying whether the friend is male or female. In Spanish, on the other hand, you *must* indicate the gender of the friend: you *must* use either "*amigo*" or "*amiga*" (and, in fact, the gender of the friend will be reinforced by both the article and adjective).

4 Language endangerment is a topic of considerable, and growing, concern among linguists. The estimates of the numbers of languages that are in danger of extinction in the next century vary considerably; some linguists believe that half of the languages spoken in the world today may be extinct within a hundred years. David Crystal is even more pessimistic, suggesting that as few as 600 languages (roughly, 10% of the languages that are spoken today) may be considered to be safe from extinction (see Crystal, 2000). For further discussions of language endangerment and language extinction, see Evans (2010), Grenoble and Whaley (1998a, 1998b, 2006), Krauss (1992, 2006), Mithun (1998) and Tsunoda (2006).

5 Since AAE is not a single variety of language but rather a collection of varieties, it would actually be more accurate for us to discuss it in the plural – as the "varieties of AAE." The same, of course, is true of all languages, though, and so for purposes of ease of reading, we have decided to write *as if* AAE constitutes a single, monolithic language variety, with the understanding that this is not actually the case. We have followed the same convention in talking about other languages, such as Spanglish, ASL, standard Spanish, SAE, and so on, in the remainder of this chapter.

6 In fact, in some contexts it is AAE that takes on the role of the high status language variety, and SAE becomes the "marked" variety (see Fordham, 2008).

7 One of the more common names used for AAE, and certainly one of the most popular, is "Ebonics." This label, which comes from combining "Ebony" with "Phonics," is deeply problematic from a linguistic perspective because of how broadly it is sometimes used. Robert Williams, for instance, has suggested that the term "Ebonics" refers to "the linguistic and paralinguistic features which on a concentric continuum represents the communicative competence of the West African, Caribbean, and the United States slave descendant of African origin. It includes the various idioms, patois, argots, ideolects [*sic*], and social dialects of Black people, especially those who have been forced to adapt to colonial circumstances. Ebonics derives its form from ebony (black) and phonics (sound, the study of sound) and refers to the study of the language of Black people" (Williams, 1975, p. vi). Carol Blackshire-Belay has gone even further than this; in her work, she says, "I extend the term Ebonics to include *all* languages of African people on the continent and in the [d]iaspora that have created new languages based on their environmental circumstances" (Blackshire-Belay, 1996, p. 20). The problem with this definition, as Baugh has observed, is that it "elevates racial unity, but it does so at the expense of linguistic accuracy .... [this creates] elastic definitions of Ebonics that ultimately undermine scientific validity" (Baugh,

2000, pp. 23–24). There may well be excellent reasons for discussing elements of all of the languages spoken by all of those of African descent, regardless of whether they are in Africa or in the diaspora – but these reasons are not *linguistic* ones, nor are they likely to be particularly helpful in addressing the challenges of speakers of AAE (a very specific set of closely related language varieties) in the context of public education in the U.S.

8 Tió actually created two words to describe this phenomenon; the other, less known term, was "*Inglañol*." In contemporary Spanish, Spanglish is called "*el espanglés*" – a term that generally speaking has the same negative connotations as its English equivalent.

9 Although our focus here is on the impact of different varieties of Spanish on the development of varieties of Spanglish, the varieties of English that are spoken around speakers of Spanglish would also have an impact on their particular variety of Spanglish. Presumably, the reverse may also be true: that is, varieties of Spanglish may have an impact on different varieties of Spanish with which they have contact.

10 The use of Spanglish is also not the same as the use of what Ofelia García and others have called "translanguaging," which refers to the dynamic process by which bilingual and multilingual speakers use their multiple languages as an integrated communication system (see García, 2009; García & Kleyn, 2016; García & Li Wei, 2014; MacSwan, 2017), though there is certainly overlap between translanguaging and Spanglish.

11 The use of the asterisk is a linguistic convention indicating that a particular form is ungrammatical (in a linguistic sense) in the language being discussed.

12 We have used "Spanish" to describe articles such as *el*, *la*, *los*, *las*, and so on, as well as in talking about nouns and verbs, but in fact given the argument presented here they might just as easily – and perhaps more accurately – be termed Spanglish articles, nouns, and adjectives.

13 There is not, of course, a single "standard Spanish," any more than there is a "standard English." In discussing the differences between Spanglish as it is spoken in the Southwest and a more standardized variety of the language, we are using the generic label "standard Spanish" to refer to the different national Spanish*es* spoken in Latin America (which are themselves incredibly diverse). This is an important note, because there are elements of Spanglish that may also be found in some regional varieties of Mexican Spanish, but which would not be accepted as standard either in Mexico or elsewhere in Latin America.

14 Historically, the term "deaf" was virtually always used to described individuals with audiologically impaired hearing. As awareness of ASL grew, so too did an understanding of ASL users as members of a distinctive linguistic and cultural community. In order to indicate the difference between individuals who were audiologically deaf, and those who were culturally and linguistically deaf, in the 1960s and 1970s it became common to adopt a distinction between *d*eaf and *D*eaf: the former referring to *d*eafness solely as an audiological condition, while the latter referring to *D*eafness as a linguistic and cultural condition. Although this is a valuable distinction, it is also an oversimplification. More recently, writers have tried to address this problem by using the term d/Deafness, indicating both groups. Even this solution, though, is problematic much of the time, and so we have chosen to simply use "deaf," with the recognition that in some instances the term is referring solely to an audiological condition, while in others it refers to a membership in a cultural and linguistic community.

15 At the national level, more than 50 countries now grant some sort of official recognition of their associated sign languages – sometimes constitutionally, sometimes legislatively, and sometimes through other policies or regulations (see Reagan, 2010).

References

Ardila, A. (2005). Spanglish: An Anglicized Spanish dialect. *Hispanic Journal of Behavioral Sciences*, 27(1): 60–81.

Armstrong, D. (1988). Some notes on ASL as a "foreign" language. *Sign Language Studies*, 59: 231–239.

Azevedo, M. (1992). *Introducción a la lingüística española*. Englewood Cliffs, NJ: Prentice Hall.

Bahan, B. (1992). American Sign Language literature: Inside the story. In *Deaf studies: What's up? Conference proceedings* (pp. 153–164). Washington, DC: College for Continuing Education, Gallaudet University.

Bailey, A. (2007). *The language demands of school: Putting academic English to the test*. New Haven, CT: Yale University Press.

Baker, A., van den Bogaerde, B. & Crasborn, O. (Eds.). (2003). *Cross-linguistic perspectives in sign language research*. Hamburg: Signum Press.

Baker, A., van den Bogaerde, B., Pfau, R. & Schermer, T. (Eds.). (2016). *The linguistics of sign language: An introduction*. Amsterdam: John Benjamins.

Ball, R. (1997). *The French-speaking world: A practical introduction to sociolinguistic issues*. New York: Routledge.

Baugh, J. (1988). Book review: *Twice as less*: Does Black English stand between black students and success in math and science? *Harvard Educational Review*, 58(3): 395–404.

Baugh, J. (1999). *Out of the mouths of slaves: African American language and educational malpractice*. Austin, TX: University of Texas Press.

Baugh, J. (2000). *Beyond Ebonics: Linguistic pride and racial prejudice*. Oxford: Oxford University Press.

Blackshire-Belay, C. (1996). The location of Ebonics within the framework of the Africological paradigm. *Journal of Black Studies*, 27(1): 5–23.

Bourdieu, P. (1971). Reproduction culturelle et reproduction sociale. *Social Science Information*, 10(2): 45–79.

Bourdieu, P. (1972). *Esquisse d'une théorie de la pratique*. Geneva: Libraire Droz.

Bourdieu, P. (1975). Le langage autorisé (Note sur les conditions sociales de l'efficacité du discours rituel). *Actes de la recherche en sciences sociales*, 1(5–6):183–190.

Bourdieu, P. (1979). *La distinction: Critique sociale du jugment*. Paris: Editions de Minuit.

Bourdieu, P. (1980). *Le sens pratique*. Paris: Éditions de Minuit.

Bourdieu, P. (1982). *Ce que parler veut dire: L'économie des échanges linguistiques*. Paris: Fayard.

Bourdieu, P. (1984). *Homo academicus*. Paris: Éditions de Minuit.

Bourdieu, P. (2001). *Langage et pouvoir symbolique*. Paris: Éditions Points.

Bourdieu, P. & J.-C. Passeron. (1970). *La reproduction: Éléments pour une théorie du système d'enseignement*. Paris: Éditions de Minuit.

Bourdieu, P. & Passeron, J-C. (1997). Language and relationship to language in the teaching situation. *Beogradski Krug*, 3–4(1–2): 64–78.

Bowie, R. & Bond, C. (1994). Influencing future teachers' attitudes toward Black English: Are we making a difference? *Journal of Teacher Education*, 45(2): 112–118.

Crystal, D. (2000). *Language death*. Cambridge: Cambridge University Press.

Cummins, J. (1986). Empowering minority students: A framework for intervention. *Harvard Educational Review*, 56(1): 18–37.

Cummins, J. (1996). *Negotiating identities: Education for empowerment in a diverse society*. Ontario, CA: California Association for Bilingual Education.

Cummins, J. (2000). *Language, power and pedagogy: Bilingual children in the crossfire*. Clevedon: Multilingual Matters.

Cutler, C. (2002). Yorkville Crossing: White teens, hip hop and African American English. *Journal of Sociolinguistics*, 3(4): 428–442.

del Valle, J. & García, O. (2013). Introduction to the making of Spanish: U.S. perspectives. In J. del Valle (Ed.), *A political history of Spanish: The making of a language* (pp. 249–259). Cambridge: Cambridge University Press.

Deutscher, G. (2010). *Through the language glass: Why the world looks different in other languages*. New York: Metropolitan Books.

Díaz-Campos, M. (2014). *Introducción a la sociolingüística hispánica*. Malden, MA: Wiley Blackwell.

Diringer, E. & Olszewski, L. (1996). Critics may not understand Oakland's Ebonics plan: Goal is to teach black kids Standard English. *SF Gate* (December 21). Downloaded from www.sfgate.com/news/article/Critics-May-Not on June 3, 2018.

Dixon, R. (2016). *Are some languages better than others?* Oxford: Oxford University Press.

Dolnick, E. (1993). Deafness as culture. *The Atlantic*, 272: 37–53.

Eder, D. (1995). *School talk: Gender and adolescent culture*. New Brunswick, NJ: Rutgers University Press.

Escobar, A. M. & Potowski, K. (2015). *El español en los Estados Unidos*. Cambridge: Cambridge University Press.

Evans, N. (2010). *Dying words: Endangered languages and what they have to tell us*. Oxford: Wiley-Blackwell.

Fairclough, N. (2015). *Language and power* (3rd ed.). New York: Routledge.

Fordham, S. (2008). Dissin' "the standard": Ebonics as guerrilla warfare at Capital High. *Anthropology and Education*, 30(3): 272–293.

Frishberg, N. (1988). Signers of tales: The case for literary status of an unwritten language. *Sign Language Studies*, 59: 149–170.

Fromkin, V., Rodman, R. & Hyams, N. (2014). *An introduction to language* (10th ed.). Boston: Wadsworth.

García, O. (2009). *Bilingual education in the 21st century: A global perspective*. Oxford: Wiley-Blackwell.

García, O. & Kleyn, T. (Eds.). (2016). *Translanguaging with multilingual students: Learning from classroom moments*. New York: Routledge.

García, O. & Li Wei. (2014). *Translanguaging: Language, bilingualism and education*. New York: Palgrave Macmillan.

García-Nevarez, A., Stafford, M. & Arias, B. (2005). Arizona elementary teachers' attitudes toward English language learners and the use of Spanish in classroom instruction. *Bilingual Research Journal*, 29(2): 295–317.

Gayles, J. & Denerville, D. (2007). Counting language: An exercise in stigmatization. *Multicultural Education*, 15(1): 16–22.

Green, L. (1993). Topics in African American English: The verb system analysis. Unpublished Ph.D. dissertation, University of Massachusetts Amherst, Amherst, Massachusetts.

Green, L. (2002). *African American English: A linguistic introduction*. Cambridge: Cambridge University Press.

Green, L. (2004). African American English. In E. Finegan & J. Rickford (Eds.), *Language in the U.S.A.: Themes for the twenty-first century* (pp. 76–91). Cambridge: Cambridge University Press.

Green, L. (2011). *Language and the African American child*. Cambridge: Cambridge University Press.

Grenoble, L. & Whaley, L. (Eds.). (1998a). *Endangered languages: Current issues and future prospects*. Cambridge: Cambridge University Press.

Grenoble, L. & Whaley, L. (1998b). Toward a typology of language endangerment. In L. Grenoble & L. Whaley (Eds.), *Endangered languages: Current issues and future prospects* (pp. 22–54). Cambridge: Cambridge University Press.

Grenoble, L. & Whaley, L. (2006). *Saving languages: An introduction to language revitalization*. Cambridge: Cambridge University Press.

Grosjean, F. (2010a). Bilingualism, biculturalism, and deafness. *International Journal of Bilingual Education and Bilingualism*, 13(2): 133–145.

Grosjean, F. (2010b). *Bilingual: Life and reality*. Cambridge, MA: Harvard University Press.

Hale, T. (1999). Francophone African literature and the hexagon: Building bridges for the new millennium. *The French Review*, 72(3): 444–455.

Hernandez, R. (1996). Never mind teaching Ebonics: Teach proper English. *The Hartford Courant* (December 26): A-21.

Hughes, A., Trudgill, P. & Watt, D. (2012). *English accents and dialects* (5th ed.). New York: Routledge.

Ivanič, R. (1998). *Writing and identity: The discoursal construction of identity in academic writing*. Amsterdam: John Benjamins.

Jacobs, R. (1996). Just how hard is it to learn ASL? The case for ASL as a truly foreign language. In C. Lucas (Ed.), *Multicultural aspects of sociolinguistics in deaf communities* (pp. 183–226). Washington, DC: Gallaudet University Press.

Johnson, S. (1998). *Exploring the German language*. London: Arnold.

Johnston, T. & Schembri, A. (2007). *Australian Sign Language (Auslan): An introduction to sign language linguistics*. Cambridge: Cambridge University Press.

Kemp, M. (1998a). An acculturation model for learners of ASL. In C. Lucas (Ed.), *Pinky extension and eye gaze: Language use in deaf communities* (pp. 213–230). Washington, DC: Gallaudet University Press.

Kemp, M. (1998b). Why is learning American Sign Language a challenge? *American Annals of the Deaf*, 143(3): 255–259.

Klee, C. (1998). Communication as an organizing principle in the national standards: Sociolinguistic aspects of Spanish language teaching. *Hispania*, 81(2): 339–351.

Komesaroff, L. (2008). *Disabling pedagogy: Power, politics and deaf education*. Washington, DC: Gallaudet University Press.

Krauss, M. (1992). The world's languages in crisis. *Language*, 68(1): 4–10.

Krauss, M. (2006). Classification and terminology for degrees of language endangerment. In M. Brenzinger (Ed.), *Language diversity endangered* (pp. 1–18). Berlin: Mouton de Gruyter.

Kuper, A. (2017). *The invention of primitive society: Transformations of an illusion* (2nd ed.). New York: Routledge.

Lane, H. (1984). *When the mind hears: A history of the deaf*. New York: Random House.

Lippi-Green, R. (2012). *English with an accent: Language, ideology, and discrimination in the United States* (2nd ed.). New York: Routledge.

Lipski, J. (2008). *Varieties of Spanish in the United States*. Washington, DC: Georgetown University Press.

Lipski, J. (2012). Geographic and social varieties of Spanish: An overview. In J. I. Hualde, A. Olarrea & E. O'Rourke (Eds.), *The handbook of hispanic linguistics* (pp. 1–26). Oxford: Wiley-Blackwell.

Lodge, R., Armstrong, N., Ellis, Y. & Shelton, J. (1997). *Exploring the French language*. London: Arnold.

López Morales, H. (Ed.). (2009). *Enciclopedia del español en los Estados Unidos*. Madrid: Instituto Cervantes.

López Morales, H. & Domínguez, C. (2009). Introducción a la demografíá hispánica en los Estados Unidos. In H. López Morales (Ed.), *Enciclopedia del español en los Estados Unidos* (pp. 83–103). Madrid: Instituto Cervantes.

MacSwan, J. (2017). A multilingual perspective on translanguaging. *American Educational Research Journal*, 54(1): 167–201.

Markowicz, H. (1980). Myths about American Sign Language. In H. Lane & F. Grosjean (Eds.), *Recent perspectives on American Sign Language* (pp. 1–6). Hillsdale, NJ: Lawrence Erlbaum Associates.

Mar-Molinero, C. (1997). *The Spanish-speaking world: A practical introduction to sociolinguistic issues*. New York: Routledge.

Mar-Molinero, C. (2000). *Politics of language in the Spanish-speaking world*. New York: Routledge.

Martínez, R. (2010). Spanglish as literacy tool: Toward an understanding of the potential role of Spanish-English code-switching in the development of academic literacy. *Research in the Teaching of English*, 45(2): 124–149.

Martínez, R. (2013). Reading the world in Spanglish: Hybrid language practices and ideological contestation in a sixth-grade English language arts classroom. *Linguistics and Education, 24(3)*: 276–288.

Martínez, G. & Petrucci, P. (2004). Institutional dimensions of cultural bias on the Texas-Mexico border: Linguistic insecurity among heritage language learners. *Critical Inquiry in Language Studies*, 1(2): 89–104.

Mayr, A. (Ed.). (2008). *Language and power: An introduction to institutional discourse*. London: Continuum.

McKee, R. & McKee, D. (1992). What's so hard about learning ASL? Students' and teachers' perceptions. *Sign Language Studies*, 75: 129–157.

McKee, D., Rosen, R. & McKee, R. (Eds.). (2014). *Teaching and learning signed languages*. London: Palgrave Macmillan.

McWhorter, J. (1998). *The word on the street: Fact and fable about American English*. New York: Plenum.

McWhorter, J. (2001). *The power of Babel: A natural history of language*. New York: W. H. Freeman.

McWhorter, J. (2011). *What language is (and what it isn't and what it could be)*. New York: Gotham Books.

Meir, I. & Sandler, W. (2013). *A language in space: The story of Israeli Sign Language*. New York: Psychology Press.

Mitchell, R., Young, T., Bachleda, B. & Karchmer, M. (2006). How many people use ASL in the United States? Why estimates need updating. *Sign Language Studies*, 6(3): 390–401.

Mithun, M. (1998). The significance of diversity in language endangerment and preservation. In L. Grenoble & L. Whaley (Eds.), *Endangered languages: Current issues and future prospects* (pp. 163–191). Cambridge: Cambridge University Press.

Natsis, J. (1999). Legislation and language: The politics of speaking French in Louisiana. *The French Review*, 73(2): 325–331.

Neidle, C., Kegl, J., MacLaughlin, D., Bahan, B. & Lee, R. (2000). *The syntax of American Sign Language: Functional categories and hierarchical structure*. Cambridge, MA: The MIT Press.

Olson, D., Torrance, N. & Hildyard, A. (1985). *Literacy, language and learning: The nature and consequences of reading and writing*. Cambridge: Cambridge University Press.

Orr, E. (1987). *Twice as less: Black English and the performance of black students in mathematics and science*. New York: W. W. Norton.

Otheguy, R. & Stern, N. (2011). On so-called Spanglish. *International Journal of Bilingualism*, 15(1): 85–100.

Peters, C. (2000). *Deaf American literature: From carnival to the canon*. Washington, DC: Gallaudet University Press.

Ramsey, C. (2004). What does culture have to do with the education of students who are deaf or hard of hearing? In B. Brueggemann (Ed.), *Literacy and deaf people: Cultural and contextual perspectives* (pp. 47–58). Washington, DC: Gallaudet University Press.

Reagan, T. (2010). *Language policy and planning for sign languages*. Washington, DC: Gallaudet University Press.

Reagan, T. (2011). Ideological barriers to American Sign Language: Unpacking linguistic resistance. *Sign Language Studies*, 11(4): 594–624.

Reagan, T. (2016). The conceptualization of "language legitimacy." *Critical Inquiry in Language Studies*, 13(1): 1–19.

Reagan, T. (2019). *Linguistic legitimacy and social justice*. London: Palgrave Macmillan.

Reeves, J. (2006). Secondary teacher attitudes toward including English-language learners in mainstream classrooms. *The Journal of Educational Research*, 99(3): 131–143.

Rickford, J. (1998). The creole origins of African American Vernacular English: Evidence from copula absence. In S. Mufwene, J. Rickford, G. Bailey & J. Baugh (Eds.), *African American English: Structure, history and use* (pp. 154–200). New York: Routledge.

Rickford, J. (1999). The Ebonics controversy in my backyard: A sociolinguist's experiences and reflections. *Journal of Sociolinguistics*, 3(2): 267–275.

Rickford, J. (2006). *Linguistics, education, and the Ebonics firestorm. In S. Nero Dialects, Englishes, creoles, and education* (pp. 71–92). Mahwah, NJ: Lawrence Erlbaum Associates.

Rickford, J. & Rickford, R. (2000). *Spoken soul: The story of Black English*. New York: John Wiley.

Roca, A. & Lipski, J. (Eds.). (1993). *Spanish in the United States: Linguistic contact and diversity*. Berlin: Mouton de Gruyter.

Ronkin, M. & Karn, H. (1999). Mock Ebonics: Linguistic racism in parodies of Ebonics on the Internet. *Journal of Sociolinguistics*, 3(3): 360–380.

Sánchez, R. (2008). Our linguistic and social context. In I. Stavans (Ed.), *Spanglish* (pp. 3–41). Westport, CT: Greenwood Press.

Santiago, B. (2008). *Pardon my Spanglish: One man's guide to speaking the habla.* Philadelphia, PA: Quirk Books.

Sayer, P. (2008). Demystifying language mixing: Spanglish in school. *Journal of Latinos and Education*, 7(2): 94–112.

Scancarelli, J. (1994). Another look at a "primitive language." *International Journal of American Linguistics*, 60(2): 149–160.

Scott, J. (1998). The serious side of Ebonics humor. *Journal of English Linguistics*, 26(2): 137–155.

Simms, L. & Thumann, H. (2007). In search of a new, linguistically and culturally sensitive paradigm in deaf education. *American Annals of the Deaf*, 152(3): 302–311.

Skutnabb-Kangas, T. (2008). Bilingual education and sign language as the mother tongue of deaf children. In C. Bidoli & E. Ochse (Eds.), *English in international deaf communication* (pp. 75–94). Bern: Peter Lang.

Skutnabb-Kangas, T. & Phillipson, R. (1989). "Mother tongue": The theoretical and sociopolitical construction of a concept. In U. Ammon (Ed.), *Status and function of languages and language varieties* (pp. 450–477). New York: Walter de Gruyter.

Snoddon, K. (2014). Hearing parents as plurilingual learners of ASL. In D. McKee, R. Rosen & R. McKee (Eds.), *Teaching and learning signed languages* (pp. 175–196). London: Palgrave Macmillan.

Stavans, I. (2000). Spanglish: Tickling the tongue. *World Literature Today*, 74(3): 555–558.

Stavans, I. (2004). *Spanglish: The making of a new American language*. New York: Harper Collins.

Stavans, I. (2008). The gravitas of Spanglish. In I. Stavans (Ed.), *Spanglish* (pp. 64–71). Westport, CT: Greenwood.

Stevenson, P. (1997). *The German-speaking world: A practical introduction to sociolinguistic issues*. New York: Routledge.

Stewart, M. (1999). *The Spanish language today*. New York: Routledge.

Stokoe, W. (1993). *Sign language structure*. Silver Spring, MD: Linstok Press (Original work published 1960)

Stotsky, S. (1999). *Losing our language: How multiculturalism undermines our children's ability to read, write and reason*. San Francisco, CA: Encounter Books.

Sutton-Spence, R. & Woll, B. (1999). *The linguistics of British Sign Language: An introduction*. Cambridge: Cambridge University Press.

Tailor, L. (2019). Eva Mendes says she and Ryan Gosling are struggling to teach their kids Spanish – here's why. *ET* (May 20). Downloaded from www.msn.com/en-us/movies/celebrity/eva-mendes-says-she-and-ryan-gosling-are-struggling-to-teach-their-kids-spanish-heres-why/ar-AABDXzq?ocid=spartandhp on May 21, 2019.

Tamasi, S. & Antieau, L. (2015). *Language and linguistic diversity in the U.S.: An introduction*. New York: Routledge.

Trask, R. (1999). *Language: The basics* (2nd ed.). New York: Routledge.

Trudgill, P. (2016). *Dialect matters: Respecting vernacular language*. Cambridge: Cambridge University Press.

Tsunoda, T. (2006). *Language endangerment and language revitalization: An introduction*. Berlin: Mouton de Gruyter.

Valdman, A. (2000). Comment gérer la variation dans l'enseignement du français langue étrangère aux Etats-Unis. *The French Review*, 73(4): 648–666.

Valli, C., Lucas, C., Mulrooney, J. & Villanueva, M. (2011). *Linguistics of American Sign Language* (5th ed.). Washington, DC: Gallaudet University Press.

Walker, A., Shafer, J. & Iiams, M. (2004). "Not in my classroom": Teacher attitudes towards English language learners in the mainstream classroom. *NABE Journal of Research and Practice*, 2(1): 130–160.

Walter, H. (1988). *Le français dans tous les sens*. Paris: Éditions Robert Laffont.

Wardhaugh, R. & Fuller, J. (2015). *Introduction to sociolinguistics* (7th ed.). Malden, MA: Wiley Blackwell.

Weiher, G. & Tedin, K. (2006). Minority student achievement. *Review of Policy Research*, 23(5): 963–967.

Wilcox, S. (1990). The structure of signed and spoken languages. *Sign Language Studies*, 67: 141–151.

Williams, J. (1975). *Origins of the English language: A social and linguistic history*. New York: Free Press.

Wodak, R. (2012). Language, power and identity. *Language Teaching*, 45(2): 215–233.

Wolfram, W. & Thomas, E. (2002). *The development of African American English*. Oxford: Blackwell.

Woolard, K. (1992). Language ideology: Issues and approaches. *Pragmatics*, 2(3): 235–249.

Zentella, A. (2008). The grammar of Spanglish. In I. Stavans (Ed.), *Spanglish* (pp. 42–63). Westport, CT: Greenwood Press.

Zuidema, L. (2005). Myth education: Rationale and strategies for teaching against linguistic prejudice. *Journal of Adolescent and Adult Literacy*, 48(8): 666–676.

Part II

Learning Language

4 Why Study a Foreign Language?

The Case for World Language Education

Writing about the value in studying a foreign language, some forty years ago Sylvia Porter suggested that:

> With a language skill added to your other skills, you might double the chances of getting the job you want. There are openings for an auto mechanic who also speaks Arabic, an electronic radio expert who knows Japanese, a chef (even a woman chef) who understands French. It even could be a foreign language would be more useful to you during the next ten years than a college diploma ... Language is, in fact, your hidden job insurance.
>
> (Quoted in Jarvis, 1980, pp. 31–32)

Although this passage was written with the intention of providing students and parents with a compelling case for the study of foreign languages, like many such arguments it has a fundamental flaw: while it may have a certain degree of face validity for world language educators and our supporters, it is not in fact true. Or, to put it perhaps a bit more gently, it is not compatible with the life experiences of most of our students (or, for that matter, with the life experiences of most of their parents or most public school educators). The United States, regardless of how one might personally feel about it, is in fact a profoundly monolingual society *ideologically* if not empirically, and relatively few students (or parents or most public school educators) really believe that foreign language skills are necessary in either the domestic or international marketplaces. Indeed, when Barack Obama, during his presidential campaign, suggested that every U.S. student should study a foreign language (a position long held by ACTFL, and many others as well, and hardly a particularly radical idea on its own merits), there was a considerable backlash to the idea, with some going so far as to question both his patriotism and his Americanism. Similarly, when he was presenting testimony related to the impeachment of Donald Trump, Lt. Col. Alexander Vindman's loyalty and patriotism were questioned in 2019 – both because his family immigrated to the U.S. when he was a young child, and in part because of his ability to speak Ukrainian (a skill arguably essential to his job) (see Bump, 2019).

Claims about language skills being job insurance, in short, are viewed with considerable skepticism in a society in which monolingualism in English is normative. One major problem with such arguments is the issue of language competence: the level of language competence required in jobs that do require language skills are far beyond what students can be expected acquire in a typical world language program at the secondary level. Even if a student *had* been fortunate enough to study Arabic for two or three years at the high school level, and had also had the benefit of appropriate automotive training, it is hardly likely that s/he would be able to function as an Arabic-speaking auto mechanic, although to be sure even minimal skills (greetings and the like) might be useful.

The experience of Lt. Col. Vindman also reflects another challenge with respect to language competence in some languages, and especially those languages that are learned and/or used for purposes of national security. It is fairly common for others to be suspicious of those who speak a language that is considered to be a "language of the enemy"; this especially true of heritage and native speakers of such languages, but it is also not uncommon for native speakers of English who have become fluent in such languages. This was true, of course, of German in both the First and Second World Wars, and later of Russian. Today it is found with respect to a variety of languages, including Arabic, Farsi, and so on. Among recent examples of this unfortunate tendency has been "a new federal restriction that bars universities with Confucius Institutes from Defense Department funding for Chinese-language study" (see Economist, 2020, p. 14).

Our comments thus far might lead one to suspect that we were hostile to the study and teaching of languages other than English in the American context, but in fact nothing could be further from the truth. The fact that there are structural, organizational and ideological barriers that generally hinder successful foreign language learning in our society, not to mention the development of positive attitudes and dispositions toward the learning of languages other than English, merely serves to help to explain *why* world language education in the United States has been, and remains, relatively unsuccessful. The challenge before us is to find arguments that are compelling for those outside the field of world language education, and then, to find ways of ensuring the effective teaching and learning of additional languages.

It is interesting that of all of the academic subjects normally offered in U.S. public schools, no other discipline is asked to defend its existence in the way that world language education is routinely challenged. Imagine, for a moment, applying some of the common arguments against the study of world languages to other subjects in the curriculum – be they mathematics, science, reading, geography, history, literature, or whatever. How seriously would we, as a society and as educators, take claims such as the following:

- I studied algebra, geometry and calculus in school, and have forgotten all I learned. I don't think that I have ever had any practical use for anything that I had to study in a mathematics class in high school or college, and I can't see any reason to make today's students study such things.
- History may be of interest to a small number of individuals, and they should be allowed to study it, so long as there are enough of them to make it economically defensible. The average person has no need for history or historical knowledge, though.
- It's pretty clear that most Americans know almost nothing about geography. Many can't even name the state capitals! Since we seem to do such a poor job teaching geography, maybe we'd be better off just not offering it at all.
- What is the point of studying earth science, anyway? I've never really needed to know what I learned in those classes in high school. Why would I care if I could identify different kinds of rocks? I'm not a geologist, after all.

All of these arguments are fundamentally absurd, we would suggest, and would be rejected out of hand if they were seriously made in public. They confuse the practical utility of a subject for a specific individual or group of individuals with its *social* and *educational* purposes. More than this, they trivialize the disciplines at issue and why we, as a society, believe that children should study them. They also beg the question of what, exactly, is encompassed by the term "educated person" – a concept on which there is a vast literature in the philosophy of education (see, for example, Barrow & Woods, 1988; Hamm, 1989; Hirst, 1974; Peters, 1966, 1967a, 1973a, 1973b). When applied to world language study, though, such arguments in our society all too often seem to take on a legitimacy that would not be seen as reasonable if applied to any other subject matter. This double standard creates a very real need for us to offer a more powerful set of justifications for precisely *why* foreign languages should be an important and integral component of the curriculum for *all* students, and it is to the task of outlining such a justification that we now turn.

Traditional Rationales for Foreign Language Study

Advocates for the study of world languages in the United States have traditionally offered a number of arguments and rationales for the desirability of students learning a foreign language. In general, these arguments have been concentrated in five broad areas:

- commercial and business needs;
- national security requirements;

- promoting cultural understanding;
- facilitating travel and tourism; and
- the transfer of skills.

Commercial and Business Needs

There is a common assumption among supporters of world language education in U.S. society that studying a foreign language will increase the individual's competitive advantage in the marketplace – along the lines suggested in the quotation from Sylvia Porter with which this chapter begins (for a more recent example of this view, see New American Economy, 2017). As globalization increases, this is not at all an unreasonable expectation: in its *Lost in Translation* report about the need for foreign language competence in the workforce, the New American Economy think-tank asserted that, "Foreign language skills represent an advantage for individuals who possess these abilities, the businesses who employ these workers, and the American economy as a whole" (New American Economy, 2017, p. 4). This is true as far as it goes as a general claim, but the reality of the workplace does not provide particularly compelling empirical data to support it. In its examination of nearly 28 million job positions that were advertised online in 2015, for instance, *Lost in Translation* determined that fewer than 5% of these positions indicated a desire for an individual with bilingual skills. That works out to under 1.5 million jobs – a substantial number, as the authors of the report note, but given the total number of positions, perhaps less than an overwhelming number. It is also important here to note that for these positions, bilingual skills were *desired* – but not, in many cases, actually *required*. Further, in many of these cases, a fairly low skill level in the language other than English was deemed acceptable – of the 25 positions examined in *Lost in Translation*, 10 required a high skill level, 4 required a medium skill level, and 11 required a low skill level (New American Economy, 2017, p. 8). Finally, the location of jobs for which foreign language skills were desired was not only strongly skewed, but was also reflective of parts of the country where large numbers of non-native speakers of English are concentrated (see Table 4.1) – which suggests *both* that many of the positions that have such requirements are service positions for jobs that involve working with local, often non-English-speaking, populations rather than with international business positions, *and* that for many of these positions there are native speakers who may well be more qualified than native speakers of English who have learned the language as a second language.

In terms of the mid-level and senior-level language requirements in business, a good way to get a sense of what such requirements are is to look at the case of MBA programs. Although the QS MBA *Jobs and Salary Trends Report 2015/16* does suggest that "language skills and

Table 4.1 Geographic Concentration of Jobs Requiring Bilingual Skills in the U.S.

Concentration of Bilingual Jobs	*Percentage of Non-English Native Speakers (2013)*
Very High Concentration of Bilingual Job Postings	
Arizona	26.8%
California	43.8%
Florida	27.4%
Oregon	14.9%
High Concentration of Bilingual Job Postings	
Colorado	16.7%
New Mexico	36.0%
Texas	34.7%
Average Concentration of Bilingual Job Postings	
Connecticut	21.5%
Illinois	22.7%
Utah	14.1%
Maryland	17.0%
Massachusetts	22.4%
New Jersey	30.4%
Rhode Island	21.3%
Virginia	14.9%
Washington	18.9%
Low Concentration of Bilingual Job Postings	
Georgia	13.6%
Idaho	10.9%
Nebraska	10.5%
Very Low Concentration of Bilingual Job Postings	
All Other States (exc. Alaska and Hawaii)	7.1%
TOTAL UNITED STATES	**20.8%**

Source: Based on New American Economy (2017, p. 18); Camarota & Zeigler (2014)

international awareness are among the top things employers look for in MBA hires," this is not actually reflected in the training included in such programs. Although there are a small number of MBA programs with foreign language requirements, these tend to be programs that either are located in non-English speaking contexts or which seek to prepare their graduates to work in such settings (e.g., the Hautes Études Commerciales de Montréal in Québec, the McCombs School of Business in Austin, Texas, the University of Miami, etc.). Rather, what is clearly the norm in MBA programs – both in Anglophone and non-Anglophone countries – is for the programs to be offered through the medium of English, and for there to be expectations that students will be fluent in English. Competence in other languages may be desirable, but it is rarely required (see QS MBA, 2016).

One interesting exception to this general tendency among graduate programs in business is Arizona State University's Thunderbird School of Global Management, which, unlike most schools of business, requires a minimum of four semesters of language study (or demonstrated equivalence in terms of language proficiency) (see Grosse, 2004). In an in-depth study of Thunderbird's graduates, Christine Grosse found that although the majority of respondents did indicate that they used their language skills on either a daily or at least frequent basis, there was a noteworthy exception – those individuals employed in the United States. As two different respondents commented,

> Unless you work abroad, U.S. companies do not value foreign language skills. Even then [in positions abroad] they expect everyone else to speak English …
>
> I would say that language skills are most useful in a career overseas. Language skills are not appreciated as much in the U.S. In my career, when I was working in the U.S. my ability to speak Japanese was treated as an interesting skill, but it was a very rare situation where it actually made a difference in my job. Within U.S. companies, I have never seen ability to speak a foreign language result in better pay.
>
> (Quoted in Grosse, 2004, p. 364)

Furthermore, in the same study several of the respondents noted that the benefits of foreign language study were closely related to the degree to which the individual was actually *fluent* in the target language:

> I have found that language skills are not as important in business unless one is truly fluent in the language. My language skills have never been good enough to negotiate in, but they gave me an understanding of the people I was negotiating with, and even a few words of the language gave people I was doing business with some comfort that I was interested in them and their way of business.
>
> I don't speak Spanish well enough for there to have been any value or different opportunities for me.
>
> (Quoted in Grosse, 2004, p. 357)

These comments are supported by the fact that over 70% of the respondents indicated that living abroad was the most valuable source for learning a foreign language. As three respondents noted,

> I believe that any … language program must include a 1- or 2-month stay in the country after the first 3 months of training.

> I think you have to live in the country to really learn the language.
>
> Languages are learned in the country, in the culture … if this type of environment can be created in the educational system then learning of the language is strengthened.
>
> (Quoted in Grosse, 2004, p. 355)

Interestingly, one of the more common themes that emerged in Grosse's study were the ties between language and culture, and the need to understand other cultures.

In fact, in spite of Grosse's findings, as a general rule it is far more common for both employers and employees in the business world to believe that while language competence is certainly a good thing, it is not in fact really *necessary* for most employees – although there is a belief that a knowledge of a small number of greetings and the like can be socially advantageous. More common, though, is the view that Tsedal Neeley has put forth in the *Harvard Business Review*:

> Ready or not, English is now the global language of business. More and more multinational companies are mandating English as the common corporate language – Airbus, Daimler-Chrysler, Fast Retailing, Nokia, Renault, Samsung, SAP [*Systeme, Anwendungen und Produkte in der Datenverarbeitung*, Systems, Applications & Products in Data Processing], Technicolor, and Microsoft in Beijing, to name a few – in an attempt to facilitate community and performance across geographically diverse functions and business endeavors …. Adopting a common mode of speech isn't just a good idea; *it's a must*, even for an American company with operations overseas …. A global language change takes perseverance and time, but if you want to surpass your rivals, *it's no longer a matter of choice*.
>
> (Neeley, 2012; our emphasis)

Finally, there is something of a Catch-22 with respect to any expectation of the importance of language for a particular occupation: as Cyrus Mehta has noted:

> The Department of Labor … has usually frowned upon an employer including a language requirement in an advertisement that was used to test the U.S. labor market to establish a shortage of domestic workers. An employer is usually required to justify the language requirement by showing it arose from business *necessity*.
>
> (Mehta, 2008, our emphasis)

National Security Requirements

The United States has a variety of both domestic and international needs and obligations that require personnel with competence (often a high level of competence) in different languages. As the Linguistic Society of America (LSA) noted in a brochure entitled *Linguistics and National Security*,

> The U.S. government relies on linguists for much of its expertise in communications intelligence – that is, the collection and transmission of information that's important for national security. Our country's messages must reach their destinations without being intercepted and understood by any other country; at the same time, we want to be able to interpret any messages that we intercept from other countries concerning espionage, military build-ups, or other activities that could threaten the United States. For this reason, the government hires language specialists to translate, analyze, and summarize intercepted messages.
>
> (Birner, 2020, p. 1)

Further, as Patti Koning has commented,

> The largest employer for language professionals in [the United States] is the U.S. Department of Defense – a fact that might surprise many people. In fact, national security is a fast-growing and exciting career area for those with strong foreign language skills, offering a wide variety of opportunities ... The Federal Bureau of Investigation (FBI), Central Intelligence Agency (CIA), and National Security Agency (NSA) all hire hundreds of foreign language professionals each year to work as agents, linguists, and language analysts.
>
> (Koning, 2009, p. 32)

The key here is the focus on *strong* language skills. There is, in fact, a huge shortage of highly competent language professionals available for these positions. Michael Nugent, the director of the Pentagon's Defense Language and National Security Education Office, has suggested that the shortage of such individuals actually constitutes a national emergency, arguing that "It's very, very important that the [U.S.] presence when they're out there, whether it's [the U.S. Department of Defense] or [the U.S. Department of] State or any of the other agencies, that they understand the culture and the region with which they are working" (quoted in Zietlow, 2017). It was with just such concerns in mind that in 1985 the U.S. government identified a list of some 169 "critical languages," languages which "would promote important scientific research or security interests of a national or economic kind" (Crystal, 1987, p. 342). The National Security Education Program (NSEP), which was established in 1991 under the auspices of the U.S. Department of Defense, currently supports the study of more than 60 of these critical languages by U.S. students at both the undergraduate and graduate levels (see Table 4.2), as well as supporting nine Language Training Centers (LTCs) at different universities (see Table 4.3). At the same time, the Critical Language Scholarship program (CLS)

Table 4.2 Critical Languages Supported by the NSEP

Albanian	African Languages (all)	Akan/Twi	Amharic
Arabic (all dialects)	Armenian	Azerbaijani (Azeri)	Bahasa Indonesia
Bambara	Belarusian	Banla (Bengali)	Bosnian
Bulgarian	Cambodian	Cantonese	Croatian
Czech	Gan	Georgian	Haitian
Hausa	Hebrew	Hindi	Hungarian
Japanese	Javanese	Kanarese	Kazakh
Khmer	Korean	Kurdish	Kyrgyz
Lingala	Macedonian	Malay	Malayalam
Mandarin	Moldovan	Pashto	Persian
Polish	Portuguese	Punjabi	Romanian
Russian	Serbian	Sinhala	Slovak
Slovenian	Swahili	Tagalog	Tajik
Tamil	Telegu	Thai	Turkmen
Turkish	Uighur	Ukrainian	Urdu
Uzbek	Vietnamese	Wolof	Yoruba
Zulu			

Table 4.3 Language Training Centers

University Site	*Languages*
California State University, Long Beach	Arabic, Chinese (Mandarin), French, Persian and Russian
Concordia College	Arabic, Chinese (Mandarin), French, Korean, Persian, Portuguese, Russian and Spanish
George Mason University	English (Advanced Writing for Non-Native Speakers of English)
George Washington University	Foreign Area Officer Regional Skill Sustainment Initiative
North Carolina State University	Arabic, Chinese (Mandarin), French, Korean, Russian and Spanish
San Diego State University	Arabic, Chinese (Mandarin), French, Georgian, German, Hebrew, Italian, Japanese, Korean, Mixtec, Pashto, Persian, Portuguese, Russian, Spanish, Tagalog, Turkish, Vietnamese and Zapotoc
University of Kansas	Arabic, Chinese (Mandarin), French, German, Italian, Japanese, Korean, Persian, Portuguese, Russian and Spanish
University of Montana	Arabic, Bahasa Indonesian, Chinese (Mandarin), Korean, Pashto and Persian
University of Utah	Arabic, Chinese (Mandarin), French, Japanese, Korean, Persian, Portuguese, Russian and Spanish

operated by the Department of State supports the study of 14 of these languages, including Arabic, Azerbaijani (Azeri), Bangala (Bengali), Chinese, Hindi, Indonesian, Japanese, Korean, Farsi (Persian), Punjabi, Russian, Swahili, Turkish and Urdu.

The challenge with this particular concern for the learning of foreign languages in the U.S. is twofold: first, many of the languages involved are less commonly taught languages (LCTLs) which are virtually never offered in either PK-12 or even university settings,[1] and second, they tend to be languages which are very difficult to acquire. Furthermore, although the concern about the need for speakers of languages for national security purposes is both common and understandable, it is also at least potentially problematic, especially for non-heritage learners, since it can be seen to promote the learning of a language as learning the "language of the enemy" – hardly an ideal motivation for the study of any language (see Geisherik, 2004; Husseinali, 2009; Kuntz, 1996). In the case of some languages (most notably, the status of the Russian language following the dissolution of the U.S.S.R. in 1991), the disestablishment or marginalization of a language has created significant challenges both within countries and in regional contexts. The problem, in a nutshell, is one that is articulated by Bezberezhyeva, who has pointed out that, "My language is not my enemy" (Bezberezhyeva, 1998); a point worth noting both in the Baltic countries and throughout most of what was formerly Soviet Central Asia, both areas where the Russian language has seen a decline in both status and utility in various domains (see Reagan, 2019).[2]

Promoting Cultural Understanding

Supporters of world language education often cite the goal of increased cultural understanding as a powerful justification for studying languages other than one's own. Such goals are extremely broad in nature, and are often worded in a variety of different ways. Sometimes it is claimed that language study will create positive attitudes, and reduce or even eliminate prejudice, toward other groups. While such results are, we believe, extremely desirable, and while language study *may* have such results, they are by no means a *guaranteed* outcome of language study. A related claim is that language study will assist students in living and functioning in an increasingly diverse, multilingual and multicultural American society. Again, we believe that this is a worthy educational goal, but the evidence that language study will have such an outcome is far from clear. It is also claimed that the study of languages other than one's own can provide access to many aspects of art, music, literature, film, and so on that would be difficult (if not impossible) to gain only through the medium of English. This is true, we believe, but – however much we might believe that this is a desirable end – it is far from obvious that this is (or is likely to become) a powerful motivator for most students, parents or policy-makers in our society. Such cultural understanding also requires a relatively high level of language competence, of course – a higher level of competence than most students in world language classes are currently likely to achieve. In short, arguments about the power of language study to promote cultural understanding seem to be somewhat exaggerated, at best.

Facilitating Travel and Tourism

The value of having studied a language is sometimes tied to its practical utility with respect to travel and tourism. The most common argument here is that by learning another language, international travel becomes much easier, perhaps cheaper, and will certainly give one access to people in another society which cannot be gained if one must rely only on English. All of these claims, in our experience, are absolutely true. By being able to communicate in French, German, Spanish, Russian, or some other language, one is far more likely to have a more pleasant experience travelling in areas where those languages are spoken. There is, though, the question of *which* language one should study, since no single language will be useful in more than a very limited number of places. It is worth noting here, as well, that using the rationale of facilitating travel and tourism is most likely to lead to support for French and Spanish rather than for any other language. Finally, there is a question here of the degree of fluency that is needed to accomplish the ends imagined here. In many cases, a very limited, survival level of competence in a foreign language is likely to prove sufficient for many people – a kind of guidebook language skill, which is certainly preferable to no language competence, but only marginally so.

Transfer of Skills

Last, one of the arguments that has historically been used to defend world language education has been the claim that, quite apart from the specific advantages of learning a second language, the study of a foreign language has a number of benefits that transfer to other kinds of skills. The idea of the "transfer of skills" is an old one, and basically refers to the idea that there are some skills and abilities that are relevant and useful in a variety of different settings – and thus, by acquiring these skills in one setting, there will be benefits in other settings (see Tozer, Violas & Senese, 1993, pp. 34, 67). Typical examples of transferable skills would include things like organizational skills, time management, the ability to communicate clearly in both oral and written styles, and so on. In the case of the study of world languages, common claims are that the study of a language will increase a student's scores on standardized tests such as the SAT or ACT, that they will improve communicative skills more generally, etc. Perhaps most common is the widely heard claim is that by studying a language, the student learns more about the structure of her or his own language. To some extent, of course, this is bound to be true: the formal study of *any* language will increase one's understanding of language writ large. However, at the same time, if our goal is simply for English-speaking students to better understand the structure of English, then perhaps focusing on English rather than on another language might be more efficient and make more sense.

Commentary and Critique

The traditional rationales for language study, in short, while all certainly true to some extent, do not constitute a sufficient justification for many students in U.S. society to study a world language. Further, while the traditional rationales for world language education do nevertheless have some force to them, this is the case only insofar as the study of a world language actually leads to *competence* in that language. The problem here is that traditional language *study* has often been confused or conflated with some meaningful degree of *bilingualism* (see Reagan, 2004). This is, of course, a very important distinction, since the vast majority of students studying a language, at either the secondary school or university level, are unlikely ever to develop a significant degree of competence in that language, at least as current world language teaching and learning results suggest. This is an important difference, since most people in Anglophone settings have direct experience only with the latter – and all too often, these experiences have been both frustrating and largely unsuccessful. The 19th-century American humorist Mark Twain commented extensively on his own problems learning (or, perhaps more accurately, *not* learning) both German and French (see Thomas, 1988). In an essay on "Taming the Bicycle," Twain wrote that,

> It [learning to ride a bicycle] is not like studying German, where you mull along, in a groping, uncertain way, for thirty years; and at last, just as you think you've got it, they spring the subjunctive on you, and there you are. No – I see now, plainly enough, that the great pity about the German language is, that you can't fall off it and hurt yourself.
>
> (Quoted in Loeb, 1996, p. 35)

In *The Innocents Abroad*, Twain discussed the problems of communicating with native speakers in French, observing, as perhaps have many others, that, "In Paris they just simply opened their eyes and stared when we spoke to them in French! We never did succeed in making those idiots understand their own language" (Twain, 1966, p. 484).

In short, although initially appealing, the practical rationales for language study are simply not terribly strong ones in most cases and for most people in the U.S. This does not mean that these objectives could not be achieved for most students; to do so, however, would require a significant commitment on the part of the society with respect to a variety of different kinds of resources and policies. The issue is not *whether* American students could learn world languages – they are more than capable of doing so – but rather, *whether* we are willing to invest in this process in the ways that would make such learning likely.

For the most part, there is not outright hostility toward world language education, although it is unfortunately not altogether absent in U.S. society. Sometimes such hostility is grounded in xenophobic fears ("This is America – speak English!"), sometimes in overly narrow and simplistic assumptions about the nature and purposes of education, sometimes in mere bloody-mindedness. An excellent example of such hostility was provided by the conservative economist Bryan Caplan, the author of the highly polemical book *The Case Against Education: Why the Education System is a Waste of Time and Money* (Caplan, 2018), who dismisses world language education by arguing that it basically results in little more than "several years of pain and suffering" for most students, and that claims about the value of foreign language education are basically "romantic" and the result of élite biases in our society. Caplan's argument, we believe, is flawed on a number of grounds, not the least of which are naïve and misguided assumptions about both the purposes of education generally and of world language study in particular.

In short, to a considerable degree the status of world language education in the United States is in many ways parallel to the status of the Irish language in contemporary Ireland: it tends to be considerably more popular with the general public as a theoretical construct in principle than it is as a practical reality when funding, time and space in the curriculum are limited, as they inevitably are in the real world of education and educational institutions. As the sociolinguist Suzanne Romaine quoted one Irish interviewee as saying, "although we are all *for* Irish as we are for cheaper bus fares, heaven and the good life, nobody of the masses is willing to make the effort" to learn and use the language (quoted in Romaine, 2000, p. 43). So, too, are most people in the United States in favor of world language education – it is conceded to be a good thing so long as it doesn't raise taxes or interfere with the "real" job of education, and often so long as *they* are not the ones expected to do the learning (see Osborn, 2000; Osborn & Reagan, 1998; Reagan, 2002; Reagan & Osborn, 1998).

Alternative Rationales for Foreign Language Study

If the traditional arguments for studying foreign languages in the U.S. are not sufficiently compelling for many students, then why should they be encouraged to devote the necessary time and energy to doing so? There are, we believe, three sets of reasons for encouraging students to study languages other than their own: epistemological arguments, sociopolitical arguments, and interpersonal arguments. In this part of the chapter, we will explore each of these. Further, we will attempt to do this through the lens of what has been called the "ideal of the educated person" – the goal of liberal education and liberal arts study in the Western tradition.

The "Educated Person" and Foreign Languages

The concept of the "educated person," and its relationship to liberal education, has been a matter of considerable interest to philosophers throughout Western history. In the decades since the 1960s, several different approaches have been taken to understanding what the educated person should know and be able to do. Even in the more detailed and developed discussions of this topic, however, the role of the study of world languages has been largely minimized or even ignored altogether. We believe that this is a very important oversight, both in terms of its implications for what is meant by the concept of the educated person and because the concept of the educated person, as it has been developed and articulated, actually provides an extremely powerful argument for the value of language study.

At the outset of our discussion here, it is important to note that the ideals of both the educated person and of liberal education more broadly are neither static nor immutable; indeed, both are clearly socially constructed, and both have changed (and will continue to change) over time, and from place to place and community to community. We would argue that not only what constitutes an educated person is necessarily tied to time and place, but further, that there cannot be any neutral conception of either education or the educated person (see Levinson, Foley & Holland, 1996; Reagan, 2018). What constituted an educated person in Athens during the time of Plato was radically different than what constituted an educated person during the time of St. Thomas Aquinas, as it would have been from that of 17th-century colonial America, or indeed from our own 21st-century Anglophone North American perspective. It is important to note that we are concerned here solely with the contemporary Western educational tradition, and that our argument is focused on that tradition, especially (although not exclusively) as it is manifested in the U.S. context. While we do believe that some elements of a liberal education are likely to be of more universal value (including, in fact, the study of languages) for virtually any society, the argument presented here is very much culturally and temporally grounded and specific.

The Western tradition of liberal education historically centered in large part on language. As Leo van Lier has noted, "There was a time, from the ancient Greeks to the late Middle Ages, when language was central in educational practices, in the form of the three branches of the *trivium:* grammar, logic, and rhetoric" (van Lier, 1995, pp. 7–8). There were a number of reasons for the centrality of language in this curriculum: the

Classical languages were the languages of the literature of antiquity, and Latin remained the language not only of the Church but also of diplomacy, science, and scholarship (see Dangel, 1995; Ostler, 2007; Waquet, 1998). Latin functioned as the unifying *lingua franca* for the social, cultural, economic and political élite. In addition, there was a strongly embedded assumption, from Classical antiquity, that the educated person must be one who could use language well and effectively to influence others – that is, the educated person should be a master of rhetoric (see Joyal, McDougall & Yardley, 2009). Whether in 5th-century BCE Athens or in the Roman Senate, the ability to persuade and convince was a deeply valued and prized skill. To be sure, from the time of the Sophists there had been concerns about individuals who were *merely* skilled in their use of language; the objective of education was not simply rhetorical skill, but deeper philosophical, political and moral understanding. As Werner Jaeger (1967, 1971a, 1971b; see also Park, 1984) noted in his landmark work *Paideia: The Ideals of Greek Culture*:

> It has been said that what was new in the [S]ophistic movement, and at the same time common to all its members, was the educational ideal of rhetoric, τὸ ευ λέγειν: for they all cultivated oratory, but differed in their estimate of everything else: and there were some [S]ophists who were rhetors pure and simple, and taught nothing else whatever: like Gorgias. But that is clearly a superficial judgment. In fact, what was common to them all was that they taught political *arête*, and all wished to instill it by increasing the powers of the mind through training – whatever they took the training to be.
>
> (Jaeger, 1967, p. 293)

Even so, Plato had been very critical of the role of rhetoric, especially earlier in his career, when he referred to it merely as a "knack" (*Gorgias* 463a6–b6), though later on he seemed to recognize its value at least as a rational skill (i.e., *techné*) (see *Phaedrus* 270b1–10; *Laws* 937e3–938a4). By the time of the late Roman Republic, rhetoric was playing an increasingly important (though not uncontroversial) role in upper class Roman education, and by the time of the Empire, it had become the core of the curriculum. As Mark Joyal, Iain McDougall and John Yardley have noted,

> By the late 1st century [CE], the landscape had altered completely. So successfully had Greek learning penetrated Roman culture, especially élite culture, that the emperor Vespasian not only established an official position in Rome for teachers of Latin and Greek rhetoric but exempted *rhetores* and *grammatici* from taxes as well. By now, rhetoric had proved itself to the Romans to be a supremely useful skill. It was also the focus of minute study and discussion, above all by Cicero and Quintillian, whose writings on the subject

> form the basis of what we know about the theory and practice of rhetoric from the 1st century [BCE] to the 1st century [CE] (and well beyond).
>
> (Joyal et al., 2009, p. 203)

Not only was rhetoric at the heart of the Roman curriculum, of course, but so too was the Greek language. Although the Roman Empire was profoundly multilingual in nature (see Adams, 2003), the two universal languages of the élite were Latin and Greek:

> Upper class Romans were by choice learners of Greek, and some are said to have achieved great competence in the second language … Upper class Romans who could not speak Greek (whether genuinely or allegedly) are sometimes disparaged, as Verres by Cicero: *Verr.* 4.127 *epigramma Graecum pernobile incisum est in basi, quod iste eruditus homo et Graeculus, qui haec subtiliter indicat, qui solus intellegit, si unam litteram Graecam scisset, certe non sustulisset* ("it had a notable Greek inscription on its pedestal, which this learned exponent of Greek culture, with his delicate critical sense and unique appreciation of these matters, would certainly not have removed if he had known a single Greek letter"). There is also a good deal of anecdotal and other evidence for fluent bilingualism (in Greek and Latin) among upper class Romans …
>
> (Adams, 2003, p. 9)

With the fall of the western Roman Empire, generally dated to 476 CE, the only remaining centralizing authority that existed throughout western Europe was the Roman Catholic Church, which became in essence the sole multinational power of the time. The Church performed not only religious functions, but also secular ones, not the least of which were educational, diplomatic, and administrative tasks. All of these undertakings took place in the language of the Church, Latin – although a variety of Latin that had evolved considerably from Classical norms (see Clackson & Horrocks, 2007, pp. 265–302; Collins, 1985; Harrington, 1997; Souter, 1949). In addition, since this Latin was no longer passed on intergenerationally as a native language, an important function of education was to ensure competence in it as the common *lingua franca* of (western) Christendom (see Janson, 2004, pp. 107–115). This meant, of course, that since virtually all educated people knew Latin, the language of scholarship and science would inevitably be Latin as well. Classical Greek reemerged as an important language during the Humanistic era, especially following the fall of Constantinople to the Ottoman Turks in 1453 CE and the influx to the West of many Greek scholars (and, not unimportantly, Greek manuscripts). For a time, Arabic was also a very important language of scholarship – much of the secular and scientific literature from Classical antiquity that we possess today originally came to us through Arabic translations (see Rosenthal, 1992; see also Carter, 2010; Chejne, 1969; Fischer, 2002; Stetkevych, 2006). Indeed, the role of Arabic in preserving the Western cultural and intellectual heritage is often overlooked. Arabic played a key role in cultural transmission during this period, especially since the Hellenism preserved in the Byzantine Empire was not that of Classical Greece, but rather was one that was the product of a mix of elements of that Classical heritage with Orthodox Christian culture (see Horrocks, 1997, pp. 131–204; Moleas, 1991, pp. 29–34; Saïd & Trédé, 1990, pp. 154–182). As Franz Rosenthal noted, "At the beginning of the 7th century, this was a Hellenism which no longer embraced the whole culture of [C]lassical antiquity, but was largely restricted by the new religious outlook to a rather narrow selection" (1992, p. 2). Instead, "most of the works that found their way to the West and there strengthened the much weakened ties with [C]lassical antiquity were the fruits of the Graeco-Arabic translation activity, the result of the process that saw to the survival of classical antiquity in Islam" (Rosenthal, 1992, p. 14). Finally, Hebrew remained a religious language *par excellence*, not only for Jews, but for anyone wishing direct access to the Torah (תּוֹרָה i.e., the Hebrew Bible) (see DeLange, 2001; Hoffman, 2004; Sáenz-Badillos, 1988). The Middle Ages, in short, for the relatively tiny educated élite was a period of fairly active and intense multilingualism.

Although the study of Latin, Greek and to a somewhat lesser extent Hebrew remained common and necessary parts of education throughout the 18th century, by the 19th century, French and German had increasingly come to play these roles to at least some extent. And yet, the study of the Classics was still deemed essential for an educated person, in part because of the view, grounded in faculty psychology (see Tozer, Violas & Senese, 2009, pp. 42–43; Watzke, 2003), that the study of more difficult subjects would strengthen the mind in general (thus making the study of Latin, and even more, of Greek, invaluable).

The 20th century saw the rise of the dominance – and, increasingly, the hegemony – of English as *the* global language. The dominance of English in the worlds of politics and diplomacy, commerce, pop culture, and even scholarship has meant that monolingual English speakers are increasingly secure and complacent in their monolingualism, and the ability to function in a second language is less and less seen as a characteristic, let alone as a necessary condition, of being an educated person. At the same time, the increasingly ubiquity of English has led to a situation in which, "English has also become a *lingua franca* to the point that any literate educated person is in a very real sense deprived if he [*sic*] does not know English. Poverty, famine, and disease are instantly recognized as the cruelest and least excusable forms of deprivation. Linguistic deprivation is a less easily noticed condition, but one nevertheless of great significance" (Burchfield, 1985, p. 160). In other words, while monolingualism for the native speaker of English is normative, bilingualism (with English as a second language) has become the expectation for most other educated persons (see Ammon, 1990, 2003). Concomitantly with the rise of the status of English internationally has come an increasing decline in the study of languages in the English-speaking world. Native speakers of English are increasingly monolingual, and efforts to teach world languages at all levels of the education systems of English-speaking countries are under threat.

With respect to the conceptualization of the educated person, the role of world language study has been largely missing from the discussion, and where present, has been somewhat misleading at best. In the 1960s, 1970s and 1980s, the work of R. S. Peters, Paul Hirst, and others (see Barrow, 1976, 1981; Barrow & Woods, 1988; Brent, 1978; Chambers, 1983; Dearden, Hirst, & Peters, 1972a, 1972b, 1972c; Doyle, 1973; Elvin, 1977; Hamlyn, 1978; Hirst, 1974, 1993; Hirst & Peters, 1970; Lloyd, 1976; Peters, 1973a, 1973b; Schofield, 1972; Straughan & Wilson, 1983) focused on articulating the nature and characteristics of the "educated man." The Peters-Hirst ideal of the "educated man," as it was called, was based on the idea that the student should be exposed to the various forms of knowledge, which included pure mathematics and logic, physical (empirical) sciences, history and human sciences, aesthetics, morals, philosophy, and religion (see Hamm, 1989, pp. 67–71). This approach emphasized theoretical rather than practical knowledge, as a number of critics noted (see Pring, 1976), and ultimately led Hirst himself to re-evaluate the forms of knowledge (see Hirst, 1993). What is important for our purposes here is that the study of language (both native and foreign) was, and remained, fundamentally excluded altogether from the discussion.

A form of knowledge, on Hirst's account, is far more than merely knowledge or skill *per se*; it is a very particular *type* of knowledge and skill, and one which meets certain clear criteria. Specifically, Hirst argued that:

> By a form of knowledge is meant a distinct way in which our experience becomes structured round the use of accepted public symbols. The symbols thus having public meaning, their use is in some way testable against experience and there is the progressive development of series of tested symbolic expressions. In this way experience has been probed further and further by extending and elaborating the use of the symbols, and by means of these it has become possible for the personal experience of individuals to become more fully structured, more fully understood. The various forms of knowledge can be seen in low-level developments within the common area of our knowledge of the everyday world. From this there branch out the developed forms which, taking certain elements in our common knowledge as a basis, have grown in distinctive ways.
>
> (Hirst, 1973, p. 102)

This means, as Robin Barrow has explained, that the forms of knowledge are characterized by three criteria:

> - They have their own distinctive concepts, as, for example, gravity, accelerations and hydrogen are characteristic of the sciences.
> - They have their own logical structure. That is to say, largely because of the meanings of the distinctive concepts, there is a limit to what may meaningfully be said employing such concepts. (Ways of talking that may make sense in one form [of knowledge] do not necessarily make sense in another.)
> - They have their own distinctive manner of testing the truth of their claims.
>
> (Barrow, 1981, p. 40)

And where would the study of a language fit with respect to the forms of knowledge? The study of language is not generally included as a particular form of knowledge in the philosophical literature, and is only rarely discussed at all. We believe, though, that the brief discussions of foreign language study that are present in the philosophical literature on this topic are nevertheless enlightening. The British philosopher Michael Oakeshott, for instance, has suggested that:

> The educational engagement in respect of languages is to initiate learners into a language as a source and repository of human understandings and sentiments, and it was this which the collegiate and grammar schools of England and their equivalents elsewhere undertook in respect of Latin and Greek and, to a lesser extent, in respect of a native language. What the learner submitted himself [*sic*] to was not a "linguistic discipline" but an initiation into exactitudes of thought and generosities of feeling, into literatures and into histories in which the "fact of life" was illuminated by a "quality of life."
>
> (Oakeshott, 1972, p. 41)

Along similar lines, John Passmore argued that:

> By means of sheer drill a driving instructor can teach a pupil to sit in a stationary car and change gear, but this inculcation of mechanical habits is not itself instruction in driving; nor is it of the slightest use except as a preliminary stage in such instruction. Similarly, there is no point in a child's learning by heart the French equivalents of English names for parts of the body, or the eccentric behaviour of irregular verbs, except as part of the process of learning to speak, read or write the French language …
>
> (Passmore, 1972, p. 37)

Perhaps the most critical perspective of the place of world language education in the curriculum comes from Barrow, who argued that:

> I turn now to ... modern languages. They gain a place as options largely on the score of complexity. They are pursuits which many may wish to undertake and in respect of which a teacher may prove of no little benefit. (If there is truth in the empirical claim that personal tuition in this sphere is of no great value and that language laboratories can do the job well and quickly, I would argue for dropping modern languages from the curriculum altogether. The expense of equipping all schools with language laboratories to cope with an option when they are available elsewhere, hardly seems justified.) They also have limited social usefulness and relevance .... I see no warrant whatsoever for the claim that "the ability to understand at least one foreign language, and to communicate in it, at however modest a level, has an educational value."
>
> (Barrow, 1976, p. 154)

In all three of these cases, we believe that the critiques of world language teaching and learning are based on a fundamental misunderstanding of what ought to be the real purpose of such study. Furthermore, one could argue that what is being critiqued is not so much language teaching at all so much as *poor* language teaching. Concerning this even the most stalwart advocate for language study would agree: much language teaching is of poor quality, and needs to be improved. This does not, however, rule out the study of language as a potential form of knowledge, any more than the fact that much of the teaching of mathematics is poor would rule out the study of mathematics.

The Peters–Hirst ideal has been critiqued on a number of grounds: Marxists and neo-Marxists quite correctly argued that it was based in and derived from a class-based set of principles and an educational tradition that was grounded firmly in a particular social class system (see Matthews, 1980). Even more powerful has been the feminist critique, offered most cogently by Jane Roland Martin and others (Martin, 1984, 1985, 1986, 1994, 2000; Mulcahy, 2002, 2008). Martin argued that the "educated man" represented by the Peters-Hirst ideal was just that: an ideal that presupposed certain gender-specific assumptions. Her emphasis on the reproductive elements of education and the educated person, although important, still left language out of the equation altogether. More recent efforts to address the complexities of identifying a justifiable conceptualization of the educated person and of liberal education more broadly – for example, by thinking about liberal education as preparation for life (see Mulcahy, 2008; see also Campbell, 2009) – while constituting significant improvements on earlier discussions, still remain incomplete, especially with respect to the place of world language study. Although we are sympathetic to Richard Pring's observation that, "I cannot lay down what precisely should be the content of the curriculum" (Pring, 1976, p. 115) because of the varying needs of distinct individuals, we nevertheless do believe that there are core areas of knowledge – along the lines of the forms of knowledge – that can, and indeed must, be identified. There are, in short, certain things (both in terms of propositional and performative knowledge) that all students should indeed master, and world languages – at least to a limited degree – are one of these.

Epistemological Arguments

One of the reasons for studying a variety of disciplines in the tradition of liberal education is that each discipline approaches problems in its own unique manner. Thus, by studying history students learn something about the way in which historians think, just as by studying biology, they learn how biologists think. To be sure, initial study in a discipline does not mean that students master the epistemological approaches used in the discipline – that comes only with in-depth, long-term study – but the basic idea in liberal education is that the student should gain a clearer understanding of how each discipline organizes the world. Study of language can contribute to such understanding on two levels.

First, the formal study of a language provides students with a metalanguage for discussing the characteristics of any language, including their native language. Second, and more important, language study is more fundamental epistemologically than the study of almost any other discipline, since different languages construct reality in different ways (see Lee, 1996; Reagan, 1999; Williams & Burden, 1999). Although linguistic relativism remains a somewhat controversial topic, there is growing acceptance among linguistics that, at least in a weak form, "human perceptions of reality are structured and constrained – not controlled, but structured and constrained – by human languages, in interesting and significant ways" (Elgin, 2000, p. 52; see also Lee, 1996; Soltis, 1979, pp. 7–8).[3] Further, as Michel Foucault has argued, even the effort to name things is, ultimately, about issues of power, control, and, ultimately, violence (see Ball, 1990). In short, language can and does play an important role in how we perceive and understand reality, and recognition of this role of human language can be an important outcome of the study of *any* language. It also provides, we believe, a powerful argument for the need for world language study as part of a liberal education, and for the study of language to be accepted as a legitimate form of knowledge.

What does it mean, though, to discuss a language – *any* language – as a form of knowledge? Is it a special kind of theoretical or scientific knowledge, a unique mode of understanding, a kind of practical knowledge, or an interpretive skill? We believe that it is all of these, and that examples of each can be provided. The study of a world language *does* function as a kind of initiation, in Peters's words, into a particular body of knowledge (that is, into the understanding and use of the new language). It also provides a unique mode of understanding, insofar as no two languages map reality in quite the same way. For instance, while English has one verb "to be," Spanish has two, *ser* and *estar*, whose use is differentiated based on semantic relationships. Other examples of the problems of linguistic mapping from one language to another abound; one of the challenges in understanding the *New Testament* and certain aspects of Christian theology, for instance, has to do with differences between English and Greek. For instance, while English has only one word for "love," Classical Greek has four (αγαπη, ερως, φιλια, and στοργη), two of which (αγαπη and φιλια) are primarily used in the *New Testament*. The differences among these terms are significant; there are serious practical and theological differences involved in how and why they are used. For instance, in John 21:15–17, Jesus asks Simon Peter two times whether he (Simon Peter) loves him (Jesus), and Simon Peter answers twice that he does. However, Jesus deliberately uses the term αγαπη, implying an unconditional love of the sort to be given to God; Simon Peter replies both times using φιλια, suggesting brotherly affection or love.[4] Just as we have already noted that in Russian there is no single word for "blue," but rather two terms that are not interchangeable (синий and голубой), in Zulu there is a single term that encompasses both "green" and "blue" (*-luhlaza*).

Although somewhat similar in some ways, it is important to note that such epistemological arguments are not synonymous with arguments grounded in the idea of the transfer of training discussed earlier in this chapter. Transfer of training suggests a pragmatic linkage between particular sets of skills, while the epistemological arguments are far deeper in nature, and have to do not with specific skills, but rather, with the overall understanding of the nature of human knowledge.

Sociopolitical Arguments

The sociopolitical arguments for language study, especially for native speakers of English, are important because they focus on raising the language awareness of students (see Andrews, 2006; Benesch, 2001; Fairclough, 1992; McKay & Hornberger, 1996). In essence, the sociopolitical arguments are concerned with helping students to understand issues of power, domination, and subordination related to language, language use, language status, and language attitudes, both in the student's own society and in international contexts. Although such understanding can develop in monolingual settings, as in the use of academic discourse (see Bartolomé, 1998; Bourdieu, Passeron & de Saint Martin, 1994), it is both more powerful and clearer when explored in a bilingual or multilingual context – as can be the case in the world language classroom (see Reagan, 2016). While the epistemological arguments for language study emphasize the ways in which different languages construct reality, the sociopolitical arguments emphasize the impact of political and social reality (especially with respect to differences in power) on language and language use. The sociopolitical arguments in favor of language study are concerned with helping students to appreciate the social contexts of language use, especially with respect to the roles played by language and language use in establishing and maintaining differential power relations in society (see Reagan & Osborn, 1998; Thomas & Wareing, 1999). As Lourdes Ortega noted, one of the challenges in the field of world language education has been its failure "to recognize the fact that both societal attitudes towards languages and power struggles resulting from ownership of a language and a culture by particular groups are inextricably embedded in the definition of goals for language education" (Ortega, 1999, p. 243). The sociopolitical arguments for language study require that world language education be reconceptualized, so that the study of language incorporates not only a focus on the target language, but also addresses issues of social justice both broadly conceived and in the specific context of the world language classroom (see Corson, 1999, pp. 6–27; Ehrenreich, 2003; Kubota, Austin & Saito-Abbott, 2003; Osborn, 2000; Osborn & Reagan, 1998; Reagan, 2016).

Interpersonal Arguments

In any communicative interaction in which one person is speaking her or his native language, and the other is using that language as a foreign language (fairly typical in linguistic encounters of native English speakers with speakers of other languages), the former have a huge advantage over the latter (see Ammon, 2003). This fundamental inequity in linguistic interactions between native and non-native speakers is both powerful and problematic. As David Jordan has commented, "If [a language] is unequally known, as between native and non-native speakers, the negotiation [of meaning] is not 'fair' ... Linguistic competence becomes a political resource; leadership falls to the better speakers" (Jordan, 1997, p. 39). In other words, differential linguistic and communicative ability in a foreign language seems inevitably to result in differences both in terms of perceptions of competence and with respect to real differences in situational power and control. To be sure, this type of linguistic inequity is by no means eliminated or even reduced by language study, but the process of language study may at the very least make the native speaker of English more aware of and sensitive to her or his dominance in a particular communicative situation.

None of these three arguments replaces the traditional arguments for foreign language study, of course. There are extremely good reasons for any person to learn a foreign language, and many people will continue to do so, certainly in non-Anglophone settings, but even in Anglophones

ones, in spite of the challenges that one faces in doing so. What the epistemological, sociopolitical, and interpersonal arguments provide are different *kinds* of rationales, rationales for why simply *studying* a foreign language – whether or not one becomes competent in the language – might nevertheless prove to be an incredibly valuable part of the curriculum for all students.

Conclusion

In this chapter, we have attempted to review the traditional arguments which have been used to defend and promote the study of languages in our society, and have suggested that they do not seem to have been particularly effective. We have also sought to explain why this might be the case. Finally, we have offered three different kinds of justifications for the study of foreign languages – justifications that differ in significant ways from the more traditional arguments. Underlying our arguments has been the idea that education in general, and world language education in particular, can either be employed to empower and liberate students, or to oppress and disempower them.

It is not enough, however, to simply make the case that the study of languages can accomplish the objectives that have been outlined here. There is a deeper question that must be answered: not *whether* such study *could* accomplish these objectives, but whether it in fact *does* do so. We would be the first to admit that some language instruction is poor – that methodologically there are often problems in the teaching of world languages, that textbooks and materials (especially for the LCTLs) are sometimes not what one might wish, and that all too many world language educators do not themselves possess adequate competence in the target language. None of these issues, though, is unique to world language education. The teaching of various STEM subjects, for instance, suffers similar challenges – and yet, no one questions the basic need for such instruction. The question, rather, is what needs to be done to do a more effective job. Given the centrality of language in human life, it is, at the very least, inconsistent (though not of course particularly surprising) to find that the same is not true for the study of world languages.

For us, perhaps the most powerful argument for the need for students to study languages other than their own is that the point of education is to introduce and initiate the individual into our common, human social and cultural heritage, and that this cannot be done adequately without some exposure to the different ways in which human beings, in various times and places, have constructed an amazingly wide variation of languages to meet their needs. If becoming educated is, as many scholars have suggested, the process by which one learns to join in the "human conversation," then language skills will inevitably be required if one wishes to join the conversation at anything more than the most basic and trivial level. On an even deeper level, one can argue that it is in the study of human language – both as an abstract entity and in terms of specific human languages – that one comes closest to what Noam Chomsky has called "the human essence" (quoted in Fromkin, Rodman & Hyams, 2003, p. 3). Indeed, one of the more fascinating outcomes of the study of human language over the past few centuries has been the discovery that there is no such thing as a "primitive" language, that each and every human language is a full, complete and rule-governed entity capable of serving its users and their needs. Further, there has been a recognition that in spite of their many differences, all human languages also share a number of significant common features – that is, what linguists call linguistic universals. It is in these linguistic universals that we may come closest to identifying what it is, exactly, that makes us human.

The study of languages other than one's own cannot only serve to help us understand what we as human beings have in common, but can also assist us to understand the diversity which underlies not only our languages, but also our ways of constructing and organizing knowledge, and the many different realities in which we live and interact. Such understanding has profound implications not only epistemologically, but also with respect to developing a critical awareness of language and social relationships. In studying languages other than our own, we are seeking to understand (and, indeed, in at least a weak sense, to become) the "Other." We are, in short, attempting to enter into realities that have, to some degree, been constructed by others and in which many of the fundamental assumptions about the nature of knowledge and society may be (and often are) different from our own. We are, in fact, creating new "selves" in an important sense. Such creation and *re*-creation forces each of us to reflect more deeply on many of the core questions related to being an educated person, as well as requiring that we become not merely *tolerant* of differences, but truly *understanding* of differences (linguistic and otherwise), and the implications of such differences. The sort of humility that is gained from studying a language other than one's own is a valuable possession in its own right, though of course language learning is by no means the only arena in which humility can be learned.

Of course, this applies only in those instances in which we conceive of the end purpose of education to be the emergence of the educated person. To the extent to which this is *not* our goal, of course, the argument fails – but then we are faced with what are far more serious problems, at least for those of us committed to any sort of democratic ideals. In other words, the case for the study of world languages rests on the view that *all* people in a democratic society are entitled to the best and most complete sort of education possible. As the philosopher of education John Dewey so cogently asserted, "What the best and wisest parent wants for his own child, that must the community want for all of its children" (Dewey, 1943, p. 7). The study of human languages *must* be a part of such education, we would argue, if one is truly concerned with *both* democratic education and education for democracy (see Goodlad, 1994, 1997; Gutman, 1999; Soder, 1996). In *Mein Kampf*, Hitler argued that:

> One can, for instance, not see why millions of people, in the course of the years, have to learn two or three foreign languages which thereafter only a fraction of which they can use and which therefore the majority of them forget again completely, for out of a hundred thousand pupils who, for instance, learn French, hardly two thousand will later on be able to use it actually, while ninety-eight thousand, throughout their entire future course of life, will no longer be in a situation where they can make use of what they have learned. During their youth, therefore, they have devoted thousands of hours to a matter which later is of no value or significance to them ... Thus for the sake of two thousand people for whom the knowledge of this language is of use, actually ninety-eight thousand have to be tortured in vain and sacrifice valuable time.
>
> (Hitler, 1940, p. 627)

We find the underlying rejection of the values of liberal education in general, and of world language study in particular, to be deeply disturbing both educationally and with respect to the implications of such views for democracy and a democratic society.

Questions for Reflection and Discussion

1 If it were possible to provide 100% accurate machine translation for all languages, would there still be reasons to study foreign languages? What might these reasons be? What does this suggest to you with respect to the providing a justification for a place for foreign language in the curriculum?
2 Can you restate the epistemological rationale for studying a foreign language in a way that would make sense to a high school student? To the student's parents? To Board of Education members?
3 Although the authors argue that there is a tie between democratic education and the need for foreign language study, many very repressive societies have been bilingual or even multilingual, while many contemporary democratic societies (including the United States) are, or seek to be, monolingual. How would you explain this discrepancy? What lessons can this teach us about foreign language teaching and learning?
4 What kinds of changes might you consider in your classroom to help students understand the value of studying a foreign language? What are the implications of the changes that you have identified for the curriculum?

5 The authors distinguish between *becoming bilingual* and *studying a foreign language*. What are the implications of this difference for the foreign language classroom?

Notes

1 Although the basic argument here is sound, it is nevertheless important to note that there are in fact several commonly taught languages included, most notably both French and Spanish.
2 A fascinating exception to this widespread tendency has been Kazakhstan, where Russian continues to have semi-official status and is extremely widely used throughout the country and by virtually all ethnolinguistic groups (see Reagan, 2015, 2019).
3 Although there is a clear connection between language and thought, it is very easy (and extremely common) to overemphasize this connection. As John McWhorter has noted, "a connection between language and thought *does* exist. The problem is how that connection has percolated into public discussion … most [linguists] would consider it a fair assessment that … language's effect on thought is distinctly subtle and, overall, minor" (McWhorter, 2014, p. xiv, our emphasis).
4 Although the *New Testament* was originally written in Greek, it is important to remember that Jesus and Peter would not, of course, have been speaking Greek – rather, they would probably have been speaking Aramaic.

References

Adams, J. (2003). *Bilingualism and the Latin language*. Cambridge: Cambridge University Press.

Ammon, U. (1990) German or English? The problems of language choice experienced by German-speaking scientists. In P. Nelde (Ed.), *Language conflict and minorities* (pp. 33–51). Bonn: Dümmler.

Ammon, U, (2003). Global English and the non-native speaker: Overcoming disadvantage. In H. Tonkin & T. Reagan (Eds.), *Language in the 21st century* (pp. 23–34). Amsterdam: John Benjamins.

Andrews, L. (2006). *Language exploration and awareness: A resource book for teachers* (3rd ed.). Mahwah, NJ: Lawrence Erlbaum Associates.

Ball, S. (Ed.). (1990). *Foucault and education: Disciplines and knowledge*. New York: Routledge.

Barrow, R. (1976). *Common sense and the curriculum*. London: George Allen & Unwin.

Barrow, R. (1981). *The philosophy of schooling*. Brighton: Harvester Press.

Barrow, R. & Woods, R. (1988). *An introduction to philosophy of education* (3rd ed.). New York: Routledge.

Bartolomé, L. (1998). *The misteaching of academic discourses: The politics of language in the classroom*. Boulder, CO: Westview Press.

Benesch, S. (2001). *Critical English for academic purposes: Theory, politics, and practice*. Mahwah, NJ: Lawrence Erlbaum Associates.

Bezberezhyeva, Y. (1998). My language is not my enemy. In *Estonia and Russia: More cheese from New Zealand?* (EuroUniversity Series, International Relations, Volume 1) (pp. 31–32). Tallinn: The Olof Palme International Center, The EuroUniversity, and the Institute of International and Social Studies.

Birner, B. (2020). Linguistics and national security. Downloaded from www.linguisticsociety.org/content/linguistics-and-national-security on January 10, 2020.

Bourdieu, P., Passeron, J. & de Saint Martin, M. (1994). *Academic discourse*. Stanford, CA: Stanford University Press.

Brent, A. (1978). *Philosophical foundations for the curriculum*. London: George Allen & Unwin.

Bump, P. (2019). The fundamentally un-American attacks on Alexander Vindman. *The Washington Post* (October 29). Downloaded from www.washingtonpost.com/politics/2019/10/29/fundamentally-un-american-attacks-alexander-vindman/ on November 20, 2019.

Burchfield, R. (1985). *The English language*. Oxford: Oxford University Press.

Camarota, S. & Zeigler, K. (2014). One in five US residents speaks foreign language at home, record 61.8 million Spanish, Chinese, and Arabic speakers grew most since 2010. Center for Immigration Studies (October). Downloaded from https://cis.org/files/camarota-language.pdf on May 4, 2019.

Campbell, E. (2009). The educated person. *Curriculum Inquiry*, 39(3): 371–379.

Caplan, B. (2018). *The case against education: Why the education system is a waste of time and money*. Princeton, NJ: Princeton University Press.

Carter, M. (2010). *A history of the Arabic language*. Cambridge: Cambridge University Press.

Chambers, J. (1983). *The achievement of education*. New York: Harper & Row.

Chejne, A. (1969). *The Arabic language: Its role in history*. Minneapolis, MN: University of Minnesota Press.

Clackson, J. & Horrocks, G. (2007). *The Blackwell history of the Latin language*. Oxford: Blackwell.

Collins, J. (1985). *A primer of Ecclesiastical Latin*. Washington, DC: Catholic University of America Press.

Corson, D. (1999). *Language policy in schools: A resource for teachers and administrators*. Mahwah, NJ: Lawrence Erlbaum Associates.

Crystal, D. (1987). *The Cambridge encyclopedia of language*. Cambridge: Cambridge University Press.

Dangel, J. (1995). *L'histoire de la langue latine*. Paris: Presses Universitaires de France.

Dearden, R., Hirst, P. & Peters, R. S. (Eds.). (1972a). *Education and the development of reason, Part 1: A critique of current educational aims*. London: Routledge & Kegan Paul.

Dearden, R., Hirst, P. & Peters, R. S. (Eds.). (1972b). *Education and the development of reason, Part 2: Reason*. London: Routledge & Kegan Paul.

Dearden, R., Hirst, P. & Peters, R. S. (Eds.). (1972c). *Education and the development of reason, Part 3: Education and reason*. London: Routledge & Kegan Paul.

DeLange, N. (2001). *Hebrew scholarship and the medieval world*. Cambridge: Cambridge University Press.

Dewey, J. (1943). *The child and the curriculum / The school and society*. Chicago, IL: University of Chicago Press. (Original works published in 1902 and 1900)

Doyle, J. (Ed.). (1973). *Educational judgments*. London: Routledge & Kegan Paul.

Economist. (2020). The new Red Scare. *The Economist* (January 4): 13–15.

Ehrenreich, S. (2003). Abroad and back home: How can foreign language teacher education help develop intercultural competence? In R. Tormey (Ed.), *Teaching social justice* (pp. 161–172). Dublin: Centre for Educational Disadvantage Research, Mary Immaculate College, and Ireland Aid.

Elgin, S. (2000). *The language imperative*. Cambridge, MA: Perseus Books.

Elvin, L. (1977). *The place of commonsense in educational thought*. London: George Allen & Unwin.

Fairclough, N. (Ed.). (1992). *Critical language awareness*. London: Longman.

Fischer, W. (2002). *A grammar of Classical Arabic* (3rd rev. ed.). New Haven, CT: Yale University Press.

Fromkin, V., Rodman, R. & Hyams, N. (2003). *An introduction to language* (7th ed.). Boston: Thomson Heinle.

Geisherik, A. (2004). The role of motivation among heritage and non-heritage learners of Russian. *Canadian Slavonic Papers/Revue Canadienne des Slavistes*, 46 (1–2): 9–22.

Goodlad, J. (1994). *Educational renewal: Better teachers, better schools*. San Francisco, CA: Jossey-Bass.

Goodlad, J. (1997). *In praise of education*. New York: Teachers College Press.

Grosse, C. (2004). The competitive advantage of foreign languages and cultural knowledge. *The Modern Language Journal*, 88(4): 351–373.

Gutman, A. (1999). *Democratic education* (rev. ed.). Princeton, NJ: Princeton University Press.

Hamlyn, D. (1978). *Experience and the growth of understanding*. London: Routledge & Kegan Paul.

Hamm, C. (1989). *Philosophical issues in education: An introduction*. New York: Falmer Press.

Harrington, K. (Ed.). (1997). *Medieval Latin* (2nd ed.). Chicago, IL: University of Chicago Press.

Hirst, P. (1973). Liberal education and the nature of knowledge. In R. S. Peters (Ed.), *The philosophy of education* (pp. 87–111). Oxford: Oxford University Press.

Hirst, P. (1974). *Knowledge and the curriculum*. London: Routledge & Kegan Paul.

Hirst, P. (1993). Education, knowledge and practices. In R. Barrow & P. White (Eds.), *Beyond liberal education* (pp. 184–199). New York: Routledge.

Hirst, P. & Peters, R. S. (1970). *The logic of education*. London: Routledge & Kegan Paul.

Hitler, A. (1940). *Mein Kampf: Complete and unabridged*. New York: Reynal & Hitchcock.

Hoffman, J. (2004). *In the beginning: A short history of the Hebrew language*. New York: New York University Press.

Horrocks, G. (1997). *Greek: A history of the language and its speakers*. London: Longman.

Husseinali, G. (2009). Who is studying Arabic and why? A survey of Arabic students' orientations at a major university. *Foreign Language Annals*, 39(3): 395–412.

Jaeger, W. (1967). *Paideia: The ideals of Greek culture, volume I: Archaic Greece: The mind of Athens* (2nd ed.). Oxford: Oxford University Press.

Jaeger, W. (1971a). *Paideia: The ideals of Greek culture, volume II: In search of the divine center*. Oxford: Oxford University Press.

Jaeger, W. (1971b). *Paideia: The ideals of Greek culture, volume III: The conflict of cultural ideals in the age of Plato*. Oxford: Oxford University Press.

Janson, T. (2004). *A natural history of Latin*. Oxford: Oxford University Press.

Jarvis, G. (1980). The value of second-language learning. In F. Grittner (Ed.), *Learning a second language: Seventy-ninth yearbook of the National Society for the Study of Education, Part* II (pp. 26–43). Chicago, IL: National Society for the Study of Education.

Jordan, D. (1997). *Esperanto and Esperantism: Symbols and motivations in a movement for linguistic equality*. In H. Tonkin (Ed.), Esperanto, interlinguistics, and planned language (pp. 38–65). Lanham, MD: University Press of America, in conjunction with the Center for Research and Documentation on World Language Problems.

Joyal, M., McDougall, I. & Yardley, J. (2009). *Greek and Roman education*. New York: Routledge.

Koning, P. (2009). Using languages in national security. *The Language Educator* (February): 32–37. Downloaded from www.actfl.org/sites/default/files/tle/career-focus/TLE_01NatSecure.pdf on March 20, 2019.

Kubota, R., Austin, T. & Saito-Abbott, Y. (2003). Diversity and inclusion of sociopolitical issues in foreign language classrooms: An exploratory survey. *Foreign Language Annals*, 36(1): 12–24.

Kuntz, P. (1996). Students of Arabic: Beliefs about foreign language learning. *Al-'Arabiyya*, 29: 153–176.

Lee, P. (1996). *The Whorf theory complex: A critical reconstruction*. Amsterdam: John Benjamins.

Levinson, B., Foley, D. & Holland, D. (Eds.). (1996). *The cultural production of the educated person*. Albany, NY: State University of New York Press.

Lloyd, D. (Ed.) (1976). *Philosophy and the teacher*. London: Routledge & Kegan Paul.

Loeb, A. (Ed.). (1996). *The wit and wisdom of Mark Twain*. New York: Barnes & Noble.

Martin, J. R. (1984). Bringing women into educational thought. *Educational Theory*, 34(4): 341–353.

Martin, J. R. (1985). *Reclaiming a conversation: The ideal of the educated woman*. New Haven, CT: Yale University Press.

Martin, J. R. (1986). Redefining the educated person: Rethinking the significance of gender. *Educational Researcher*, 15(6): 6–10.

Martin, J. R. (1994). *Changing the educational landscape: Philosophy, women, and curriculum*. New York: Routledge.

Martin, J. R. (2000). *Coming of age in academe: Rekindling women's hopes and reforming the academy*. New York: Routledge.

Matthews, M. (1980). *The Marxist theory of schooling: A study of epistemology and education*. Brighton, UK: Harvester Press.

McKay, S. & Hornberger, N. (Eds.). (1996). *Sociolinguistics and language teaching*. Cambridge: Cambridge University Press.

McWhorter, J. (2014). *The language hoax: Why the world looks the same in any language*. Oxford: Oxford University Press.

Mehta, C. (2008). Requiring a foreign language under PERM. (May 16). Downloaded from https://cyrusmehta.com/blog/2008/05/16/requiring-a-foreign-language-under-perm-3/ on March 20, 2019.

Moleas, W. (1991). *The development of the Greek language*. Bristol, UK: Bristol Classical Press.

Mulcahy, D. (2002). *Knowledge, gender, and schooling*. Westport, CT: Bergin & Garvey.

Mulcahy, D. (2008). *The educated person: Toward a new paradigm for liberal education*. Lanham, MD: Rowman & Littlefield.

Neeley, T. (2012). Global business speaks English. *Harvard Business Review* (May). Downloaded from https://jbr.org/2012/05/global-business-speaks-english on March 20, 2019.

New American Economy. (2017). Not lost in translation: The growing importance of foreign language skills in the U.S. job market. (March). Downloaded from http://research.newamericaneconomy.org/wp-content/uploads/2017/03/NAE_Bilingual_V9.pdf on May 15, 2019.

Oakeshott, M. (1972). Education: The engagement and its frustration. In R. Dearden, P. Hirst & R. S. Peters (Eds.), *Education and the development of reason, Part* 1 (pp. 17–47). London: Routledge & Kegan Paul.

Ortega, L. (1999). Language and equality: Ideological and structural constraints in foreign language education in the U.S. In T. Huebner & K. Davis (Eds.), *Sociopolitical perspectives on language policy and planning in the U.S.A.* (pp. 243–266). Amsterdam: John Benjamins.

Osborn, T. A. (2000). *Critical reflection and the foreign language classroom*. Westport, CT: Bergin & Garvey.

Osborn, T. A. & Reagan, T. (1998). Why Johnny can't *hablar, parler*, or *sprechen:* Foreign language education and multicultural education. *Multicultural Education*, 6(2): 2–9.

Ostler, N. (2007). *Ad infinitum: A biography of Latin*. New York: Walker & Co.

Park, C. (1984). A reconsideration: Werner Jaeger's *Paideia*. *Modern Age*, 28(2): 152–155.

Passmore, J. (1972). On teaching to be critical. In R. Dearden, P. Hirst & R. S. Peters (Eds.), *Education and the development of reason, Part* 3 (pp. 25–43). London: Routledge & Kegan Paul.

Peters, R. S. (1966). *Ethics and education*. London: George Allen & Unwin.

Peters, R. S. (Ed.). (1967a). *The concept of education*. London: Routledge & Kegan Paul.

Peters, R. S. (Ed.). (1973a). *The concept of education*. London: Routledge & Kegan Paul.

Peters, R. S. (Ed.). (1973b). *The philosophy of education*. Oxford: Oxford University Press.

Pring, R. (1976). *Knowledge and schooling*. London: Open Books.

QS MBA. (2016). Language requirements for MBA admissions around the world. (October 6). Downloaded from www.topmba.com/admissions/language-requirements-mba-admissions-around-world on January 15, 2020.

Reagan, T. (1999). Constructivist epistemology and second/foreign language pedagogy. *Foreign Language Annals*, 32(4): 413–425.

Reagan, T. (2002). *Language, education and ideology*. Westport, CT: Praeger.

Reagan, T. (2004). "Don't know much about the French I took": A contemporary case for second language study in the liberal arts. *Arts and Humanities in Higher Education*, 3(2): 231–241.

Reagan, T. (2015). Language policy in education in Kazakhstan: Practical and ideological constraints. In F. Touchon (Ed.), *Language education policy unlimited: Global perspectives and local practices* (pp. 77–93). Blue Mounds, WI: Deep University Press.

Reagan, T. (2016). Language teachers in foreign territory: A call for a critical pedagogy-infused curriculum. In L. Cammarata, T. Osborn & D. Tedick (Eds,), *Content-based foreign language teaching: Curriculum and pedagogy for developing advanced thinking and literacy skills* (pp.173–191). New York: Routledge.

Reagan, T. (2018). *Non-western educational traditions: Alternative approaches to educational thought and practice* (4th ed.). New York: Routledge.

Reagan, T. (2019). Language planning and language policy in Khazakhstan. In A. Kirkpatrick & A. J. Liddicoat (Eds.), *The Routledge international handbook of language education Policy in Asia* (pp. 442–451). New York: Routledge.

Reagan, T. & Osborn, T. A. (1998). Power, authority and domination in foreign language education: Toward an analysis of educational failure. *Educational Foundations*, 12(2): 45–62.

Romaine, S. (2000). *Language in society: An introduction to sociolinguistics* (2nd ed.). Oxford: Oxford University Press.

Rosenthal, F. (1992). *The classical heritage in Islam*. New York: Routledge.

Sáenz-Badillos, A. (1988). *Historia de la lengua hebrea*. Sabadell, Spain: Editorial AUSA.

Saïd, S. & Trédé, M. (1990). *A short history of Greek literature*. New York: Routledge.

Schofield, H. (1972). *The philosophy of education*. London: George Allen & Unwin.

Soder, R. (Ed.). (1996). *Democracy, education and the schools*. San Francisco, CA: Jossey-Bass.

Soltis, J. (1979). *Education and the concept of knowledge*. New York: Teachers College Press, Columbia University.

Souter, A. (1949). *A glossary of later Latin to 600 A.D.* Oxford: Clarendon Press.

Stetkevych, J. (2006). *The modern Arabic literary language*. Washington, DC: Georgetown University Press.

Straughan, R. & Wilson, J. (1983). *Philosophizing about education*. London: Cassell.

Thomas, L. & Wareing, S. (1999). *Language, society and power*. New York: Routledge.

Thomas, U. (1988). Mark Twain's German language learning experiences. In D. Beseler, W. Lohnes & V. Nollendorfs (Eds.), *Teaching German in America: Prolegomena to a history* (pp. 133–143). Madison, WI: University of Wisconsin Press.

Tozer, S., Violas, P. & Senese, G. (1993). *School and society: Educational practice as social expression*. New York: McGraw-Hill.

Tozer, S., Violas, P. & Senese, G. (2009). *School and society: Historical and contemporary perspectives* (6th ed.). Boston: McGraw-Hill.

Twain, M. (1966). *The innocents abroad*. New York: Signet Classics. (Original work published 1869)

van Lier, L. (1995). *Introducing language awareness*. London: Penguin English.

Waquet, F. (1998). *Le latin ou l'empire d'un signe*. Paris: Editions Albin Michel.

Watzke, J. (2003). *Lasting change in foreign language education: A historical case for change in national policy*. Westport, CT: Praeger.

Williams, M. & Burden, R. (1999). *Psicología para profesores de idiomas: Enfoque del constructivismo social*. Cambridge: Cambridge University Press.

Zietlow, A. (2017). Foreign language "emergency" hinders U.S. economy and foreign policy, report warns. *The Washington Times* (June 15). Downloaded from www.washingtontimes.com/news/2017/jun/15/foreign-language-learning-disparity-an-american-em/ on March 20, 2019.

5 Learning Languages

Constructivism and World Language Education

One of the more puzzling and complex concepts with which world language educators must deal is the question of what it actually means to "know" a language. Although people who speak a single language often believe that this must be an easy matter to determine, most of us who are bilingual or multilingual know better. When we say that a person "knows" another language, we might mean a number of very different things. We might, for instance, mean that they have native competence at a very high level, or that they have the necessary communicative skills required to function on a daily basis in a society in which the language is used, or even that they have some basic language skills that allow them to cope with relatively simple tasks in the language – or anything in between these very different kinds of competence. In the same way, when we talk about an individual being "bilingual," we are dealing not with a clearly defined sort of competence, but rather with a continuum of quite different *degrees* of competence.[1] The notion of "knowing" a language is in fact highly problematic, as is the notion of "learning" a language. This is an especially important point for world language educators to understand, since underlying all pedagogical practice, ultimately, are questions of epistemology – that is, questions concerned with the nature of knowledge. The ways in which we think about what it means to "know" a language are directly linked to all aspects of how we teach.

In this chapter, we will explore the epistemological foundations of learning and teaching as these relate to the case of world language education. We will then discuss the use of metaphors and metaphorical language as windows into our own understanding of what it means to "know" a language, and what the implications of such metaphorical language for our teaching practice are. Next, we will examine the role and place of learning theories in world language education, and will briefly explore some of the major historical approaches to the teaching of foreign languages. The focus of the chapter, though, will be on constructivist learning theory, and the implications of constructivism for both the learning and the teaching of world languages. We will consider the potential contributions of constructivism to world language teaching and learning by providing a broad overview of its core assumptions and concepts, and then explore the ways in which constructivism can inform and promote effective pedagogical practice.

Epistemology and Education

Epistemology and epistemological concerns are at the heart of education (see Scott, 2010; Siegel, 2010; Slezak, 2010). In essence, epistemology refers to the branch of philosophy that addresses questions of knowledge, belief, the justification of beliefs (including the nature of justified belief), and what it means when we say that one "knows" something. As Peter Paul and Donald Moores have explained,

> As a branch of philosophy, epistemology entails the study of a construct labeled *knowledge* ... Traditionally, the foci have been on the conditions, sources, and limits of knowledge. Debate has centered on perspectives involving the relationship between the knower and what is known – between subject/agent and object, or between the observer and the object of observation ... Pertinent questions include the following: Is there a separation of the two entities such that what is known can be shared with and agreed upon by others regardless of conditions (or qualifications) such as location or time? Are these two entities so intertwined that insights can only be personally or socially constructed, influenced by time and context? Is the framing of this issue erroneous, limited, or simply meaningless with no true or specific response or resolution?
>
> (Paul & Moores, 2012, p. 5)

At its core, then, epistemology can be understood to be the attempt to address the questions surrounding the relationship between the knower and the known; the term itself is sometimes even used synonymously with "a way of knowing" or a "worldview."[2] Historically, in the Western intellectual tradition there has been an assumption that there is a single, universal epistemological stance that would describe and explain all aspects of knowledge. More recently, there have been powerful and compelling arguments that only a model that takes into account the possibility of *multiple* epistemologies (such as feminist epistemologies, black epistemologies, latinx epistemologies, queer epistemologies, indigenous epistemologies, and so on) can be appropriate. Such arguments have important implications for understanding learning and learning theories as well as for what it means to "know" a language, as we shall see. A good way to come to grips with these developments in epistemological theory is by examining the relationship between epistemology and the philosophy of science, and it is to this relationship that we now turn.

Epistemology and the Philosophy of Science

During much of the modern era, positivistic approaches to epistemology dominated the philosophy of science, as well as educational discourse.[3] By the 1960s, though, the dominance of positivism was beginning to come under attack in the work of such individuals as Thomas Kuhn, Michel Foucault and Paul Feyerabend, among others, each of whom presented distinct challenges to positivistic epistemology. Kuhn's *The Structure of Scientific Revolutions* (Kuhn, 1970) introduced the related concepts of "paradigms," "paradigm shifts", and "normal science," which allowed for the distinction between periods of normal science during which a dominant paradigm exists in a particular discipline and times of paradigm shifts during which major scientific revolutions take place (Kuhn, 1970, 1972, 1977).[4]

Foucault focused on the ways in which societies delegitimize and marginalize the knowledges of various groups (Foucault, 1975, 1976, 2000, 2008). As Philip Stokoes noted,

> The theme that underlies all Foucault's work is the relationship between power and knowledge, and how the former is used to control and define the latter. What authorities claim as "scientific knowledge" are really just means of social control. Foucault shows how, for instance, in the 18th century "madness" was used to categorise and stigmatise not just the mentally ill but the poor, the sick, the homeless and, indeed, anyone whose expressions of individuality were unwelcome.
>
> (Stokoes, 2004, p. 187)

Conceptualizing "power" dynamically, and focusing on the relationship between power and discourse, especially vis-à-vis the role of disciplines in the determination of what constitutes "legitimate" understandings, Foucault sought to stress the notion that "philosophy today is entirely political" (Foucault, 2001, p. 266, our translation).

Finally, the philosopher of science Feyerabend sought to take Kuhn's work to what he considered its logical conclusion: not merely epistemological relativism (of which Kuhn was misleadingly accused by many), but rather epistemological *anarchy* – the idea, in Fereyabend's own words, that in science "anything goes" (Fereyabend, 1970, 1981a, 1981b, 1983, 1991, 1995, 2002a, 2002b, 2006, 2010; see also Wolfmeyer, 2017). As Feyerabend argued in *Against Method*:

> *Science is an essentially anarchic enterprise: theoretical anarchism is more humanitarian and more likely to encourage progress than its law-and-order alternatives ... anarchism*, while perhaps not the most attractive *political* philosophy, is certainly excellent medicine for *epistemology*, and for the *philosophy of science*.
>
> (Feyerabend, 2010, p. 1, emphasis in original)

By the last quarter of the 20th century, the epistemological debates in the philosophy of science had spread to the social sciences as well as to education, and by 1987 they had become widespread, leading to the appearance of what came to be termed "social epistemology." In essence, social epistemology can be understood to be a:

> field of intellectual inquiry or discipline in which the epistemic agents like traditional epistemology [are] still individual, but, the fundamental attempt stresses the multiple dimensions of knowledge with the fact that the acquisition and justification of our beliefs and knowledge is determined by various forms of social interaction or the translation of knowledge or justification from one person to another.
>
> (Jha & Devi, 2014, pp. 12–13)

Ethnoepistemology

The recognition that knowledge is both individually and socially constructed has extremely significant implications for education, and this is especially true for historically marginalized groups. In the 1970s and early 1980s, challenges to traditional approaches to epistemology arose from two directions: first, feminist scholars raised a number of powerful critiques of academe, not only with respect to existing organizational, structural and personal biases, but also about the actual *content* of disciplinary knowledge: which questions were asked (and which were *not* asked), what methods were used (and which were *not* used) to answer them, what criteria should be (and which should *not* be) used to evaluate research results, and so on (see Alcoff & Potter, 1993; Anderson, 1995; Duncan, 2005; García, 2013; Lennon & Whitford, 1994). In their landmark work *Women's Ways of Knowing*, Mary Belenky, Blythe Clinchy, Nancy Goldberger and Jill Tarule argued that "gender is a major social, historical, and political category that affects the life choices of all women in all communities and cultures" (Belenky et al., 1997, p. 13). Furthermore, they identified five epistemological perspectives that are essential in reconceptualizing epistemology to take women's perspectives into account:

> *Silence*: A position of not knowing in which the person feels voiceless, powerless, and mindless.
>
> *Received Knowing*: A position at which knowledge and authority are construed as outside the self and invested in powerful and knowing others from whom one is expected to learn.
>
> *Subjective Knowing*: A position in which knowing is personal, private, and based on intuition and/or feeling states rather than on thought and articulated ideas that are defended with evidence.

> *Procedural Knowing*: A position at which techniques and procedures for acquiring, validating, and evaluating knowledge claims are developed and honored. There are two distinct kinds of procedural knowledge: *separate knowing* and *connected knowing*.
>
> *Constructed Knowing*: A position at which truth is understood to be contextual – knowledge is recognized as tentative rather than as absolute, and it is believed that the knower is part of (constructs) the known.
>
> (Goldberger, Tarule, Clinchy & Belenky, 1996, pp. 4–5)

We would suggest here that these epistemological perspectives are also not just relevant to, but are essential for, taking into account the epistemological perspectives of other marginalized and oppressed groups as well.

At the same time that feminist critiques of traditional epistemology were coming to the fore, non-Western scholars, working in post-colonial settings and in indigenous contexts, began to argue that what had been taken to be epistemology was in fact only *Western* epistemology – a single, particular "folk epistemology" that ought to be taken to be equivalent to, but not necessarily superior to, other folk epistemologies (see Abu-Saad & Champagne, 2006; Christie, 2006; Gélinas & Bouchard, 2014; Laughlin, 2013; Mazzocchi, 2018; Vanier, 2011). As James Maffie has explained, such *ethnoepistemology* requires us to view "Western epistemology as one among many possible, contingent epistemological undertakings pursued by human beings … [an] approach [which] decenters and provincializes the aims, norms, problems, intuitions, and conclusions of Western epistemology since it no longer regards these as inevitable, universal, or definitive of the epistemology standpoint *per se*" (Maffie, 2013, p. 278). Such an approach to epistemology, which is based on the idea that "different ethnic groups have their own implicit, informal theories of knowledge and that these ethnotheories form the assumptions on which the explicit formal theories are based" (Zambrano & Greenfield, 2004, p. 251), has profound implications for education as well as other disciplines. As Michelle Salazar Pérez and Cinthya Saavedra have suggested,

> Epistemology refers to what can be known, and the relationship between the knower and the known … however … "epistemology is more than a 'way of knowing'"; rather it encompasses a "system of knowing" that has historically privileged Euro-American perspectives as if they are "the only legitimate way to view the world." This epistemological dominance has had devastating consequences for marginalized children both in their educational experiences and everyday encounters with the world.
>
> (Salazar Pérez & Saavedra, 2017, p. 3)

Furthermore, it is not merely the case that dominated and marginalized groups have their own distinctive epistemologies, but that there are also multiple, overlapping epistemologies. For example, it is not the case that there is a single "feminist epistemology"; rather,

> Most feminists of color recognize that gender, race, class, and sexual orientation – *not* gender alone – determine the allocation of power and the nature of any individual's identity, status, and consequence … Therefore, "endarkened" feminist epistemologies are crucial, as they speak to the failures of traditional patriarchal and liberal educational scholarship and examine the intersection of race, class, gender and sexuality.
>
> (Bernal, 1998, p. 556, our emphasis)

The debate about the relationship between the knower and the known which underlies these epistemological concerns is based, in part, on differences of opinion related to the notions of objectivity and relativism (Paul & Moores, 2012, p. 5), and we now turn to a brief discussion of these matters.

Objectivism and Relativism

In the traditional conception of epistemology, science "is a cumulative enterprise to find a true theory that is the key to nature. The received view claims epistemic foundationalism in its efforts toward a logic of justification: Each scientific theory can be (re)formulated by rules of correspondence between the language of theory and the language of observation" (De Clerck, 2016, p. 38). In other words, science is objective to the extent that its results and conclusions are free from the biases, assumptions and concerns of the scientist. The commitment to objectivism understood in this way is at the heart of positivism and positivistic epistemology. As we have already seen, this view of epistemology has come under attack in recent decades. Essentially, as Goedele De Clerck has argued,

> Situating knowledge production in a cultural, social, political, and historical context is often discussed as a form of cognitive relativism; this differs from objectivism, which seeks universals … Pinxten (1991) distinguishes between a traditional objectivism and a more recent (post-Kantian) objectivism: Whereas traditional objectivism refers to an ontological foundation for the evaluation of statements about the world, post-Kantian objectivism situates the foundation for statements of truth in the theoretical consensus that scientists have reached. Pinxten distinguishes four versions of relativism:
>
> 1 *Kuhn's conception of the incommensurability of paradigms.* Because we do not have a universal language of observation, facts are theory-laden.
> 2 *Science is conducted from within a Weltanschauung.*

3 *Worldviews and theories are relativistic.* Underneath these superficial differences, as an *a priori* criterion of universality (including truth and logic) provides cross-cultural understanding. Barnes … states that this universal foundation cannot be found in truth or rationality; rather it can be found in "an unproblematic baseline of normality" … This is problematic because the concept of what is normal is relativistic.
4 *Science may have cultural components* … Values of the socio-cultural context in which science is produced constitute knowledge production and need to be taken into account in the study of epistemic practices.

(De Clerck, 2016, p. 39)

For our purposes here, the key epistemological concern that needs to be addressed is what it means to know a language, and how such knowledge can be developed in the target language classroom, and we now turn to a discussion of these points.

The Nature of Knowledge

In a work concerned with critical pedagogy, there are a number of significant epistemological distinctions that should be noted. One useful concept in this regard is the idea of tacit knowledge. Michael Polyani first wrote about tacit knowledge in his book *Personal Knowledge* (Polyani, 1958), and later in *The Tacit Dimension* (Polyani, 1966). Tacit knowledge, which can be contrasted with explicit knowledge, has been defined as the skills, ideas, concepts, and experiences that we possess, but which are not codified, and which may not be easily expressed – indeed, we may not even be aware of our tacit knowledge. What is especially interesting and valuable is that it is in a community of practice – such as a community of classroom teachers – where such tacit knowledge can often be most clear, and also where it can be most effectively passed from one person to another.

A second way of conceptualizing knowledge that is of special relevance in a critical context is by borrowing the anthropological distinction between emic and etic knowledge. In essence, emic knowledge refers to knowledge, understanding and interpretations that come from *within* a particular cultural community, while etic knowledge refers to knowledge, understanding and interpretations that are proposed by those *outside* of the community. Finally, Jürgen Habermas and others have noted that knowledge can take three distinct forms: technical knowledge, practical knowledge, and emancipatory knowledge (McLaren, 2003, p. 197; see also Holub, 1991; Outhwaite, 2009). Technical knowledge is the sort which can be measured and quantified, and which comes principally from the natural sciences. Practical knowledge is concerned with describing and analyzing social situations, and comes mainly from the social sciences. Emancipatory knowledge is knowledge that seeks to understand social relationships, and especially seeks to understand how such relationships are distorted by power and inequitable power relations in society.

Knowing a Language

A number of years ago, we were working together in the Middle East as consultants in a technical university's TESOL program. One of the faculty in the program, an extremely fluent non-native speaker of English, asked for help in understanding an aspect of English grammar about which he indicated he had never been completely clear, and he assumed that, as native speakers and as language educators, we would be able to help him. The question was about the difference between the first, second and third conditionals in English, and when each should be used. As native speakers of English, using these forms correctly was presumably no problem at all for either of us – but the issue was that this did not provide any insight at all about *what*, exactly, the first, second and third conditionals actually *were*. [5] This actually demonstrates both the advantages and disadvantages of the native speaker of a language as a world language educator of her or his own language. The native speaker knows how the language works, what forms are appropriate and what forms are not appropriate, and so on – but without formal study, we are not as likely as the non-native speaker to understand *why* particular forms are correct and others are incorrect. The non-native speaker who has learned the target language as a second language, on the other hand, will probably never reach the degree of linguistic fluency of a native speaker, but may very well be more understanding and aware of the challenges faced by other non-native speakers in learning the language – and may also be more effective in teaching many aspects of the target language.

The Components of Knowledge in the World Language Education Context

What, then, does it actually mean when we say that the native speaker "knows" her or his native language? What is the *kind* of knowledge that we are thinking about when we make such a claim? These questions are important, especially in the context of the world language classroom, since they have huge implications for the content of the curriculum, the most appropriate teaching methodologies to be used, the kinds of pedagogical and extra-curricular materials that the teacher will utilize, the nature of assessment, and finally, what should (and should not) be included in any national content area standards that are to be used in the field. We would suggest that the answers to these questions are far broader, more inclusive and more complex than world language educators typically assume. Specifically, we would argue that there are five quite different kinds of knowledge that need to be taken into account in world language education: linguistic knowledge, metalinguistic knowledge, sociolinguistic knowledge, discourse knowledge, and strategic/pragmatic knowledge. Each of these types of knowledge is explained below:

- *Linguistic Knowledge*. Linguistic knowledge includes an understanding of the fundamental structures and components of the target language: its phonology, morphology, and syntax, as well as its lexicon. Issues related to the orthography of the language being taught – spelling and punctuation conventions, the alphabet (or its equivalent), and so on – are also included here as an important part of linguistic knowledge where they are relevant (they would not be relevant, for instance, in a class in which the target language is an unwritten language or a sign language such as ASL). It is with such knowledge that world language educators have traditionally been primarily, if not almost exclusively, concerned. Such linguistic knowledge is, of course, essential in learning a new language, and there is no question that it will continue to be a central focus of the world language classroom – but to focus *only* on such knowledge leads to a technicist view not only of language, but also of what can often be an inability to use the target language properly and appropriately.
- *Metalinguistic Knowledge*. Metalinguistic knowledge refers to an understanding of the common elements that are typically taught in world language classes *regardless* of the target language. Perhaps the most obvious example of metalinguistic knowledge is simply the terminology used to describe the various components of a language: nouns, verbs, adjectives, adverbs, conjunctions, singular, plural, tense, mood, aspect, gender, conjugation, declension, and so on. Such metalinguistic knowledge, it should be pointed out, is by no means *necessary* for learning a language, but is nevertheless extremely useful in doing so. As we have noted, such knowledge is also cited by many people as one of the more useful outcomes of having studied a language in school – that is, it provides them with a vocabulary that can be used not only with respect to the target language, but also in talking about their native language.
- *Sociolinguistic Knowledge*. Sociolinguistic knowledge is the awareness of variation in the target language, which can include regional variation, ethnic variation, social class or SES variation, gender variation, religious variation, or virtually any other kind of variation that characterizes differences among speakers of the target language. Sociolinguistic knowledge is already mentioned in a few contexts in world language education (most notably, in Spanish classes where we typically at least mention differences between Peninsular and Latin American Spanish, or in classes teaching a language such as Arabic, which is characterized by extensive regional variation), but for the

most part we only scratch the surface in discussions about such differences. For understandable reasons, we have historically focused only on the standard variety of the target language, but we would argue that students should arguably be also taught about non-standard varieties of the language (though this does not mean that they would need to be taught to actually use such varieties most of the time). The inclusion of sociolinguistic knowledge in the world language classroom is an area in which there is significant potential for incorporating more critical perspectives.

- *Discourse Knowledge*. Language use is more than simply the coding and decoding of messages. When we use a language we are engaged in a process in which meaning is co-produced with our interlocuter(s); that is, there is a give and take in which the ideas, assumptions and biases of both the speaker and the listener play a role. Meaning, in other words, is in practice actually negotiated between users of the language. It is important for students as non-native speakers of the target language to understand this process, and to be able to negotiate not only meaning, but also the process of meaning construction itself.
- *Strategic/Pragmatic Knowledge*. There is an entire branch of linguistics, called pragmatics, which is concerned with what might be considered to be the non-linguistic or extra-linguistic elements of human communication (see Birner, 2013; Yan Huang, 2014, 2017). This strategic or pragmatic knowledge includes the "rules" we assume in engaging in conversations, the strategies that we employ in both producing meaning and understanding the meanings of others, what methods we use to gain and organize knowledge linguistically, how we question and, if necessary, repair communicative breakdown, and a host of other factors. Included here, and very valuable in the context of the world language classroom, would be information about how to begin and end conversations, issues of formality and informality, matters of politeness, personal space preferences and norms, and so on.

Linguistic Competence and Linguistic Performance

Another useful way in which knowledge of language can be conceptualized is by distinguishing between what Noam Chomsky, in *Aspects of the Theory of Syntax* (1965), called "linguistic competence" and "linguistic performance," which basically refer to two very different kinds of linguistic ability. This distinction was actually in some sense a response to an earlier distinction suggested by Ferdinand de Saussure in 1916. In his *Cours de Linguistique Générale*, de Saussure had suggested that language is fundamentally a system of linguistic signs. This system of signs is the result of a general social consensus about how these signs are used, and de Saussure called this consensus *langue*. He distinguished *langue* from *parole*, which was how *langue* was actually manifested in speech, and argued that it was possible to understand the structure of *langue* by studying *parole* (Chomsky, 1965, pp. 36–43). In developing his theory of generative grammar, Chomsky replaced this distinction between *langue* and *parole* with that of linguistic competence and linguistic performance. In essence, the concept of linguistic competence refers to the innate, and unconscious, knowledge of the individual speaker of her or his language, while the concept of linguistic performance is used to describe the individual's actual (often flawed) use of language. For Chomsky and other linguists working in generative linguistics, it was linguistic competence that was by far of greater significance.[6] It is worth noting here that although we believe that the distinction between linguistic competence and linguistic performance is a useful one in discussing the teaching and learning of world languages, within the discipline of linguistics proper it has been widely criticized, and is no longer universally accepted as a valid representation of the nature of linguistic knowledge.

Language Acquisition and Language Learning

As we mentioned in Chapter 2, there is an important distinction between *language acquisition* and *language learning* (see Pinker, 2009; Van Patten & Williams, 2015). Language acquisition refers to the informal process by which an individual acquires her or his first language, and, depending on the context, may describe the acquisition of other languages. Language learning, on the other hand, refers to a more formal process – typically, what takes place in school settings, for instance, as students study a second or additional language. We know that language can be acquired, because virtually all human beings do in fact acquire a language, but it is also true that language is learnable – that is, it is possible for us to engage in a formal process by which we learn a second or additional language. Thus, while language acquisition has at least elements that appear to be almost instinctive in nature, language learning is comparable to the learning of any other skill. Needless to say, this has incredibly important implications for teaching and learning in the world language classroom.

Metaphors in Educational Discourse

Metaphors are widely used in education and in other kinds of public discourse, and often play key roles in discussion and debates. Thomas Green has suggested that, "it may be that metaphors are necessary if we are to think about important matters at all. No major philosopher in the history of the subject has escaped their use and no major field of knowledge in the modern world can do without them" (Green, 1971, p. 56). Metaphors, at root, are basically unstated analogies, involving the implicit comparison of two different kinds of things, one of which is intended by the speaker to be taken literally, the other figuratively. Examples of common educational metaphors would include the claims that "education is growth," "critical thinking is a tool," and "teachers mold and shape children." Taken literally, each of these claims is clearly not only false, but absurd (see Scheffler, 1960, pp. 49–59; see also Scheffler, 1979). However, it is nevertheless true that we do in fact understand each of these statements quite clearly in the non-literal way in which each is intended. Metaphors, in short, are used because they have value to us. As Green noted:

> The main virtue of the metaphor is that it calls our attention to certain similarities between two things. It carries the mind over from one thing to another by calling attention to resemblances. In other words, a metaphor is a way of establishing "thought-full" relations between [and among] things.
>
> (Green, 1971, p. 57)

We commonly use metaphors and metaphorical language to describe such concepts as teaching, learning and knowing, and such metaphors are extremely important.[7] By their very nature, metaphors are intended to be non-literal (see Lakoff & Johnson, 1980), and yet, they reflect underlying beliefs and attitudes and, even more, themselves take on significant pedagogical power. There is a wealth of metaphorical language in the discourse of classroom teachers that relates directly and indirectly to pedagogy and pedagogical issues. As Steven Miller and Marcel Fredericks have argued, the use of metaphors is a worthwhile topic for our attention since, "Metaphorical expressions are so pervasive in ordinary and academic life ... they must reflect a 'fundamental core' of shared meaning. By using these expressions, people must assign meaning. Metaphors are not simply random events but are ways of 'structuring' and extending experience" (Miller & Fredericks, 1988, pp. 263–264).

Metaphors and metaphorical language function in part to structure the individual's construction of reality, as well as to mediate her or his experiences with underlying, and often implicit, assumptions, values and beliefs. As George Lakoff and Mark Johnson have suggested:

> Metaphors may create realities for us, especially social realities. A metaphor may thus be a guide for future action. Such actions will, of course, fit the metaphor. This will, in turn, reinforce the power of the metaphor to make experience coherent. In this sense metaphors can be self-fulfilling prophecies.
>
> (Lakoff & Johnson, 1980, p. 156)

If it is indeed the case that metaphors not only play a role in the way in which individuals construct their realities, but also serve as guides for practice, then it would seem to be evident that the study of the *kinds* of metaphors and metaphorical language employed by teachers and other educators about teaching and learning ought to be of considerable concern to anyone interested in understanding and improving educational practice (see Nattinger, 1993). Siegelman (1990), for instance, believes that metaphors have the potential to generate new ideas and meanings between listener and speaker. Thus, if the goal is to help people better communicate their personal realities, metaphors can provide an infrastructure for supporting shared cultures (see Nuessel, 2000).

The analysis of metaphors in educational discourse can provide us with useful insights, and the use of metaphors can help us to develop clearer understandings and appreciations of complex issues and concepts. Consider, for instance, the kinds of metaphors that are often used by teachers to describe the concept of "teaching." In a fascinating study of classroom teacher discourse, Miller and Fredericks found that four broad "families" of metaphors were commonly used:

- teaching as a conduit (the "transfer of knowledge");
- teaching as a biological process (the "growth of students");
- teaching as a process of building (the "construction of knowledge and understanding"); and
- teaching as war ("working in the trenches").

(Miller & Fredericks, 1988)

The metaphor chosen to describe teaching tells us a great deal about the teacher. The frequent use of war or military metaphors, for instance, suggests that the teacher perceives the classroom as something of a battleground. Insofar as this is the case, we would expect (and indeed would be likely to find) that concerns of classroom management and control are at the top of such a teacher's worries. This, in turn, will be reflected in the approach to students, teaching methods, assessment, and so on taken by the teacher.

Theories of Learning and World Language Education

Since at least the time of Plato in the 4th and 5th centuries BCE, philosophers have sought to understand how human beings learn. Most of the discussion that took place in this "on-going human conversation" before the 19th century, though, was basically limited to what might be called "armchair theorizing" – that is, it consisted of hypotheses for which there was really no empirical evidence. Toward the end of the 19th century, this began to change as the new science of psychology emerged, and throughout the 20th and now early 21st centuries a number of interesting models of human learning – each with its own implications for classroom practice – have been suggested by psychologists, based on experimental, empirical and increasingly neurological evidence (see, for example, National Research Council, 2000). Entire books have been written about particular learning theories, and whole courses in teacher education programs are devoted to the subjects of educational psychology and learning theories, and it is neither possible nor appropriate for us to cover all of the different learning theories and their implications for world language educators here. However, it is nonetheless true, as Marion Williams and Robert Burden have noted, that:

> The educational process is one of the most important and complex human undertakings ... There exists a common idea that teaching is carried out by a person, the teacher, who is standing in front of the classroom in front of a group of students and transmitting information to these students who are attempting to absorb it ... this vision simplifies a very complex process that involves a complicated interaction among the learning process itself, the goals and actions of the teacher, the personality, culture and background of the learner, the learning environment, and many other variables. The effective educator ought to be one who understands the complexities of the teaching-learning process and who can use this knowledge to empower his or her students both in and beyond the classroom.
>
> (Williams & Burden, 1999, p. 15, our translation)

In the next part of the chapter, we will briefly summarize what we take to be two of the more important sets of learning theories that are generally taken to be in competition with constructivist learning theories, which are the focus of the chapter and to which we will return. It is important to note that our comments here are necessarily overly simplified, and that not only is each of these theories far more complex than suggested here, but that within each of these theories are actually multiple (and often competing) theories.

Behaviorism

Behaviorism is the oldest of the different learning theories that we will discuss, and it has had a huge impact on both psychology and education (see Baum, 2017; O'Neil, 1995; Slavin, 2018). Behaviorism first developed in the late 19th century, and was really the first approach to understanding learning that was based on experimental hypotheses and tests. In essence, behaviorism is grounded in the idea that all behaviors – whether human or animal – are in some manner responses to stimuli that the individual is exposed to (in its simplest version, called Stimulus–Response Theory). Among the earliest of the modern psychologists interested in understanding the nature of learning was the Russian physician and physiologist Ivan Pavlov, who is credited with first identifying what is called classical conditioning, which serves in many ways as the foundation for contemporary behavioral learning theories. Pavlov is best known for an important, but also fairly simple, set of experimental results that originated from informal observations that he made while conducting studies on the digestive processes of dogs. When given food, dogs salivate. This is a natural (and necessary) part of the eating process. What Pavlov noticed, though, was that his test animals salivated whenever they saw the laboratory technician who fed them – whether or not they were actually being fed. This was an *unconditioned* stimulus which led to an *unconditioned* response. Pavlov further discovered, however, that he could produce a *conditioned* response in the dogs in a deliberate fashion, and that there were certain things that increased the speed at which the conditioned response would develop. The conditioned response here is basically learning, and it takes place not only in dogs and other animals, but can also be used with people in a variety of ways and for a number of different purposes.

The American psychologist Edward Thorndike added to the concept of classical conditioning by demonstrating that responses to stimuli that produced pleasant consequences tended to be repeated, while those produced unpleasant consequences were less likely to be repeated – which is called the "Law of Effect" (see Beatty, 1998; O'Neil, 1995; Thorndike, 2000). John Watson, in the early decades of the 20th century, sought to develop "methodological behaviorism" by focusing only on behaviors, events and outcomes that could actually be measured, thus effectively eliminating thoughts and feelings from an understanding of learning (see Watson, 1970). Beginning in the 1930s, another American psychologist, B. F. Skinner, critiqued both the idea that classical conditioning could adequately explain much of human behavior and elements of Thorndike's work (especially Thorndike's references to mental states which could not be observed), and expanded the application of the "Law of Effect" into what came to be known as operant conditioning. For Skinner, operant conditioning refers to how learning can be strengthened or weakened as a result of either positive reinforcement or negative reinforcement (see Skinner, 1971, 1974); Skinner's approach to behaviorism is commonly called "radical behaviorism" (Chiesa, 1992, 1994; Johnson, 2014).

There are a number of very direct implications for educational practice that emerge from behaviorist learning theory, including:

> - an emphasis on producing observable and measurable outcomes in students (including the use of behavioral objectives, task analysis, and criterion-referenced assessments);
> - pre-assessment of students to determine where instruction should begin;
> - emphasis on mastering early steps before progressing to more complex levels of performance (sequencing of instruction, mastery learning);
> - use of reinforcement to impact performance; and
> - use of cues, shaping and practice to ensure a strong stimulus–response association.
>
> (Ertmer & Newby, 2013, pp. 49–50)

It has become fairly common in some educational circles to view behaviorism very critically, but it is important to understand that behaviorist approaches in many areas have proven to be extremely effective. This is especially true in terms of the application of behaviorism in applied behavioral analysis, including not only in the field of special education (where it is widely utilized), but also in different cognitive-behavioral therapies including in the treatment of mood disorders, phobias, and post-traumatic stress disorder. Basically, behaviorism is most useful in

> facilitating learning that involves discriminations (recalling facts), generalizations (defining and illustrating concepts), associations (applying explanations), and chaining (automatically performing a specified procedure) ... however, it is generally agreed that behavior principles cannot adequately explain the acquisition of higher level skills or those that require a greater depth of processing (e.g., language development, problem solving, inference generating, critical thinking).
>
> (Ertmer & Newby, 2013, p. 49)

It is also the case, however, that in terms of understanding language learning and improving on language teaching, behaviorism has been less successful than in many other areas, as we will see when we discuss the Audiolingual Method.

Cognitivism

Beginning in the 1960s, there was a move away from behaviorism and toward what has come to be called "cognitivism," although this transition actually began far earlier and was in some ways embedded in some of the major limitations of behaviorism (see Mandler, 2002). As George Mandler noted,

> The well-documented cognitive "revolution" was, to a large extent, an evolving return to attitudes and trends that were present prior to the advent of behaviorism and that were alive and well outside of the United States, where behaviorism had not developed any coherent support. The behaviorism of the 1920 to 1950 period was replaced because it was unable to address central issues in human psychology, a failure that was inherent in part in J. B. Watson's founding manifesto with its insistence on the seamless continuity of human and nonhuman animal behavior. The "revolution" was often slow and piecemeal ... With the realization that different approaches and concepts were needed to address a psychology of the human, developments in German, British, and Francophone psychology provided some of the fuel of the "revolution."
>
> (Mandler, 2002, p. 339)

Perhaps the single most important distinction between behaviorist approaches and cognitivist approaches to understanding learning is how "thinking" is conceptualized. For behaviorists, thinking is a behavior, while for cognitivists it is far more than merely a behavior – it is foundational, and must be far more than merely a behavior (see Lilienfeld, Lynn, Namy, Woolf, Jamieson, Marks & Slaughter, 2015, pp. 31–32). In other words:

> according to cognitivists, predictions of behavior based solely on rewards and punishments from the environment will never be adequate, because our interpretation of rewards and punishments is a crucial determinant of our behaviour ... Without understanding how people evaluate information, cognitivists maintain, we will never fully grasp the causes of their behaviour.
>
> (Lilienfeld, Lynn, Namy, Woolf, Jamieson, Marks & Slaughter, 2015, p. 31)

Cognitivism focuses on such concepts as memory, perceptions, thinking, knowing and problem-solving, and defines learning as changes in the learner's mental schemata. It is often suggested that cognitivism views the mind as a "black box" – a "black box" that we wish to open and understand. Prior to learning, we are in a state of equilibrium, and learning is, on Jean Piaget's account, basically the process of "adaptation." Adaptation involves the state of equilibrium being challenged by a new situation which challenges our existing schemata, leading to disequilibrium. Disequilibrium leads, in turn, to accommodation and ultimately assimilation (see Piaget, 1928, 1932, 1948a, 1948b, 1976, 1979, 1993, 1996, 2012; Sinclair, Berthoud, Gerard & Venesiano, 1985). Essentially, what this means, as Peggy Ertmer and Timothy Newby have explained, is that "the real focus of the cognitive approach is on *changing the learning by encouraging his/her to use appropriate learning strategies*" (Ertmer & Newby 2013, p. 52, emphasis in original).

Cognitivism, like behaviorism, has a number of implications for educational practice, including:

> - an emphasis on the active involvement of the learner in the learning process;
> - the use of hierarchical analyses to identify and illustrate prerequisite relationships;
> - an emphasis on structuring, organizing, and sequencing information to facilitate optimal processing; and
> - the creation of learning environments that allow and encourage students to make connections with previously learned material.
>
> (Ertmer & Newby, 2013, p. 53)

To a very considerable extent, cognitivism can be best thought of as analogous to the way that a computer operates – and, indeed, cognitivists often use the metaphor of "mind as a computer" to explain the core assumptions of cognitivism.

Approaches to Teaching World Languages

In addition to different learning theories, in the preparation of future teachers of world languages we often teach students about various approaches that have been and can be used in the teaching of languages: the Grammar-Translation Method, the Direct Method, the Audiolingual Method, Communicative Language Teaching, Total Physical Response, the Silent Way, Suggestopedia, and so on. In fact, it is quite common for language teaching textbooks to include sections in which each of the major approaches to the teaching of world languages are explicitly discussed, sometimes in considerable detail (see Brown, 2001; Curtain & Dahlberg, 2004; Horowitz, 2008; Larsen-Freeman, 2000; Lessow-Hurley, 2009; Omaggio Hadley, 1993; Richard-Amato, 1996; Shrum & Glisan, 2016) (see Figure 5.1 for a comparison of the different approaches to teaching foreign languages). This is somewhat different from how teachers of other subject areas are typically prepared; in most disciplines, although there may be different broad approaches to teaching, the clear demarcation that we assume in world language education is not common. To be sure, this is somewhat misleading, since it suggests that in world language classrooms we are likely to employ only a single method, rather than use different elements from different approaches (which is probably the most common way in which languages are actually taught). Nevertheless, in world language education we continue to identify particular approaches to teaching languages, and such differentiations are very much part of our discipline in a way that they are not for other subjects. We turn now to brief descriptions of a number of the more common approaches to the teaching of world languages in the contemporary U.S. setting.

The Grammar-Translation Method

The Grammar-Translation Method has its origins in the teaching of the Classical languages, and in the teaching of Latin in particular. Traditionally in the United States, Latin was taught through the medium of English, and the goals of such instruction were two-fold: first, to allow the student to translate texts from Latin into English accurately, and second, as a way of strengthening cognitive skills. Grammar was taught deductively, and the focus of classroom activity was on translation. Minimal, if any, concern was given to oral communication in the target language. When modern languages (especially French and German) began to be taught in public schools, initially the Grammar-Translation Method was

Teaching Approach	*Theory of Language Learning*	*Objectives*	*Typical Activities*	*Role of Teacher*	*Role of Learner*
Grammar-Translation Method	It is not really clear that any particular theory of language learning underlies the Grammar-Translation method.	The primary object of the Grammar-Translation method is for students to be able to read the target language. A secondary objective is to develop mental discipline.	Translation activities; focus on grammatical rules.	The teacher serves as an expert and reference on the structure of the target language, and to be able to judge the accuracy of translations.	The student must memorize the grammatical rules of the target language as well as vocabulary items, in order to be able to translate texts (most often from the target language into their native language).
Direct Method	The essence of language is meaning. Vocabulary, not grammar, is the heart of language, and is thus the focus of the Direct Method.	The Direct Method is designed to give learners basic communicative skills.	Activities allowing comprehensible input about things in the here-and-now. The focus of activities is on meaning rather than form.	The teacher is the primary source of comprehensible input. She or he must create a positive, low-anxiety climate in the classroom, and must choose and orchestrate a rich mixture of classroom activities.	Students should not try to learn language in the usual sense of "learning," but rather should try to lose themselves in activities involving meaningful communication.

(Continued)

(Cont.)

Teaching Approach	*Theory of Language Learning*	*Objectives*	*Typical Activities*	*Role of Teacher*	*Role of Learner*
Audiolingual Method	Language is seen as a system of rule-governed structures that are hierarchically arranged.	The objectives of the Audiolingual Method include providing students with control of the structures of sound, form, and order in the target language. Mastery of the language – and ultimately, native speaker mastery of the language – is the goal of the Audiolingual Method.	Dialogues and drills, repetition and memorization, and pattern practice are characteristic activities associated with the Audiolingual Method.	The teacher's role is central and active; the Audiolingual Method is clearly teacher-dominated. The teacher provides a model, and controls direction and pace.	Students are conceptualized as "organisms" that can be directed by skilled training techniques to produce correct responses.
Communicative Language Teaching	Language is fundamentally a system for the expression of meaning; the primary function of language is interaction and communication.	The objectives of Communicative Language Teaching reflect the needs of the learners. They include functional as well as linguistic goals.	Communicative Language Teaching seeks to engage learners in communication, involve processes such as information sharing, negotiation of meaning, and interaction.	The teacher is the facilitator of the communicative process, participants tasks, and texts; needs analyst, counselor, process manager.	The learner is seen as negotiator, interactor, and as giving as well as taking.
Total Physical Response	Basically, Total Physical Response is a structuralist, grammar-based view of language.	Total Physical Response seeks to teach oral proficiency to produce learners who can communicate without inhibitions and intelligibly with native speakers.	Imperative drills to elicit physical actions are the most common kinds of activities in Total Physical Response.	The teacher has an active and direct role; the "director of a stage play" with students as actors.	The role of the student is to be both a listener and a performer, with little influence over the actual content of learning.

The Silent Way	The Silent Way assumes that each and every language is composed of elements that give it a unique rhythm and spirit.	Near-native fluency, correct pronunciation, basic practical knowledge of the grammar of the target language are the major objectives of the Silent Way. In essence, the learner learns *how* to learn a language.	In the Silent Way, learner response to commands, questions, and visual cues. Activities encourage and shape oral responses without grammatical explanation or modeling by the teacher.	Teachers must (i) teach to the test, (ii) test, and then (iii) get out of the way. The teacher should remain impassive, and resist temptation to model, remodel, assist, direct, or exhort learners.	Since learning is a process of personal growth, students are responsible for their own learning and must develop independence, autonomy, and responsibility.
Suggestopedia	The underlying theory of language for Suggestopedia is fairly conventional, although memorization of whole meaningful texts is recommended.	The primary objective of Suggestopedia is to develop advanced conversational competence quickly. Learners are required to master prodigious lists of vocabulary, although the goal is understanding rather than memorization.	Initiatives, question and answer, role play, and listening exercises under deep relaxation are characteristic of Suggestopedia.	The principal task of the teacher is to create situations in which the learner is most suggestible and present material in a way most likely to encourage positive reception and retention. The teacher should exude authority and confidence.	Learners must maintain a passive state and allow the materials to work on them (rather than vice versa).

Figure 5.1 Comparison of Approaches to Teaching Foreign Languages
(Based on Brown, 2001, pp. 34–35; Larsen-Freeman, 2000)

used to teach them as well. It would be an understatement to say that the Grammar-Translation Method is not particularly well-suited to teaching modern languages; as Jack Richards and Theodore Rodgers have commented,

> Though it may be true to say that the Grammar-Translation Method is still widely practiced, it has no advocates. It is a method for which there is no theory. There is no literature that offers a rationale or justification for it or that attempts to relate it to issues in linguistics, psychology, or educational theory.
>
> (Richards & Rodgers, 2001, p. 7)

Whether the Grammar-Translation Method is in fact "still widely practiced" is debatable, but insofar as it is used, it is almost always cited as an example of poor language teaching.[8] Typical of the criticisms of the Grammar-Translation Method is the story of François Gouin, as it was recounted by Karl Diller:

> François Gouin, a 19th century Latin teacher from France ... decided to teach himself German. Gouin began by memorizing a German grammar book and 248 irregular verbs, an effort that took him ten days. Despite these efforts, he was unable to understand a word of spoken German. Convinced, however, that he was on the right track and only needed to broaden his knowledge, he set about memorizing 800 German roots. At that point, unable to engage in even simple conversation or to translate written German, he purchased a dictionary and proceeded to memorize 30,000 words in 30 days, an effort that all but destroyed his eyesight, but failed to make him proficient in German .... Imagine his surprise to find that his three-year-old nephew had learned to speak French during a three-month vacation in France!
>
> (Quoted in Lessow-Hurley, 2009, pp. 90–91)

To be fair, though, there are several problems with the critiques of the Grammar-Translation Method that should be taken into account. Camilo Andrés Bonilla Carvajal has pointed out that to a considerable degree the "Grammar-Translation Method" was not really so much a distinctive and unified approach to teaching languages as it has been a kind of "straw man" created by more recent methodologists to defend their own approaches to the teaching of languages. As Carvajal suggests, the "assertion that Grammar-Translation did exist, and that it is the negative model of teaching practices that should be better avoided at all costs, might reflect an unconstructive and unfounded ideological interest of mainstream theoreticians and unsuspecting teachers" (Carvajal, 2013, p. 243). This is not to suggest that we would advocate the use of a methodology similar to that encompassed under the label of the Grammar-Translation Method, but rather, merely that claims about Grammar-Translation probably need to be taken somewhat carefully (see Larsen-Freeman, 2000, pp. 11–22).

The Direct Method

The Direct Method, which is also sometimes called the Natural Method, developed in the early 20th century as a response to the Grammar-Translation Method (see Brown, 2001, pp. 18–22; Horowitz, 2008, pp. 52–57; Larsen-Freeman, 2000, pp. 23–33; Richard-Amato, 1996, pp. 12–13). Unlike the Grammar-Translation Method, the Direct Method is focused explicitly on the development of oral skills in the target language. One of the central characteristics of the Direct Method is that classroom interactions take place only in the target language; neither the student nor the teacher is to use the student's native language, and translation of any type is discouraged. Grammatical constructs are taught indirectly and inductively, and spoken language is central to instruction utilizing the Direct Method. The Direct Method is widely used in international language schools, such as Berlitz, as well as in language learning programs at the U.S. State Department's Foreign Service Institute. The Direct Method has a number of advantages, including that it:

- can facilitate the development of speech fluency in the target language;
- provides a relatively rapid way to increase and expand vocabulary knowledge in the target language;
- reduces the linguistic interference and inhibitions from the learner's L1;
- discourages students from relying on translation, and encourages them to begin to operate in the target language from the beginning of the learning experience;
- can assist the student in developing "language sense" in the target language; and
- assists the student in bridging the gap between the theory and practice gap in the language learning experience.

In addition, actual teaching in the Direct Method often makes extremely good use of audiovisual and other materials and realia.

At the same time, though, there are limitations that have been identified with the Direct Method. Specifically, the Direct Method:

- may result in less emphasis on the written language, and thus impact the development of both reading and writing in the target language;
- supports the acquisition of basic vocabulary, but not more advanced vocabulary items that are less concrete;
- requires extremely skilled and linguistically competent teachers;

- is not well-suited to situations in which large numbers of students must be taught together, as in many public school settings;
- does not allow grammar to be taught systematically;
- can be somewhat slow in real-life situations; and
- can sometimes be problematic in teaching students with special needs.

In spite of these challenges and limitations, there is little doubt that the Direct Method can be an extremely effective approach to language teaching, and it offers a number of useful insights for the classroom teacher.

The Audiolingual Method

The Audiolingual Method (ALM) is an especially interesting case in the development of teaching methodologies in world language education (see Chastain, 1976, pp. 109–129; Larsen-Freeman, 2000, pp. 35–51; Littlewood, 1984, pp. 17–21). It arose as the result of the convergence of two extremely powerful forces, one intellectual and one social. ALM is grounded in behaviorist psychology, and specifically, in B. F. Skinner's view that all behavior – including human language – is learned through repetition and reinforcement. Thus, the rise and dominance of behaviorism in the mid-20th century provided the intellectual foundation for the emergence of the ALM. At the same time, following World War II and during the Cold War – and especially after the 1957 launch of *Sputnik*, which led many to believe that the United States was falling behind the Soviet Union in many technical and military fields – there was a concern with the serious shortage of Americans with necessary skills in languages other than English.[9] The result of this latter development was the passage of the National Defense Education Act (NDEA) in 1958, which provided substantial federal funding for instructional equipment and materials, teacher training, and so on, for mathematics and science education as well as for foreign language education. NDEA funding made possible a number of radical changes in the teaching of foreign languages as the ALM method gained prominence in the 1960s.

The ALM was characterized by a number of distinctive features. Each of the four skills (listening, speaking, reading and writing) is taught separately, and while all four skills are taught, there is a clear emphasis on speaking and listening. Although the rejection of the learner's L1 is not as complete as is the case with the Direct Method, in general in the ALM the use of the mother tongue is minimized to as great an extent as possible. Dialogue is a central feature of ALM, and linguistic features of the target language are typically introduced in dialogues. Students memorize and practice dialogues, and then engage in various kinds of drills that are used to reinforce the linguistic features being taught. ALM dialogues were most often introduced without any translation, and students memorized the dialogues, which provided an introduction to vocabulary as well as introducing specific grammatical forms that were to be acquired. An example of an ALM drill from the *ALM Russian Level 1* textbook is:

Поход в горы

КОЛЯ: Ну как? Всё готово?
ВАНЯ: Да. Вот мой рюкзак. Палатка и одеяло там.
КОЛЯ: Одеяло оставь. Оно не нужно. У нас есть лишний спальный мешок.
ВАНЯ: Как так?
КОЛЯ: Витя в поход не идёт.

ВАНЯ: А где же провизия?
КОЛЯ: Она внизу. Полная корзина – хлеб, лимонад, пирожки …
ВАНЯ: А фотоаппарат где?
КОЛЯ: Он у меня. Спеши, ребята ждут!
ВАНЯ: Пошли! Я готов.

A Trip to the Mountains

KOLYA: Well, how's it going? Is everything ready?
VANYA: Yes. Here's my knapsack. The tent and blanket are over there.
KOLYA: Leave the blanket. You won't need it. (It isn't necessary.) We have an extra sleeping bag.
VANYA: How come?
KOLYA: Vitya is not going on the trip.

VANYA: But where's the food?
KOLYA: It's downstairs. A whole basketful (a full basket) – bread, lemonade, *pirozhki*…
VANYA: And where's the camera?
KOLYA: I have it. Hurry up, the kids are waiting!
VANYA: Let's go! I'm ready.

(ALM Russian, 1969, p. 61)

In this dialogue, the specific grammatical points taught include the gender of nouns, possessive adjectives, and the possessives его (his), её (her) and их (their). In addition to the vocabulary included in the dialogue itself, in the supplement to the dialogue and in the various drills, the following additional vocabulary is covered:

(лишний) билет	(extra) ticket
бутерброды	sandwiches
варенье	jam
вещи	things
девочки	girls
деньги	money

закуска	snacks
зонтик	umbrella
кошелёк	wallet (change-purse)
куртка	jacket
лодка	boat
мальчики	boys
место	place
очки	glasses
пальто	coat
перчатки	gloves
печенье	cookies
плащ	raincoat
полотенце	towel
проигрыватель	record player
свитер	sweater
спички	matches
сумка	pocketbook
чай	tea

In addition to the memorization of the dialogue, the ALM makes extensive use of a variety of different kinds of drills. These drills range from very simple to quite complex in nature. There are several major kinds of drills used in ALM teaching, including the following.

Repetition Drills

Repetition drills are used at the beginning of a lesson or unit, and consist of the teacher modeling a line from the dialogue, and students attempting to repeat what the teacher has said as accurately and quickly as possible. This is done based entirely on aural input; students do not see the written text that they are learning at this point. In repetition drills, the teacher corrects student errors in pronunciation and grammar. Repetition drills are used to assist students in memorizing the initial dialogue of the lesson or unit.

Substitution Drills

Substitution drills involve the student repeating a line from the dialogue which the teacher has provided, and substituting the "cue" into the line in its proper place:

> Paul is reading the book. → newspaper → Paul is reading the newspaper.
> magazine → Paul is reading the magazine.

In the case of the Russian dialogue provided above, an example of a substitution drill would be:

Teacher: Зонтик не нужен.
Teacher: Свитер.
Student 1: Свитер не нужен.
Teacher: Зонтик не нужен.
Teacher: Спальный мешок.
Student 2: Спальный мешок не нужен.

Teacher: You don't need an umbrella.
Teacher: Sweater.
Student 1: You don't need a sweater.
Teacher: You don't need an umbrella.
Teacher: Sleeping bag.
Student 2: You don't need a sleeping bag.

Expansion Drills

Expansion drills are employed when a long line in a dialogue is presenting students with difficulty. In an expansion drill, the teacher breaks down the line into smaller parts, and the students then repeat each part of the sentence. Then, following the teacher's cue, the students expand on what they are repeating. The goals of expansion drills are to keep the intonation of the line as natural as possible, while also drawing the students' attention to the end of the sentence where new information is often presented. An example of an expansion drill, for the sentence "My mother is a teacher who works in a school and teaches children," is:

Teacher: My mother is a teacher.
Students: My mother is a teacher.
Teacher: She works in a school.
Students: She works in a school.
Teacher: She teaches children.
Students: She teaches children.
Teacher: My mother is a teacher who works in a school. (etc.)

Chain Drill

A chain drill is a technique used in the world language classroom when students, one by one, ask and answer questions of one another. The teacher begins the chain by greeting a particular student, or by asking the student a question. The student responds appropriately, and then turns to another student in the class and asks that student the same question. Thus, a chain drill might look as follows:

Teacher to Student 1: ¡Hola! ¿Cómo se llama usted?
Student 1: Me llamo Juan.

Student 1 to Student 2: ¡Hola! ¿Cómo se llama usted?
Student 2: Me llamo María.
Student 2 to Student 3: ¡Hola! ¿Cómo se llama usted? (etc.)

Question–Answer Drill

Question–Answer drills are drills in which the teacher, after modeling the desired behavior, asks a question for which there is either a "yes" or "no" response option for the student. For example:

Teacher: Vas-tu au magasin? (Shows a picture of a store.)
Teacher: Oui, je vais au magasin.
Teacher to Student 1: Vas-tu au parc? (Shows a picture of a park.)
Student 1: Oui, je vais au parc.
Teacher to Student 2: Vas-tu au théâtre? (Shows a picture of a skyscraper.)
Student 2: Non, je ne vais pas au théâtre. (etc.)

Transformation Drill

In a transformation drill, the teacher asks students to change the type of sentence in the dialogue. For instance, this might entail changing a positive sentence to a negative one, turning a statement into a question, or changing a sentence in the active voice to the passive voice. In the following Russian case, the student is being asked to change the gender of the perfective past tense form of the verb:

Teacher: Она прочитала книгу.
Student 1: Он прочитал книгу.
Teacher: Он пошел в магазин.
Student 2: Она пошла в магазин.

Teacher: She read the book.
Student 1: He read the book.
Teacher: He went to the store.
Student 2: She went to the store.

The ALM has both strengths and weaknesses. On the one hand, it can be fairly easily used with larger classes, correct pronunciation and structure are emphasized, there are well-developed pedagogical materials for many commonly taught languages available, and it is very much a teacher-centered approach. Last, one of the more visible and lasting results of the widespread adoption of the ALM method in public schools in the 1950s and 1960s was the development and implementation of language laboratories in many schools. At the same time, precisely because it is a teacher-centered approach, the learner has very little control over the material studied or any other aspect of the learning environment and experience. Further, ALM pays very little attention to communicative competence (as opposed to linguistic competence), and even with respect to linguistic competence, emphasizes form over meaning. It is an extremely mechanical method that is based primarily on pattern practice, drill and memorization, all of which can be demotivating for many students.

Communicative Language Teaching

Communicative language teaching (CLT), which is also sometimes called the "communicative approach," presupposes that the most appropriate goal for language learning is the ability to actually communicate in the target language (see Breen & Candlin, 1980; Larsen-Freeman, 2000, pp. 121–136; Lee & VanPatten, 2003; Nunan, 1991; Savignon, 1983; Widdowson, 1978). This means that there is inevitably less focus in CLT on grammatical competence, and more on interaction between the teacher and students, and among students, in the classroom. It is also the case that in CLT oral skills (listening and speaking) precede reading and writing skills, which are often seen as of less importance. One of the challenges in discussing CLT is that it is not a narrow or rigid approach; indeed, even defining it clearly is problematic. As H. Douglas Brown has commented:

> It is difficult to offer a definition of CLT. It is a unified but broadly based, theoretically well-informed set of tenets about the nature of language and language learning and teaching. From the earlier seminal works in CLT … up to more recent teacher education textbooks … we have definitions enough to send us reeling.
>
> (Brown, 2001, p. 43)

This does not mean, though, that we cannot offer a generally viable definition of CLT. Brown himself does so, suggesting that the following interconnected characteristics provide a useful working description of CLT:

- Classroom goals are focused on all of the components (grammatical, discourse, functional, sociolinguistic, and strategic) of communicative competence. Goals therefore must intertwine the organizational aspects of language with the pragmatic.
- Language techniques are designed to engage learners in the pragmatic, authentic, functional use of language for meaningful purposes. Organizational language forms are not the central focus, but rather aspects of language that enable the learner to accomplish those purposes.
- Fluency and accuracy are seen as complementary principles underlying communicative techniques. At times fluency may have to take on more importance than accuracy in order to keep learners meaningfully engaged in language use.

- Students in a communicative class ultimately have to use the language, productively and receptively, in unrehearsed contexts outside the classroom. Classroom tasks must therefore equip students with the skills necessary for communication in those contexts.
- Students are given opportunities to focus on their own learning process through an understanding of their own styles of learning and through the development of appropriate strategies for autonomous learning.
- The role of the teacher is that of facilitator and guide, not an all-knowing bestower of knowledge. Students are therefore encouraged to construct meaning through genuine linguistic interaction with others.

(Brown, 2001, p. 43)

There are a number of concepts that often overlap CLT. Each of these concepts, it should be noted, can and is used to support other approaches to language learning and teaching, but they are most often associated with CLT. This is perhaps understandable, since CLT is arguably the dominant approach to the teaching of world languages in the United States today. These concepts include:

- learning-centered instruction.
- cooperative learning.
- collaborative learning.
- interactive learning.
- whole language education.
- content-based instruction.
- task-based instruction.

(Brown, 2001, pp. 46–51)

Finally, among the common activities in the CLT classroom are role-playing, interviews, group work, scavenger hunts, filling information gaps, sharing of opinions, and so on.

Other Approaches to Language Teaching

In addition to the major approaches to language teaching that we have discussed thus far, there are several other distinctive approaches that are sometimes employed in the world language classroom. Each of these approaches tends to have been developed by a single individual, and all are typically used in conjunction with other teaching methods. The three additional approaches to language teaching that we will briefly discuss here are Total Physical Response, the Silent Way, and Suggestopedia.

Total Physical Response

Total Physical Response (TPR) was developed by James Asher, a psychology professor at San José State University (see Asher, 1966, 1969, 1996). It is based on the coordination of language and physical movement; teachers give students commands in the target language, and students respond with the appropriate actions (Brown, 2001, pp. 34–35; Richard-Amato, 1996, pp. 116–125). Asher based TPR on first language acquisition, and offered three hypotheses for language learning: (i) students learn language primarily by listening, (ii) language learning is based in the right hemisphere of the brain, and (iii) language learning should be stress-free. TPR is often used with younger language learners, and is generally used in conjunction with other approaches to language teaching. One of the more significant contributions of TPR to world language teaching has been its emphasis on listening as a major component of language learning and teaching (Brown, 2001, p. 247).

The Silent Way

The Silent Way was developed by the innovative mathematics educator Caleb Gattegno, and initially introduced in 1963 (Gattegno, 1963; Young, 2011). The Silent Way emphasizes student autonomy and active participation in the learning process, and is based on the idea that *teacher silence* can be used to promote language learning; ideally, in a setting in which the Silent Way is being utilized, the students will do 90% or more of the talking (Brown, 2001, pp. 28–29, 34–35). The feature of the Silent Way that is perhaps most widely recognized is the use of "Cuisenaire rods," which are colored wooden rods that come in ten different lengths and a variety of different colors. These Cuisenaire rods are an important tool in the Silent Way, and can be used in teaching a variety of things from very basic language skills to quite complex skills. The Silent Way has never been a particularly popular method of teaching foreign languages among foreign language educators, no doubt in part because Gattegno was "not one of us." The challenges faced by the Silent Way are discussed quite sympathetically in a review of the 1972 second edition of *Teaching Foreign Languages in Schools: The Silent Way* by Earl Stevick (a figure who was indeed very much "one of us"):

> This is another book by an outsider … Caleb Gattegno does language teaching as a by-product and special case of a professional commitment which is broader than language teaching as such … [he] makes no mention of those who are conspicuous in the field; in turn, his own published works are cited only rarely in our books and journals. The first edition of this book received no serious reviews in the United States, and as far as I am aware, the second edition has thus far been entirely ignored

> .... It is not hard to understand how this has happened. I myself found the first chapter of the first edition so annoying that I refused to read further.
>
> (Stevick, 1974, p. 305)

To his credit, Stevick goes on to indicate that as a result of his exposure to and experiences with the Silent Way, he found "the second edition exciting and utterly charming from cover to cover" (Stevick, 1974, p. 305). To be sure, there are many problems with the Silent Way as a pedagogical approach to teaching languages, but there can be little doubt that there is also a good deal that we can learn from it.

Suggestopedia

Suggestopedia is a method of foreign language instruction that was developed by the Bulgarian psychotherapist Georgi Lozanov in the 1970s. Suggestopedia emphasizes the importance of ensuring that students feel comfortable, relaxed and confident in the learning setting, and employs art, music (especially baroque music), and so on to create a positive learning environment (Brown, 2001, pp. 34–35; Lessow-Hurley, 2009, p. 93). Suggestopedia lessons are structured around three broad steps: deciphering, during which the grammar and vocabulary of the lesson are introduced, the concert session, which involves first a passive and then an active part, and finally, elaboration (see Lozanov, 1978; Lozanov & Gateva, 1988). Although extremely popular with its advocates, Suggestopedia has been severely criticized, and even labeled "pseudoscience" by its critics (see Brown, 2001, p. 28).

Constructivist Learning Theory

In recent years, a number of academic disciplines, not the least of which are mathematics and science, have undergone significant changes in the epistemology which underlies their pedagogical practice, moving increasingly toward constructivist approaches to epistemology and learning theory (see Boudourides, 2003; Cooper, 1993; Fensham, Gunstone & White, 1994; Gil-Pérez, Guisasola, Moreno, Cachapuz, Pessoa de Carvalho, Torregrosa, Salinas, Valdés, González, Duch, Dumas-Carré, Tricárico & Gallego, 2002; Jones & Brader-Araje, 2002; Larochelle, Bednarz & Garrison, 1998; Matthews, 1993, 2002; Mintzes, Wandersee & Novak, 1997; Nelson, 1996; Nola, 1997; Oxford, 1997; Spivey, 1997; Stanovich, 1994; Steffe, Cobb & Von Glasersfeld, 1988; Steffe & Kieren, 1994; Tobin, 1993; Von Glasersfeld, 2002; Wood, Cobb & Yackel, 1995). This change in learning theory has, in essence, involved a change in the *metaphors* that we use to conceptualize knowledge, teaching, learning and knowing (see Tarsitani, 1996). Although to some extent arguably implicit in many contemporary discussions about communicative language teaching, and often fairly clearly embodied in actual world language teaching practice, constructivist approaches to epistemology and learning theory have only recently, and relatively rarely, been explicitly examined in terms of their implications for world language teaching and learning (see Blyth, 1997; Craig, 1995; Kaufman & Grennon Brooks, 1996; Kumaravadivelu, 1994; Nyikos & Hashimoto, 1997; Reagan, 1999, 2002; Stevick, 1996; Williams & Burden, 1999).

Constructing Constructivism

Although constructivism has gained considerable attention in the educational literature, there is no clear definition or consensus of what is meant by the term (see Duffy & Jonassen, 1992; Fosnot, 1996a; Kafai & Resnick, 1996; Merrill, 1992; Nicaise & Barnes, 1996; Schwandt, 1994; Steffe & Gale, 1995). As Virginia Richardson has noted, "One cannot think of constructivist teaching … as a monolithic, agreed-upon concept …. There are fundamental theoretical differences in the various constructivist approaches" (Richardson, 1997b, p. 3). Indeed, there is even debate about whether constructivism is best understood as an epistemology, an educational philosophy, a pedagogical approach, a theory of teaching, or a theory of learning (see Kaufman & Grennon Brooks, 1996, p. 234). Arguably the best articulation of the nature of constructivism in the educational literature remains that of Catherine Fosnot, who compellingly suggests that, "Constructivism is not a theory about teaching. It's a theory about knowledge and learning" (Fosnot, 1993, p. vii). Some general principles of learning derived from constructivism may be helpful to keep in mind, however, as we rethink and reform our educational practices (Fosnot, 1996b, p. 29). Such a view of constructivism essentially confirms its status as an epistemology — a theory of knowledge and learning, rather than a theory of teaching (see Von Glasersfeld, 1993, pp. 23–24). As an epistemology, constructivism entails the rejection of traditional transmission-oriented views of learning, as well as behaviorist models of learning. Instead, emphasis is placed on the individual learner's construction of her or his knowledge. Beyond this, though, constructivism assumes not only that learning is constructed, but also that the learning process is a personal and individual one, that learning is an active undertaking, that learning is collaborative in nature, and that all learning is situated (see Merrill, 1992, p. 102). In other words, what constructivism offers is a radically different view of the nature of the learning process — a view that is grounded in a rejection of what Von Glasersfeld has called the "domination of a mindless behaviorism" (Von Glasersfeld, 1995a, p. 4). This view includes, as Fosnot notes, a number of general principles of learning, including:

- Learning is not the result of development; learning *is* development. It requires invention and self-organization on the part of the learner.
- Disequilibrium facilitates learning. "Errors" need to be perceived as a result of learners' conceptions and therefore not minimized or avoided ... Contradictions, in particular, need to be illuminated, explored, and discussed.
- Reflective abstraction is the driving force of learning. As meaning-makers, humans seek to organize and generalize across experiences in a representational form.
- Dialogue within a community engenders further thinking. The classroom needs to be seen as a "community of discourse engaged in activity, reflection, and conversation."
- Learning proceeds toward the development of structures. As learners struggle to make meaning, progressive structural shifts in perspective are constructed – in a sense, "big ideas" ... These "big ideas" are learner-constructed, central organizing principles that can be generalized across experiences and that often require the undoing or reorganizing of earlier conceptions. This process continues throughout development.

(Fosnot, 1996b, pp. 29–30)

It is important to stress here that constructivist epistemology is more than simply an alternative to other approaches to epistemology; rather, it entails a rejection of some of the core assumptions that have been shared by Western epistemology for some two and a half millennia (see Gergen, 1982, 1995). As Von Glasersfeld has argued, "the crucial fact [in understanding constructivism is] that the constructivist theory of knowing breaks with the epistemological tradition in philosophy" (Von Glasersfeld, 1995a, p. 6), which is why it has been labeled not merely postmodernist, but *post-epistemological* by some writers (see Noddings, 1990).

Up to this point, we have discussed constructivism as a single entity, while simultaneously trying to keep in mind Richardson's warning that it is in fact far from monolithic. In reality, it has become fairly commonplace in discussions of constructivism to distinguish between what are often taken to be two fundamentally distinct, competing *types* of constructivism (see Cobb, 1994, 1996; Magadla, 1996). The first type of constructivism, radical constructivism, is fundamentally an epistemological construct that has been most clearly and forcefully advocated in the work of Von Glasersfeld (1984, 1989, 1993, 1995a, 1995b, 1996). Radical constructivism has its philosophical roots in Piaget's genetic epistemology (Piaget, 1928, 1932, 1948a, 1948b, 1976, 1979, 1993, 1996, 2012; see also Sinclair, Berthoud, Gerard & Venesiano, 1985), and is essentially a cognitive view of learning in which "students actively construct their ways of knowing as they strive to be effective by restoring coherence to the worlds of their personal experience" (Cobb, 1996, p. 34). Radical constructivism is premised on the belief that an individual's knowledge can never be a "true" representation of reality (in an observer-independent sense), but is rather a construction of the world that s/he experiences. In other words, knowledge is not something that is passively received by the learner; it is, quite the contrary, the result of active mental work on the part of the learner. Thus, from a radical constructivist perspective, knowledge is not something that can merely be conveyed from teacher to student, and any pedagogical approach that presumes otherwise must be rejected.

The alternative to radical constructivism is social constructivism, which has as its primary theoretical foundation the work of Lev Vygotsky (2005a, 2005b, 2008; see also Frawley, 1997; Lantolf, 2000; Moll, 1990). Social constructivism, while accepting the notion that the individual does indeed construct her or his own knowledge, argues that the *process* of knowledge construction inevitably takes place in a sociocultural context, and that therefore knowledge is in fact *socially* constructed. As Rosalind Driver, Hilary Asoko, John Leach, Philip Scott, and Eduardo Mortimer have argued with respect to science education, "it is important ... to appreciate that scientific knowledge is both symbolic in nature and also socially negotiated ... The objects of science are not phenomena of nature but constructs that are advanced by the scientific community to interpret nature" (Driver et al., 1994, p. 5).

The tension between radical and social constructivism, between the personal and the social construction of knowledge, is to a significant extent more apparent than real, and in any event, is certainly amenable to resolution on a practical level, criticisms to the contrary notwithstanding (see, for example, Cobern, 1993; Confrey, 1995). As Paul Cobb has asserted, "the sociocultural and cognitive constructivist perspectives each constitute the background for the other" (Cobb, 1996, p. 48), and Von Glasersfeld has recognized that "we must generate an explanation of how 'others' and the 'society' in which we find ourselves living can be conceptually constructed on the basis of our subjective experiences" (Von Glasersfeld, 1995a, p. 12).

Perhaps the most reasonable way to articulate the common, shared elements of radical and social constructivism is to talk about learning as "socially mitigated but personally constructed," a formulation which at the very least moves us away from a strong bifurcation of radical and social constructivism and allows us to move on to a discussion of the implications of constructivist epistemology in general for teaching practice.

Constructivist Teaching

While it is obviously important to keep in mind that constructivism is not, and could not be, a pedagogical theory or approach *per se*, it is also true that certain characteristics of the constructivist-based classroom can be identified. For example, Dorit Kaufman and Jacqueline Grennon

Brooks have identified eight characteristics that have been observed in constructivist classrooms. Teachers in such classrooms:

- Use raw data and primary sources, along with manipulative, interactive, and physical materials.
- When framing tasks, use cognitive terminology, such as *classify, analyze, predict, create*, and so on.
- Allow student thinking to drive lessons. Shift instructional strategies or alter content based on student responses.
- Inquire about students' understandings of concepts before sharing your own understandings of those concepts.
- Ask open-ended questions of students and encourage students to ask questions of others.
- Seek elaboration of students' initial responses.
- Engage students in experiences that might engender contradictions to students' initial hypotheses and then encourage a discussion.
- Provide time for students to construct relationships and create metaphors.

(Kaufman & Grennon Brooks, 1996, p. 235; see also Grennon Brooks & Brooks, 1993)

What these characteristics, taken together, are all about really focuses on what could be called "guided discovery" or, more accurately, "structured induction" both in and as the learning process. These characteristics function both as descriptive and normative attributes in that they have not only been observed in practice, but in that they have also been used for evaluation purposes. It is important to note here, incidentally, that "Many of these attributes are not unique to constructivist teaching but are representative of good teaching in general" (Kaufman & Grennon Brooks, 1996, p. 235) — a point which would seem to confirm Von Glasersfeld's claim that, "Constructivism does not claim to have made earth-shaking inventions in the area of education; it merely claims to provide a solid conceptual basis for some of the things that, until now, inspired teachers had to do without theoretical foundation" (Von Glasersfeld, 1995a, p. 15). Furthermore, while it is the case that "constructivist principles of learning do not automatically engender principles of teaching … [since] learners construct meaning on their own terms no matter what teachers do" (Winitzky & Kauchak, 1997, p. 62), it is also true that:

> Constructivist theorists would maintain … that learning is better or more effective when teachers use constructivist teaching methods, like culturing … bacteria as opposed to lecturing about bacteria. Constructivist teaching typically involves more student-centered, active learning experiences, more student-student and student-teacher interaction, and more work with concrete materials and in solving

> realistic problems ... Nevertheless, students still create their own meanings based on the interaction of their prior knowledge with instruction, and the meanings they make may not be the ones the teacher had in mind, no matter how constructivist the instruction ... Teachers create constructivist learning experiences for students based necessarily on what they, the teachers, find salient. But what is salient to the teacher is not necessarily so to the learner.
>
> (Winitzky & Kauchak, 1997, pp. 62–63)

With this significant caveat in mind, then, we are ready to turn to an examination of the implications of constructivist epistemology for the specific case of world language education.

Constructivism in World Language Education

Constructivism has a wide range of implications for world language educators, both in terms of its significance for research and its relevance for pedagogical practice. With respect to the former, studies of the social nature of language learning and acquisition are increasingly grounded in constructivist epistemological positions. Writing about developments in bilingual education, for instance, Christian Faltis has noted that "a shift toward the constructivist, social nature of learning and language acquisition is also increasingly evident in new research efforts" (Faltis, 1997, p. 194). Similarly, the veritable explosion in discourse studies is ultimately, albeit often implicitly, linked to constructivist approaches to understanding, whether one is concerned with academic discourse (see Achard, 1993; Bourdieu, Passerson & de Saint Martin, 1994; Fairclough, 1992, 1995, 2015; Reagan, 1999, 2002), classroom discourse (see Bartolomé, 1998; Craig, 1995; Measures, Quell & Wells, 1997; van Lier, 1996; Woods, 1996), or scientific discourse (see Boulter, 1997; Gunnarsson, Linell & Nordberg, 1997). Indeed, Britt-Louise Gunnarsson has gone so far as to suggest that:

> The complexity of the construction of knowledge has been focused on by scholars dealing with scientific discourse. Proceeding from ideas within the social constructivist tradition, they have developed a methodology for the purpose of understanding how science is created through discourse .... the social construction of scientific facts [has been described] as an antagonistic struggle among scientists, leading to a deliberate diminishing of the results of others and a leveling up — to a generalized level — of one's own results. Scientific facts are regarded as mere works; rhetoric determines what become scientific facts.
>
> (Gunnarsson, 1997, p. 111)

The implications of such a view of the nature and role of scientific discourse for the classroom are significant:

> It is the growing recognition of the significance of the social construction of conceptual understanding in science that has coincided with the development of a suitable methodology for investigating social situations involving talk. Science is now often seen within science education research as intimately constructed, through discourse, within communities of knowers. The following themes in research and discourse in science teaching and learning arise from the synthesis of constructivism and sociolinguistic methodology and can be seen in the major work in progress:
>
> - The *complexity* of classroom discourse which has complex interactions with the ways teachers teach, the resources they use and with the particular phenomenon of science being studied;
> - *Communities* in science and science classrooms having characteristic discourse patterns;
> - *Collaboration* in classroom settings allowing the authentic practice of science and the development of appropriate discourse;
> - *Critiques* of science, its methodology, its boundaries, its status, and its language as a cultural construct.
>
> (Boulter, 1997, p. 242)

Such research foci emphasize, not surprisingly, the social construction of language and discourse, but there is room as well for concern with the personal or individual construction of language. One powerful way in which we can conceptualize the personal construction of language has to do with the linguistic notion of idiolects: "The unique characteristics of the language of an individual speaker are referred to as the speaker's *idiolect*. English may then be said to consist of 400,000,000 idiolects, or the number equal to the number of speakers of English" (Fromkin & Rodman, 1993, p. 276). In other words, a transfer or transmission-based view of language learning is simply incompatible with the final outcome of such learning, since each individual speaker (whether native or non-native) in fact constructs her or his own understanding of the target language, which will, in turn, be modified and can be evaluated by comparison with other speakers of the language. This is not, of course, to minimize in any way the key role played by interaction in the process of language learning; as Katherine Nelson has cogently observed:

> Competence in constructing and using culturally defined categories of entities (objects, events, properties, etc.) has been shown to involve a number of different linguistic components, including superordinate labels and the vocabulary of inclusive hierarchies.

> These verbal components can account for aspects of conceptual development previously held to be perceptually based (e.g., grouping along lines of shape similarity) or logically based (e.g., set relations). The verbal contributions to the development of cultural categories are integrated with experientially derived categories ... The coordination and integration processes involved in the assembling of cultural taxonomies ... exemplify the more general problem encountered during the preschool years of reconfiguring individual experientially based representations established independently of linguistic input to accommodate knowledge systems displayed in language. This reconfiguration cannot be accomplished through individual constructive processes alone, but requires implicit and explicit collaboration with knowledge bearers ...
>
> (Nelson, 1996, p. 332)

Although Nelson's focus was on language acquisition in early childhood, the same general claim would apply, we believe, to world language learning with respect to the complementary and interactive roles of the individual and the social construction of language. This is an important aspect of a constructivist approach to understanding world language learning, since it emphasizes not only the individual construction of meaning, but also, the potential for the *misconstruction* of meaning and therefore the need for collaboration and interaction with the "knowledge bearer" – that is, generally speaking, the teacher.[10] This brings us to the implications of constructivist epistemology for second language pedagogy.

In the context of the world language classroom, the application of constructivist epistemology would necessarily undergird virtually all classroom practice. As Williams and Burden have explained,

> The literature on the teaching of languages offers exhaustive commentaries on the different methodologies for the teaching of languages, and is rich with ideas and techniques for language teaching. Without exception, what is clear to us is that the most important thing for teachers to understand is the process of learning that should inform our language teaching. The conceptions that teachers hold about the learning, and about what affects learning, will impact everything that happens in the classroom. At the same time, in order to be able to make informed decisions in their daily teaching, teachers must be consciously aware of their beliefs about learning and teaching.
>
> (Williams & Burden, 1999, pp. 11–12, our translation)

This is true, as far as it goes, not only of world language teaching, but of all teaching. To be sure, world language pedagogy does indeed have many common features with other sorts of teaching – but it is also distinct in some key ways. Successful world language learning entails far more for the learner than merely learning content and skills. Robert Gardner has suggested that, "Languages are unlike any other subject taught in a classroom in that they involve the acquisition of skills and behaviour patterns which are characteristic of another community" (Gardner, 1985, p. 146), while David Crookall and Rebecca Oxford argue that, "Learning a second language is ultimately learning to be another social person" (Crookall & Oxford, 1988, p. 136). It is this need for the learner to reconstruct one's personal identity that is at the heart of world language learning, and it is in this process of reconstruction, rather than merely in terms of learning vocabulary and grammatical forms, that constructivist epistemology may be most useful. It is also a constructivist perspective that allows us to recognize, as Jan Anward has argued, that certain kinds of world language pedagogy are in fact internally contradictory: "Put bluntly, we could say that in the context of language drills students are often taught language resources that cannot be used in that very context" (Anward, 1997, p. 129).

Constructivist epistemology has clear implications for classroom practice, the curricula, student evaluation and assessment, and, indeed, virtually all aspects of the teaching/learning process (see Henning, 1995; Zietsman, 1996). It also has the potential to impact in significant ways the preparation of world language educators (see Condon, Clyde, Kyle & Hovda, 1993; Rainer & Guyton, 1994; Richardson, 1997a) and the challenge of preparing such educators to engage in reflective and analytic classroom practice (see Parker, 1997; Reagan, Case & Brubacher, 2000; Richards & Lockhart, 1994; Zeichner & Liston, 1987, 1996). The ultimate purpose of taking constructivist epistemology seriously in world language education, though, is its potential for helping teachers empower students to acquire language more effectively. An additional point that needs to be stressed here is that constructivist epistemology, while certainly having clear implications for classroom practice, is concerned first and foremost with helping us to understand the learning process itself, rather than with dictating pedagogical practice. Much of the common pedagogical practice of world language teachers is fully compatible with constructivist learning theory; the power of constructivist epistemology for world language education may well be more in its explanatory, legitimating and justificatory power than in terms of any specific implications that it may have for classroom practice.

Conclusion

In this chapter, we have explored a number of topics that are central to learning and teaching languages. Underlying the whole chapter is the question, "What does it mean to 'know' a language?" In order to answer this question, we began with a discussion of the role of epistemology in education generally, and in world language education in particular. In this discussion, we considered the role of epistemology in the philosophy of science, and examined the work of three very important 20th-century philosophers: Thomas Kuhn, Michel Foucault, and Paul Feyerabend. We also discussed ethnoepistemology, the tension between objectivism and relativism, and the nature of knowledge broadly conceived – including the distinctions between tacit and explicit knowledge, between emic and etic knowledge, and among technical, practical and emancipatory knowledge.

We then turned to an explicit consideration of what "knowing a language" actually entails in the context of world language education. After identifying and discussing five components of knowledge in world language education – linguistic knowledge, metalinguistic knowledge, sociolinguistic knowledge, discourse knowledge, and strategic/pragmatic knowledge – we also considered the distinction between linguistic competence and linguistic performance, and revisited the distinction between language acquisition and language learning. We also explored the uses of metaphors and metaphorical language in educational discourse, and with respect to learning theories.

An important element of epistemology in education is how one conceptualizes learning, and we next discussed two major approaches to understanding learning in the context of world language education: behaviorism and cognitivism. We then explored a number of the major historical approaches to the teaching of world languages, including the Grammar-Translation approach, the Direct Method, the Audiolingual Method, Communicative Language Teaching, as well as Total Physical Response, the Silent Way, and Suggestopedia. Finally, we conclude with a detailed examination of constructivism as a learning theory, and of the implications of constructivist learning theories for both the learning and the teaching of world languages.

Questions for Reflection and Discussion

1. What, in your view, is the difference among "knowing Spanish," "speaking Spanish," "studying (or having studied) Spanish," and "knowing about Spanish"? How would our goals in the world language classroom be reflected (or not reflected) in each of these different kinds of "knowing"?
2. In this chapter, David Crookall and Rebecca Oxford are quoted as suggesting that, "Learning a second language is ultimately learning to be another social person." Based on your own experiences as a second language learner, do you agree or disagree with this claim? What are the implications of this view for world language teaching and learning?
3. When, and why, are student errors beneficial in the context of the world language classroom? What are the implications of your answer for teaching methods in world language education?
4. What can you, as a world language teacher, do to encourage *oral* language practice as students engage in the construction of their own

knowledge of the target language? What barriers discourage oral language practice, and how can you minimize these?

5 What can you, as a world language teacher, do to encourage *written* language practice as students engage in the construction of their own knowledge of the target language? What barriers discourage written language practice, and how can you minimize these?

Notes

1 The concept of "bilingual education" in the U.S. context is an especially noteworthy example of what is rather odd ordinary language use in the context of the public schools. When students are initially placed in bilingual education programs, they typically speak their native language but little or no English. In general (although there are some important exceptions), bilingual education programs in the U.S. continue to be largely transitional in nature, with the objective of preparing the child to be ready to be transitioned to the "regular" English-medium classroom. Thus, once the child has actually become at least minimally competent in English (and hence in at least some sense bilingual), she or he is moved to a monolingual classroom and is no longer considered to be eligible for bilingual education.

2 Until recently, the German term *Weltanschauung* was commonly used to describe this phenomenon, and it was typically asserted that we needed to use the German word because there was no equivalent in English. This was indeed arguably the case in the past, but it seems fairly clear to us that the word "worldview" in English is now fully comparable to the German *Weltanschaung*.

3 This is in fact an oversimplification. There are a number of different kinds of positivism (logical positivism, logical empiricism, etc.), many different scholars associated with different sorts of positivism (e.g., Karl Popper, Quine, Durkheim, Wittgenstein, etc.), and positivism in different academic disciplines also varies to a considerable extent. However, there are nevertheless core ideas that hold positivism together as a distinctive paradigm, albeit one in which various theories and perspectives compete.

4 The example of a "paradigm shift" best associated with Thomas Kuhn is the case of the transition in cosmology from a Ptolemaic system to a Copernican one, but others would include the replacement of Galen's miasma theory with the germ theory of disease in medicine, the transition from Aristotelian mechanics to classical mechanics and then the subsequent transition to quantum mechanics, and so on.

5 In fact, upon further discussion, it turned out that we actually *did* know about what was being asked, but had learned these forms, respectively, as the "future conditional" and "present conditional," and "past conditional." For those not familiar with these labels, the first conditional (or the future conditional) is the form *if* + *present* + *will* (e.g., "If I have the money, I will take a vacation"), the second conditional (or the present conditional) is the form *if* + *past simple* + *would* (e.g., "If I had the money, I would take a vacation"), and the third conditional (or the past conditional) is the form *if* + *past pluperfect* + *would have* ("If I had had the money, I would have taken a vacation") (see Larsen-Freeman & Celce-Murcia, 2016, pp. 575–604).

6 It is worth noting that as the Chomskian paradigm in linguistics developed, the distinction between linguistic competence and linguistic performance was largely replaced by that of I-Language (the internalized innate knowledge of

the language) and E-Language (the externalized output produced by the speaker) (see Chomsky, 1986).

7 It is important to emphasize that our concern here, and the focus in the literature on metaphors in discourse, is on *metaphorical language* rather than simply on metaphors. Thus, included in this discussion are not only pure metaphors, but also similes and other forms of metaphorical language. For an extended discussion and explanation of this matter, see Lakoff and Johnson (1980); also of interest are Ortony (1980), Smith (1981), and Taylor (1984).

8 Although the Grammar-Translation Method does have its origins in the teaching of the Classical languages, even in the contemporary teaching of Latin and Greek it has become far less common than it once was (see, for instance, Balme & Lawall, 1990a, 1990b; Mastronarde, 1993; Saffire & Freis, 1999; Traupman, 1997).

9 The close role of the military in the development of the ALM also led it to be called, in some settings, the "Army Method."

10 The idea that students can *misconstruct* knowledge is an important one. The concept of knowledge construction does not in any way entail that *all* constructions of knowledge are equally valid, nor that some are not demonstrably false. For instance, the student in a beginning Spanish class who says, *Yo vas a mi casa* instead of *Yo voy a mi casa* has not simply constructed knowledge *differently*, she or he has made an error – the produced form is simply not acceptable or correct in Spanish.

References

Abu-Saad, I. & Champagne, D. (Eds.). (2006). *Indigenous education and empowerment: International perspectives*. Lanham, MD: Rowman & Littlefield.

Achard, P. (1993). *La sociologie du langage*. Paris: Presses Universitaires de France.

Alcoff, L. & Potter, E. (Eds.). (1993). *Feminist epistemologies*. New York: Routledge.

ALM Russian. (1969). *ALM Russian Level 1* (2nd ed.). New York: Harcourt Brace Jovanovich.

Anderson, E. (1995). Feminist epistemology: An interpretation and a defense. *Hypatia: A Journal of Feminist Philosophy*, 10(3): 50–84.

Anward, J. (1997). Parameters of institutional discourse. In B. Gunnarsson, P. Linell & B. Nordberg (Eds.), *The construction of professional discourse* (pp. 127–150). London: Longman.

Asher, J. (1966). The learning strategy of the Total Physical Response: A review. *The Modern Language Journal*, 50(2): 79–84.

Asher, J. (1969). The Total Physical Response approach to second language learning. *The Modern Language Journal*, 53(1): 3–17.

Asher, J. (1996). *Learning another language through actions* (5th ed.). Los Gatos, CA: Sky Oaks Productions.

Balme, M. & Lawall, G. (1990a). *Athenaze: An introduction to ancient Greek* (rev. ed.). New York: Oxford University Press.

Balme, M. & Lawall, G. (1990b). *Teacher's handbook – Athenaze: An introduction to ancient Greek* (rev. ed.). New York: Oxford University Press.

Bartolomé, L. (1998). *The misteaching of academic discourses: The politics of language in the classroom*. Boulder, CO: Westview Press.

Baum, W. (2017). *Understanding behaviorism: Behavior, culture, and evolution* (3rd ed.). Oxford: Wiley Blackwell.

Beatty, B. (1998). From laws of learning to a science of values: Efficiency and morality in Thorndike's educational psychology. *American Psychologist*, 53(10): 1145–1152.

Belenky, M., Clinchy, B., Goldberger, N. & Tarule, J. (1997). *Women's ways of knowing: The development of self, voice, and mind*. New York: Basic Books. (Original publication 1986)

Bernal, D. (1998). Using a chicana feminist epistemology in educational research. *Harvard Educational Review*, 68(4): 555–582.

Birner, B. (2013). *Introduction to pragmatics*. Oxford: Wiley-Blackwell.

Blyth, C. (1997). A constructivist approach to grammar: Teaching teachers to teach aspect. *The Modern Language Journal*, 81(1): 50–66.

Boudourides, M. (2003). Constructivism, education, science, and technology. *Canadian Journal of Learning and Technology/La Revue Canadienne de l'Apprentissage et de la Technologie*, 29(3). Downloaded from www.learntechlib.org/p/43187 on November 25, 2019.

Boulter, C. (1997). Discourse and conceptual understanding in science. In B. Davies & D. Corson (Eds.), *Encyclopedia of language and education, volume 3: Oral discourse and education* (pp. 239–248). Dordrecht: Kluwer.

Bourdieu, P., Passeron, J. & de Saint Martin, M. (1994). *Academic discourse*. Stanford, CA: Stanford University Press.

Breen, M. & Candlin, C. (1980). The essentials of a communicative curriculum. *Applied Linguistics*, 1(2): 89–112.

Brown, H. D. (2001). *Teaching by principles: An interactive approach to language pedagogy* (2nd ed.). White Plains, NY: Longman.

Carvajal, C. (2013). "Grammar-Translation" Method: A linguistic historic error of perspective – Origins, dynamics and in consistencies. *Praxis y Saber*, 4(8): 243–263.

Chastain, K. (1976). *Developing second-language skills: Theory to practice* (2nd ed.). Chicago, IL: Rand McNally.

Chiesa, M. (1992). Radical behaviorism and scientific frameworks: From mechanistic to relational accounts. *American Psychologist*, 47(11): 1287–1299.

Chiesa, M. (1994). *Radical behaviorism: The philosophy and the science*. Boston, MA: Authors Cooperative.

Chomsky, N. (1965). *Aspects of the theory of syntax*. Cambridge, MA: MIT Press.

Chomsky, N. (1986). *Knowledge of language*. New York: Praeger.

Christie, M. (2006). Transdisciplinary research and Aboriginal knowledge. *The Australian Journal of Indigenous Education*, 35: 78–89.

Cobb, P. (1994). Where is the mind? Constructivist and socioculturalist perspectives on mathematical development. *Educational Researcher*, 23(7): 13–20.

Cobb, P. (1996). Where is the mind? A coordination of sociocultural and cognitive constructionist perspectives. In C. Fosnot (Ed.), *Constructivism* (pp. 34–52). New York: Teachers College Press.

Cobern, W. (1993). Contextual constructivism: The impact of culture on the learning and teaching of science. In K. Tobin (Ed.), *The practice of constructivism in science education* (pp. 51–69). Hillsdale, NJ: Lawrence Erlbaum Associates.

Condon, M., Clyde, J., Kyle, D. & Hovda, R. (1993). A constructivist basis for teaching and teacher education: A framework for program development and research on graduates. *Journal of Teacher Education*, 44(4): 273–278.

Confrey, J. (1995). How compatible are radical constructivism, sociocultural approaches, and social constructivism? In L. Steffe & J. Gale (Eds.), *Constructivism in education* (pp. 185–225). Hillsdale, NJ: Lawrence Erlbaum Associates.

Cooper, J. (1993). *Literacy: Helping children construct meaning* (2nd ed.). Boston, MA: Houghton Mifflin.

Craig, B. (1995). Boundary discourse and the authority of language in the second-language classroom: A social-constructionist approach. In J. Alatis, C. Straehle, B. Gallenberger & M. Ronkin (Eds.), *Georgetown University Round Table on Languages and Linguistics 1995: Linguistics and the education of language teachers* (pp. 40–54). Washington, DC: Georgetown University Press.

Crookall, D. & Oxford, R. (1988). Review essay. *Language Learning*, 31: 128–140.

Curtain, H. & Dahlberg, C. (2004). *Languages and children, making the match: New languages for young learners, grades K-8* (3rd ed.). Boston, MA: Pearson.

De Clerck, G. A. M. (2016). *Deaf epistemologies, identity and learning: A comparative perspective*. Washington, DC: Gallaudet University Press.

De Saussure, F. (1965). *Cours de linguistique générale*. Paris: Payot. (Original publication 1916)

Driver, R., Asoko, H., Leach, J., Scott, P. & Mortiner, E. (1994). Constructing scientific knowledge in the classroom. *Educational Researcher*, 23(7): 5–12.

Duffy, T. & Jonassen, D. (Eds.). (1992). *Constructivism and the technology of instruction: A conversation*. Hillsdale, NJ: Lawrence Erlbaum Associates.

Duncan, G. A. (2005). Critical race ethnography in education: Narrative, inequality and the problem of epistemology. *Race, Ethnicity and Education*, 8(1): 93–114.

Ertmer, P. & Newby, T. (2013). Behaviorism, cognitivism, constructivism: Comparing critical features from an instructional design perspective. *Performance Improvement Quarterly*, 26(2): 43–71.

Fairclough, N. (Ed.). (1992). *Critical language awareness*. London: Longman.

Fairclough, N. (1995). *Critical discourse analysis: The critical study of language*. London: Longman.

Fairclough, N. (2015). *Language and power* (3rd ed.). New York: Routledge.

Faltis, C. (1997). Bilingual education in the United States. In J. Cummins & D. Corson (Eds.), *Encyclopedia of language and education, volume 5: Bilingual education* (pp. 189–197). Dordrecht: Kluwer.

Fensham, P., Gunstone, R. & White, R. (Eds.). (1994). *The content of science: A constructivist approach to its teaching and learning*. London: Falmer Press.

Feyerabend, P. (1970). Consolations for the specialist. In I. Lakatos & A. Musgrave (Eds.), *Criticism and the growth of knowledge* (pp. 197–230). Cambridge: University of Cambridge Press.

Feyerabend, P. (1981a). *Probleme des Empirismus: Schriften zur Theorie der Efklärung, der Quantentheorie und der Wissenschaftsgeschichte, Ausgewählte Schriften, Band 2*. Braunschweig: F. Vieweg & Sohn.

Feyerabend, P. (1981b). *Realism, rationalism and scientific method: Philosophical papers, volume 1*. Cambridge: Cambridge University Press.

Feyerabend, P. (1983). *Science in a free society*. London: Verso. (Original publication 1978)

Feyerabend, P. (1991). *Three dialogues on knowledge*. Oxford: Basil Blackwell.

Feyerabend, P. (1995). *Killing time: The autobiography of Paul Feyerabend*. Chicago, IL: University of Chicago Press.

Feyerabend, P. (2002a). *Against method: Outline of an anarchistic theory of knowledge* (3rd ed.). London: Verso. (Original publication 1975)

Feyerabend, P. (2002b). *Farewell to reason* (2nd ed.). London: Verso. (Original publication 1987)

Feyerabend, P. (2006). *Paul K. Feyerabend: Knowledge, science and relativism* (3 vols.). Cambridge: Cambridge University Press. (Original publication 1999)

Feyerabend, P. (2010). *Against method* (4th ed.). London: Verso.

Fosnot, C. (1993). Preface. In J. Grennon Brooks & M. Brooks, *The case for constructivist classrooms* (pp. vii–viii). Alexandria, VA: Association for Supervision and Curriculum Development.

Fosnot, C. (Ed.). (1996a). *Constructivism: Theory, perspectives, and practice*. New York: Teachers College Press.

Fosnot, C. (1996b). Constructivism: A psychological theory of learning. In C. Fosnot (Ed.), *Constructivism* (pp. 8–33). New York: Teachers College Press.

Foucault, M. (1975). *Surveiller et punir: Naissance de la prison*. Paris: Éditions Gallimard.

Foucault, M. (1976). *Histoire de la folie à l'âge classique*. Paris: Éditions Gallimard.

Foucault, M. (2000). *Naissance de la clinique*. Paris: Presses Universitaires de France.

Foucault, M. (2001). *Dits et écrits, vol. 2*. Paris: Gallimard.

Foucault, M. (2008). *L'archéologie du savoir*. Paris: Éditions Gallimard.

Frawley, W. (1997). *Vygotsky and cognitive science: Language and the unification of the social and computational mind*. Cambridge, MA: Harvard University Press.

Fromkin, V. & Rodman, R. (1993). *An introduction to language* (5th ed.). Fort Worth, TX: Harcourt Brace Jovanovich.

García, R. B. (2013). De los sistemas orgánicos a los sistemas simbólicos. La cultura y la articulación de lo real apuntes para una etnoepistemología desde Wittgenstein. *Revista de Filosofía*, 74(2): 43–70.

Gardner, R. (1985). *Social psychology and language learning: The role of attitudes and motivation*. London: Edward Arnold.

Gattegno, C. (1963). *Teaching foreign languages in schools: The Silent Way* (2nd ed.). New York: Educational Solutions.

Gélinas, C. & Bouchard, Y. (2014). An epistemological framework for indigenous knowledge. *Revista de Humanidades de Valparaíso*, 4: 47–62.

Gergen, K. (1982). *Towards transformation in social knowledge*. New York: Springer.

Gergen, K. (1995). Social construction and the educational process. In L. Steffe & J. Gale (Eds.), *Constructivism in education* (pp. 17–39). Hillsdale, NJ: Lawrence Erlbaum Associates.

Gil-Pérez, D., Guisasola, J., Moreno, A., Cachapuz, A., Pessoa de Carvalho, A., Torregrosa, J., Salinas, J., Valdés, P., González, E., Duch, A., Dumas-Carré, A., Tricárico, H. & Gallego, R. (2002). Defending constructivism in science education. *Science and Education*, 11(6): 557–571.

Goldberger, N., Tarule, J., Clinchy, B., & Belenky, M. (1996). *Knowledge, difference, and power: Essays inspired by women's ways of knowing*. New York: Basic Books.

Green, T. (1971). *The activities of teaching*. New York: McGraw-Hill.

Grennon Brooks, J., & Brooks, M. (1993). *The case for constructivist classrooms*. Alexandria, VA: Association for Supervision and Curriculum Development.

Gunnarsson, B. (1997). Language for special purposes. In G. Tucker & D. Corson (Eds.), *Encyclopedia of language and education, volume 4: Second language education* (pp. 105–117). Dordrecht: Kluwer.

Gunnarsson, B., Linell, P. & Nordberg, B. (Eds.). (1997). *The construction of professional discourse*. London: Longman.

Henning, E. (1995). Problematising the discourse of classroom management from the view of social constructivism. *South African Journal of Education*, 15(3): 124–129.

Holub, R. (1991). *Jurgen Habermas: Critic in the public sphere*. New York: Routledge.

Horowitz, E. (2008). *Becoming a language teacher: A practical guide to second language learning and teaching*. Boston, MA: Pearson.

Jha, A. & Devi, R. (2014). Social epistemology and social constructivist pedagogy for school reforms. *Pedagogy of Learning*, 2(1): 12–18.

Johnson, J. (2014). *Radical behaviorism for ABA practitioners*. Cornwall-on-Hudson, NY: Sloan Educational Publishing.

Jones, M. & Brader-Araje, L. (2002). The impact of constructivism on education: Language, discourse, and meaning. *American Communication Journal*, 5(3). Downloaded from https://pdfs.semanticscholar.org/11e2/5b4e83ec8d804d125a4eddf02ceaca39d6fd.pdf?_ga=2.261817163.772962529.1574727270-522058878.1574727270 on November 25, 2019.

Kafai, Y. & Resnick, M. (Eds.). (1996). *Constructivism in practice: Designing, thinking, and learning in a digital world*. Mahwah, NJ: Lawrence Erlbaum Associates.

Kaufman, D. & Grennon Brooks, J. (1996). Interdisciplinary collaboration in teacher education: A constructivist approach. *TESOL Quarterly*, 30(2): 231–251.

Kuhn, T. (1970). *The structure of scientific revolutions* (2nd enlarged ed.). Chicago, IL: University of Chicago Press. (Original publication 1962)

Kuhn, T. (1972). *La structure des revolutions scientifiques*. Paris: Flammarion.

Kuhn, T. (1977). *The essential tension*. Chicago, IL: University of Chicago Press.

Kumaravadivelu, B. (1994). The postmethod condition: (E)merging strategies for second/foreign language teaching. *TESOL Quarterly*, 28(1): 27–48.

Lakoff, G. & Johnson, M. (1980). *Metaphors we live by*. Chicago, IL: University of Chicago Press.

Lantolf, J. (2000). Introducing sociocultural theory. In J. Lantolf (Ed.), *Sociocultural theory and second language learning* (pp. 1–26). Oxford: Oxford University Press.

Larochelle, M., Bednarz, N. & Garrison, J. (Eds.). (1998). *Constructivism and education*. Cambridge: Cambridge University Press.

Larsen-Freeman, D. (2000). *Techniques and principles in language teaching* (2nd ed.). Oxford: Oxford University Press.

Larsen-Freeman, D. & Celce-Murcia, M. (2016). *The grammar book: Form, meaning, and use for English language teachers*. Boston, MA: National Geographic Learning.

Laughlin, C. (2013). The ethno-epistemology of transpersonal experience: The view from transpersonal anthropology. *International Journal of Transpersonal Studies*, 32(1): 43–50.

Lee, J. & VanPatten, B. (2003). *Making communicative language teaching happen* (2nd ed.). Boston, MA: McGraw-Hill.

Lennon, K. & Whitford, M. (Eds.). (1994). *Knowing the difference: Feminist perspectives in epistemology*. New York: Routledge.

Lessow-Hurley, J. (2009). *The foundations of dual language instruction* (5th ed.). Boston, MA: Pearson.

Lilienfeld, S., Lynn, S., Namy, L., Woolf, N., Jamieson, G., Marks, A. & Slaughter, V. (2015). *Psychology: From inquiry to understanding* (2nd ed.). Melbourne, Victoria: Pearson Australia.

Littlewood, W. (1984). *Foreign and second language learning: Language acquisition research and its implications for the classroom*. Cambridge: Cambridge University Press.

Lozanov, G. (1978). *Suggestopedia and outlines of Suggestopedia*. New York: Gordon & Breach.

Lozanov, G. & Gateva, E. (1988). *The foreign language teacher's Suggestopedia manual*. New York: Gordon & Breach.

Maffie, J. (2013). Ethno-epistemology. In B. Kaldis (Ed.), *Encyclopedia of philosophy and the social sciences* (pp. 277–279). Los Angeles, CA: Sage.

Magadla, L. (1996). Constructivism: A practitioner's perspective. *South African Journal of Higher Education*, 10(1): 83–88.

Mandler, G. (2002). Origins of the cognitive (r)evolution. *Journal of the History of the Behavioral Sciences*, 38(4): 339–353.

Mastronarde, D. (1993). *Introduction to Attic Greek*. Berkeley, CA: University of California Press.

Matthews, M. (1993). Constructivism and science education: Some epistemological problems. *Journal of Science Education and Technology*, 2(1): 359–370.

Matthews, M. (2002). Constructivism and science education: A further appraisal. *Journal of Science Education and Technology*, 11(2): 121–134.

Mazzocchi, F. (2018). Why "integrating" western science and indigenous knowledge is not an easy task: What lessons could be learned for the future of knowledge? *Journal of Futures Studies*, 22(3): 19–34.

McLaren, P. (2003). *Life in schools: An introduction to critical pedagogy in the foundations of education* (4th ed.). Boston, MA: Allyn and Bacon.

Measures, E., Quell, C. & Wells, G. (1997). A sociocultural perspective on classroom discourse. In B. Davies & D. Corson (Eds.), *Encyclopedia of language and education, volume 3: Oral discourse and education* (pp. 21–29). Dordrecht: Kluwer.

Merrill, M. (1992). Constructivism and instructional design. In T. Duffy & D. Jonassen (Eds.), *Constructivism and the technology of instruction* (pp. 99–114). Hillsdale, NJ: Lawrence Erlbaum Associates.

Miller, S. & Fredericks, M. (1988). Uses of metaphor: A qualitative case study. *International Journal of Qualitative Studies in Education*, 1(3): 263–272.

Mintzes, J., Wandersee, J. & Novak, J. (Eds.). (1997). *Teaching science for understanding: A human constructivist view*. San Diego, CA: Academic Press.

Moll, L. (Ed.). (1990). *Vygotsky and education: Instructional implications and applications of sociocultural psychology*. Cambridge: Cambridge University Press.

National Research Council. (2000). *How people learn: Brain, mind, experience, and school*. Washington, DC: National Academy Press.

Nattinger, J. (1993). Communicative language teaching: A new metaphor. In L. Cleary & M. Linn (Eds.), *Linguistics for teachers* (pp. 599–612). New York: McGraw-Hill.

Nelson, K. (1996). *Language in cognitive development: The emergence of the mediated mind*. Cambridge: Cambridge University Press.

Nicaise, M. & Barnes, D. (1996). The union of technology, constructivism, and teacher education. *Journal of Teacher Education*, 47(3): 205–212.

Noddings, N. (1990). Constructivism in mathematics education. In R. Davis, C. Maher & N. Noddings (Eds.), *Constructivist views on the teaching and learning of mathematics* (pp. 7–18). Reston, VA: National Council of Teachers of Mathematics.

Nola, R. (1997). Constructivism in science and science education: A philosophical critique. *Science and Education*, 6(1–2): 55–83.

Nuessel, F. (2000). The use of metaphor to comprehend and explicate scientific theory. In P. Perron, L. Sbrochhi, P. Colilli & M. Danesi (Eds.), *Semiotics as a bridge between the humanities and the sciences* (pp. 479–500). New York: Legas.

Nunan, D. (1991). *Language teaching methodology: A textbook for teachers*. New York: Prentice-Hall.

Nyikos, M. & Hashimoto, R. (1997). Constructivist theory applied to collaborative learning in teacher education: In search of ZPD. *The Modern Language Journal*, 81(4): 506–517.

Omaggio Hadley, A. (1993). *Teaching language in context* (2nd ed.). Boston, MA: Heinle & Heinle.

O'Neil, W. (1995). American behaviorism: A historical and critical analysis. *Theory and Psychology*, 5(2): 285–305.

Ortony, A. (Ed.). (1980). *Metaphor and thought*. Cambridge: Cambridge University Press.

Outhwaite, W. (2009). *Habermas: A critical introduction* (2nd ed.). Cambridge: Polity Press.

Oxford, R. (1997). Constructivism: Shape-shifting, substance, and teacher education applications. *Peabody Journal of Education*, 72(1): 35–66.

Parker, S. (1997). *Reflective teaching in the postmodern world: A manifesto for education in postmodernity*. Buckingham: Open University Press.

Paul, P., & Moores, D. F. (2012). Toward an understanding of epistemology and deafness. In P. Paul & D. Moores (Eds.), *Deaf epistemologies: Multiple perspectives on the acquisition of knowledge* (pp. 3–15). Washington, DC: Gallaudet University Press.

Piaget, J. (1928). Logique génétique et sociologie. *Revue Philosophique de la France et de l'Étranger*, 105: 167–205.

Piaget, J. (1932). *The moral judgment of the child*. London: Routledge & Kegan Paul.

Piaget, J. (1948a). *Le langage et la pensée chez l'enfant* (new ed.). Paris: Delachaux et Niestlé. (Original publication 1923)

Piaget, J. (1948b). *La naissance de l'intelligence chez l'enfant* (new ed.). Paris: Delachaux et Niestlé. (Original publication 1923)

Piaget, J. (1976). *Psychologie et epistémologie*. Paris: Editions Gonthier. (Original publication 1970)

Piaget, J. (1979). *L'epistémologie génétique* (3rd ed.). Paris: Presses Universitaires de France. (Original publication 1950)

Piaget, J. (1993). *Le jugement et le raisonnement chez l'enfant* (8th ed.). Paris: Delachaux & Niestlé.

Piaget, J. (1996). *La construction du réel chez l'enfant* (6th ed.). Neuchatel: Delachaux & Niestlé. (Original publication 1950)

Piaget, J. (2012). *La psychologie de l'intelligence* (3rd ed.). Paris: Armand Collin. (Original publication 1947)

Pinker, S. (2009). *Language learnability and language development*. Cambridge, MA: Harvard University Press.

Pinxton, R. (1991). Objectivism versus relativism: What are we arguing about? In D. Raven, I. Van Vucht Tijssen & J. De Wolf (Eds.), *Cognitive relativism and social science* (pp. 181–191). New York: Transaction Press.

Polyani, M. (1958). *Personal knowledge: Towards a post-critical philosophy*. Chicago, IL: University of Chicago Press.

Polyani, M. (1966). *The tacit dimension*. Chicago, IL: University of Chicago Press.

Rainer, J. & Guyton, E. (1994). Developing a constructivist teacher education program: The policy-making stage. *Journal of Teacher Education*, 45(2): 140–146.

Reagan, T. (1999). Constructivist epistemology and second/foreign language pedagogy. *Foreign Language Annals*, 32(4): 413–425.

Reagan, T. (2002). "Knowing" and "learning" a foreign language: Epistemological reflections on classroom practice. In T. Osborn (Ed.), *The future of foreign language education in the United States* (pp. 45–61). Westport, CT: Bergin & Garvey.

Reagan, T., Case, C. & Brubacher, J. (2000). *Becoming a reflective educator: How to build a culture of inquiry in the schools* (2nd ed.). Thousand Oaks, CA: Corwin.

Richard-Amato, P. (1996). *Making it happen: Interaction in the second language classroom, from theory to practice* (2nd ed.). White Plains, NY: Longman.

Richards, J. & Lockhart, C. (1994). *Reflective teaching in second language classrooms*. Cambridge: Cambridge University Press.

Richards, J. & Rodgers, T. (2001). *Approaches and methods in language teaching* (2nd ed.). Cambridge: Cambridge University Press.

Richardson, V. (Ed.). (1997a). *Constructivist teacher education: Building a world of new understandings*. London: Falmer Press.

Richardson, V. (1997b). Constructivist teaching and teacher education: Theory and practice. In V. Richardson (Ed.), *Constructivist teacher education* (pp. 3–14). London: Falmer Press.

Saffire, P. & Freis, C. (1999). *Ancient Greek alive* (3rd ed.). Chapel Hill, NC: University of North Carolina Press.

Salazar Pérez, M. S., & Saavedra, C. (2017). A call for onto-epistemological diversity in early childhood education and care: Centering global south conceptualizations of childhood/s. *Review of Research in Education*, 41(1): 1–29.

Savignon, S. (1983). *Communicative competence: Theory and classroom practice*. Reading, MA: Addison-Wesley.

Scheffler, I. (1960). *The language of education*. Springfield, IL: Charles C. Thomas.

Scheffler, I. (1979). *Beyond the letter: A philosophical inquiry into ambiguity, vagueness and metaphor in language*. London: Routledge & Kegan Paul.

Schwandt, T. (1994). Constructivist, interpretivist approaches to human inquiry. In N. Denzin & Y. Lincoln (Eds.), *Handbook of qualitative research* (pp. 118–137). Thousand Oaks, CA: Sage.

Scott, D. (2010). *Education, epistemology and critical realism*. New York: Routledge.

Shrum, J. & Glisan, E. (2016). *Teacher's handbook: Contextualized language instruction* (5th ed.). Boston, MA: Cengage Learning.

Siegel, H. (2010). Knowledge and truth. In R. Bailey, R. Barrow, D. Carr & C. McCarthy (Eds.), *The Sage handbook of philosophy of education* (pp. 283–295). Los Angeles, CA: Sage.

Siegelman, E. (1990). *Metaphor and reasoning in psychotherapy*. New York: Guilford Press.

Sinclair, H., Berthoud, I., Gerard, J. & Venesiano, E. (1985). Constructivisme et psycholinguistique génétique. *Archives de Psychologie*, 53(204): 37–60.

Skinner, B. F. (1971). *Beyond freedom and dignity*. Indianapolis, IN: Hackett.

Skinner, B. F. (1974). *About behaviorism*. New York: Random House.

Slavin, R. (2018). *Educational psychology: Theory and practice* (12th ed.). New York: Pearson.

Slezak, P. (2010). Radical constructivism: Epistemology, education and dynamite. *Constructivist Foundations*, 6(1): 102–111.

Smith, N. (Ed.). (1981). *Metatphors for evaluation: Sources of new methods*. Beverly Hills, CA: Sage.

Spivey, N. (1997). *The constructivist metaphor: Reading, writing and the making of meaning*. San Diego, CA: Academic Press.

Stanovich, K. (1994). Constructivism in reading education. *The Journal of Special Education*, 28(3): 259–274.

Steffe, L., Cobb, P. & Von Glasersfeld, E. (1988). *Construction of arithmetical meanings and strategies*. New York: Springer.

Steffe, L. & Gale, J. (Eds.). (1995). *Constructivism in education*. Hillsdale, NJ: Lawrence Erlbaum Associates.

Steffe, L. & Kieren, T. (1994). Radical constructivism and mathematics education. *Research in Mathematics Education*, 25: 711–733.

Stevick, E. (1996). *Memory, meaning, and method: A view of language teaching* (2nd ed.). Boston, MA: Heinle & Heinle.

Stevick, E. (1974). Reviewed work: Teaching foreign languages in schools. *TESOL Quarterly*, 8(3): 305–314.

Stokoes, P. (2004). *Philosophy: 100 essential thinkers*. New York: Enchanted Lion Books.

Tarsitani, C. (1996). Metaphors in knowledge and metaphors of knowledge: Notes on the constructivist view of learning. *Interchange*, 27(1): 23–40.

Taylor, W. (Ed.). (1984). *Metaphors of education*. London: Heinemann.

Thorndike, E. (2000). *Animal intelligence: Experimental studies*. New York: Routledge. (Original publication 1911).

Tobin, K. (Ed.). (1993). *The practice of constructivism in science education*. Hillsdale, NJ: Lawrence Erlbaum Associates.

Traupman, J, (1997). *Conversational Latin for oral proficiency* (2nd ed.). Wauconda, IL: Bolchazy Carducci Publishers.

Vanier, F. (2011). Une conception naturaliste et normative de l'axiologie scientifique contemporaine: Analyse et dépassement de la théorie de Laudan. Unpublished M.A. thesis, Université de Montréal, Montréal.

van Lier, L. (1996). *Interaction in the language curriculum: Awareness, autonomy and authenticity*. London: Longman.

Van Patten, B. & Willliams, J. (Eds.). (2015). *Theories in second language acquisition: An introduction* (2nd ed.). New York: Routledge.

Von Glasersfeld, E. (1984). An introduction to radical constructivism. In P. Watzlawick (Ed.), *The invented reality* (pp. 17–40). New York: Norton.

Von Glasersfeld, E. (1989). Cognition, construction of knowledge, and teaching. *Synthese*, 80(1):121–140.

Von Glasersfeld, E. (1993). Questions and answers about radical constructivism. In K. Tobin (Ed.), *The practice of constructivism in science education* (pp. 23–38). Hillsdale, NJ: Lawrence Erlbaum Associates.

Von Glasersfeld, E. (1995a). A constructivist approach to teaching. In L. Steffe & J. Gale (Eds.), *Constructivism in education* (pp. 3–15). Hillsdale, NJ: Lawrence Erlbaum Associates.

Von Glasersfeld, E. (1995b). *Radical constructivism: A way of knowing*. London: Falmer Press.

Von Glasersfeld, E. (1996). Footnotes to "The many faces of constructivism." *Educational Researcher*, 25(6): 19.

Von Glasersfeld, E. (Ed.). (2002). *Radical constructivism in mathematics education*. New York: Kluwer.

Vygotsky, L. S. (2005a). ***Мышление и речь*** [Thinking and speech]. Moscow: Labirint.

Vygotsky, L. S. (2005b). *Психология развития ребенка* [Psychology of the child's development]. Moscow: Eksmo.

Vygotsky, L. S. (2008). *Психология искусства* [Psychology of art]. Moscow: Labirint.

Watson, J. B. (1970). *Behaviorism*. New York: W. W. Norton. (Original publication 1924)

Widdowson, H. (1978). *Teaching language as communication*. Oxford: Oxford University Press.

Williams, M. & Burden, R. (1999). *Psicología para profesores de idiomas: Enfoque del constructivismo social*. Cambridge: Cambridge University Press.

Winitzky, N. & Kauchak, D. (1997). Constructivism in teacher education: Applying cognitive theory to teacher learning. In V. Richardson (Ed.), *Constructivist teacher education* (pp. 59–83). London: Falmer Press.

Wolfmeyer, M. (2017). Anarchist epistemologies and the separation of science and state: The critique and relevance of Paul Feyerabend to educational foundations. *Educational Studies*, 53(4): 327–341.

Wood, T., Cobb, P. & Yackel, E. (1995). Reflections of learning and teaching mathematics in elementary school. In L. Steffe & J. Gale (Eds.), *Constructivism in education* (pp. 401–422). Hillsdale, NJ: Lawrence Erlbaum Associates.

Woods, D. (1996). *Teacher cognition in language teaching: Beliefs, decision-making and classroom practice*. Cambridge: Cambridge University Press.

Yan Huang. (2014). *Pragmatics*. Oxford: Oxford University Press.

Yan Huang. (Ed.). (2017). *The Oxford handbook of pragmatics*. Oxford: Oxford University Press.

Young, R. (2011). *L'anglais avec l'approche Silent Way*. Paris: Hachette.

Zambrano, I. & Greenfield, P. (2004). Ethnoepistemologies at home and school. In R. Sternberg & E. Grigorenko (Eds.), *Culture and competence: Contexts of life success* (pp. 251–272). Washington, DC: American Psychological Association.

Zeichner, K. & Liston, D. (1987). Teaching student teachers to reflect. *Harvard Educational Review*, 57(1): 23–48.

Zeichner, K. & Liston, D. (1996). *Reflective teaching: An introduction*. Mahwah, NJ: Lawrence Erlbaum Associates.

Zietsman, A. (1996). Constructivism: Super theory for all educational ills? *South African Journal of Higher Education*, 10(1): 70–75.

Part III

Teaching Language

6 When Methodology Fails

A Critical Look at World Language Education

The French-American historian and philosopher Jacques Barzun, in critiquing the teaching of foreign languages in the United States, once wrote that,

> Boys and girls "take" French or Spanish or German ... for three, four, or five years before entering college, only to discover there that they cannot read, speak, or understand it. The word for this type of instruction is not "theoretical" but "hypothetical." Its principle is "If it were possible to learn a foreign language in the way I have been taught, I should now know that language."
>
> (Barzun, 1954, p. 119)

As educators who have spent our personal and professional lives studying, learning, using, and teaching a variety of languages, we find Barzun's criticism of our discipline every bit as true today as it was when he first wrote it more the half a century ago. Unfortunately, little seems to have changed: as Dennis Baron has written, "Anglo-Americans ... will continue for the most part to resist learning other languages either in school or after school ... or they will learn foreign languages imperfectly" (Baron, 1990, p. 200). Not only do Americans generally not learn foreign languages, but the problem, as Richard Brecht, of the University of Maryland's Center for Advanced Study of Language, has suggested, goes even deeper than this: "It isn't that people don't think language education is important. *It's that they don't think it's possible*" (quoted in Friedman, 2015, our emphasis). And yet, in spite of such pessimism, the reality of contemporary world language education in the U.S. is paradoxical.

The "foreign language paradox" in the U.S. is the combination of the incredible progress that the field of world language education has made, coupled with its ongoing and continuing failures. On the one hand, there have been dramatic, and extremely positive, changes in many ways. The national standards for world language learning produced by ACTFL – originally the *Standards for Foreign Language Learning: Preparing for the 21st*

Century (National Standards in Foreign Language Education Project, 1996) and the *Standards for Foreign Language Learning in the 21st Century* (National Standards in Foreign Language Education Project, 2006), and more recently, the *World-Readiness Standards for Language Learning* [National Standards Collaborative Board, 2015) – are among the best of the various disciplinary standards documents produced in recent years.[1] Textbooks and other teaching materials, especially for the more commonly taught languages (especially French and Spanish), are qualitatively superior to any that have existed before, and for the most part create excellent opportunities for the inclusion of appropriate technology in the world language classroom, as well as being explicitly tied to and integrating the ACTFL *Standards*. And last, if not universally true, for the most part world language educators are better prepared as language educators than at any time in our history. Finally, although far from successful, there are individuals who do in fact become fluent in languages other than English – indeed, if you are reading this book, you are almost certainly such a person.

At the same time there is a growing shortage of well-qualified world language teachers (U.S. Department of Education, 2016), budgetary limitations increasingly threaten world language education programs (especially at the elementary and middle school levels) (Skorton & Altschuler, 2012), student enrollments in world languages at all levels are declining (see Tables 6.1 and 6.2), sometimes precipitously (Looney & Lusin, 2018; Pufahl & Rhodes, 2011), the percentage of universities that require world language study continues to decrease (Looney & Lusin, 2018; Skorton & Altschuler, 2012), offerings in many less commonly taught languages (LCTLs) (including, for instance, Arabic, Hebrew, Japanese, and Russian) are being reduced or eliminated altogether (Skorton & Altschuler, 2012), and program articulation remains a major concern (see Pufahl & Rhodes, 2011, p. 267). At the K-12 level, only 20.7% of students in the United States study a world language (American Academy of Arts & Sciences, 2016, p. viii). Finally, although roughly 20% of the U.S. population report speaking a second language (in comparison to 26% of Canadians and 66% of Europeans), less than 1% of American adults are proficient in the language that they studied in a U.S. classroom (Friedman, 2015). Further contributing to this paradox are a number of apparent contradictions: for example, although it is true that a near-record number of students in universities are studying a world language, it is also true that in recent years the percentage of such students has been declining – by more than 15% between 2009 and 2016, and by more than 9% just between Fall 2013 and Fall 2016 (Looney & Lusin, 2018, p. 2). Further, although the raw number of students in higher education studying a world language may appear to be impressive, with almost 1.5 million students engaged in world language study, this number represents only 7% of all university students (Friedman, 2015; New American Economy, 2017, p. 1) – in 2016, only 7.5 of every 100 tertiary-level students were enrolled in a world language course (compared with 16.5 of every 100 in 1965) (Looney & Lusin, 2018, p. 12). Finally, in considering the percentage of Americans proficient in a world language, the difference between the 18% and the 1% is largely due to the fact that the larger percentage includes individuals whose first language is a language other than English.

The challenge that we have set for ourselves in this book is to try to explain why this situation exists in our society, and to offer some suggestions for what world language teachers need to know to be able to address it. We take as a given that world language education in American public schools is largely unsuccessful at producing individuals competent in second languages. Based on our own teaching experience, we do not believe that this is the case for any reason related to students themselves; students in U.S. schools are every bit as bright, capable and talented as those anywhere else in the world. We also take as a given that this lack of success in world language learning is not due to any particular methodological or pedagogical failure on the part of world language teachers. To be sure, some teachers are better than others, some are more competent in the languages that they teach than are others, and some world language programs are better designed and implemented than others. These factors alone do not, and cannot, though, explain the overwhelming failure to achieve our articulated goals. Rather, to explain *why* world language education is relatively unsuccessful in contemporary U.S. society, we need to look more critically at the social, political, cultural, historical, economic and ideological contexts in which world language education takes place. Only by contextualizing the experience of the world language learner and teacher, we believe, can one begin to understand both *what* is taking place in world language education and *why* it is taking place.

It is this contextualization of world language education which we believe is so essential for the world language teacher to understand. The classroom world language educator must not only have competence in the target language, but must also understand the nature of human language more generally, and must be sensitive to the political, ideological and sociocultural aspects of language and language use. In other words, the world language educator must be able to function in a classroom setting as something of a critical, applied linguist. In the late 1960s, the British philosopher of education Richard Peters, in an effort to explain why teachers needed to be familiar with philosophy of education, argued that:

> There was a time, I suppose, when the view was defensible that teachers could pick up their art entirely on an apprenticeship system from experienced practitioners on the job. Education had relatively few agreed upon aims; procedures were more or less standardized; few fundamental questions were raised about principles underlying school organization, class management and the curriculum; the

Table 6.1 Number and Percentage of K-12 Students Enrolled in Foreign Language Courses

State	*Percentage of Students Enrolled in Foreign Language Courses*	*Number of Students Enrolled in Foreign Language Courses*	*Total Student Enrollment*
Alabama	7.38%	54,557	739,327
Alaska	22.46%	29,056	129,350
Arizona	10.76%	121,925	1,132,808
Arkansas	11.58%	53,930	465,631
California	14.63%	917,074	6,268,293
Colorado	15.54%	120,639	776,339
Connecticut	18.41%	102,431	556,370
Delaware	20.16%	24,872	123,364
Florida	17.90%	466,414	2,605,738
Georgia	18.56%	298,795	1,609,681
Hawai'i	13.08%	20,885	159,719
Idaho	11.21%	30,164	269,165
Illinois	15.28%	311,038	2,034,962
Indiana	15.46%	160,123	1,035,442
Iowa	16.67%	78,779	472,625
Kansas	16.01%	77,684	485,161
Kentucky	17.13%	115,031	671,466
Louisiana	15.80%	103,405	654,407
Maine	26.78%	50,200	187,450
Maryland	25.72%	210,539	818,521
Massachusetts	23.73%	222,173	936,328
Michigan	14.80%	243,595	1,645,742
Minnesota	20.17%	166,346	824,783
Mississippi	8.49%	40,917	482,004
Missouri	19.60%	175,103	893,562
Montana	14.06%	20,165	143,405
Nebraska	25.88%	72,637	280,697
Nevada	9.34%	40,166	429,954
New Hampshire	14.70%	29,079	197,856
New Jersey	27.58%	350,622	1,271,481
New Mexico	17.71%	57,313	323,688
New York	29.59%	771,767	2,608,408
North Carolina	22.36%	325,393	1,455,021
North Dakota	26.88%	25,688	95,549
Ohio	17.97%	349,017	1,941,875
Oklahoma	15.94%	96,115	602,995
Oregon	14.62%	82,395	563,392

Table 6.1 (Cont.)

State	*Percentage of Students Enrolled in Foreign Language Courses*	*Number of Students Enrolled in Foreign Language Courses*	*Total Student Enrollment*
Pennsylvania	22.61%	404,185	1,787,501
Rhode Island	16.24%	23,824	146,701
South Carolina	24.86%	174,247	700,824
South Dakota	24.23%	29,338	121,089
Tennessee	11.46%	107,931	941,866
Texas	20.48%	912,054	4,453,772
Utah	15.94%	85,711	537,653
Vermont	17.37%	15,540	89,482
Virginia	17.93%	215,651	1,202,933
Washington	18.22%	186,153	1,021,834
West Virginia	21.75%	58,630	269,513
Wisconsin	30.66%	256,593	836,860
Wyoming	17.28%	14,788	85,578
Washington, DC	27.29%	6,524	23,904
National Mean	18.51%		
TOTAL		8,907,201	48,112,069

Table 6.2 Percentage Change in Foreign Language Enrollments at the University Level, 2009–2015

Language	*Change 2009–2015*	*2013 Enrollments*
Spanish	–8.2%	790,756
French	–8.1%	197,757
ASL	+19.1%	109,577
German	–9.3%	86,700
Italian	–11.3%	71,285
Japanese	–7.8%	66,740
Chinese*	+2.0%	61,055
Arabic	–7.5%	32,286
Latin	–16.2%	27,192
Russian	–17.9%	21,962
Ancient Greek	–35.5%	12,917
Biblical Hebrew	–8.7%	12,551
Portuguese	+10.1%	12,415
Korean	+44.7%	12,229
Modern Hebrew	–19.4%	6,698
Other Languages	–2.6%	40,059
TOTAL	–6.7%	1,562,176

> general standards of the community, which they were meant to pass on in training the character of children, were relatively stable; and little was known about the psychology of children and the social conditions under which they lived which transcended common-sense .... I do not want to minimize the importance of this learning on the job under skilled direction. Indeed I think we would all agree that it must be the lynchpin of any system of training. I need hardly comment much either on its limitations as a sufficient type of training under modern conditions. The point is that nowadays just about none of the conditions obtain which provided the milieu in which the old apprenticeship system was viable. Education no longer has agreed aims; procedures are constantly under discussion and vary according to what different people conceive themselves as doing in teaching the various subjects; fundamental questions concerned with principles underlying school organization, class management and the curriculum are constantly being raised; and in the area of moral education the task is made more perplexing by the variations of standards which characterize a differentiated society. The question therefore is not *whether* a modern teacher indulges in philosophical reflection about what he [or she] is doing; it is rather *whether he [or she] does it in a sloppy or a rigorous manner* ...
>
> (Peters, 1967, pp. 152–153, our emphasis)

The same is true, we would suggest, with respect to the classroom teacher (and especially the world language educator) and applied linguistics. There is no question about *whether* teachers function as applied linguists; they *do* function in this way. The question is, rather, whether they are doing so well or poorly. The role of the world language teacher, then, is not merely that of a guide to the target language and culture, but also, and perhaps more importantly, that of a mentor and colleague in the students' development of critical language awareness. Our purpose in writing this book is to help both current and future world language teachers to develop their own critical language awareness, as well as a sensitivity to linguistic issues, that will help them become more effective mentors for their own students.

The Monolingual Norm

One of the most powerful ways in which dominance is expressed and maintained in any society is through the establishment and maintenance of social norms (see Cummins, 1996, 2000; Sleeter & McLaren, 1995; Spring, 2000). In other words, what counts as "normal" functions also to determine what is "not normal." Although this process is by no means deliberate much of the time, it is nevertheless quite real, and the identification and critique of the implicit dominance in such normativization is an important aspect of the empowerment, as well as of the *dis*empowerment, of both individual students and groups. For example, in contemporary U.S. society, the dominant norm in racial terms is white; other racial identities are "Other" (there is an extensive literature that has developed in recent years dealing with what is called critical race theory that addresses just this issue; see Cole, 2009; Delgado & Stefancic, 2017; Taylor, Gillborn & Ladson-Billings, 2009; Zamudio, Russell, Rios & Bridgeman, 2011). Such norms are significant because they in effect legitimize one group over others (see Sleeter, 2001). As Peter McLaren and Juan Muñoz argue:

> Our attention has been drawn to the fact that the term *ethnic* is rarely applied to populations commonly described as "white." If you are white you occupy a space that seemingly transcends ethnicity. Whiteness miraculously becomes the "oneness" without which otherness could not exist – the primogenitor of identity, the marker against which otherness defines itself. Whiteness functions as a frozen state – a dead zone where "traits" associated with skin color, phenotype, race, class, and gender characteristics historically associated with Anglo-Europeans are held to be perpetually raceless. Whiteness has been positioned as the backdrop against which alternative or unconventional social practices and cultural formations are judged, thus ascribing an unprecedented degree of authority and power to its membership and its ethnocentric cultural, social, and ideological expressions, while at the same time repositioning the "other" as deviant. Whiteness has become the laboratory which ethnicities are given defining characteristics, assembled, and categorized. Schools are the clinics which "treat" these ethnic groups, police their behavior, and assimilate them.
>
> (McLaren & Muñoz, 2000, pp. 32–33)

This process is especially disempowering when it takes place with groups that have been historically marginalized – whether on the basis of race, ethnicity, gender, sexual preference, age, language, disability, or whatever (see Hollins, 2008; Larson & Ovando, 2001; Sleeter & McLaren, 1995). As Lennard Davis commented in his seminal work on disability studies,

> We live in a world of norms. Each of us endeavors to be normal or else deliberately tries to avoid that state. We consider what the average person does, thinks, earns, or consumes. We rank our intelligence, our cholesterol level, our weight, height, sex drive, bodily dimensions along some conceptual line from subnormal to above-average. We consume a daily balance of vitamins and nutrients based on what an average human should consume. Our children are ranked in school and tested to determine where they fit into a normal curve

> of learning, of intelligence. Doctors measure and weigh them to see if they are above or below average on the height and weight curves. There is probably no area of contemporary life in which some idea of a norm, mean, or average has not been calculated ... To understand the disabled body, one must return to the concept of the norm, the normal body.
>
> (Davis, 1995, p. 23)

In the case of language, the common assumption in U.S. society is that monolingualism in English is both typical and normal. Thus, bilingualism or multilingualism are atypical and, in some sense, abnormal. This is especially interesting given how unusual it is from a global perspective. An additional aspect of normative monolingualism in contemporary U.S. society is the overlap of assumptions about social class and monolingualism. Although there is some expectation that very well-educated individuals may have at least a limited knowledge of a foreign language (almost always another language of wider communication), bilingualism and multilingualism are most commonly associated with groups and individuals at the lower end of the socioeconomic continuum. This association, in turn, simply reinforces the idea that bilingualism and multilingualism are in some manner problematic. As Viv Edwards has pointed out,

> Language teaching is full of paradoxes. The foreign languages taught in school enjoy high status with the dominant English-speaking group; the heritage languages associated with minority groups are regularly marginalized. The problem comes when the same language is both a foreign language and a heritage language. It is especially difficult to understand why Spanish, the language of a poor and marginalized community in the U.S.A., is the most popular choice for foreign language study.
>
> (Edwards, 2004, p. 144).

In truth, the paradox that Edwards identifies here is considerably less of a problem than it might at first appear. Although one might argue that languages studied in school are high status in the British context (which is the context in which Edwards in writing), this is considerably less so in the American context. Further, the Spanish that is taught in U.S. schools is generally not the same variety as that used locally – thus reinforcing an ideology of linguistic difference, and further marginalizing the relevant linguistic minority communities. And, finally, there is the question of whether competence in the foreign languages that we teach is actually one of our educational goals – especially given such factors as *when* we begin teaching foreign languages, *how* we teach them, and *how much time* we allocate to teaching them. In short, while there is certainly an apparent paradox here, it may well be less of a real paradox than it might appear.

Assumptions about the normalcy of monolingualism, especially in English-speaking societies, are often the result of historical power relations which are, in turn, reinforced by ideological beliefs (see Silverstein, 1996; Woolard, 1992). The idea that competence in more than one language is non-normative contradicts significant aspects of the human experience. Especially pernicious in this regard are beliefs about the cognitive and psychological costs of bilingualism and multilingualism. Although the empirical evidence about the positive effects of bilingualism and multilingualism is overwhelming (see Bialystok, 2007; Calvo & Bialystok, 2014; Cenoz & Genesee, 1998; Cunningham-Andersson & Andersson, 1999; Elgin, 2000; Poulin-Dubois, Blaye, Coutya & Bialystok, 2011; Tokuhama-Espinosa, 2001), it continues to be the case that there are continuing concerns among parents and others (including even educators) about the perceived or feared negative effects that might come from bilingualism and multilingualism.

The Realities of Contemporary World Language Education in the United States

There are a large number of constraints in the public schools that tend to work against the effectiveness of contemporary world language education programs in the United States (see Osborn & Reagan, 1998; Reagan, 2019; Reagan & Osborn, 1998, 2019, pp. 315–346). Among these constraints are the amount of time actually devoted to world language teaching and learning, the poor articulation of world language instruction from one level to the next (e.g., middle school to high school, high school to university), the lack of significant extracurricular institutional support for foreign language learning, institutional and individual biases with respect to which languages are offered and who takes which language, the public justifications and rationales for world language education (and the limitations of such justifications and rationales, as they were discussed in Chapter 4), the articulated goals of world language education, and finally, what might be termed the "social expectation of failure" with respect to the learning of languages other than English in the U.S. context.

Although various kinds of programs involving the teaching of foreign languages in the elementary school were gaining popularity in many parts of the U.S. prior to the passage and implementation of the *No Child Left Behind Act* in 2001 (see Curtain & Pesola, 1994; Lipton, 1992), since then the growing focus on accountability, especially in terms of reading and mathematics, has significantly reduced the presence of world language programs in many elementary schools (see Rhodes & Pufahl, 2010) – although at the same time, the number of immersion foreign language programs in the country actually seems to have risen, from only 3 in 1971 to 528 in 2011. For the most part, though, foreign language education programs in the U.S. typically begin at either the middle or secondary school level (see Rhodes & Branaman, 1999; Rhodes & Pufahl, 2010). From a linguistic and language learning perspective, this is counter-intuitive at the very least. Although the measurable merits of early world language instruction can be debated, there is little doubt that the earlier one begins studying a second language, the better.[2] In societies in which language learning is considered to be an essential component of a child's education, children routinely begin the study of world languages very early in their schooling (see Baldauf, 1993; Beardsmore, 1993a, 1993b; Dominguez & Pessoa, 2005; Ervin, 1991; Nikolov, 2009; Nikolov & Djiunović, 2006). Further, *when* foreign language learning begins is only one part of the broader picture. Perhaps even more important is the *amount* of time actually devoted to language teaching and learning. Typically in American schools, foreign language classes meet one period a day, allowing in most school districts for a maximum of fewer than 150 hours of language study per year – a maximum that does not take into account the many factors that inevitably impinge on this total, including teacher and student absences, fire drills, pep rallies, snow days, and so on, all of which reduce the amount of real time actually devoted to language teaching and learning.

This hypothetical 150 hours of language study is actually very telling, since we *do* in fact know roughly how much time is needed to acquire different levels of competence in different languages (see Lett, 2005; Liskin-Gasparro, 1982; Stansfield, Gao & Rivers, 2010). Using the expected levels of speaking proficiency guidelines from the Foreign Service Institute, in order to achieve a level 1 to 1+ on the 5-point Interagency Language Roundtable (ILR) scale (which basically indicates survival proficiency), students with *average* aptitude for language learning require a *minimum* of 240 hours of instruction in French and Spanish, 480 hours for German, and even longer in the cases of most of the LCTLs, such as Arabic, Chinese, Japanese and Russian (Omaggio Hadley, 1993, p. 28; see also Brecht & Walton, 1994; Everson, 1993; Lett, 2005; Stansfield, Gao & Rivers, 2010; Walker, 1989) (see Table 6.3), which indicates the minimum time required to reach Level 3 Proficiency). In other words, given the time required for the learning of different languages, the time allocated to foreign language instruction in schools in effect ensures that students, over the course of two years of study, will have had sufficient exposure to the target language to achieve *at best* minimal, survival levels of competence in the target language, and are in fact very unlikely to achieve even that.

These time-related constraints on world language education are illuminating because they so clearly conflict with what is known empirically about what is required for successful language learning. It would seem, then, that since no one could seriously expect the current approach to world language education to succeed, the system must in fact be expected, at least to some degree, to fail.[3] This is, on its own, an intriguing insight, but again, it is far from the whole picture.

The time constraints in world language education are further exacerbated by the lack of significant external institutional support for foreign

Table 6.3 The U.S. Defense Language Institute Language Learning Difficulty Scale

Category of Difficulty	*Duration of Instruction Required**	*Class Hours Needed*	*Languages*
I	26 weeks	575–600	French, Italian, Portuguese, Spanish
II	34 weeks	900	German, Indonesian
III	48 weeks	1,100	Dari/Persian Farsi, Hebrew, Hindi, Russian, Serbian/Croatian, Tagalog, Thai, Turkish, Uzbek, Urdu
IV	64 weeks	2,200	Arabic, Cantonese, Japanese, Korean, Mandarin, Pashto

*To achieve Level 3 General Professional Proficiency in Speaking and Reading for the average native English speaker.

language learning. Voluntary language clubs and the occasional school-sponsored field trip notwithstanding, students of languages other than English in U.S. schools have very few real opportunities to actually utilize the target language in meaningful ways outside of the classroom context. Content courses (that is, courses in social studies, literature, mathematics, the sciences, and so on) are virtually never taught in foreign languages in public schools.[4] Even the growing popularity of interdisciplinary curricular and instructional approaches in public schools has had little impact on world language education in most school districts. In short, in the typical middle and secondary school, world language education is very much seen by students and by non-foreign language educators alike as peripheral to the "real" school experience, and continues, all too often, to exist in a sort of curricular silo, cut off from other subjects.

Both subtle and blatant biases also impact world language instruction in the schools. A clear Eurocentric bias continues to be reflected in the languages most commonly offered in U.S. public schools, with the vast majority of students enrolled in Spanish and French, and to significantly lesser degrees, in Latin and German. Further, social class background often affects the student's decision to study a world language at all, and folk wisdom about the relative ease or difficulty of particular languages, as well as assumptions about the appropriateness of different languages for particular students, also affect which language the student is likely to choose (or to be advised by school personnel and others to take). In our experience, Spanish is generally seen as a relatively easy option by students, parents, counselors, and other teachers, while German and Latin are seen as more difficult and thus suited to more capable students.[5] Thus, it could be argued that the foreign language offerings of the school are grounded in historic sociopolitical power relationships, and that the selection of the language to be studied by the student is further constrained by her or his social and educational background and expected life outcomes.

The Ideological Limitations on World Language Education in the United States

The ideological content of both the formal and hidden curricula is well-established and well-documented in general terms (see Altbach, Kelly, Petrie & Weis, 1991; Apple, 1990, 1995; Apple & Weiss, 1983; Kentli, 2009; Lynch, 1989). Extensive scholarly analysis has been done on such subject areas as social studies, the literary canon in English, sexism and racism in textbooks, and so on (see Jay, 2003; Luke, 1988; Woodward, Elliot & Nagel, 1988). As Michael Apple and Linda Christian-Smith noted almost 30 years ago, "During the past two decades, a good deal of progress has been made on answering the question of whose knowledge becomes socially legitimate in schools" (Apple & Christian-Smith, 1991, p. 1). Although the fundamental issue here is one of epistemology (see Steedman, 1988; Steffe, 1995), normative issues of value and bias also play significant roles in the establishment and maintenance of ideological hegemony in U.S. society (see Beyer & Apple, 1988).

Teachers and other educators have been made very aware of and sensitive to explicit issues of bias in the curriculum, and teacher education students are commonly taught to identify and rectify such biases in the curriculum (see, for example, Banks, 1994, pp. 117–121; Gollnick & Chinn, 1994, pp. 320–326; Jay, 2003; Nieto, 2000). There is, at the very least, a rhetorical commitment to eliminating blatant bias in the curriculum in U.S. public education. Nonetheless, as Jean Anyon observed in her classic study of U.S. social studies textbooks, the textbook:

> suggests a great deal about the society that produces and uses it. It reveals which groups have power and demonstrates that the views of these groups are expressed and legitimized in the school curriculum. It can also identify social groups that are not empowered by the economic and social patterns in our society and do not have their views, activities, and priorities represented in the school curriculum … Omissions, stereotypes, and distortions that remain in "updated" social studies textbook accounts of Native Americans, Blacks, and women reflect the relative powerlessness of these groups.
> (Anyon, 1979, p. 382)

In the case of world language education, although obvious bias has been largely (though by no means completely) eliminated in textbooks and instructional materials, many underlying ideological and cultural biases remain unexamined and unaddressed. Although this is no doubt true of the wider curriculum as well, in the case of world language education the biases that can be identified are most often concerned with the content and purpose of the formal curriculum, and have the effect of essentially nullifying important elements of the formal curriculum, a point to which we will return later in this book.

An important aspect of the ideological content and functions of the curriculum is visible in the national standards movement. The debate about the content of the national standards in social studies, for instance, has been largely one informed by and grounded in competing ideological perspectives (see, e.g., Cochran-Smith & Fries, 2001; McCollum-Clark, 1995; Nash, Crabtree & Dunn, 1997; Tuinamuana, 2011; Zajda, 2010). In the case of world language education, the national standards have been far less controversial, in part because the standards themselves are the product of world language educators who took their task seriously and produced standards that presupposed a commitment to meaningful language learning (see National Standards Collaborative Board, 2015). It is with this assumption, though, that the problem arises, since it is by no means clear that the general public shares this commitment.

In addition, as we saw in Chapter 3, the concept of linguistic legitimacy (that is, what counts and what does not count as a "real" language) underlies world language education in a variety of ways (see Reagan, 2016, 2019). Not only are most human languages excluded from serious consideration as "real" languages for the purposes of world language study in U.S. schools, but even more, the *variety* of the target language tends to be very selectively chosen. Thus, some Spanish classes in the United States continue to employ Peninsular Spanish as their norm (although certainly less so than in the past), just as French classes use Parisian French as their model. Although there may be compelling reasons for such choices, they nonetheless have important consequences for the world language student. First, even where there are local opportunities for students to actually use the target language (Spanish in the Southwest, French in parts of the Northeast, etc.), the language of the classroom tends to differ dramatically from the local variety, thus again emphasizing the "Otherness" of the classroom language, and minimizing its actual usefulness for students.

An additional problem in this regard is that posed by the growing numbers of native or heritage language learners in the world language classroom (see Brinton, Kagan & Bauckus, 2008; Clyne, Fernandez, Chen & Summo-O'Connell, 1997; Kagan, 2005; Valdés, 2005). It is not uncommon for native speakers of Spanish, for instance, to have difficulties in basic Spanish language classes, largely because of the differences between the normative language employed in the classroom and the language variety of the native speaker (see Ruíz, 1991; Valdés, Lozano & García-Moya, 1981). Our point here is a simple one: it is not necessarily the native speaking student who should be seen as the problem, but rather, the attitudes and values related to language held by the school and teachers (including, unfortunately, some world language teachers). As Guadalupe Valdés has noted,

> it is a fact that a surprising number of Spanish-speaking students … are still being placed in beginning Spanish classes for non-speakers to help them "unlearn" their "bad" habits and begin anew as foreign speakers. It matters not that the student is fluent and has internalized every single grammar rule that the teacher may hope to present. If he says *traiba* for *traía*, many schools will make him "begin from the beginning" … every day teachers of Spanish casually enroll native Spanish-speaking students in beginning Spanish classes for non-speakers, in which the materials used have been designed exclusively for teaching English-speaking students. The students are expected, in the process, to acquire the standard Spanish dialect as opposed to that normally used in their own speech communities.
>
> (Valdés, 1981, p. 7)

Chet Bowers and David Flinders have argued that "the language processes of the class can be understood as an ecology of power that advantages certain groups of students over others" (Bowers & Flinders, 1990, p. 26), and nowhere is this more apparent than in the world language classroom. While all teachers are empowered to some extent by their presumed expertise (just as students are essentially *disempowered* by their lack of expertise in the subject-matter being studied), in the case of the world language teacher not only is *content* at issue but so too is the ability to communicate in what is in essence the language medium of the classroom. This difference alone makes the world language class different from others, and implies a different and even more significant power differential between world language educators and their students. As Barbara Craig has noted:

> Traditionally, the [world language] teacher's role has been seen as that of an authoritative expert. This view is based on the conception of knowledge as a quantifiable intellectual commodity. The teacher, as an expert in a field of inquiry or as an expert speaker of a language, has more of this knowledge than his or her students have. Because this knowledge has a separate existence outside of its knowers, it can be given, or taught, to the learners by the teacher-expert.
>
> (Craig, 1995, p. 41)

The world language teacher occupies a unique position in the context of public schooling. The language teacher is often called upon to be the school's unofficial translator/interpreter for foreign documents as well as for dealing with non-English-speaking parents and visitors. Furthermore, since most administrators and supervisors do not possess the language skills to assess a teacher's proficiency, the evaluation of such teachers is sometimes more limited in nature than might be the case in other subject areas. In fact, in our experience world language teachers have been known to use code switching as a strategy to increase the difficulty an administrator may have when observing a lesson. The hope, as we have heard it expressed, is that supervisors will *assume* that since they hear a foreign language being used, sound and effective instruction must be taking place. At the same time, we have seen monolingual administrators assume that all is well in the foreign language classroom as long as all that they hear is in the target language, and we have also seen instances in which the world language teacher switches to English to teach a world language class during an observation so that the supervisor can understand what is taking place.

After initial certification, a world language classroom teacher's own language proficiency is rarely evaluated, and then usually in a fairly perfunctory manner. This is especially true in the case of the LCTLs, where the teacher is likely to be the sole speaker of the target language in the school. Where there are other speakers of the language on staff, as is sometimes the case with bilingual education teachers, it is not uncommon to find world language teachers engaged in subtle disputes about relative language competence, especially where other speakers of the language may speak a less prestigious or non-standard variety of the language. In some school districts, world language teachers replace guidance counselors in the role of placement advisor with respect to world language classes, and have been known to use this power to guide native speaking students (and heritage language learners) into independent study courses, thus isolating the student and protecting the teacher from any challenge to her or his linguistic authority in the classroom. This is especially significant, since the native speaker could just as easily – though at far greater risk to the teacher – be validated by the classroom teacher as a "knower" in the foreign language classroom context. Far from just a language issue, the refusal to recognize the native speaker as a "knower" can function as a strategy to make such students invisible, thus preserving and legitimizing the dominant group's way of viewing what is language and who is a language user. The world language teacher controls, to a significant extent, not only the content of the world language curriculum, but also serves as the arbitrator of what counts as correct and incorrect use in the target language, as well as preferred lexical and grammatical choices. In addition, the teacher has the opportunity to employ what could be called the *official code switch*. The world language teacher decides when classroom conversation should be in English, and when it must be in the target language, thus effectively controlling classroom discourse (see Gee, 1996; Heath, 1983; Hymes, 1996).

Language and Politics

Another powerful way to conceptualize the ideological aspect of the marginalization of world language education is by taking into account what Dell Hymes has identified as the core assumptions about language in the United States. Hymes suggests that these core assumptions, which are most often tacit rather than clearly articulated, include the ideas that:

- Everyone in the United States speaks only English.
- Monolingualism is normal and healthy, while bilingualism is inherently unstable, perhaps injurious, and possibly unnatural.
- It is acceptable for native speakers of English to study foreign literary languages and high-status foreign languages, but not local or domestic language varieties.
- Since virtually everyone else in the world is learning English, there is no reason to learn other languages.
- There are correct and incorrect language varieties. Incorrect language varieties have no inherent value, except as entertainment.

(Hymes, 1996, pp. 84–85)

Each of these assumptions, as Hymes stresses, is fundamentally flawed, and the list as a whole is grounded in a lack of understanding of the nature of language, a confusion of historical mythology with historical fact, and is replete with both factual and normative errors. This having been said, the list nevertheless does, we believe, fairly accurately reflect commonly held beliefs and myths about language in the United States. To be sure, not everyone accepts these core assumptions, but they do appear to have significant impacts on educational and social policy and thought.

Conclusion

The marginalization of world language education is by no means unique in public education. It is a situation shared by art and music education, among other disciplines, and reflects widely held social and cultural values and beliefs. What makes the case of world language education unusual is the ideological aspect of its marginalization. In addition, given what we take to be the lack of success in achieving world language learning for the overwhelming majority of students at all educational levels in the United States, we believe that it is time for a radical rethinking of the nature, purposes, and goals of world language education in our society. We have already suggested here that world language education programs in the United States do not, in even a very limited sense, accomplish the most commonly articulated goals and objectives for language study. Furthermore, we have argued that, given the way in which world language education programs are designed and implemented, this can hardly be a surprise (see Osborn & Reagan, 1998; Reagan

& Osborn, 1998). There appears to be what might be called a "social expectation of failure" – not only is world language education not particularly successful much of the time, but most people in our society do not *expect* it to be successful. We do not believe that world language education in the United States can be turned into a success story without a number of fundamental changes that will affect virtually every part of the field. Essentially, what is needed is a paradigm shift that will create a significantly different approach to the ways in which world languages are taught, our expectations for students in world language classes, the scheduling, organization and articulation of world language courses and programs, the kinds of teaching and learning materials used with different groups of students, and our goals for world language education. Perhaps most important, we need to build critical perspectives and critical pedagogy into world language education. In the remainder of this book, we will be exploring different aspects of the paradigm shift that we believe remains necessary in our field.

Questions for Reflection and Discussion

1 The claim that world language education in the U.S. is not generally very successful raises a very important question: as a person who has presumably learned a world language in the U.S., how can your own success at language learning be explained?
2 If policy makers in the U.S. decided to make a sincere commitment to promoting world language learning, what changes might they seek to make in world language education? Consider in your answer changes in curriculum, methodology, assessment, and teacher preparation.
3 What motivated you to decide to become a world language educator? What does this tell you about what kind of world language teacher you are likely to be? What does it tell you about what you will expect from your students?
4 Do you genuinely believe that all students can learn a world language? Why or why not? What are the implications of your beliefs about world language learning for your own teaching practice?
5 Examine a copy of a common first or second year textbook in the language (or languages) that you plan to teach. Can you identify any ideological or political biases in the textbook? How might such biases be dealt with in the context of the world language classroom?

Notes

1 See Phillips and Abbott (2011). More critical perspectives on the ACTFL *Standards* can be found in both Fox and Diaz-Greenberg (2006) and Magnan (2008).
2 Although there are clear benefits of early second language learning, it is important to note that much of the scholarly literature in the field may have overplayed such benefits, and have underestimated effective second language learning in older students (see, for example, Marinova-Todd, Marshall &

Snow, 2000; Samway & McKeon, 1999, pp. 20–21). Further, the fact that there are certainly benefits to learning a second language early in life, does not mean that older individuals cannot or should not also seek to do so.

3 The interesting aspect of this, in our view, is *not* the fact that most students do not acquire a high degree of competence in the target language, but rather, is the fact that some *do*. Given the barriers that they face, it is truly remarkable that some individuals do learn second languages in the U.S. school and university context. This is the case, we imagine, for most of the readers of *this* book – given all of the barriers and constraints, how did you still manage to become competent in a second language? Such criticisms are by no means new or novel, of course. Similar concerns were raised in the discourse surrounding the NDEA in the late 1950s, and more recently in National Commission on Excellence in Education's *A Nation at Risk: The Imperative for Educational Reform* in 1983 (see Watzke, 2003).

4 The exception to this general rule occurs in the context of bilingual education. Content subject matter is taught in languages other than English in such settings, and in dual immersion and two-way bilingual education programs, such instruction is an especially valuable component of the second language learning process.

5 There is a core of truth here, of course. The estimates provided by the Foreign Language Institute for gaining varying degrees of proficiency in different languages makes quite clear the fact that some languages are indeed more difficult than are others for native speakers of English to learn than are others. However, in our experience the assumptions made about the relative ease of different languages in the secondary school context are based largely on bias and misinformation rather than any sound empirical evidence.

References

Altbach, P., Kelly, G., Petrie, H. & Weis, L. (Eds.). (1991). *Textbooks in American society: Politics, policy, and pedagogy*. Albany, NY: State University of New York Press.

American Academy of Arts and Sciences. (2016). *The state of languages in the U.S.: A statistical portrait*. Cambridge, MA: Author.

Anyon, J. (1979). Ideology and United States social studies textbooks. *Harvard Educational Review*, 49(3): 361–386.

Apple, M. (1990). *Ideology and curriculum* (2nd ed.). New York: Routledge.

Apple, M. (1995). *Education and power* (2nd ed.). New York: Routledge.

Apple, M. & Christian-Smith, L. (1991). The politics of the textbook. In M. Apple & L. Christian-Smith (Eds.), *The politics of the textbook* (pp. 1–21). New York: Routledge.

Apple, M. & Weiss, L. (Eds.). (1983). *Ideology and practice in schooling*. Philadelphia, PA: Temple University Press.

Baldauf, R. (1993). Fostering bilingualism and national development through school second language study. *Journal of Multilingual and Multicultural Development*, 14(1/2): 121–134.

Banks, J. (1994). *An introduction to multicultural education*. Boston, MA: Allyn & Bacon.

Baron, D. (1990). *The English-only question: An official language for Americans?* New Haven, CT: Yale University Press.

Barzun, J. (1954). *Teacher in America*. Garden City, NY: Doubleday Anchor Books.

Beardsmore, H. (1993a). European models of bilingual education: Practice, theory and development. *Journal of Multilingual and Multicultural Development*, 14(1/2): 103–120.

Beardsmore, H. (Ed.). (1993b). *European models of bilingual education*. Clevedon: Multilingual Matters.

Beyer, L. & Apple, M. (Eds.). (1988). *The curriculum: Problems, politics and possibilities*. Albany, NY: State University of New York Press.

Bialystok, E. (2007). Cognitive effects of bilingualism: How linguistic experience leads to cognitive change. *International Journal of Bilingual Education and Bilingualism*, 10(3): 210–223.

Bowers, C. & Flinders, D. (1990). *Responsive teaching: An ecological approach to classroom patterns of language, culture, and thought*. New York: Teachers College Press.

Brecht, R. & Walton, A. (1994). National strategic planning in the less commonly taught languages. In R. Lambert (Ed.), *Foreign language policy* (pp. 190–212). Thousand Oaks, CA: Sage.

Brinton, D., Kagan, O. & Bauckus, S. (Eds.). (2008). *Heritage language education: A new field emerging*. New York: Routledge.

Calvo, A. & Bialystok, E. (2014). Independent effects of bilingualism and socioeconomic status on language ability and executive functioning. *Cognition*, 130(3): 278–288.

Cenoz, J. & Genesee, F. (Eds.). (1998). *Beyond bilingualism: Multilingualism and multilingual education*. Clevedon: Multilingual Matters.

Clyne, M., Fernandez, S., Chen, I. & Summo-O'Connell, R. (1997). *Background speakers: Diversity and its management in LOTE programs*. Belconnen, Australia: Language Australia.

Cochran-Smith, M. & Fries, M. (2001). Sticks, stones, and ideology: The discourse of reform in teacher education. *Educational Researcher*, 30(8): 3–15.

Cole, M. (2009). *Critical race theory and education: A Marxist response* (2nd ed.). London: Palgrave Macmillan.

Craig, B. (1995). Boundary discourse and the authority of language in the second-language classroom: A social-constructionist approach. In J. Alatis, C. Straehle, B. Gallenberger & M. Ronkin (Eds.), *Georgetown University Round Table on Languages and Linguistics 1995: Linguistics and the education of language teachers* (pp. 40–54). Washington, DC: Georgetown University Press.

Cummins, J. (1996). *Negotiating identities: Education for empowerment in a diverse society*. Ontario, CA: California Association for Bilingual Education.

Cummins, J. (2000). *Language, power and pedagogy: Bilingual children in the crossfire*. Clevedon, UK: Multilingual Matters.

Cunningham-Andersson, U. & Andersson, S. (1999). *Growing up with two languages: A practical guide*. New York: Routledge.

Curtain, H. & Pesola, C. (1994). *Languages and children, making the match: Foreign language instruction for an early start, grades K-8* (2nd ed.). White Plains, NY: Longman.

Davis, L. (1995). *Enforcing normalcy: Disability, deafness, and the body*. London: Verso.

Delgado, R. & Stefancic, J. (2017). *Critical race theory: An introduction* (3rd ed.). New York: New York University Press.

Dominguez, R. & Pessoa, S. (2005). Early versus late start in foreign language education: Documenting achievements. *Foreign Language Annals*, 38(4): 473–480.

Edwards, V. (2004). *Multilingualism in the English-speaking world*. Oxford: Basil Blackwell.

Elgin, S. (2000). *The language imperative*. Cambridge, MA: Perseus Books.

Ervin, G. (Ed.). (1991). *International perspectives on foreign language teaching*. Lincolnwood, IL: National Textbook Company, in conjunction with the American Council on the Teaching of Foreign Languages.

Everson, M. (1993). Research in the less commonly taught languages. In A. Omaggio Hadley (Ed.), *Research in language learning* (pp. 198–228). Lincolnwood, IL: National Textbook Company, in conjunction with the American Council on the Teaching of Foreign Languages.

Fox, R. & Diaz-Greenberg, R. (2006). Culture, multiculturalism, and foreign/world language standards in U.S. teacher preparation programs: Toward a discourse of dissonance. *European Journal of Teacher Education*, 29(3): 401–422.

Friedman, A. (2015). America's lacking language skills. *The Atlantic* (May 10). Downloaded from www.theatlantic.com/education/archive/2015/05/filling-americas-language-education-potholes/392876 on March 13, 2017.

Gee, J. (1996). *Social linguistics and literacies: Ideology in discourse* (2nd ed.). London: Taylor & Francis.

Gollnick, D. & Chinn, P. (1994). *Multicultural education in a pluralistic society* (4th ed.). New York: Merrill.

Heath, S. B. (1983). *Ways with words: Language, life and work in communities and classrooms*. Cambridge: Cambridge University Press.

Hollins, E. (2008). *Culture in school learning: Revealing the deep meaning* (2nd ed.). New York: Routledge.

Hymes, D. (1996). *Ethnography, linguistics, narrative inequality: Toward an understanding of voice*. London: Taylor and Francis.

Jay, M. (2003). Critical race theory, multicultural education, and the hidden curriculum of hegemony. *Multicultural Perspectives*, 5(4): 3–9.

Kagan, O. (2005). In support of a proficiency-based definition of heritage language learners: The case of Russian. *International Journal of Bilingual Education and Bilingualism*, 8(2/3): 213–221.

Kentli, F. (2009). Comparison of hidden curriculum theories. *European Journal of Education*, 1(2): 83–88.

Larson, C. & Ovando, C. (2001). *The color of bureaucracy: The politics of equity in multicultural school communities*. Belmont, CA: Wadsworth.

Lett, J. (2005). Foreign language needs assessment in the U.S. military. In M. Long (Ed.), *Second language needs analysis* (pp. 105–124). Cambridge: Cambridge University Press.

Lipton, G. (1992). *Practice handbook to elementary foreign language programs* (2nd ed.). Lincolnwood, IL: National Textbook Company.

Liskin-Gasparro, J. (1982). *ETS oral proficiency testing manual*. Princeton, NJ: Educational Testing Service.

Looney, D. & Lusin, N. (2018). Enrollments in languages other than English in United States institutions of higher education, Summer 2016 and Fall 2016: Preliminary report. Modern Language Association (February). Downloaded from https://files.eric.ed.gov/fulltext/ED590075.pdf on May 15, 2019.

Luke, A. (1988). *Literacy, textbooks and ideology*. Philadelphia, PA: Falmer Press.

Lynch, K. (1989). *The hidden curriculum: Reproduction in education, a reappraisal*. London: Falmer Press.

Magnan, S. (2008). Reexamining the priorities of the national standards for foreign language education. *Language Teaching*, 41(3): 349–366.

Marinova-Todd, S., Marshall, D. & Snow, C. (2000). Three misconceptions about age and L2 learning. *TESOL Quarterly*, 34(1): 9–34.

McCollum-Clark, K. (1995). National Council of Teachers of English, corporate philanthropy, and national education standards: Challenging the ideologies of English education reform. Unpublished Ph.D. dissertation, The Pennsylvania State University, University Park, Pennsylvania.

McLaren, P. & Muñoz, J. (2000). Contesting whiteness: Critical perspectives on the struggle for social justice. In C. Ovando & P. McLaren (Eds.), *The politics of multiculturalism and bilingual education: Students and teachers caught in the cross fire* (pp. 23–49). Boston, MA: McGraw-Hill.

Nash, G., Crabtree, C. & Dunn, R. (1997). *History on trial: Culture wars and the teaching of the past*. New York: Alfred A. Knopf.

National Commission on Excellence in Education. (1983). *A nation at risk: The imperative for educational reform*. Washington, DC: Government Printing Office.

National Standards Collaborative Board. (2015). *World-readiness standards for learning languages* (4th ed.). Alexandria, VA: Author.

National Standards in Foreign Language Education Project. (1996). *Standards for foreign language learning: Preparing for the 21st century*. Lawrence, KS: Allen Press.

National Standards in Foreign Language Education Project. (2006). *Standards for foreign language learning in the 21st century* (3rd ed.). Lawrence, KS: Allen Press.

New American Economy. (2017). Not lost in translation: The growing importance of foreign language skills in the U.S. job market. *New American Economy* (March). Downloaded from http://research.newamericaneconomy.org/wp-content/uploads/2017/03/NAE_Bilingual_V9.pdf on May 15, 2019.

Nieto, S. (2000). *Affirming diversity: The sociopolitical context of multicultural education* (3rd ed.). New York: Longman.

Nikolov, M. (Ed.). (2009). *Early learning of modern foreign languages: Processes and outcomes*. Bristol: Multilingual Matters.

Nikolov, M. & Djiunović, J. (2006). Recent research on age, second language acquisition, and early foreign language learning. *Annual Review of Applied Linguistics*, 26: 234–260.

Omaggio Hadley, A. (1993). *Teaching language in context* (2nd ed.). Boston, MA: Heinle & Heinle.

Osborn, T. A. & Reagan, T. (1998). Why Johnny can't *hablar*, *parler*, or *sprechen*: Foreign language education and multicultural education. *Multicultural Education*, 6(2): 2–9.

Peters, R. S. (1967) The place of philosophy in the training of teachers. *Paedagogica Europa*, 3: 152–153.

Phillips, J. & Abbott, M. (2011). *A decade of foreign language standards: Impact, influence, and future directions*. Report of Grant Project # P017A080037, Title VII, International Research Studies, U.S. Department of Education to the American Council on the Teaching of Foreign Languages. Washington, DC: Author.

Poulin-Dubois, D., Blaye, A., Coutya, J. & Bialystok, E. (2011). The effects of bilingualism on toddlers' executive functioning. *Journal of Experimental Child Psychology*, 108(3): 567–579.

Pufahl, I. & Rhodes, N. (2011). Foreign language instruction in U.S. schools: Results of a national survey of elementary and secondary schools. *Foreign Language Annals*, 44(2): 258–288.

Reagan, T. (2016). The conceptualization of "language legitimacy." *Critical Inquiry in Language Studies*, 13(1): 1–19.

Reagan, T. (2019). *Linguistic legitimacy and social justice*. London: Palgrave Macmillan.

Reagan, T. & Osborn, T. A. (1998). Power, authority and domination in foreign language education: Toward an analysis of educational failure. *Educational Foundations*, 12(2): 45–62.

Reagan, T. & Osborn, T. A. (2019). Time for a paradigm shift in U.S. foreign language education? Revisiting rationales, evidence and outcomes. In D. Macedo (Ed.), *Decolonizing foreign language education: The misteaching of English and other colonial languages* (pp. 73–110). New York: Routledge.

Rhodes, N. & Brananman, L. (1999). *Foreign language instruction in the United States: A national survey of elementary and secondary schools*. McHenry, IL: Delta Systems, for the Center for Applied Linguistics.

Rhodes, N. & Pufahl, I. (2010). *Foreign language teaching in U.S. schools: Results of a national survey*. Washington, DC: Center for Applied Linguistics.

Ruíz, R. (1991). The empowerment of language minority students. In C. Sleeter (Ed.), *Empowerment through multicultural education* (pp. 217–227). Albany, NY: State University of New York Press.

Samway, K. & McKeon, D. (1999). *Myths and realities: Best practices for language minority students*. Portsmouth, NH: Heinemann.

Silverstein, M. (1996). *Monoglot "Standard" in America: Standardization and metaphors of linguistic hegemony*. Boulder, CO: Westview Press.

Skorton, D. & Altschuler, G. (2012). America's foreign language deficit. *Forbes* (August 27). Downloaded from www.forbes.com/sites/collegeprose/2012/08/27/americas-foreign-language-deficit/#73b6b39f4ddc on March 13, 2017.

Sleeter, C. (2001). Epistemological diversity in research on preservice teacher preparation for historically underserved children. In W. Secada (Ed.), *Review of research in education: 25* (pp. 209–250). Washington, DC: American Educational Research Association.

Sleeter, C. & McLaren, P. (Eds.) (1995). *Multicultural education, critical pedagogy, and the politics of difference*. Albany, NY: State University of New York Press.

Spring, J. (2000). *The intersection of cultures: Multicultural education in the United States and the global economy* (2nd ed.). Boston, MA: McGraw-Hill.

Stansfield, C., Gao, J. & Rivers, W. (2010). A concurrent validity study of self-assessments and the federal Interagency Language Roundtable oral proficiency interview. *Russian Language Journal/Русский язык*, 60: 299–315.

Steedman, P. (1988). Curriculum and knowledge selection. In L. Beyer & M. Apple (Eds.), *The curriculum* (pp. 119–139). Albany, NY: State University Press of New York.

Steffe, L. (1995). Alternative epistemologies: An educator's perspective. In L. Steffe & J. Gale (Eds.), *Constructivism in education* (pp. 489–523). Hillsdale, NJ: Lawrence Erlbaum Associates.

Taylor, E., Gillborn, D. & Ladson-Billings, G. (Eds.). (2009). *Foundations of critical race theory in education*. New York: Routledge.

Tokuhama-Espinosa, T. (2001). *Raising multilingual children: Foreign language acquisition and children*. Westport, CT: Bergin & Garvey.

Tuinamuana, K. (2011). Teacher professional standards, accountability, and ideology: Alternative discourses. *Australian Journal of Teacher Education*, 36(12): 72–82.

U.S. Department of Education. (2016). *Teacher shortage areas: Nationwide listing, 1990–91 through 2016–2017*. Washington, DC: U.S. Department of Education, Office of Postsecondary Education.

Valdés, G. (1981). Pedagogical implications of teaching Spanish to the Spanish-speaking in the United States. In G. Valdés, A. Lozano & R. García-Moya (Eds.), *Teaching Spanish to the Hispanic bilingual* (pp. 3–20). New York: Teachers College Press.

Valdés, G. (2005). Bilingualism, heritage language learners, and SLA research: Opportunities lost or seized? *The Modern Language Journal*, 89(3): 410–426.

Valdés, G., Lozano, A. & García-Moya, R. (Eds.). (1981). *Teaching Spanish to the Hispanic bilingual: Issues, aims, and methods*. New York: Teachers College Press.

Walker, G. (1989). The less commonly taught languages in the context of American pedagogy. In H. Lepke (Ed.), *Northeast Conference on the Teaching of Foreign Languages: Shaping the future* (pp. 111–137). Middlebury, VT: Northeast Conference on the Teaching of Foreign Languages.

Watzke, J. (2003). *Lasting change in foreign language education: A historical case for change in national policy*. Westport, CT: Praeger.

Woodward, A., Elliott, D. & Nagel, K. (Eds.). (1988). *Textbooks in school and society*. New York: Garland.

Woolard, K. (1992). Language ideology: Issues and approaches. *Pragmatics*, 2(3): 235–249.

Zajda, J. (Ed.). (2010). *Globalisation, ideology and educational policy reforms*. Dordrecht: Springer.

Zamudio, M., Russell, C., Rios, F. & Bridgeman, J. (2011). *Critical race theory matters: Education and ideology*. New York: Routledge.

7 The World Language Educator and Critical Reflective Practice

Toward Emancipatory Knowledge

The idea of the teacher as reflective practitioner is not a new one. John Dewey wrote about the need for reflective thinking as early as 1903, and dealt with the role of reflection extensively in both *How We Think* (Dewey, 1910, 1933) and *Logic: The Theory of Inquiry* (Dewey, 1938). For Dewey, logical theory and analysis was a generalization of the reflective process in which we all engage from time to time. Dewey recognized that we can "reflect" on a whole host of things in the sense of merely "thinking about" them; however, logical, or *analytic*, reflection can take place only when there is a real problem to be solved. As he explained,

> The general theory of reflection, as over against its concrete exercise, appears when occasions for reflection are so overwhelming and so mutually conflicting that specific adequate response in thought is blocked. Again, it shows itself when practical affairs are so multifarious, complicated, and remote from control that thinking is held off from successful passage into them.
>
> (Dewey, 1976, p. 300)

In other words, *true* reflective practice can be said to take place only when the individual is faced with a *real* problem or situation that she or he needs to resolve, and seeks to resolve that problem in a rational manner.

In 1983, Donald Schön published the first edition of his *The Reflective Practitioner: How Professionals Think in Action*. Schön's focus in that work was not exclusively on teachers, but rather on professionals in a host of fields including architecture, social services, and various health service professions (social work, architecture, and nursing). In all of these areas, it had a huge impact, but arguably nowhere was its impact greater than in teacher education. Indeed, nearly 40 years after the initial publication of *The Reflective Practitioner*, most teacher preparation programs include among their explicit and articulated goals the development of "reflective practitioners" – although precisely what that phrase means is often less than crystal clear. Most recently, the idea that our goal should be not simply preparing teachers to be reflective practitioners, but rather *critical* reflective practitioners, has gained support, especially among those committed to critical pedagogy more generally (see Fook, 2006). In this chapter, we will begin with a discussion of the traditional debate about whether teaching is best understood as an art or as a science, and will suggest that this dichotomy is misleading, and that the concept of reflective practice offers a solution to this apparent dilemma. We will then discuss the knowledge basis that is necessary for an individual to become an effective world language educator, and then turn to an analysis of the real-world tasks of the world language teacher. Next, we will focus on the meaning and implications of reflective practice in general, and then of *critical* reflective practice in particular, as these are manifested in the world language classroom. Finally, the special situation of world language teacher who is a native language speaker of the target language will be briefly explored in light of the earlier discussion of critical reflective practice.

The Art and Science of Teaching

There has been a long-standing debate about the nature of teaching. This debate usually takes the form of a dichotomy: is teaching best understood as an art, or rather, should we consider teaching to be a science? For those who advocate the former view, in which teaching is conceptualized as a kind of artistic endeavor, the teacher's role is seen as roughly comparable to that of the painter, composer or creative writer. If one accepts this view of teaching, then the best preparation to become a teacher is probably based on some sort of apprenticeship model, in which the future teacher works under the supervision of an experienced, master teacher. If, on the other hand, one conceptualizes teaching as essentially an application of particular set of technical and scientific principles in specific classroom settings, then a different approach to teacher preparation (one similar to the traditional normal school model) probably makes sense. At its heart, this dichotomy is grounded in the question of whether teachers are born or made – or, perhaps, even if *some* (relatively few) teachers are *born*, others (the vast majority) can be *made*. This is a very important matter, since most classroom teachers are almost certainly *not* born teachers. As Mark Van Doren insightfully commented,

> Good teachers have always been and will always be, and there are good teachers now. The necessity henceforth is that fewer of them be accidents. The area of accident is reduced when there is a design which includes the education of teachers. Not the training – a contemporary term that suggests lubricating oil and precision parts, not to say reflexes and responses.
>
> (Van Doren, 1959, pp. 170–171)

However, much of what every classroom teacher actually does during the school day actually involves making judgments and decisions, often with limited and insufficient information. Rather than thinking about the role of the teacher in terms of whether teaching is best understood as an art form, a set of technical skills, or some combination of these two, we would suggest that teaching can be more accurately and usefully conceptualized in terms of the role of the teacher as a decision-maker – a point to which we will return shortly.

The Knowledge Base of the World Language Educator

What does a person need to know in order to be an effective teacher? Although it is often suggested that a knowledge of the subject matter to be taught is sufficient to teach the subject, this is clearly not really the case. In the case of world language education, not every person who speaks a language is capable of teaching the language; in fact, most speakers of a language are *not* likely to be effective teachers of the language without additional training. There is in fact an entire constellation of knowledge, skills and dispositions that are required to be effective in the classroom (see Ghaye, 2010; Jay & Johnson, 2002; Loughran, 1996, 2002; van Manen, 1995). Some years ago, the educational psychologist Lee Shulman identified seven broad categories of knowledge which would, taken together, constitute the major components of the knowledge base for the classroom teacher, and Shulman's categories have remained largely unchallenged since he proposed them. Shulman argued that any teacher should have mastered:

- the appropriate content knowledge;
- general pedagogical knowledge, with special reference to those broad principles and strategies of classroom management and organization that appear to transcend subject matter;
- curriculum knowledge, with particular grasp of the materials and programs that serve as "tools of the trade" for teachers;
- pedagogical content knowledge, that special amalgam of content and pedagogy that is uniquely the province of teachers, their own special form of professional understanding;
- knowledge of learners and their characteristics;
- knowledge of educational contexts, ranging from the workings of the group or classroom, the governance and financing of school districts, to the character of communities and cultures; and
- knowledge of educational ends, purposes, and values, and their philosophical and historical grounds.

(Shulman, 1987, p. 54)

Shulman's conceptualization of the teacher education knowledge base is, by its nature, very general and non-specific. If it is to be useful to us, we need to move this knowledge base to the next level of specificity: how is this knowledge base manifested in the case of the world language educator? It is to a discussion of this matter that we now turn.

Content knowledge is at the top of Shulman's conceptualization of the teacher education knowledge base, and this is obviously as it should be. Clearly one must know a subject in order to teach it effectively. In the context of world language education, this means that the world language teacher should have achieved a high degree of competence in the target language. This would seem to be axiomatic; it is somewhat puzzling to imagine a language being taught by someone who is unable to speak it well – and yet, in all too many cases, that is the case that we find in many language classrooms. In addition to language competence, content knowledge for the world language educator includes an array of other aspects of language knowledge (see Byram, 2012; Franklin, Laurence & Welles, 1999; Guntermann, 1993; Richards, 1998; Wallace, 1991). The world language educator should not only speak, understand, read and write the target language well, but should be familiar with the language from both linguistic and sociolinguistic perspectives. A formal understanding of the phonology, morphology and syntax of the language is essential for the effective world language educator, as is an awareness of the social and cultural contexts in which the target language is used. A knowledge of the historical development of the language is also valuable, as is a broad and deep knowledge of the literature of the language. What this all amounts to is that the world language teacher must be thoroughly and deeply familiar with the target language and its speaker community (or communities), and must be so at both the pragmatic and theoretical levels. The amount and diversity of knowledge required of the world language teacher, we believe, provides a powerful rationale for why any future world language educator should be expected to have lived for at least a reasonable period of time in a setting in which the target language is the dominant, daily language. To be sure, such an experience is not always required of future world language teachers, but it is only through such experiences that the kind of deep knowledge of and familiarity with the target language and culture can be achieved. Finally, native speakers certainly have some advantages in this regard, but merely *being* a native speaker of a language in no way prepares one to teach it.

Beyond content knowledge, there is general pedagogical knowledge which is necessary for effective teaching practice regardless of one's area of specialization. Included here, on Shulman's account, "are those broad principles and strategies of classroom management and organization that appear to transcend subject matter" (Shulman, 1987, p. 54). Such principles and strategies are not particularly difficult to identify; they include the knowledge and skills that often allow us to differentiate between successful and unsuccessful classroom teachers. An individual may well be a competent user of the target language without being effective in (or even in control of) the classroom. Among the principles and strategies that are core pedagogical knowledge and skills are instructional planning, lesson presentation skills, questioning skills, interpersonal communication skills, classroom management skills, and knowledge of evaluation approaches and strategies. Although for the most part general pedagogical knowledge is shared across disciplines, in the case of world language education there are a number of specific characteristics of such knowledge that are unique. For example, while all teachers need to understand issues of evaluation, the world language educator must understand not only general principles of assessment and evaluation, but also specific issues related to how a student's fluency and oral proficiency in the target language can be best assessed (see Curtain & Dahlberg, 2004, pp. 160–204; Hedge, 2000, pp. 378–401; Richard-Amato, 1996, pp. 93–114). Another example of the unique general pedagogical knowledge of the world language teacher is the variety of ways in which the target language can be used in the classroom, including how code mixing, code switching and translanguaging are utilized (see Macaro, 2002).

Like all classroom teachers, the world language educator requires not only content and pedagogical knowledge, but also needs specific curriculum knowledge. In other words, it is important for the teacher not only to be competent in the target language, but also to know what aspects of the language are generally taught at different levels in the school context. An individual might be very well versed and knowledgeable about specific linguistic aspects of the target language, but in the classroom context, this specialized knowledge must, to a certain extent, be subjugated to the established and generally accepted curriculum. Thus, in a basic Spanish course, a detailed discussion of the historical evolution of the subjunctive mood would be both inappropriate and arguably extremely poor pedagogy, regardless of the accuracy or quality of the presentation. Similarly, the vocabulary taught at different levels of world language instruction will generally move from most general to increasingly specialized (see Schmitt, 2000).[1] Color terminology, for instance, is an appropriate focus for a beginning world language class, as would be vocabulary to describe family relationships, foods, body parts and so on; terminology used to describe complex scientific or technical issues is arguably less so.[2] Finally, an important part of curriculum knowledge on the part of the classroom teacher is an awareness of the ancillary materials generally used by world language teachers – authentic texts, music, and other realia.

This brings us to what Shulman called pedagogical content knowledge, which is a powerful combination of content, pedagogical and curricular knowledge. This combination, though, is an instance in which the whole is greater than the sum of its parts, since it refers to the specialized articulated and unarticulated knowledge that world language educators are able to manifest in classroom practice. This knowledge goes far beyond merely content or pedagogical knowledge; it is, at its base, the understanding not only of the target language, but also of how particular features of the target language are most likely to be acquired by learners. John Watzke has argued that pedagogical content knowledge in world language education is constructed by teachers from four core sources: prior knowledge that frames instructional decisions, attitudes toward teacher control in the classroom, instructional goals for daily lessons, and considerations for responding to student affect (Watzke, 2007, p. 63). In addition, pedagogical content knowledge includes an awareness of how learners make sense (or do not make sense) of elements of the target language, and of ways of assisting them master the language. A good example of where pedagogical content knowledge might be useful would be in teaching English native speakers to distinguish between *ser* and *estar*, or between *por* and *para*, in Spanish. These features of Spanish differ in significant ways from English, but are typically taught very early in the introductory Spanish curriculum and are often somewhat challenging for students. In the languages that we most commonly teach in U.S. public schools – French, Spanish and German – helping students to understand and use correctly gender and gender agreement in nouns and adjectives is another example in which pedagogical content knowledge is invaluable. Since nouns in English do not show gender, assisting students to transition from English to languages in which gender is mandatory is extremely important. In English, you can say, "My friend has a book" – leaving unspecified whether my friend is male or female. In Spanish, you simply do not have this option; you *must* indicate your friend's gender (*Mi amigo tiene un libro* or *Mi amiga tiene un libro*). This may not seem to be terribly important, but it is in fact an essential feature of learning to speak Spanish (or French, German, Russian, or many other languages). For instance, a powerful example of the role of both pedagogical content knowledge and the value of instructional technology has been provided by June Phillips, who reports that in an e-mail exchange between a U.S. student in New York and a Chilean student:

> when [the] U.S. youngster, named Chema, sent a message of introduction to [the] Chilean keypal, some of the adjectives used in the message ended in *o* and some ended in *a* in spite of the student's record of more accurate responses on the worksheets, audio tapes, and computerized drills that came with the classroom text package. Chema received a response that said, *Me alegré mucho de recibir tu mensaje, pero aclárame amigo o amiga. ¿Cuál es tu sexo?* "I'm really glad to receive your message, but make it clear whether you are a [male] friend or [female] friend. Are you male or female?" Maybe, like so many language learners in the past, Chema will never travel to a country where Spanish is spoken, but today's student will communicate real messages with users of the target language. That single instance caused learning to occur for Chema, her teacher reported that she never again made an agreement error when talking about herself.
>
> (Phillips, 1998, p. 27)

The effective language educator must also have a detailed and in-depth knowledge of learners, learning and teaching styles, and possible barriers to learning. One example of what might be included here, for instance, would be an understanding of Howard Gardner's work on "multiple intelligences," which has the potential to revolutionize the teaching of languages (and much else) (see Gardner, 1983, 1991, 1993; Reid, 1998). Gardner argues that human intellectual competence is far too complex to be captured by a single conception of intelligence, and instead, he proposes a model of a number of distinct kinds of intelligence: verbal/linguistic intelligence, musical intelligence, mathematical/logical intelligence, visual/spatial intelligence, bodily/kinesthetic intelligence, intrapersonal intelligence, interpersonal intelligence, naturalist intelligence, existential intelligence, and moral intelligence (see Figure 7.1). Each of these "intelligences" can be effectively utilized in world language education, and good world language teaching will involve all of them in various contexts and settings (see Christison, 1998).

The world language educator must also be familiar with the broader social and cultural context in which she or he is to teach. This includes not only an understanding of the interpersonal interactions among students, but also the power relations in the classroom, the school, and society in general. In order to function effectively as an advocate for world language education, the world language educator needs to understand issues of educational governance, financing, and the politics and policies in her or his community that impact world language teaching and learning. Finally, the world language educator must be able to demonstrate a clear knowledge of educational ends, purposes, and values, especially with respect to the teaching and learning of foreign languages. In

Figure 7.1 The Theory of Multiple Intelligences

Type of Intelligence
Musical-Rhythmic
Visual-Spatial
Verbal-Linguistic
Logical-Mathematical
Bodily-Kinesthetic
Interpersonal
Intrapersonal
Naturalistic
Existential*
Moral*

*In 2009, Gardner added Existential Intelligence and Moral Intelligence to his original list of multiple intelligences.
(Based on Gardner, 1983, 1993)

other words, the world language educator should be able to clearly and forcefully articulate the rationale for world language study, and should be able to explain the ties of world language study to other aspects and goals of both liberal education and career education.

All of this taken together constitutes the knowledge base for the world language educator (see Freeman & Johnson, 2012; Watzke, 2007). It is important to understand that this compilation is in fact merely a heuristic device, since each individual world language educator will inevitably construct her or his own knowledge base. Thus, although an impressive (and even, perhaps, intimidating) summary, this conceptualization of the knowledge base is still inadequate, because it relies on an idealized, and simplistic, conception of what the world language educator actually does, and indeed only hints at what the real tasks of the world language educator in the classroom actually are.

The Real World of the Classroom Teacher

We have already suggested that much of what the classroom teacher does during the school day is to act as a decision-maker. In fact, Richard Shavelson has gone so far as to suggest that, "any teaching act is the result of a decision, either conscious or unconscious ... What distinguishes the exceptional teacher is not the ability to ask, say, a higher-order question, but the ability to decide when to ask such a question" (Shavelson, 1973, pp. 143–145). Consider the many different kinds of judgments and decisions that the typical teacher makes during her or his normal, daily routine. Every teacher makes curricular decisions, methodological decisions, decisions about individual children, their needs and problems, decisions about classroom management and organization, decisions about both personal and professional ethics, and so on – all areas that are reflected in and that are reflective of the knowledge base for teaching as a profession. The educational philosopher Robert Fitzgibbons has suggested that teachers make three types of decisions: those concerned with *educational outcomes* (that is, with what the goals or results of the educational experience should be), those concerned with the *matter of education* (that is, with *what* is, could be, or should be taught), and those concerned with the *manner of education* (that is, with *how* teaching should take place) (Fitzgibbons, 1981, pp. 13–14).

When a teacher makes decisions, she or he is doing more than merely taking a course of action or acting in a certain way. The process of decision-making should be a rational one, which means that the teacher (whether consciously or unconsciously) considers and weighs alternatives, and employs criteria to select a given option or course of action. Unfortunately, as Jere Brophy, a well-known educational researcher, once reported, "most studies of teachers' interactive decision-making portray it as more reactive than reflective, more intuitive than rational, and more routinized than conscious" (quoted in Irwin, 1987, p. 1).[3] *Good* teaching, however, inevitably requires reflective, rational and conscious decision-making. As Charles Silberman argued almost 50 years ago in his book *Crisis in the Classroom*, "We must find ways of stimulating public school teachers … to think about what they are doing and why they are doing it" (Silberman, 1971, p. 380). An important element in this process of reflective, rational and conscious decision-making is that we should be able to expect a teacher to be able to justify her or his decisions and actions in the classroom. Justification of decisions and actions, as Cornel Hamm explains, is actually a fairly simple and straightforward matter: "To provide a justification for a course of action is to provide good reasons or grounds for that course of action" (Hamm, 1989, p. 163). To be able to provide such justification, the teacher cannot rely either on instinct alone or on prepackaged sets of techniques. Instead, she or he must think about what is taking place and what options are available in a critical, analytic way. In other words, the teacher must engage in *reflection* about her or his practice.

Reflective Practice in World Language Education

Reflective practice can be understood as a cyclical process, moving from *reflection-for-practice* through *reflection-in-practice* and to *reflection-on-practice*, which then leads on to new *reflection-for-practice* (see Killion & Todnem, 1991; Norlander-Case, Reagan & Case, 1999; Reagan, Case & Brubacher, 2000; Richards & Lockhart, 1994; Schön, 1983, 1987).[4] Reflection-for-practice refers to the reflective planning and preparation that precedes the classroom teaching event. Included here are not only the formal lesson and unit planning engaged in by the teacher, but also, and arguably more important, the teacher's analysis of likely pedagogical, learning and management problems and challenges that might emerge in a particular class when dealing with a specific topic. All teachers, to some extent, engage in reflection-for-practice, though they do so with varying degrees of thoroughness and effectiveness. Reflection-on-practice takes place at the other end of the classroom teaching event; it refers to retrospective reflection on what took place, both positive and negative, during the classroom teaching event. All teachers engage in reflection-on-practice, though again, they do so in very different ways, some of which are far more productive and useful than others. Good reflection-on-practice leads, of course, to new reflection-for-practice, thus completing the cycle of reflective practice.

Distinct in kind from reflection-for-practice and reflection-on-practice is *reflection-in-practice*, which is concerned with the application of what Michael Polanyi has called "tacit knowledge" in the classroom setting (Polanyi, 1958, 1966). Reflection-in-practice involves the teacher's ability to utilize her or his unarticulated (and often unconscious) knowledge about content, pedagogy, and learners in the classroom context. It is this ability to engage in reflection-in-practice that, to a very significant extent, distinguishes the experienced master teacher from the novice. Both may well engage in effective, even exemplary, reflection-for-practice and reflection-on-practice, but only the experiential base of the master teacher allows for consistently effective reflection-in-practice. This experiential base develops only as a result of practice; it helps to explain why no new teacher is likely to be as effective as many more experienced classroom teachers.

Another way of thinking about the relationships among the different kinds of reflective practice is to note that both reflection-in-practice and reflection-on-practice are essentially *reactive* in nature, being distinguished primarily by *when* reflection takes place – with reflection-in-action referring to reflection in the midst of practice, and reflection-on-practice referring to reflection that takes place after an event. Reflection-for-action, on the other hand, is: "the desired outcome of both previous types of reflection. We undertake reflection, not so much to revisit the past or to become aware of the metacognitive process one is experiencing (both noble reasons in themselves), but to guide future action (the more practical purpose)" (Killion & Todnem, 1991, p. 15). In other words, reflection-for-practice is *proactive* in nature.

All three of these types of reflection – reflection-for-practice, reflection-on-practice, and reflection-in-practice – will be necessary components of reflective practice on the part of the world language teacher (see Akbari, 2007; Akbari, Behzadpoor & Dadvand, 2010; Farrell, 2014; Geyer, 2009; Pacheco, 2011). It is important to note that the relative significance of each of these three components of reflective practice may change over the course of a teacher's career; thus, as was noted earlier, for the novice teacher, reflection-for-practice and reflection-on-practice may be the most obvious ways in which her or his practice is distinguished, while for the more experienced teacher, reflection may be most clearly manifested in her or his reflection-in-practice. Further, the process of engaging in reflection-for-practice should be seen not as a linear one, but as an ongoing spiral, in which each of the elements of reflective practice are constantly involved in an interactive process of change and development. As we have seen, reflective practice involves what the teacher does *before* entering the classroom (in terms of her or his planning and preparation, for instance), *while* in the classroom (both while functioning as an educator and in all of the other roles expected of the classroom teacher), and retrospectively, *after* she or he has left the classroom.

A useful way of thinking about both the reflective teacher and the nature of the reflective practice in which she or he will engage has been provided by Judee Irwin, who has suggested that:

> A reflective/analytic teacher is one who makes teaching decisions on the basis of a conscious awareness and careful consideration of (1) the assumptions on which the decisions are based and (2) the

> technical, educational, and ethical consequences of those decisions. These decisions are made before, during and after teaching actions. In order to make these decisions, the reflective/analytic teacher must have an extensive knowledge of the content to be taught, pedagogical and theoretical options, characteristics of individual students, and the situational constraints in the classroom, school and society in which they work.
>
> (Irwin, 1987, p. 6)

Notice that this description includes virtually all of the issues that have been discussed thus far. We see that the reflective teacher is first and foremost a decision-maker, who must make her or his decisions consciously and rationally. Further, the reflective teacher must base her or his decisions and judgments on a solid body of content, including both technical and content knowledge, which are organized and reinterpreted according to her or his unique experiences.

From Reflective Practice to *Critical* Reflective Practice

What we have been discussing thus far is reflective practice and its implications for the classroom teacher. However, given the focus of this book, reflective practice on its own – whatever its many benefits may be – is not our ultimate objective. Rather, we are concerned with practice that is not merely reflective, but which is *both* reflective *and* critical. One way of thinking about this important distinction was provided in the 1970s by Max van Manen, who suggested a hierarchical model of *levels of reflectivity* (van Manen, 1977, pp. 205–208). He argued that there are three distinct levels of reflective practice, which can be seen, at least ideally, as paralleling the growth of the individual teacher from novice to expert or master teacher. The first level is concerned with the effective application of skills and technical knowledge in the classroom setting. At this first level, reflection entails the appropriate selection and use of instructional strategies and the like in the classroom. The second level involves reflection about the assumptions underlying specific classroom practices, as well as about the consequences of particular methodological strategies, curricula, and assessment approaches. In other words, at this second level of reflectivity teachers begin to apply educational criteria to teaching practice in order to make individual and independent decisions about pedagogical matters. Finally, the third level of reflectivity (the level at which the reflection becomes *critical reflection*) entails the questioning of moral, ethical and other types of normative criteria related directly and indirectly to the classroom (see Irwin, 1996). At this level, we are concerned not only with pedagogical matters, but with issues of equity, social justice, ethics, and so on. It is also at this level of reflectivity that we would expect the classroom teacher to become an active advocate for the role and place of world language study both in the curriculum and in our society more generally.

Another way of conceptualizing the distinction between reflective practice and critical reflective practice is to view reflective practice not in a hierarchical manner, but rather to focus on elements that appear to play significant roles in fostering reflection and reflective practice on the part of the classroom teacher. Georgea Sparks-Langer and Amy Colton, in a synthesis of the research on teachers' reflective thinking, have argued that there are three such elements: the *cognitive element*, the *narrative element*, and the *critical element* (Sparks-Langer & Colton, 1991). The cognitive element of reflective thinking is concerned with the knowledge that teachers need to master in order to make good decisions in and about the classroom situation. It is important to recognize that while all teachers, whether novice or expert, will for the most part have similar bodies of knowledge at their disposal, the *organization* and *structuring* of this knowledge may differ radically. Research conducted by cognitive psychologists has suggested that the *schemata*, or organized networks of facts, concepts, generalizations and experiences, of beginning and experienced teachers are very different in significant ways (see Sparks-Langer & Colton, 1991, pp. 37–38; Berliner, 1986). Since such *schemata* are constructed by teachers over time as a result of their experiences, it is not surprising that those who have been teaching for longer periods of time will often be able to make sense of and respond to a problematic or challenging situations in the classroom more quickly and effectively than are novices.[5] Studies which suggest that expert teachers are able to deal with changes in lesson plans and classroom situations far more successfully than are new teachers can be explained, according to Sparks-Langer and Colton, "because (1) many of the routines and the content were available [to the expert teachers] in memory as automatic scripts and (2) their rich schemata allowed the experts to quickly consider cues in the environment and access appropriate strategies" (Sparks-Langer & Colton, 1991, p. 38). *Schemata* of the sort discussed here are constructed naturally over time, but their development can be encouraged and supported by reflective practice. In other words, while good teaching practice does indeed depend on a strong experiential base, reflective practice can help us to speed up the development of such an experiential base in new teachers. At the same time that experience can, and frequently does, help the expert teacher to respond to changes and challenges in the classroom, it is important to note that there is also a risk of "negative socialization" – the process by which new teachers are assimilated into existing, traditional models and approaches in the school context, in spite of whatever they might have learned in their teacher preparation programs. As John Watzke has noted:

> Similar to research findings in other subject disciplines, the instructional practices of beginning [world language] teachers may initially be considered traditional, outdated, or even antithetical to their

> preservice preparation as control over students and the instructional content serve as a proxy for perceptions of successful teaching. Professional development of beginning teachers must support the ongoing transformation of pedagogical content knowledge in order to ensure that these early characteristics do not become lasting traits in long-term teaching careers.
>
> (Watzke, 2007, p. 63)

The second element of reflective thinking, the *narrative element*, has to do with teachers' narratives – that is, with their ability to describe and analyze what has taken place in their classroom, why it has taken place, what might have been done to change what took place, and what should be done following particular classroom events (see Connelly & Clandinin, 1990; Goswami & Stillman, 1987; Zeichner & Liston, 1987, 1996). Teacher accounts of their own experiences in the classroom take many forms, and serve a variety of different functions. A pre-service student's journal is an example of one fairly common type of narrative (see Vélez-Rendón, 2008a, 2008b). Other kinds of narrative discourse on the part of teachers include descriptions of critical events in the classroom, various types of logs and journals, conference reports completed jointly by teachers and supervisors or mentors, self-interviewing, peer observations followed by collaborative and cooperative discussions, and so on. The key aspect of the narrative element of reflective thinking is that such narratives, whatever their form, serve to contextualize the classroom experience both for the teacher himself or herself and for others, and by so doing, provide us with a much richer understanding of what takes place in the classroom and of the teacher's construction of reality than would otherwise be possible. Narrative accounts are extremely common, especially in the preparation of teachers as well as in qualitative research on classroom practices (see Antonek, McCormick & Donato, 2011; Bolton, 2010; Orland-Barak & Yinon, 2007), and there can be little doubt that they provide one of the most effective ways in which reflective practice can be encouraged and promoted.

The third element of reflective thinking is the *critical element*, which is concerned with "the moral and ethical aspects of social compassion and justice" (Sparks-Langer & Colton, 1991, p. 39). Concerns with issues of social justice and ethics in education have been common to educators and educational theorists throughout the history of education, and are clearly manifested in such common and important distinctions made by educators as that between educational *product goals* (that is, what we want to achieve in the classroom or the school) and *process goals* (that is, the restrictions that exist on how our product goals can be achieved) (see Teal & Reagan, 1973). Further, as part of her or his concern with critical reflective practice, the world language educator teacher must also demonstrate both ethical behavior and sensitivity as well as sociocultural awareness.[6] As Charles Case, Judith Lanier and Cecil Miskel have noted, "The attendant characteristics of professions include conditions of practice that allow professionals to apply this knowledge freely to the practical affairs of their occupation and to use their knowledge, judgment, and skill within the structures of the ethical code of the profession" (Case, Lanier & Miskel, 1986, p. 36). The critical element of reflective practice is a necessary part of all reflective practice, but as we shall see, *critical* reflective practice takes this element to a new and more powerful level – one more in keeping with our earlier discussion of critical pedagogy and world language education.

Such a conceptualization of the reflective practitioner makes clear how much is being expected of the classroom teacher by advocates of reflective practice. Why, one might ask, should a teacher devote so much time and energy to becoming a reflective practitioner? What are the benefits of reflective practice? There are in fact a number of benefits to be gained from reflective practice, but perhaps among the more compelling is that reflective practice is useful in helping to *empower* classroom teachers. As Catherine Fosnot has noted, "An empowered teacher is a reflective decision maker who finds joy in learning and in investigating the teaching/learning process – one who views learning as construction and teaching as a facilitating process to enhance and enrich development" (Fosnot, 1989, p. xi). Most important, though, reflective practice is a tool for individual teachers to improve their own teaching practice, and to become better, more proficient and more thoughtful professionals in their own right (see Wallace, 1991; Zeichner & Liston, 1987, 1996) – and hence, to improve student learning (Osterman & Kottkamp, 2004; Zubizarreta, 2009). *Critical* reflective practice, in short, entails all of the elements of reflective practice more generally, but also emphasizes the need to place educational practice in its social, historical and ideological context, and to deeply explore the underlying assumptions that govern both educational theory and pedagogical practice in a genuinely deep manner (see Brookfield, 2000; Howard, 2010).

Critical Literacy and World Language Education

An important part of critical reflective practice is the development of critical literacy. There is a substantial body of literature devoted to critical literacy, much of it outstanding, but it tends to focus on the nurturing and development of critical literacy for students rather than for teachers (see Cadiero-Kaplan 2002; McDaniel, 2004; Mulcahy, 2010). Although we share the concern with and commitment to promoting critical literacy in students, our concern here is more on the development of critical literacy in pre- and in-service teachers. The key facet of critical literacy is learning to read in a far different way than most of us are used to. Critical literacy is not synonymous with simply reading – it refers to a very special type of reading. Reading can be (and typically is) understood to refer to the process of decoding a text and comprehending that text. It also includes placing the text in a broader context, to ensure a clear, cogent and accurate understanding of the author's intention in producing the text. Critical literacy, however, goes far beyond this, asking us to join in what is better thought of as an on-going intellectual discussion and debate. This on-going discussion has been called the "human conversation" by some scholars, and basically means that we are placing the text not only in a particularistic context, but in a much broader one that takes into account the setting in which it was produced, the setting in which we are reading it, the socio-historical, political, and ideological frameworks in which it was developed and in which it is being read and (perhaps) applied. This means that reading a text critically is a much more in-depth process than simply reading a text.

A valuable way of conceptualizing critical literacy, at least metaphorically, is provided by the Jewish *Talmud*. Traditional study of the *Talmud* is a lifelong undertaking which involves intense study, discussion, comparison, debate, and argument (see Freedman, 2014; Küng, 1991, pp. 169–222; Steinsaltz, 1989). The *Talmud*,[7] which is the core text of Rabbinic Judaism, was produced between the third and sixth centuries CE. It constitutes the source of both *halakha* (religious law) and Jewish theology. It is not, however, collection of straightforward, logical arguments of the sort that most of us are familiar with. Rather, it employs its own unique logic and forms of reasoning.

The way that a page of *Talmud* is laid out provides us with an excellent way of thinking about what critical literacy might look like in practice. At the top of the page, all the way on the left, is the page number, while centered on the page is the page heading. In the center of the page is the Talmudic text itself. One the right-hand side of the page, next to the Talmudic text, is Rashi's commentary[8] on the text (written in a special script, called "Rashi Script"[9]). On the left-hand side of the page are commentaries by other Talmudic scholars and other references. So, on a single page one finds the basic text, the Rashi commentary on the text, several other (often disagreeing) commentaries, and additional reference materials. It is thus, as suggested earlier, an entire conversation that is taking place – but a conversation among different Rabbinic scholars that actually took place over centuries, in many different locales and among people who never actually meet one another. Although the case of the *Talmud* is an unusual one taken from a very particular religious context, the basic idea of approaching a text as part of an on-going conversation across time and place, and involving many readers, is an extremely valuable one in attempting to develop critical literacy.

Native Speakers as World Language Educators

Up to this point, we have at least implicitly been discussing the world language educator who is a native speaker of English and a second language user of the target language. Most world language teachers in the United States fall into this category, so it is understandable that this is the primary audience often addressed in the world language education literature. However, there are also significant numbers of world language educators whose first language is the target language that they teach. These teachers may themselves be immigrants, or may have grown up in the United States as speakers of a heritage language. The challenges faced by such individuals in the world language classroom are different in important ways from those faced by native speakers of English (see Schreffler, 2007). For instance, these teachers must often deal with conflicting language standards, norms, and attitudes. In addition, such teachers may face significant challenges with respect to English-medium tests designed for teacher certification. For these native or heritage language teachers, reflective practice provides a powerful means by which their own background knowledge and experiences can be utilized in contextualizing the teaching of the target language. Critical reflection is, in some ways, especially important for this group of teachers, both with respect to cultural and linguistic knowledge.

Conclusion

Writing about continuing education in the health professions, Stephen Brookfield noted:

> The concept of critical reflection is frequently invoked as a distinguishing feature of good practice ... But what exactly is critical reflection? How is it recognized? What are its benefits? How can it be incorporated into professional practice? ... the constituent elements of critical reflection ... provide an example of how a critically reflective approach can be taken toward continuous, formative evaluation.
> (Brookfield, 2005, p. 197)

In this chapter, we have attempted to follow Brookfield's suggestion with respect to its implications for world language education. Toward that end, we have examined a number of aspects of both reflective practice and critical reflective practice. We began by discussing the traditional debate about whether teaching is better understood and conceptualized as a kind of art, or rather as a kind of applied science. A case was made for the idea that this dichotomy is a misleading one, and that the concept of reflective practice can offer a useful solution to the apparent dilemma of "art or science." Next, we examined the knowledge base that is necessary for a person to become an effective classroom teacher generally, and how this applies to the specific case of the world language teacher – and to the real-world tasks of and challenges faced by the world language educator – were then explored. The idea of reflective practice as it has emerged in the educational literature was examined, and the ways in which reflective practice is both foundational for and different from critical reflective practice was discussed. The place of critical literacy was then briefly explored, and the case of the native speaker of the target language was discussed in light of the concept of critical reflective practice.

Questions for Reflection and Discussion

1 In this chapter, the authors consider the concept of the knowledge base for a world language educator in general terms. Can you add specificity to the different elements that they identify as necessary for effective teaching practice? What content have you learned in your (a) language classes, (b) education classes, (c) linguistics classes, and (d) other classes, that you believe will prove to be essential in functioning as a classroom teacher?
2 The authors assert that, "Native speakers certainly have some advantages … but merely *being* a native speaker of a language in no way prepares one to teach it." Do you agree or disagree with this view? Why?
3 What are the implications of the idea that reflective practice can occur "only when the individual [student] is faced with a *real* problem that she or he needs to resolve" for the methodology and content of the world language classroom?
4 Describe an instance in which you changed your teaching *during a lesson*. Explain your rationale for the change, and discuss the results.
5 Identify examples of knowledge related to teaching and learning a language that one does not know simply by virtue of being a native speaker of the language. What do you believe are the implications of this part of the knowledge base?

Notes

1 This observation does not apply, however, in certain specialized kinds of world language teaching and learning settings – for instance, in "language for specific purposes" programs (see Donna, 2000, p. 70).
2 We recognize, of course, that these general claims about appropriateness may not apply in specific settings. Obviously, the issue here is to ensure that the content of the learning experience is appropriate *for the particular learners being taught.*
3 It is important to note here that this criticism is not so much directed toward teachers as it is of the environment in which teachers work. For the quality of teacher decision-making to improve, more is required than simply changing teacher preparation. In addition, the many structural and organizational barriers to reflective practice must also be addressed – hence, calls for reflective practice properly understood inevitably involve concomitant changes in school organization and culture.

4 "Reflective practice" in educational contexts is, then, far more than simply "thinking about" teaching. It involves a deliberate, critical and on-going kind of self-evaluation, and is oriented not just to the understanding of classroom practice, but also toward its improvement.
5 It is important to note that we tend to assume that more experience in the classroom automatically translates into greater pedagogical skill – an assumption that is demonstrably false in many cases. There is an old saying in educational circles that there is an important difference between having 30 years of teaching experience and one year of teaching experience repeated 30 times.
6 The ethical dimensions of teaching are an incredibly important aspect of teaching as a profession. John Goodlad's discussions of the "moral dimensions of schooling" are central to this point, as are the more focused explorations of "teacher ethics" and professional codes of ethics in the teacher education literature (see Goodlad, 1994, 1997; Strike, Haller & Soltis, 1988; Strike & Soltis, 1992).
7 Although we are discussing "the" *Talmud* here, there are actually two different *Talmuds*: the *Babylonian Talmud* (*Talmud Bavli*) and the *Jerusalem Talmud* (*Talmud Yerushalmi*). The former was first produced in Babylon around the year 500 CE, although its final form was only determined later. The *Talmud Yerushalmi* was produced somewhat earlier (around the 4th century CE) in Galilee. In general, when the term *Talmud* is used, it is the *Babylonian Talmud* that is being discussed.
8 Rashi was Rabbi Shlomo Yitzchaki, a medieval French rabbi and scholar, who is generally referred to by the acronym "Rashi," Rashi wrote a comprehensive commentary of the *Talmud*, as well as one on the *Tanakh*. His work is recognized for its clear, concise and accurate approach to the fundamental meaning of texts.
9 "Rashi script" is a special typeface in which Rashi's commentaries are traditionally printed. It is, basically, a semi-cursive typeface. There is no connection between Rashi script and Rashi himself; the script was introduced by printers at some point in the 15th century CE.

References

Akbari, R. (2007). Reflections on reflection: A critical appraisal of reflective practices in L2 teacher education. *System*, 35(2): 192–207.

Akbari, R., Behzadpoor, F. & Dadvand, B. (2010). Development of English language teaching reflection inventory. *System*, 38(2): 211–227.

Antonek, J., McCormick, D. & Donato, R. (2011). The student teacher portfolio as autobiography: Developing a professional identity. *The Modern Language Journal*, 81(1): 15–27.

Berliner, D. (1986). In pursuit of the expert pedagogue. *Educational Researcher*, 15(7): 5–13.

Bolton, G. (2010). *Reflective practice: Writing and professional development* (3rd ed.). Los Angeles, CA: Sage.

Brookfield, S. (2000). The concept of critically reflective practice. In A. Wilson & E. Hayes (Eds.), *Handbook of adult and continuing education* (new ed.) (pp. 33–49). San Francisco, CA: Jossey-Bass.

Brookfield, S. (2005). Critically reflective practice. *Journal of Continuing Education in the Health Professions*, 18(4): 197–205.

Byram, M. (2012). Language awareness and (critical) cultural awareness: Relationships, comparisons and contrasts. *Language Awareness*, 21(1–2):5–13.

Cadiero-Kaplan, K. (2002). Literacy ideologies: Critically engaging the language curriculum. *Language Arts*, 79(5): 371–381.

Case, C., Lanier, J. & Miskel, C. (1986). The *Holmes Group Report*: Impetus for gaining professional status for teachers. *Journal of Teacher Education*, 37(4): 36–43.

Christison, M. (1998). An introduction to multiple intelligence theory and second language learning. In J. Reid (Ed.), *Understanding learning styles in the second language classroom* (pp. 1–14). Upper Saddle River, NJ: Prentice Hall Regents.

Connelly, F. & Clandinin, D. (1990). Stories of experience and narrative inquiry. *Educational Researcher*, 19(5): 2–14.

Curtain, H. & Dahlberg, C. (2004). *Languages and children, making the match: New languages for young learners, grades K-8* (3rd ed.). Boston, MA: Pearson.

Dewey, J. (1910). *How we think*. Boston, MA: D.C. Heath.

Dewey, J. (1933). *How we think: A restatement of the relations of reflective thinking to the educative process* (2nd rev. ed.). Lexington, MA: D.C. Heath.

Dewey, J. (1938). *Logic: The theory of inquiry*. New York: Henry Holt.

Dewey, J. (1976). The relationship of thought and its subject matter. In J. Boydston (Ed.), *John Dewey: The middle works, volume 2 (1902–1903)* (pp. 298–315). Carbondale, IL: Southern Illinois University Press. (Original work published 1903)

Donna, S. (2000). *Teach business English*. Cambridge: Cambridge University Press.

Farrell, T. (2014). *Promoting teacher reflection in second language education: A framework for TESOL professionals*. New York: Routledge.

Fitzgibbons, R. (1981). *Making educational decisions: An introduction to philosophy of education*. New York: Harcourt Brace Jovanovich.

Fook, J. (2006). *Beyond reflective practice: Reworking the "critical" in critical reflection*. Keynote address presented at the "Professional Lifelong Learning: Beyond Reflective Practice" conference held at Trinity and All Saints College, Leeds, UK, July 3.

Fosnot, C. (1989). *Enquiring teachers, enquiring learners: A constructivist approach to teaching*. New York: Teachers College Press.

Franklin, P., Laurence, D. & Welles, E. (Eds.). (1999). *Preparing a nation's teachers: Models for English and foreign language programs*. New York: Modern Language Association of America.

Freedman, H. (2014). *The Talmud: A biography*. London: Bloomsbury.

Freeman, D. & Johnson, K. (2012). Reconceptualizing the knowledge-base of language teacher education. *TESOL Quarterly*, 32(3): 397–417.

Gardner, H. (1983). *Frames of mind: The theory of multiple intelligences*. New York: Basic Books.

Gardner, H. (1991). *The unschooled mind: How children think and how schools should teach*. New York: Basic Books.

Gardner, H. (1993). *Multiple intelligences: The theory in practice*. New York: Basic Books.

Geyer, N. (2009). Reflective practices in foreign language teacher education: A view through micro and macro windows. *Foreign Language Annals*, 41(4): 627–638.

Ghaye, T. (2010). *Teaching and learning through reflective practice: A practical guide for positive action* (2nd ed.). New York: Routledge.

Goodlad, J. (1994). *Educational renewal: Better teachers, better schools*. San Francisco, CA: Jossey-Bass.

Goodlad, J. (1997). *In praise of education*. New York: Teachers College Press.

Goswami, D. & Stillman, P. (Eds.). (1987). *Reclaiming the classroom: Teacher research as an agency for change*. Portsmouth, NH: Heinemann.

Guntermann, G. (Ed.). (1993). *Developing language teachers for a changing world*. Lincolnwood, IL: National Textbook Company, in conjunction with the American Council on the Teaching of Foreign Languages.

Hamm, C. (1989). *Philosophical issues in education: An introduction*. New York: Falmer Press.

Hedge, T. (2000). *Teaching and learning in the language classroom*. Oxford: Oxford University Press.

Howard, T. (2010). Culturally relevant pedagogy: Ingredients for critical teacher reflection. *Theory into Practice*, 42(3): 195–202.

Irwin, J. (1987). What is a reflective/analytical teacher? Unpublished manuscript, University of Connecticut, School of Education, Storrs, CT.

Irwin, J. (1996). *Empowering ourselves and transforming schools: Educators making a difference*. Albany, NY: State University of New York Press.

Jay, J. & Johnson, K. (2002). Capturing complexity: A typology of reflective practice for teacher education. *Teaching and Teacher Education*, 18(1): 73–85.

Killion, J. & Todnem, G. (1991). A process for personal theory building. *Educational Leadership*, 48(6): 14–16.

Küng, H. (1991). *Das Judentum: Die religiöse Situation der Zeit*. Zürich: Piper München.

Loughran, J. (1996). *Developing reflective practice: Learning about teaching and learning through modelling*. New York: Routledge.

Loughran, J. (2002). Effective reflective practice: In search of meaning in learning about teaching. *Journal of Teacher Education*, 53(1): 33–43.

Macaro, E. (2002). Analyzing student teachers' codeswitching in foreign language classrooms: Theories and decision making. *The Modern Language Journal*, 85(4): 531–548.

McDaniel, C. (2004). Critical literacy: A questioning stance and the possibility for change. *The Reading Teacher*, 57(5): 472–481.

Mulcahy, C. (2010). *Marginalized literacies: Critical literacy in the language arts classroom*. Charlotte, NC: Information Age Publishing.

Norlander-Case, K., Reagan, T. & Case, C. (1999). *The professional teacher: The preparation and nurturance of the reflective practitioner*. San Francisco, CA: Jossey-Bass.

Orland-Barak, L. & Yinon, H. (2007). When theory meets practice: What student teachers learn from guided reflection on their own classroom discourse. *Teaching and Teacher Education*, 23(3): 957–969.

Osterman, K. & Kottkamp, R. (2004). *Reflective practice for educators: Professional development to improve student learning* (2nd ed.). Thousand Oaks, CA: Corwin.

Pacheco, A. (2011). Reflective teaching and its impact on foreign language teaching. *Actualidades Investigativas en Educación*, 5: 1–19.

Phillips, J. (1998). Media for the message: Technology's role in the Standards. *CALICO Journal*, 16: 25–36.

Polyani, M. (1958). *Personal knowledge: Towards a post-critical philosophy*. Chicago, IL: University of Chicago Press.

Polyani, M. (1966). *The tacit dimension*. Chicago, IL: University of Chicago Press.

Reagan, T., Case, C. & Brubacher, J. (2000). *Becoming a reflective educator: How to build a culture of inquiry in the schools* (2nd ed.). Thousand Oaks, CA: Corwin.

Reid, J. (Ed.). (1998). *Understanding learning styles in the second language classroom*. Upper Saddle River, NJ: Prentice Hall Regents.

Richard-Amato, P. (1996). *Making it happen: Interaction in the second language classroom, from theory to practice* (2nd ed.). White Plains, NY: Longman.

Richards, J. (1998). *Beyond training: Perspectives on language teacher education*. Cambridge: Cambridge University Press.

Richards, J. & Lockhart, C. (1994). *Reflective teaching in second language classrooms*. Cambridge: Cambridge University Press.

Schmitt, N. (2000). *Vocabulary in language teaching*. Cambridge: Cambridge University Press.

Schön, D. (1983). *The reflective practitioner: How professionals think in action*. New York: Basic Books.

Schön, D. (1987). *Educating the reflective practitioner*. San Francisco, CA: Jossey-Bass.

Schreffler, S. (2007). Hispanic heritage language speakers in the United States: Linguistic exclusion in education. *Critical Inquiry in Language Studies*, 4(4): 25–34.

Shavelson, R. (1973). What is the most basic teaching skill? *Journal of Teacher Education*, 24(2): 144–151.

Shulman, L. (1987). Knowledge and teaching: Foundations of the new reform. *Harvard Educational Review*, 57(1): 1–22.

Silberman, C. (1971). *Crisis in the classroom*. New York: Random House.

Sparks-Langer, G. & Colton, A. (1991). Synthesis of research on teachers' reflective thinking. *Educational Leadership*, 48(6): 37–44.

Steinsaltz, A. (1989). *The Talmud: The Steinsaltz edition, A reference guide*. New York: Random House.

Strike, K., Haller, E. & Soltis, J. (1988). *The ethics of school administration*. New York: Teachers College Press.

Strike, K. & Soltis, J. (1992). *The ethics of teaching* (2nd ed.). New York: Teachers College Press.

Teal, S. & Reagan, G. (1973). Educational goals. In J. Frymier (Ed.), *A school for tomorrow* (pp. 37–84). Berkeley, CA: McCutchan.

Van Doren, M. (1959). *Liberal education*. Boston, MA: Beacon Press.

van Manen, J. (1977). Linking ways of knowing with ways of being practical. *Curriculum Inquiry*, 6(3): 205–208.

van Manen, M. (1995). On the epistemology of reflective practice. *Teachers and Teaching: Theory and Practice*, 1(1): 33–50.

Vélez-Rendón, G. (2008a). From student to teacher: A successful transition, *Foreign Language Annals*, 39(2): 320–333.

Vélez-Rendón, G. (2008b). Second language teacher education: A review of the literature. *Foreign Language Annals*, 35(4): 457–467.

Wallace, M. (1991). *Training foreign language teachers: A reflective approach*. Cambridge: Cambridge University Press.

Watzke, J. (2007). Foreign language pedagogical knowledge: Toward a developmental theory of beginning teacher practices. *The Modern Language Journal*, 91(1): 63–82.

Zeichner, K. & Liston, D. (1987). Teaching student teachers to reflect. *Harvard Educational Review*, 57(1): 23–48.

Zeichner, K. & Liston, D. (1996). *Reflective teaching: An introduction*. Mahwah, NJ: Lawrence Erlbaum Associates.

Zubizarreta, J. (2009). *The learning portfolio: Reflective practice for improving student learning* (2nd ed.). San Francisco, CA: Jossey-Bass.

8 World Language Education, Critical Pedagogy and Social Justice

Toward *Conscientização* [1]

Perhaps nowhere has there been more significant change in the teaching of world languages in the past twenty years than in the tools available for bringing the insights of critical pedagogy into the classroom. ACTFL has not only created a special interest group addressing issues of social justice, but the volume published by ACTFL, *Words and Actions: Teaching Languages through the Lens of Social Justice*, is already in its second edition (Glenn, Weseley & Wassell, 2014). Professional conferences now regularly include panels and presentations on issues related to the development of a critical pedagogy for world language education, whether specific to issues of social justice or seeking to address broader emphases such as intercultural competence or content-based teaching. Finally, more and more teacher education programs – both in the U.S. and around the world – are working to incorporate critical perspectives to ensure that new teachers are not only familiar with critical pedagogy but also well-grounded in understandings of how critical pedagogy can be implemented in the classroom.

Ira Shor has suggested that critical pedagogy refers to:

> habits of thought, reading, writing, and speaking which go beneath surface meaning, first impressions, dominant myths, official pronouncements, traditional clichés, received wisdom, and mere opinions, to understand the deep meaning, root causes, social context, ideology, and personal consequences of any action, event, object, process, organization, experience, text, subject matter, policy, mass media, or discourse.
>
> (Shor, 1992, p. 129)

This is useful as far as it goes, but it is inadequate as a complete explanation of what is a very complex set of ideas. In fact, critical pedagogy is difficult to define, in part because it does not, in the words of one of its leading proponents, Peter McLaren, "constitute a homogenous set of ideas" (McLaren, 2003, pp. 185–186). Rather, critical pedagogy is conceptualized and manifested in a wide variety of ways by many different scholars and educators who, while sharing certain common assumptions and objectives, differ in many other important ways (see Darder, Torres & Baltodano, 2009; Denzin, 2003; Freire, 2002a, 2002b, 2002c, 2002d; Gay, 1995; Giroux, 1981, 1983, 1988a, 1988b, 1991, 1992a, 1992b, 1994, 1997a, 1997b, 2001a, 2001b, 2003a, 2003b, 2004, 2005, 2008, 2010, 2011; Giroux & McLaren, 1986; Giroux & Simon, 1988; Gruenewald, 2003; Kanpol, 1999; Kincheloe, 2008; McLaren, 1988, 1989, 2002, 2003, 2005, 2015; McLaren & Kincheloe, 2007; Morrow, 2002; Wink, 2000; Young, 1993). At its heart, critical pedagogy seeks "to empower the powerless and transform existing social inequalities and injustices" (McLaren, 2003, p. 186). It is, as Joan Wink suggests, "a process that enables teachers and learners to join together in asking fundamental questions about knowledge, justice, and equity in their own classroom, school, family, and community" (Wink, 2000, p. 71).

Critical pedagogy has its roots in the Frankfurt School (*Frankfurter Schule*), an intellectual movement associated with the *Institut für Sozialforschung* (Institute for Social Research) founded in Germany during the time of the Weimar Republic (1918 to 1933).[2] Essentially, the intellectuals, academics, activists, and political dissidents who constituted the Frankfurt School were seeking to understand the political milieu of their own age in an attempt to transform social reality. Building on the work of the Frankfurt School, from the late 1960s onwards progressive educators around the world have been developing both the theoretical and practical frameworks needed to apply such perspectives to the field of education. The foundation of much of contemporary critical pedagogy is Paolo Freire's 1968 book *The Pedagogy of the Oppressed*. Freire, a professor at the University of Recife in Brazil, sought in this and other works to develop a philosophy of adult education that would demonstrate solidarity with the poor and oppressed in their struggle to survive by engaging them in a dialogue of greater awareness and analysis. Freire (1973, 1974, 2002a, 2002b, 2002c, 2002d) explored the conservative role and functions of the school in considerable detail. He argued that dominant cultures (for instance, in contemporary American society, the Anglo-American culture) tend to overlook the wants and needs of dominated cultures that co-exist with these dominant cultures. Freire suggested that schools, as social institutions involved in the maintenance of the *status quo*, generally function to impose the values of the dominant culture on dominated groups in society. Basic literacy skills, such as reading and writing, can sometimes thus become for dominated groups acts of memorization and repetition, rather than acts of reflection on meaning and critical translation into the student's own culture. This insight is particularly important in the context of education in the United States. In the past half-century, an extensive body of scholarly literature has emerged dealing with almost every aspect of critical pedagogy and the application of critical pedagogy in different disciplinary fields.

Critical Pedagogy and Public Schooling

For much of our history, it has been the family that has been the primary socializing force in the United States for both children and adults (see Demos, 1971, 2000). The family was the major source of economic activity: the home was the center of work for most Americans in what was, until the mid- to late 19th century, a largely agrarian society. Parents were largely responsible for the education of their children, which entailed literacy, numeracy and religion, as well as for ensuring that children had the appropriate and necessary skills for adulthood (for boys, most often this meant farming skills, while for girls it meant preparation for their future roles as wives and mothers). Together with the church, families played a key role in both religious instruction and religious practice in a largely Protestant America. Finally, it was the family rather than institutions (and especially State institutions) that were responsible for providing different for sorts of welfare, including medical care, housing and care for the elderly, and so on. As many of these functions came to be taken over by the State, in whole or in part, this shift in responsibility from the home and family to State institutions made it increasingly possible for the government carry out a variety of social agendas, and this was nowhere clearer than in the case of education and schooling.

From its very beginnings, schooling in our society has been concerned with meeting social, political and economic needs. In understanding schooling at different times and in different places, an analytic framework that includes the nexus of a society's political economy and ideology, as well as its institutions of schooling, is extremely valuable. The political economy of a society includes its various social, economic and political institutions and processes, while its ideology includes dominant and typically shared, beliefs, values and habits of thought. As Steven Tozer, Guy Senese, and Paul Violas observed, "The interactive relationship among political economy, ideology, and schooling becomes clearer when they are examined in different historical circumstances" (Tozer et al., 2013, p. 10). This complex nexus can be seen, for instance, in colonial New England, where a theocratic agricultural and emerging merchant society sought to use educational institutions to ensure basic literacy, primarily for religious purposes – an importance that was manifested clearly in the 1647 *Old Deluder Satan Act*, which required townships to assume responsibility for the literacy education of children (principally with respect to biblical literacy) when it became clear that parents were not adequately doing so. The expansion of the country into the Old Northwest created new needs as it became increasingly important, especially following the American Revolution and the establishment of the United States as a new political entity, to create a shared national identity and culture in a country characterized by large distances and an already diverse population. In the 19th century, as American society became increasingly urbanized and industrialized, and as the population of the society became even more diverse, these social, economic and educational functions – and larger and larger parts of each – came to be seen as the responsibility of the State. At the heart of these changes were questions about the nature and future of the society that was being created: what are the role and purposes of schooling in a democratic society? To what extent are schools conservative institutions that should be dedicated to the protection of the *status quo*, and to what extent should they seek to change society and improve the general welfare of all of the people in the society? Who should control the schools? Who should determine the content of the curriculum? How should the schools be funded – by all in society, or only by those who use them? These same questions are being debated today as we reach the end of the first two decades of the 21st century. As teachers, administrators, parents and other citizens seek to come to grips with such questions, it is necessary to reflect on our values, determine individual and group positions, and then develop the kinds of schools and schooling which will not only meet the wants and aspirations of the youth in their classrooms, but also the needs of the society writ large (see Goodlad, 1994, 1997).

Emancipatory and Transformative Schooling

Education can be emancipating and transforming, not only for individuals but also for the society as a whole – and, in fact, for both the dominant and dominated cultures (see McLaren & Leonard, 1993). Although emancipatory and transformative educational experiences remain relatively uncommon in U.S. public schools, they have received significant support and attention, especially among advocates of critical pedagogy (see, for instance, Giroux, 1991, 1992a, 1992b, 1994, 1997a, 1997b). What critical pedagogy offers, basically, is the recognition that schooling – *all* schooling – is an intrinsically *political* activity, and that efforts to present it as "objective" or "neutral" are not only misguided but fundamentally misleading and even potentially dangerous. As McLaren has argued,

> critical pedagogy examines schools both in their historical context and as part of the existing social and political fabric that characterizes the dominant society. Critical pedagogy poses a variety of counterlogics to the positivistic, ahistorical, and depoliticized analysis employed by both liberal and conservative critics of schooling … Fundamentally concerned with the centrality of politics and power in our understanding of how schools work, critical theorists have produced work centering on the political economy of schooling, the state and education, the representation of texts, and the construction of student subjectivity.
>
> (McLaren, 1989, p. 159)

The various institutions dedicated to providing education in society can certainly be used to promote democracy and democratic values (see Gutman, 1999), but they can also be used to perpetuate an unjust and inequitable *status quo*. As Henry Giroux explained, "Central to the development of critical pedagogy is the need to explore how pedagogy functions as a cultural practice to *produce* rather than merely *transmit* knowledge within the asymmetrical relations of power that structure teacher–student relations" (Giroux, 1992a, p. 98). What, then, are the implications of critical pedagogy for the world language educator? World language education can certainly be analyzed from a critical perspective. As Terry A. Osborn has argued,

> the traditions that typically frame research and practice in language education have competed with the realities of growing cultural interdependence and a shift in pressure to assimilate in some areas of public life in the United States. As a result, the politics of cultural control have been either deemphasized or overlooked as most in the field have settled for technicist formulas or inquiry into the nature of language learning that springs from positivistic or interpretivistic paradigms.
>
> (Osborn, 2000, pp. 123–124)

Such perspectives on the teaching and learning of world languages are invaluable, for they force us to ask fundamental questions not only about *what* we are attempting to accomplish, but also *why* we are trying to achieve these ends. It is all too easy for us to rely on platitudes about the role of world language education for the individual and for society, just as it is far too easy for us to blame others for the lack of success that world language education so often experiences. However, critical pedagogy has implications not only for understanding our failures, but also provides us with some powerful ideas for how world language education could function as a positive and constructive force in American education.

Critical pedagogy requires that we reexamine not only the purposes of world language instruction, but even more, that we identify the hidden (and often not-so-hidden) biases about language, social class, power, and equity that underlie language use. From a critical perspective, world language education is not only about the teaching and learning of a second or additional linguistic system, but is also about social and cultural knowledge, and, perhaps even more, about helping students to develop critical approaches to examining and understanding such knowledge. As Osborn has noted:

> Indeed, most [language educators] recognize that, even under optimum conditions, non-native language learning is difficult. Every day, language teachers throughout the country enter classrooms to attempt what seems to be impossible … But in the shadow of such

> pessimistic odds, renewal of our professional vision in the 20th century occurred with surprising regularity. With such a rich history of effort behind us, the challenges of critical reflection and language education may give one pause, but the greatest traditions of the profession will drive us to rise to the challenge in the 21st century ... "[World language education] is unsurpassed in its power to liberate the mind and spirit from the prisons of cultural provincialism, servile ideological conformity, and social class distinctions, thereby freeing the individual person to think for herself or himself." This sentiment ... can begin to be more credible every day. And critical reflection in the language classroom will serve as a powerful means to that end.
>
> (Osborn, 2000, p. 124, quoting Idaho State Department of Education, 1994, p. 22)

It is, then, toward the effective utilization of this means that this book has been written, and we invite you to join with us in making such critical reflection a central part of world language teaching and learning.

When the Classroom Door Closes ...

In PK-12 school settings, we have often heard the expression that "what happens when the classroom door closes is the teacher's business." This claim, which we believe to have been far more true in the past than in the present, is intended to emphasize the autonomy of the teacher in the face of prescriptive formulas designed to constrain and control the many aspects of teaching activities. It is, when understood in this way, an effort to point to the ability of the classroom teacher to resist many of the more negative messages and mandated practices – especially those concerning languages and the learning of foreign languages – that are common in our society. It is also a recognition of the transformational power that language education can have. World language classrooms are sites of struggle, and language educators have the ability to join in this struggle in ways that advance the causes of social equity and justice.

At the same time, though, it is precisely when the classroom door closes that the world language classroom paradoxically needs to become more open, to involve the voices of others in the field, in the communities in which we teach, among our students themselves, and through honest exchanges as we invite others to join us in the dialogue and learn to listen to one another. It involves forsaking what is "foreign" about non-English languages (and even non-standard varieties of English), and seeking common ground that is more than identifying with specific national boundaries. Social justice as an orientation for world language education requires the rejection of the nation-state as the primary force in determining how curricula are established and evaluated. As Joel Spring has explained:

> Nation-states and global institutions such as the World Bank share an interest in creating an industrial and consumerist paradigm in students' minds for interpreting world events. When, in strong nation-states like Singapore and the United States, government officials refer to attacks on the nation's "way of life," they are usually referring to attacks on the ability of people to work for the consumption of goods. The industrial and consumerist paradigm results in students' evaluating world events according to their effect on economic growth and the equal opportunity to consume. The hidden curriculum of schools is the imparting to students an industrial and consumerist paradigm.
>
> (Spring, 2003, p. 165)

This consumerist paradigm is quite evident in most contemporary world language classrooms. We involve students in transactions that only thinly veil an ideology of trade. The teacher provides students with information, and students provide information back to the teacher – a fundamentally transactional model. The teacher provides information about shopping in and travelling to other places, and the students provide information about hobbies, families, school schedules, and so on. Though these are certainly part of the human experience, they are not the whole of the human experience. We can put this a different way: in the lives of those who speak other languages, how do they experience love, grief, pain, doubt, fear, and outrage? Do they experience racism, sexism, ageism, ableism, and linguicism? Do they explore their sexual identity and gender orientation? Are they even free to do so? Do they wonder about God and matters of faith? What are their views about climate change and global warming? These experiences are also human – indeed, they are profoundly human – but they are not particularly consumer-oriented, nor are they discussed in the typical curriculum of the world language classroom.

Spring contrasts the consumerist approach with those advocated by human rights and environmental educators, who call for more activist citizenship and the evaluation of world events in light of their effects on human rights or the biosphere, respectively. If we accept his argument, then we must assume a position on world language teaching that includes the evaluation of curricula based on their effects on promoting positive cross-national and cross-cultural understanding. Understandably, there will need to be a balance between the language skill and language understanding. In fact, this balance is one of the more important challenges that we face today.

Sources of Inspiration for a Social Justice Pedagogy

It should be clear by this point that a central focus of our concern with critical pedagogy is the closely related concept of social justice, and of pedagogy aimed at achieving social justice. To be sure, the idea of "social justice" is every bit as problematic as that of critical pedagogy: efforts to provide a clear and concise definition of social justice pedagogy seem to be almost certain to fail. And yet, as with critical pedagogy, this does not mean that the goal is not worthwhile (see Adams & Bell with Goodman & Yoshi, 2016; Ayers, Hunt & Quinn, 1998; Kumashiro, 2015; Hawkins, 2011). One powerful way in which we can think about social justice has been provided by Lee Anne Bell, who writes that:

> Social justice is both a goal and a process. The goal of social justice is full and equitable participation of people from all social identity groups in a society that is mutually shaped to meet their needs. The process for attaining the goal of social justice should also be democratic and participatory, respectful of human diversity and group differences, and inclusive and affirming of human agency and capacity for working collaboratively with others to create change. Domination cannot be ended through coercive tactics that recreate domination in new forms ... a "power with" vs. "power over" ... paradigm is necessary for enacting social justice goals.
>
> (Bell, 2016, p. 3)

Social justice pedagogy is at the core of *Pedagogy of the Oppressed*, but the concern with achieving the goals of social justice through education did not actually originate with Freire. One of the earliest efforts at popular education with such concerns was that of the Danish *Folkehøjskole* (the Folk High School), which spread not only to many parts of Europe but also to the United States. The original concept of the *Folkehøjskole* is credited to the Danish theologian and writer Nikolaj Grundtvig, and the first *Folkehøjskole* opened in Rødding in 1844. Basically, the *Folkehøjskole* was an effort to create a popular, democratic alternative to élite educational institutions that would provide individuals with a chance at what we would today call "lifelong learning," and which was characterized by a focus on personal development, creative and innovative pedagogy, and a degree of openness unheard of in other kinds of 19th century educational institutions. In the United States, the conception of the *Folkehøjskole* was adapted by Myles Horton when he founded the Highlander Folk School in Monteagle, Tennessee, in 1932 (see Adams, 2007; Adams, 1975; Glen, 1996; Horton, 1989; Horton & Freire, 1990). The underlying philosophical orientation of the Highlander Folk School was always something of a work in progress:

> [Highlander] is deliberately vague about its governing concepts, letting the people it serves and the times in which they live define precisely what brotherhood, democracy, mutuality, and united social action mean. These ideals change as people change. Highlander

> changes with them and avoids learning dictated from specific theory, learning that, by nature, would curtail freedom.
>
> (Adams, 1975, p. 206)

As Horton pointed out, the program at Highlander had specific features, and these features need to be kept in mind in contemplating of a new form of world language education:

> There were two kinds of pre-conditions, the School believed, to developing an educational program which could basically influence community life. First, there was the relationship between the school and the community. The school and its teachers, it was emphasized, needed to be "a natural part of community life" … The other necessary pre-condition had to originate within the community: some generally perceived crisis situation which could rouse people to want to do something …. The community program was to include, henceforth, not only discussion of subjects of concern and social and recreational activities, but direct participation in achieving an improved (if not a new) local social order.
>
> (Horton, 1989, p. 47)

Grundtvig, Horton, Freire, as well as more recent critical pedagogues, all recognize that the work of education is inherently value-laden. However, they also realize that although these values serve as motivation for educators to work to undo the negative effects of discrimination found in educational programming, a different danger emerges. As Freire has explained:

> It happens, however, that as they cease to be exploiters or indifferent spectators or simply the heirs of exploitation and move to the side of the exploited, they almost always bring with them the marks of their origin: their prejudices and their deformations, which include a lack of confidence in the people's ability to think, to want, and to know … Accordingly, these adherents to the people's cause constantly run the risk of falling into a type of generosity as malefic as that of the oppressors … They talk about the people, but they do not trust them, and trusting the people is the indispensable precondition for revolutionary change.
>
> (Freire, 2002d, pp. 55–56)

Put another way, if world language educators proceed to teach differently in an effort to engage in social justice work, they must be cautious not to do so from the standpoint of "liberator" or as the "spokesperson" for the exploited, or "comforter" of those in pain. Instead, they must trust that the voices of those who have been disenfranchised will speak for themselves. They must, to be frank, trust the people. Since trust in the people is an indispensable precondition to a pedagogy of social justice, then world language classrooms must begin to embrace the peoples in the United States and abroad as part of the study of languages in ways they have not done so before.

Implementing Social Justice Education in the World Language Classroom

There have been numerous efforts to find ways to effectively introduce concerns about social justice into the world language classroom. Since the publication of our earlier book *The Foreign Language Educator in Society: Toward a Critical Pedagogy* in 2002, and Osborn's *Teaching World Languages for Social Justice: A Sourcebook of Principles and Practices* in 2006, great strides have been made in providing teachers concrete examples based on real classroom experiences. None has been more impressive nor impactful than Cassandra Glynn, Pamela Weseley and Beth Wassell's *Words and Actions: Teaching Languages Through the Lens of Social Justice*, which was published in 2014. This volume includes an abundance of insightful connections to world language education, including products, practices, and perspectives. Products include access to tangible and intangible resources. Practices include issues that arise from interactions among people.

Describing "entry points" in the curriculum, Glenn, Weseley and Wassell (2014) argue that chapter themes, cultural blurbs, vocabulary lists and textbook activities are points at which world language teachers can introduce topics related to social justice. Specific strategies include looking at the history behind the topics that is reflective of inequalities, examining accepted truths that can be challenged, and raising differing perspectives by people from different groups. Even vocabulary lists of items in a home can situate students within a particular social class, reinforce stereotypes, even gender bias. They suggest that teachers can reconceptualize textbook chapters by using backward design. Themes of environment can be linked to ecojustice, themes of family to family structures and membership in families, and themes of food to broader issues of food production, distribution and culinary styles and preferences (as well as such matters as urban areas where food is unhealthy or unaffordable, or where there is a lack of clean water). At the elementary levels, themes such as improving our community can engage students with their own agency and responsibility for social activism.

Heather Hackman has argued that, "the question of how to teach effectively from a clear social justice perspective that empowers, encourages students to think critically, and models social change has been a consistent challenge for progressive educators" (Hackman, 2005, p. 103), and if anything this is an understatement. The gap between theory and practice in education is one that has created on-going problems in the discipline, and this has been especially true in the case of critical pedagogy and efforts to promote social justice pedagogy. This does not, however, mean that there is no way to reconcile theory and practice in education – merely that it is a difficult matter that requires considerable thought. Hackman has suggested that there are five key components necessary for bridging this gap, and these include tools for:

- content mastery;
- critical thinking;
- action and social change;
- personal reflection; and
- the awareness of multicultural group dynamics.

(Hackman, 2005, p. 103)

Underlying all of these components is the teacher's personal reflection on her or his identity, as well as on that of her or his students.

Social Justice and Multicultural Education

One very important aspect of promoting social justice education, as well as one of the key points of origin for social justice education, has been multicultural education (see Skutnabb-Kangas, Phillipson, Mohanty & Panda, 2009; Larson & Ovando, 2001; Sleeter, 1991). The presence of cultural, ethnic, racial, linguistic, and other sorts of diversity has been part of our educational history since its very beginnings, although such diversity has often been seen in negative terms. In the 1960s, however, a change began to take place. What changed was not the presence of large numbers of culturally and linguistically different students; rather, what was new was how these students were viewed, and what kinds of educational programs and responses were available to serve them. Underlying these changes was a growing recognition, as Sonia Nieto perceptively argued, that:

> Our schools reflect the sociocultural and sociopolitical context in which we live, and this context is unfair to many young people and their families. The ideologies underlying many school policies and practices are based on flawed ideas about intelligence and difference. If we want to change the situation, it means changing the curriculum and pedagogy in individual classrooms, as well as the school's practices and the ideologies undergirding them. That is, we need to create not only affirming classrooms, but also an affirming society in which racism, sexism, social class discrimination, and other biases are no longer acceptable.
>
> (Nieto, 2000, p. xx)

The creation of such affirming classrooms has been, and continues to be, a difficult undertaking, to be sure, and the creation of such an affirming society is even more difficult and daunting task – as recent developments in the broader American society have demonstrated all too clearly. It is, though, what multiculturalism education is really all about, and it is why multicultural education and education for social justice go hand in hand (Gay, 1995; McLaren & Muñoz, 2000; Skutnabb-Kangas, Phillipson, Mohanty & Panda, 2009; Sleeter & McLaren, 1995).

Social Justice and Media Literacy

One early approach to wrestling with critical approaches to world language education in the classroom focused on analyzing relevant media accounts related to language, language diversity and culture from critical perspectives (see Osborn, 2006). Media accounts inevitably include both explicit and implicit assumptions and perspectives on the world – assumptions and perspectives that are never "neutral," but which rather are grounded in ideological and political worldviews. Students may well not recognize such assumptions at all, or they may simply accept them uncritically. It is with raising student consciousness about such assumptions that critical pedagogues are, in part, concerned. For example, Robert Entman and Andrew Rojecki have argued that the images of members of minority groups held by most white Americans are derived largely from mass media (see Entman, 2007; Entman & Rojecki, 1998, 2000). Among the imagery that they have identified with respect to members of minority groups are:

- The association of minority group members with negative values and antisocial behaviors.
- Implications carried by both inclusions and exclusions that minority group members are fundamentally different from white Americans in undesirable ways.
- Depictions of minority group members as more homogeneous and less differentiated than members of the dominant group.
- Portrayals of minority group members as rarely in intimate or even moderately close and positive relationships with whites.

(Entman & Rojecki, 1998, p. 82)

Not only does the media impact how members of the dominant group see members of minority groups; it also has an effect on how members of minority groups – and especially children from those groups – often come to see themselves (see Berry & Asamen, 2001).

The case for the importance of media literacy in the curriculum generally has been made clearly and cogently by a number of scholars (see, for example, Alvermann & Hagood, 2003; Brown, 2006; Christ & Potter,

1998; Hobbs, 2005, 2011; Potter, 2010), but we would add to their work the suggestion that the world language classroom provides a uniquely powerful opportunity for such instruction. Among the key concepts of media literacy that are especially relevant for the world language curriculum are that the messages conveyed by the media, both explicitly and implicitly, are *constructed* by editorial choices, represent a reality that may or may not be valid, carry messages of sociopolitical impact (or at least purposes), and are interpreted by those who receive them. David Machin and Theo Van Leeuwen (2007) echo these concepts with characteristic issues in semiotic analysis that can be adapted for use in the world language classroom.

Depictions of individual people, as are often found in world language textbooks, commonly contain multiple layers of meaning, including showing people in groups or as individuals, from a distance or up close, and near other elements, including pictures or text in ways that also provide meaning. To these techniques of visual analysis, some elements from the realm of discourse analysis may also be helpful in illuminating underlying biases. Moira Chimombo and Robert Roseberry (1998), for example, note that media contain and rely on "frames" (that is, our experiences suggest or imply additional features not specifically stated). One example of such a frame might be a shoe store, which would immediately bring to mind shoes, of course, but would also include such things as a cash register, seats, boxes, salespersons, and so on. Social expectations of what takes place in a shoe store are also part of the frame. This having been said, all of these matters would differ in significant ways in a *zapatería* in Buenos Aires, an обувной магазин in Moscow, or a 鞋店 in Shanghai.

"Scripts" are a significant feature of discourse that include actions as opposed to items (Chimombo & Roseberry, 1998). Putting on a sneaker, for example, may include pulling up socks, pulling the shoe on the tongue, stretching the heel, pulling and tying laces. Scripts are often assumed rather than explicitly stated. Frames and scripts thus work together to create a sequence of things and events in a general sense called a schema. David Bloome refers to the impact of the schema as suggesting social relationships and identities exist in a text including both the "world-in-the-text" and the "people-in-the-text," moving readers to construct "a situation model (a mental micro-world) which of necessity requires that reader makes inferences" (Bloome, 2003, p. 295). Editorials, cartoons, and articles in the target languages accessible via the Internet a particularly good resource for finding examples of such media accounts in the United States in many languages. Products, practices, and perspectives of the target culture are rich in media accounts, and students can therefore gain cultural insights through these activities.

Intercultural Competence and Social Justice Education

In recent years, there has been increasing concern with the role of intercultural competence in world language education (see Byram, Nichols & Stevens, 2001; Deardorff, 2004, 2009; Sercu, with Bandura, Castro, Davcheva, Laskaridou, Lundgren, García & Ryan, 2005; Stier, 2006). As Michael Byram and Manuela Wagner have argued, "language teaching has long been associated with teaching in a country or countries where a target language is spoken, but this approach is inadequate" (Byram & Wagner, 2018, p. 140). It is inadequate because it is far too narrow to accurately describe both the appropriate educational goals for the world language classroom and the skill set that is most likely to be ultimately required of students in world language classes – both of which deal not so much with *cultural* competence or even *bicultural* competence, but rather with *intercultural* competence. Further, the ties between intercultural competence and social justice are extremely close. As Byram and Wagner point out,

> There are important parallels between fostering social justice and developing intercultural citizenship. Both concepts promote criticality in that educators enable students to reflect critically on language, discourse, and culture with regard to power and inequality. In both approaches, educators foster students' engagement with important societal issues by applying the skills of intercultural competence, which allow them to make critical judgments based on specific evidence.
>
> (Byram & Wagner, 2018, pp. 147–148)

Intercultural education is also, perhaps by its very nature, collaborative and interdisciplinary. For example, Fabiana Cardetti, Manuela Wagner, and Michael Byram report on a project to integrate a theory of intercultural competence and social justice into an interdisciplinary unit in mathematics, world languages and social studies. In so doing, they drew among other sources upon Claire Kramsch's work, including the observation that:

> If intercultural competence is the ability to reflect critically or analytically on the symbolic systems we use to make meaning, we are led to reinterpret the learning of foreign languages as not gaining a mode of communication across cultures, but more as acquiring a symbolic mentality that grants as much importance to subjectivity and the historicity of experience as to the social conventions and the cultural expectations of any one stable community of speakers.
>
> (Cardetti et al., 2015)

Critical Pedagogy and Conflict

Conflict is an inherent component of critical perspectives in education; critical pedagogy will inevitably lead to conflict, both internal and external, for both teachers and students. As Power explains:

> I learned that whenever you are in the classroom – and especially when you a white, middle-class teacher teaching a multiracial, multilevel group – you must think through the meanings of democracy, authority, and control. The contradictions inherent in the ideals of equality and liberty, respect for individual differences and the ethos of the group, the need for leadership and the need to share power pose as serious a challenge within a classroom as they do in the larger society.
>
> (Power, 1998, pp. 106–107)

Freire likewise contends:

> The radical, committed to human liberation, does not become a prisoner of a "circle of certainty" within which reality is also imprisoned. On the contrary, the more radical the person is, the more fully he or she can better transform it. This individual *is not afraid to confront*, to listen, to see the world unveiled. This person is not afraid *to meet the people or to enter into dialogue* with them. This person does not consider himself or herself the proprietor of history or of all people, or the liberator of the oppressed; but he or she *does* commit himself or herself, within history, to fight at their side.
>
> (Freire, 1993, p. 21, our emphasis)

Confrontation and conflict are an essential and necessary part of challenging the *status quo*. Both teachers and learners will feel a sense of discomfort as a result of this. As Angel Lin (2004) and others suggest, members of dominant groups will likely see themselves as under attack – their privileged status has generally gone unrecognized, and it comes as a significant shock that they owe their status, resources, and so on to factors that were largely unearned and undeserved. There will likely be a need to explore these claims and to openly discuss the issues related to social justice in language classrooms.

Social Justice Pedagogy and Dialectic

Social justice pedagogy is intrinsically linked to the concept of a dialectical stance. As Bill Ayers explains in the "Forward" to *Teaching for Social Justice: A Democracy and Education Reader*:

> Teaching for social justice demands a dialectical stance: one eye firmly fixed on the students – Who are they? What are their hopes, dreams,

> and aspirations? Their passions and commitments? What skills, abilities, and capacities, does each one bring to the classroom? – and the other eye looking unblinkingly at the concentric circles of context – historical flow, cultural surround, economic reality. Teaching for social justice is teaching that arouses students, engages them in a quest to identify obstacles to their full humanity, to their freedom, and then to drive, to move against these obstacles. And so the fundamental message of the teacher for social justice is: You *can* change the world.
>
> (Ayers, 1998, p. xvii, our emphasis)

Patricia Gross highlights a similar feature in collaborative curriculum design, which is the foundation for learner ownership of the curriculum:

> Joint curriculum design questions predetermined topics and emphases .... [S]tudents and teachers need to study course outlines to establish essentials, suggest options, and find areas of common and individual interest. Students and teachers need to be able to associate course concepts with prior frames of reference and move beyond them into new explorations. When probed, knowledge and the quest for knowledge do not stagnate; they thrive.
>
> (Gross, 1997, p. 66)

In short, a critically-based world language pedagogy must, at a minimum, include three features: (i) inquiry *with* (not *about* or *on*) the students and the community, which may be focused on problems; (ii) listening to hear the voices of students and other educational stakeholders; and (iii) connections to other, broader social movements.

Theater of the Oppressed

Perhaps one of the most satisfying developments for us professionally in the past two decades has been the appearance of a plethora of options offered by teachers *from* in classrooms *to* their peers *in* classrooms. Many of these options will be discussed and explored in Chapter 9, but it is worth noting one in particular here. For both pre-service and in-service world language educators, one intriguing approach to develop and deepen critical language awareness, and hence to promote critical pedagogical perspectives and pedagogies of social justice, is in the use of the Brazilian playwright Augusto Boal's "theatre of the oppressed" (see Boal, 1979, 1994, 2006; Cohen-Cruz & Schutzman, 2006). Jennifer Wooten and Melissa Cahnmann-Taylor, for instance, have presented a case study and critical analysis of how such an approach can be utilized in the preparation of world language educators:

> [Participants] identify those stories of recurring struggle that resonate with the group and then to perform, or *spect-act*, these stories. Boal's

> term *spect-actor* breaks the traditional divide between actors and audience, asking all participants – including audience members – to imagine and perform alternative courses of action for the protagonist. Each spect-actor that volunteers changes the story's end, at which point all spect-actors engage in a "reality check" to determine how realistic the change in action might be in any future context involving the story's "protagonist" and "antagonist." Each rehearsal aims to expand the protagonist's possibilities for alternative courses of action, thus expanding her/his sense of agency and options for future action, leading to an iterative cycle of action and critical reflection.
>
> (Wooten & Cahnmann-Taylor, 2014, pp. 179–195)

The use of theatre in educational settings, of course, is by no means a new idea, nor is it unique to critical pedagogy (see, for example, Redington, 1983; Somers, 1996). However, as Helen Nicholson observes, there is a natural "alliance between theatre, social justice and education [that] is politically charged and optimistic" (Nicholson, 2009, p. 58).

Language Rights as Human Rights

An important aspect of social justice, especially for the world language educator, is the role of education in the promotion of human rights. The concept of human rights is both a modern one and a Western one. In most human societies throughout history, there has been no equivalent to the idea of human rights as we now conceptualize them – at most, individuals and groups might have certain kinds of *legal* rights, but these were not inalienable, nor were they rights that were assumed for all people. Further, the concept of human rights emerged in a particular social, cultural, political, economic, historical and ideological context – specifically, during the European Enlightenment as a development of medieval concerns with natural law. Neither of these factors – the modern emergence of the concept of human rights, nor the fact that the origins of the concept of human rights is culture-specific – necessarily mean that the concept is flawed or limited, but both should make us hesitant in presupposing that the way that we conceive of human rights is inherently correct, let alone the only valid way in which human rights might be understood. This having been said, it is also the case that this Western conceptualization of human rights has been adopted widely by both Western and non-Western states, and is generally accepted (at least most of the time) in international law in the contemporary world.

In discussing human rights, it is useful to begin with a key distinction found in the discourse on human rights, originally proposed by Isaiah Berlin (1966, pp. 162–166): negative rights versus positive rights (see also Hirschl, 2000; Nelson, 2005; Young, 2017). In essence, a negative right is the right not to be subjected to an action (by either another person or by the State), while a positive right is one assumed to be tied to some benefit (most often, provided or ensured by the State). Traditional civil and political rights, such as freedom of speech, freedom of religion, and so on, constitute negative rights, as do the right to a fair trial, *habeas corpus*, and so on. Positive rights, on the other hand, include such rights as the right to protection of person and property, the right to food, housing, employment, education, and so on.

Another important aspect in the discourse on human rights, and one which has significant implications for the issue of language rights in particular, is the question of whether fundamental human rights are intrinsically *individual* in nature, or whether in some contexts they can be conceived of as *group* or *communal* rights (Coulombe, 1993; Dunbar, 2001; May, 2003; Stroud, 2010). Since the Enlightenment, human rights have been generally considered to be vested in the individual, although they are the result of a social contract that is communal in nature. The dilemma here is that in some cases – including that of language and linguistic rights – it is not at all clear what individual language rights might look like in the absence of group language rights: if the majority of members of a group chooses not to maintain its language, to what extent, and in what ways, does the individual still possess language rights? And, at the same time, if the group chooses to maintain its language, does this mean that the individual loses her or his right to decide *not* to maintain the language? These questions are not merely hypothetical in nature – they are dilemmas that current face both individual speakers and the speaker communities of hundreds, if not thousands, of languages around the world today.

Conceptualizing Linguistic Human Rights

If the concept of human rights is a fairly recent one in political thought, that of *linguistic* human rights is even more recent. Nevertheless, the idea of linguistic human rights has rapidly gained significance in the post-colonial world, especially as newly independent countries seek to select national languages and make decisions about language use. Reflecting these developments, there has been considerable discussion devoted to issues of linguistic human rights, most often with respect to concerns about the social, political, economic and educational rights of minority groups (see, for example, Grin, 2005; Guillorel & Koubi, 1999; May, 2003, 2012; Paulston, 2003; Wright, 2007). These concerns have also been reflected in a number of international declarations and agreements, beginning with the *Universal Declaration of Human Rights* (1948), and including the *Declaration on the Rights of Persons Belonging to National or Ethnic, Religious and Linguistic Minorities* (1992), the *Universal Declaration of Linguistic Rights* (commonly called the "Barcelona Declaration") (1996), the *Convention on the Rights of the Child* (1989), the *Convention Against*

Discrimination in Education (1960), the *International Covenant on Civil and Political Rights* (1966), the *Framework Convention for the Protection of National Minorities* (1988), and the *European Charter for Regional or Minority Languages* (1992). Further, many (although by no means most, let alone all) national constitutions include some kind of protection for language rights.

It has become common in the literature on the application of the concept of human rights to the case of language to distinguish between *language rights* and *linguistic human rights* (see Faingold, 2018; Grin, 2005; Hamel, 1997; Kontra, Phillipson, Skutnabb-Kangas & Várady, 1999; Skutnabb-Kangas & Phillipson with Rannut, 1995). Tove Skutnabb-Kangas (2000, pp. 482–487) has suggested that language rights differ from linguistic human rights in terms of what is *necessary*, as opposed to what is *desirable*. Linguistic human rights (that is, language rights *plus* human rights) are those which are required to meet basic human needs and to live a dignified life (such as having a language-related identity, access to one's mother tongue, the right of access to an official language, at least primary education in one's mother tongue, etc.). Although both language rights and linguistic human rights are obviously important, it is primarily with *linguistic human rights* that we are concerned here.

Violations of Linguistic Human Rights

Explicit statements of and commitments to language rights differ in significant ways from the legal and constitutional provisions governing the issue of language and linguistic human rights in the vast majority (indeed, in virtually all) of the member states of the United Nations. Even more important are the gaps between legal and constitutional protections and the reality of daily life in societies around the world. Constitutional guarantees may be rhetorically desirable, but they are by no means either necessary or sufficient to ensure social justice. In short, it is not merely issues of linguistic human rights that are relevant and important, but even more the issues of the *violation* of such rights. As the British philosopher Brenda Almond notes:

> The Second World War involved violations of human rights on an unprecedented scale but its ending saw the dawn of a new era for rights. Following their heyday in the 17th century … rights played a crucial role in the revolutions of the late 18th century. In the nineteenth and early twentieth centuries, however, appeal to rights was eclipsed by movements such as utilitarianism and Marxism which could not, or would not, accommodate them …. The contemporary period has seen a further shift in their fortunes and today they provide an accepted international currency for moral and political debate. In many parts of the world, irrespective of cultural or religious traditions, when issues or torture or terrorism, poverty or

> power are debated, the argument is very often conducted in terms of rights and their violation.
>
> (Almond, 1993, p. 259)

Examples of the violations of both individual and group language rights abound – in fact, it is difficult to find cases in which countries do not violate the language rights of at least some of their citizens. Under the best of circumstances, the recognition of minority languages[3] tends to be limited both with respect to the number of minority languages identified and in terms of what their recognition actually means in practice. Although many of the more egregious examples of the violations of linguistic human rights are tied to colonialism – the cases of the treatment of indigenous languages in North America (see McCarty, 2004, 2008; White, 2006), Latin America (see Hamel, 1995a, 1995b; Hornberger, 1998, 1999; Van Cott, 2005), and Australia (see McConvell, 2008; Nicholls, 2005) are all powerful examples here – such violations have occurred, and continue to occur, in many other settings as well.

Implications of the Concept of Linguistic Human Rights for the Classroom

What are the implications of such concerns about linguistic human rights, and the violations of such rights, for the world language classroom and for the world language teacher? Classroom discourse – essentially, the communication that takes place both formally and informally in the school context – is at the heart of the teaching and learning processes (see Cazden & Beck, 2003; Walsh, 2006, 2011; Young, 1993). As David Bloome, Stephanie Carter, Beth Christian, Sheila Otto and Nora Shuart-Faris (2004) observe, classroom discourse is also closely tied to such topics as equity, democracy, freedom, justice, racism, classism, homophobia, and sexism. The ideology of linguistic legitimacy impacts the classroom in a variety of ways: in teacher–student and student–teacher communication, in teacher (and student) judgments about language and language variation, in the assessment and evaluation of students (as well as of teachers), and in the explicit and implicit messages sent in the formal curriculum (as well as in the hidden curriculum) (Reagan, 2019). For the classroom teacher, this creates a great responsibility and entails a number of obligations. If one assumes that the school and classroom should be places that are not only physically but also emotionally safe places for all students, that the background experiences of all students should be recognized, respected and taken into account in designing and implementing the curriculum and assessment that take place in the classroom, and that pluralism – linguistic and otherwise – is a valuable and arguably necessary feature of a democratic society, then a commitment to linguistic human rights becomes not merely a desirable, but a necessary and essential component of world language education.

Conclusion

In this chapter, the related concepts of critical pedagogy and social justice education have been explored, both as theoretical constructs and with respect to how each can be implemented in terms of classroom practice. We have also discussed the emancipatory and transformative potential of critical pedagogy, as well as aspects of social justice pedagogy, with particular focus on world language teaching and learning. An important element of these discussions was an extensive review of what we have called "voices from the field": that is, ideas and practices suggested by classroom world language educators intended for their peers. Finally, the chapter ends with a detailed examination of the concept of linguistic human rights, and of the implications of linguistic human rights are for the world language classroom. Although we recognize that there is still much to be done with respect to incorporating both critical pedagogy and social justice education into world language education, we nevertheless believe that a great deal of progress has been made in the past decades.

It is also worth noting here, though, that the commitments to critical pedagogy and social justice that are presupposed in this chapter are by no means universally accepted. Educational institutions are, by their very nature, most often profoundly conservative, and certainly not all educators are progressive in their values, beliefs, and practices. This is by no means a recent phenomenon or challenge, though – resistance to change (and especially to change related to issues of social justice) has been common throughout our educational history. Such resistance has been especially fierce in debates about both social justice education and critical pedagogy, and can be expected to remain so. Nevertheless, we believe that the evidence is simply overwhelming that much of traditional public education in the United States has been, and continues to be, grounded in and supportive of the oppression of many groups of students. Lee Anne Bell has suggested that this oppression consists of a number of overlapping strands, including the fact that oppression is:

- pervasive;
- cumulative;
- durable and mutating;
- grounded in group-based categories;
- restrictive;
- intersecting;
- internalized;
- normalizing; and
- hierarchical.

(Bell, 2016, pp. 5–16)

The critiques of critical pedagogy and social justice education (as well as similar and related critiques of multicultural and anti-racist education) typically argue that these are political and ideological efforts, which ought not be reflected or manifested in public education. What this argument overlooks is that, as we have already argued, *all* education is *profoundly* political and ideological in nature. The question is not *whether* education is political, but rather, what its political orientation should be. Joe Kincheloe has argued that, "whether one is teaching in Bangladesh or Bensonhurst, Senegal or Shreveport, East Timor or West New York, education is a political activity" (Kincheloe, 2008, p. 8). Further, as Sandy Grande has argued about critical pedagogy,

> Critical pedagogy is first and foremost an approach to schooling (i.e., teaching, policy making, curriculum production) that emphasizes the political nature of education. As such, critical pedagogy aims to understand, reveal, and disrupt the mechanisms of oppression imposed by the established order, suturing the processes and aims of education to emancipatory goals.
>
> (Grande, 2007, p. 317)

The cognizance of the political and ideological nature of education is necessary to understand the fundamental nature and institutions in which children are educated. To appreciate schools and schooling – including the teaching and learning processes – we need to grasp the complex nexus of the social, cultural, economic, political, and historical contexts in which they exist. This is what critical pedagogy and social justice education are all about.

Questions for Reflection and Discussion

1 This chapter begins by noting that critical pedagogy is "difficult to define," and even quotes Peter McLaren as writing that it does not "constitute a homogenous set of ideas." If this is the case, how useful do you believe that critical pedagogy can actually be in terms of providing guidance for classroom practice? Is it necessary to have a clear definition of a pedagogical concept to make effective use of that concept?
2 Many writers have suggested that education can be both emancipatory and transformative in nature. Others have pointed out that schooling is often a profoundly conservative force in a society. How can both of these ideas be true? What are the implications of each for a world language teacher in the U.S.?
3 How would you define "language rights"? Do you agree with the authors that these rights are better thought of as "linguistic human rights"? Why or why not?

4 Locate either a news story or an editorial from a local or national newspaper from a place where the language that you teach is spoken. How might you utilize this story or editorial in promoting media literacy in a world language classroom? Could it be used in supporting a critical pedagogical approach to teaching a world language? How could it be used in terms of raising student awareness of issues of social justice?
5 Locate an editorial cartoon from a local or national newspaper from a place where the language that you teach is spoken. How might you utilize this story or editorial in promoting media literacy in a world language classroom? Could it be used in supporting a critical pedagogical approach to teaching a world language? How could it be used in terms of raising student awareness of issues of social justice?

Notes

1 *Conscientização* is the Portuguese term used by Paolo Freire. It is most often translated as "conscientization" (or "critical consciousness") in English, but this is at best a very limited and insufficient translation. Even in Portuguese, the underlying concept of *conscientização* is a complex one. Freire himself once commented, "a conscientização è um tomar posse uma ruptura da realidade," suggesting that it refers to taking a break from reality (see Freire, 2018).
2 There is an extensive body of historical and philosophical research on the history and work of the Frankfurt School. See, for instance, Arato and Gebhardt (1985), Bottomore (2002), Jay (1996), Wheatland (2009), Wiggershaus (1994) and Marcus and Tar (1984).
3 The use of the phrase "minority languages" here is problematic, since in many cases the language(s) involved are those spoken by the majority of citizens of the country, or a majority of individuals in a particular region of a country. Further, as Stephen May has pointed out, "the same language may be regarded as both a majority and minority language, depending on the context … Spanish is a majority language in Spain and many Latin American states, but a minority language in the United States" (May, 2006, p. 260).

References

Adams, A. (2007). Horton, Highlander, and leadership education: Lessons for preparing educational leaders for social justice. *Journal of School Leadership*, 17(3): 250–275.

Adams, F. (1975). *Unearthing seeds of fire: The idea of Highlander*. Salem, NC: John F. Blair.

Adams, M. & Bell, L. with Goodman, D. & Yoshi, K. (Eds.). (2016). *Teaching for diversity and social justice* (3rd ed.). New York: Routledge.

Almond, B. (1993). Rights. In P. Singer (Ed.), *A companion to ethics* (pp. 259–269). Oxford: Basil Blackwell.

Alvermann, D. & Hagood, M. (2003). Critical media literacy: Research, theory, and practice in "new times." *The Journal of Educational Research*, 93(3): 193–205.

Arato, A. & Gebhardt, E. (Eds.). (1985). *The essential Frankfurt School reader*. New York: Continuum.

Ayers, W. (1998). Popular education: Teaching for social justice. In W. Ayers, J. Hunt & T. Quinn (Eds.), *Teaching for social justice: A democracy and education reader* (pp. xvii–xxv). New York: Teachers College Press.

Ayers, W., Hunt, J. & Quinn, T. (Eds.). (1998). *Teaching for social justice: A democracy and education reader*. New York: Teachers College Press.

Bell, L. (2016). Theoretical foundations social justice education. In M. Adams & L. Bell with D. Goodman & K. Joshi (Eds.), *Teaching for diversity and social justice* (3rd ed.) (pp. 3–26). New York: Routledge.

Berlin, I. (1966). Two concepts of liberty. Inaugural Lecture, delivered before the University of Oxford, October 31, 1958. Reprinted in I. Berlin, *Four essays on liberty* (pp. 162–166). Oxford: Oxford University Press.

Berry, G. & Asamen, J. (2001). Television, children, and multicultural awareness: Comprehending the medium in a complex multimedia society. In D. Singer & J. Singer (Eds.), *Handbook of children and the media* (pp. 359–373). Thousand Oaks, CA: Sage.

Bloome, D. (2003). Narrative discourse. In A. Graesser, M. Gernsbacher & S. Goldman (Eds.), *Handbook of discourse processes* (pp. 287–319). Mahwah, NJ: Lawrence Erlbaum Associates.

Bloome, D., Carter, S., Christian, B., Otto, S. & Shuart-Faris, N. (2004). *Discourse analysis and the study of classroom language and literacy events: A microethnographic perspective*. New York: Routledge.

Boal, A. (1979). *Theatre of the oppressed*. London: Pluto Press.

Boal, A. (1994). *The rainbow of desire: The Boal method of theatre and therapy*. New York: Routledge.

Boal, A. (2006). *The aesthetics of the oppressed*. New York: Routledge.

Bottomore, T. (2002). *The Frankfurt School and its critics*. New York: Routledge.

Brown, J. (2006). Media literacy has potential to improve adolescents' health. *Journal of Adolescent Health*, 39(4): 459–460.

Byram, M., Nichols, A. & Stevens, D. (Eds.). (2001). *Developing intercultural competence in practice*. Clevedon: Multilingual Matters.

Byram, M. & Wagner, M. (2018). Making a difference: Language teaching for intercultural and international dialogue. *Foreign Language Annals*, 51(1): 140–151. Downloaded from https://onlinelibrary.wiley.com/doi/full/10.1111/flan.12319 on August 1, 2019.

Cardetti, F., Wagner, M. & Byram, M. (2015). Interdisciplinary collaboration to develop intercultural competence by integrating math, languages, and social studies. Presented at the annual Northeastern Educational Research Association conference. Downloaded from https://opencommons.uconn.edu/cgi/viewcontent.cgi?article=1006&context=nera-2015 on August 1, 2019.

Cazden, C. & Beck, S. (2003). Classroom discourse. In A. Graesser, M. Gernsbacher & S. Goldman (Eds.), *Handbook of discourse processes* (pp. 165–197). Mahwah, NJ: Lawrence Erlbaum Associates.

Chimombo, M. & Roseberry, R. (1998). *The power of discourse: An introduction to discourse analysis*. New York: Routledge.

Christ, W. & Potter, W. (1998). Media literacy, media education, and the academy. *Journal of Communication*, 48(1): 5–15.

Cohen-Cruz, J. & Schutzman, M. (Eds.). (2006). *A Boal companion: Dialogues on theatre and cultural politics*. New York: Routledge.

Coulombe, P. (1993). Language rights, individual and communal. *Language Problems and Language Planning*, 17(2): 140–152.

Darder, A., Torres, R. & Baltodano, M. (2009). *The critical pedagogy reader*. New York: Routledge/Falmer.

Deardorff, D. (2004). Internationalization: In search of intercultural competence. *International Educators*, 13(2): 13–15.

Deardorff, D. (Ed.). (2009). *The Sage handbook of intercultural competence*. Los Angeles, CA: Sage.

Demos, J. (1971). Developmental perspectives on the history of childhood. *The Journal of Interdisciplinary History*, 2(2): 315–327.

Demos, J. (2000). *A little commonwealth: Family life in Plymouth Colony* (2nd ed.). Oxford: Oxford University Press.

Denzin, N. (2003). *Performance ethnography: Critical pedagogy and the politics of culture*. Thousand Oaks, CA: Sage.

Dunbar, R. (2001). Minority language rights in international law. *International and Comparative Law Quarterly*, 50(1): 90–120.

Entman, R. (2007). Framing bias: Media in the distribution of power. *Journal of Communication*, 57(1): 163–173.

Entman, R. & Rojecki, A. (1998). Minorities in mass media: A status report. In A. Garmer (Ed.), *Investing in diversity: Advancing opportunities for minorities and media* (pp. 67–85). Washington, DC: Aspen Institute.

Entman, R. & Rojecki, A. (2000). *The black image in the white mind: Media and race in America*. Chicago: University of Chicago Press.

Faingold, E. (2018). *Language rights and the law in the United States and its territories*. Lanham, MD: Lexington Books.

Freire, P. (1973). *Education for critical consciousness*. New York: Seabury.

Freire, P. (1974). *Pedagogy of the oppressed*. New York: Seabury. (Original publication 1968)

Freire, P. (1993). *Pedagogy of the oppressed* (rev. ed.). New York: Continuum.

Freire, P. (2002a). *Cartas a quien pretende enseñar*. Buenos Aires: Siglo XXI Editores Argentina.

Freire, P. (2002b). *Pedagogía de la autonomía*. Buenos Aires: Siglo XXI Editores Argentina.

Freire, P. (2002c). *Pedagogía de la esperanza: Un reencuentro con la Pedagogía del oprimido*. Buenos Aires: Siglo XXI Editores Argentina.

Freire, P. (2002d). *Pedagogía del oprimido*. Buenos Aires: Siglo XXI Editores Argentina.

Freire, P. (2018). *Conscientização*. São Paulo: Cortez Editora.

Gay, G. (1995). Mirror images on common issues: Parallels between multicultural education and critical pedagogy. In C. Sleeter & P. McLaren (Eds.), *Multicultural education, critical pedagogy, and the politics of difference* (pp. 155–189). Albany, NY: State University of New York Press.

Giroux, H. (1981). *Ideology, culture, and the process of schooling*. Philadelphia, PA: Temple University Press.

Giroux, H. (1983). *Theory and resistance in education*. London: Heinemann.

Giroux, H. (1985). Teachers as transformative intellectuals. *Social Education*, 49(5): 376–379.

Giroux, H. (1988a). *Escola crítica e política cultural* (2nd ed.). São Paulo: Cortez Editora.

Giroux, H. (1988b). *Schooling and the struggle for public life*. Minneapolis, MN: University of Minnesota Press.

Giroux, H. (1988c). *Teachers as intellectuals: Toward a critical pedagogy of learning*. Westport, CT: Bergin & Garvey.

Giroux, H. (Ed.) (1991). *Postmodernism, feminism, and cultural politics: Redrawing educational boundaries*. Albany, NY: State University of New York Press.

Giroux, H. (1992a). *Border crossings: Cultural workers and the politics of education*. New York: Routledge.

Giroux, H. (1992b). Educational leadership and the crisis of democratic government. *Educational Researcher*, 21(4): 4–11.

Giroux, H. (1994). Doing cultural studies: Youth and the challenge of pedagogy. *Harvard Educational Review*, 64(3): 278–308.

Giroux, H. (1997a). *Pedagogy and the politics of hope: Theory, culture and schooling*. Boulder, CO: Westview Press.

Giroux, H. (1997b). Rewriting the discourse of racial identity: Toward a pedagogy and politics of whiteness. *Harvard Educational Review*, 67(2): 285–320.

Giroux, H. (2001a). *Public spaces, private lives: Beyond the culture of cynicism*. Lanham, MD: Rowman & Littlefield.

Giroux, H. (2001b). *Stealing innocence: Corporate culture's war on children*. New York: Palgrave.

Giroux, H. (2003a). *Democracy beyond the culture of fear*. New York: Palgrave Macmillan.

Giroux, H. (2003b). *La escuela y la lucha por la ciudadanía*. Buenos Aires: Siglo XXI Editores Argentina.

Giroux, H. (2004). *Terror of neoliberalism: Authoritarianism and the eclipse of democracy*. New York: Routledge.

Giroux, H. (2005). *Estudios culturales, pedagogía crítica y democracia radical*. Madrid: Editorial Popular.

Giroux, H. (2008). *La universidad secuestrada: El reto de confrontar a la alianza military-académica*. Caracas: Centro Internacional Miranda.

Giroux, H. (2010). Paulo Freire and the crisis of the political. *Power and Education*, 2(3): 335–340.

Giroux, H. (2011). *On critical pedagogy*. New York: Continuum.

Giroux, H. & McLaren, P. (1986). Teacher education and the politics of engagement: The case for democratic schooling. *Harvard Education Review*, 56(3): 213–227.

Giroux, H. & Simon, R. (1988). Critical pedagogy and the politics of popular culture. *Cultural Studies*, 2: 294–320.

Glen, J. (1996). *Highlander: No ordinary school* (2nd ed.). Knoxville, TN: University of Tennessee Press.

Glenn, C., Weseley, P. & Wassell, B. (2014). *Words and actions: Teaching languages through the lens of social justice*. Alexandria, VA: American Council on the Teaching of Foreign Languages.

Goodlad, J. (1994). *Educational renewal: Better teachers, better schools*. San Francisco, CA: Jossey-Bass.

Goodlad, J. (1997). *In praise of education*. New York: Teachers College Press.

Grande, S. (2007). Red Lake Woebegone: Pedagogy, decolonization, and the critical project. In P. McLaren & J. Kincheloe (Eds.), *Critical pedagogy: Where are we now?* (pp. 315–336). New York: Peter Lang.

Grin, F. (2005). Linguistic human rights as a source of policy guidelines: A critical assessment. *Journal of Sociolinguistics*, 9(3): 448–460.

Gross, P. (1997). *Joint curriculum design: Facilitating learner ownership and active participation in secondary classrooms*. New York: Routledge.

Gruenewald, D. (2003). The best of both worlds: A critical pedagogy of place. *Educational Researcher*, 32(4), 3–12.

Guillorel, H. & Koubi, G. (Eds.). (1999). *Langues du droit, droit des langues*. Brussels: Bruylant.

Gutman, A. (1999). *Democratic education* (rev. ed.). Princeton, NJ: Princeton University Press.

Hackman, H. (2005). Five essential components for social justice education. *Equity and Excellence in Education*, 38(2): 103–109.

Hamel, E. (1995a). Indigenous education in Latin America: Policies and legal frameworks. In T. Skutnabb-Kangas & R. Phillipson (Eds.), *Linguistic human rights* (pp. 271–287). Berlin: Mouton de Gruyter.

Hamel, E. (1995b). Linguistic rights for Amerindian peoples in Latin America. In T. Skutnabb-Kangas & R. Phillipson (Eds.), *Linguistic human rights* (pp. 289–303). Berlin: Mouton de Gruyter.

Hamel, R. (1997). Introduction: Linguistic human rights in a sociolinguistic perspective. *International Journal of the Sociology of Language*, 127(1): 1–24.

Hawkins, M. (Ed.). (2011). *Social justice language teacher education*. Bristol: Multilingual Matters.

Hirschl, R. (2000). "Negative" rights vs. "positive" entitlements: A comparative study of judicial interpretations of rights in an emerging neo-liberal economic order. *Human Rights Quarterly*, 22(4): 1060–1098.

Hobbs, R. (2005). Media literacy and the K-12 content areas. In G. Schwarz & P. Brown (Eds.), *Media literacy: Transforming curriculum and teaching* (pp. 74–99). Malden, MA: Blackwell Publishing.

Hobbs, R. (2011). The state of media literacy: A response to Potter. *Journal of Broadcasting and Electronic Media*, 55(3): 419–430.

Hornberger, N. (1998). Language policy, language education, language rights: Indigenous, immigrant, and international perspectives. *Language in Society*, 27(4): 439–458.

Hornberger, N. (1999). Maintaining and revitalising indigenous languages in Latin America: State planning vs. grassroots initiatives. *International Journal of Bilingual Education and Bilingualism*, 2(3): 159–165.

Horton, A. (1989). *The Highland Folk School: A history of its major programs, 1932–1961*. New York: Carlson.

Horton, M. & Freire, P. (1990). *We make the road by walking: Conversations on education and social change*. Philadelphia, PA: Temple University Press.

Idaho State Department of Education. (1994). *Idaho foreign language content guide and framework*. Boise, ID: Author.

Jay, M. (1996). *The dialectical imagination: A history of the Frankfurt School and the Institute of Social Research, 1923–1950*. Berkeley, CA: University of California Press.

Kanpol, B. (1999). *Critical pedagogy: An introduction* (2nd ed.). Westport, CT: Bergin & Garvey.

Kincheloe, J. (2008). *Critical pedagogy* (2nd ed.). New York: Peter Lang.

Kontra, M., Phillipson, R., Skutnabb-Kangas, T. & Várady, T. (Eds.). (1999). *Language: A right and a resource*. Budapest: Central European University Press.

Kumashiro, K. (2015). *Against common sense: Teaching and learning toward social justice*. New York: Routledge.

Larson, C. & Ovando, C. (2001). *The color of bureaucracy: The politics of equity in multicultural school communities*. Belmont, CA: Wadsworth.

Lin, A. (2004). Introducing a critical pedagogical curriculum: A feminist, reflexive account. In B. Norton & K. Toohey (Eds.), *Critical pedagogies and language learning* (pp. 271–290). Cambridge: Cambridge University Press.

Machin, D. & Van Leeuwen, T. (2007). *Global media discourse: A critical introduction*. New York: Routledge.

Marcus, J. & Tar, Z. (Eds.). (1984). *Foundations of the Frankfurt School of Social Research*. New Brunswick, NJ: Transaction Books.

May, S. (2003). Rearticulating the case for minority language rights. *Current Issues in Language Planning*, 4(2): 95–125.

May, S. (2006). Language policy and minority rights. In R. Ricento (Ed.), *An introduction to language policy: Theory and method* (pp. 255–272). Oxford: Blackwell.

May, S. (2012). *Language and minority rights: Ethnicity, nationalism and the politics of language*. New York: Routledge.

McCarty, T. (2004). Dangerous difference: A critical-historical analysis of language education policies in the United States. In J. Tollefson & A. Tsui (Eds.), *Medium of instruction policies: Which agenda? Whose agenda?* (pp. 71–96). Mahwah, NJ: Lawrence Erlbaum Associates.

McCarty, T. (2008). Native American languages as heritage mother tongues. *Language, Culture and Curriculum*, 21(3): 201–225.

McConvell, P. (2008). Language mixing and language shift in indigenous Australia. In J. Simpson & G. Wigglesworth (Eds.), *Children's language and multilingualism: Indigenous language use at home and school* (pp. 237–260). London: Continuum.

McLaren, P. (1988). Culture or canon? Critical pedagogy and the politics of literacy. *Harvard Educational Review*, 58(2): 213–235.

McLaren, P. (1989). *Life in schools: An introduction to critical pedagogy in the foundations of education*. New York: Longman.

McLaren, P. (2002). Critical pedagogy: A look at the major concepts. In A. Darder, M. Baltodano & R. Torres (Eds.), *The critical pedagogy reader* (pp. 69–96). New York: Routledge.

McLaren, P. (2003). *Life in schools: An introduction to critical pedagogy in the foundations of education* (4th ed.). Boston, MA: Allyn and Bacon.

McLaren, P. (2005). *Capitalists and conquerors: A critical pedagogy against empire*. Lanham, MD: Rowman & Littlefield.

McLaren, P. (2015). *Life in schools: An introduction to critical pedagogy in the foundations of education* (6th ed.). New York: Routledge.

McLaren, P. & Kincheloe, J. (Eds.). (2007). *Critical pedagogy: Where are we now?* New York: Peter Lang.

McLaren, P. & Leonard, P. (Eds.). (1993). *Paulo Freire: A critical encounter*. New York: Routledge.

McLaren, P. & Muñoz, J. (2000). Contesting whiteness: Critical perspectives on the struggle for social justice. In C. Ovando & P. McLaren (Eds.), *The politics of multiculturalism and bilingual education: Students and teachers caught in the cross fire* (pp. 23–49). Boston, MA: McGraw-Hill.

Morrow, R. (2002). *Reading Freire and Habermas: Critical pedagogy and transformative social change*. New York: Teachers College Press.

Nelson, E. (2005). Liberty: One concept too many? *Political Theory*, 33(1): 58–78.

Nicholls, C. (2005). Death by a thousand cuts: Indigenous language bilingual education programmes in the Northern Territory of Australia. *International Journal of Bilingual Education and Bilingualism*, 8(2–3):160–177.

Nicholson, H. (2009). *Theatre and education*. London: Red Globe Press.

Nieto, S. (2000). *Affirming diversity: The sociopolitical context of multicultural education* (3rd ed.). New York: Longman.

Osborn, T. A. (2000). *Critical reflection and the foreign language classroom*. Westport, CT: Bergin & Garvey.

Osborn, T. A. (2006). *Teaching world languages for social justice: A sourcebook of principles and practices*. Mahwah, NJ: Lawrence Erlbaum Associates.

Paulston, C. (2003). Language policies and language rights. In C. Paulston & G. Tucker (Eds.), *Sociolinguistics: The essential readings* (pp. 472–483). Oxford: Blackwell.

Potter, E. (2010). The state of media literacy. *Journal of Broadcasting and Electronic Media*, 54(4): 675–696.

Power, K. (1998). No little I's and no little you's: Language and equality in an adult literacy community. In W. Ayers, J. Hunt & T. Quinn (Eds.), *Teaching for social justice: A democracy and education reader* (pp. 102–123). New York: Teachers College Press.

Reagan, T. (2019). *Linguistic legitimacy and social justice*. London: Palgrave Macmillan.

Reagan, T. & Osborn, T. A. (2002). *The foreign language educator in society: Toward a critical pedagogy*. Mahwah, NJ: Lawrence Erlbaum Associates.

Redington, C. (1983). *Can theatre teach? An historical and evaluative analysis of theatre in education*. Oxford: Pergamon Press.

Sercu, L. with Bandura, E., Castro, P., Davcheva, L., Laskaridou, C., Lundgren, U., García, M. & Ryan, P. (2005). *Foreign language teachers and intercultural competence: An international investigation*. Bristol: Multilingual Matters.

Shor, I. (1992). *Empowering education: Critical teaching for social change*. Chicago, IL: University of Chicago Press.

Skutnabb-Kangas, T. (2000). *Linguistic genocide in education – or worldwide diversity and human rights?*Mahwah, NJ: Lawrence Erlbaum Associates.

Skutnabb-Kangas, T. & Phillipson, R. with Rannut, M. (Eds.). (1995). *Linguistic human rights*. Berlin: Mouton de Gruyter.

Skutnabb-Kangas, T., Phillipson, R., Mohanty, A. & Panda, M. (Eds.). (2009). *Social justice through multicultural education*. Bristol: Multilingual Matters.

Sleeter, C. (1991). *Empowerment through multicultural education*. Albany, NY: State University of New York Press.

Sleeter, C. & McLaren, P. (Eds.) (1995). *Multicultural education, critical pedagogy, and the politics of difference*. Albany, NY: State University of New York Press.

Somers, J. (Ed.). (1996). *Drama and theatre in education: Contemporary research*. North York, ONT: Captus University Press.

Spring, J. (2003). *Educating the consumer-citizen: A history of the marriage of schools, advertising, and media*. New York: Routledge.

Stier, J. (2006). Internationalisation, intercultural community and intercultural competence. *Journal of Intercultural Communication*, 11: 1–11.

Stroud, C. (2010). African mother-tongue programmes and the politics of language: Linguistic citizenship vs. linguistic human rights. *Journal of Multilingual and Multicultural Development*, 22(4): 339–355.

Tozer, S., Senese, G. & Violas, P. (2013). *School and society: Historical and contemporary perspectives* (7th ed.). New York: McGraw-Hill.

Van Cott, D. (2005). Building inclusive democracies: Indigenous peoples and ethnic minorities in Latin America. *Democratization*, 12(5): 820–837.

Walsh, S. (2006). *Investigating classroom discourse*. New York: Routledge.

Walsh, S. (2011). *Exploring classroom discourse: Language in action*. New York: Routledge.

Wheatland, T. (2009). *The Frankfurt School in exile*. Minneapolis, MN: University of Minnesota Press.

White, F. (2006). Rethinking Native American language revitalization. *The American Indian Quarterly*, 30(1): 91–109.

Wiggershaus, R. (1994). *The Frankfurt School: Its history, theories, and political significance*. Cambridge, MA: MIT Press.

Wink, J. (2000). *Critical pedagogy: Notes from the real world* (2nd ed.). New York: Longman.

Wooten, J. & Cahnmann-Taylor, M. (2014). Black, white, and rainbow [of desire]: The colour of race-talk of pre-service world language educators in Boalian theatre workships. *Pedagogies: An International Journal*, 9(3): 179–195.

Wright, S. (2007). The right to speak one's own language: Reflections on theory and practice. *Language Policy*, 6(2): 203–224.

Young, R. (1993). *Teoría crítica de la educación y discurso en la aula*. Barcelona: Ediciones Paidós, in collaboration with the Centro de Publicaciones del Ministerio de Educación y Ciencia.

Young, R. (2017). *Personal autonomy: Beyond negative and positive liberty*. New York: Routledge. (Original publication 1986)

9 Challenging Ideology in the Curriculum

The Role of Critical Pedagogy and Social Justice Education

In this chapter, we will address the role of critical pedagogy and social justice education in challenging the curriculum in world language education courses. The curriculum for world language education has been widely discussed in our discipline for many years, and many others have explored the area in depth and with considerable insight. What we wish to provide here is somewhat different from what is commonly available in the world language education literature, however: our focus here, as in *World Language Education as Critical Pedagogy: The Promise of Social Justice* more broadly, is on offering a perspective on the curricula used in world language education classes that is grounded in a critical perspective that goes beyond normal theoretical and practical concerns in ways that can help to promote critical pedagogy in the world language classroom. As Michael Apple has argued,

> If we have learned anything from the intense and continuing conflicts over what and whose knowledge should be declared "official" that have raged throughout the history of the curriculum in so many nations, it should have been one lesson. There is an intricate set of connections between knowledge and power. Questions of whose knowledge, who chooses, how this is justified–these are constitutive issues, not "add-ons" that have the status of afterthoughts. This construction of good education not only marginalizes the politics of knowledge but also offers little agency to students, teachers, and community members.
>
> (Apple, 2006, p. 5)

We believe that this is an excellent starting point for this chapter, and, indeed, for any effort to examine the curriculum critically.

The Curriculum and World Language Education

It has become something of a commonplace to begin discussions about curricula with references to the etymology of the term (see Wiggins & McTighe, 2005, p. 6). The word "curriculum" can be traced back to the Latin verb *currere*, which means "to run (in a race)," and so the curriculum is the course that the student "runs" in going through the educational process. Although this explanation is true to a certain extent, in our view it does not really adequately explain the contemporary use of the term "curriculum." In fact, we would suggest that it is not particularly helpful to rely on etymology here – rather, what seems to us to make the most sense is simply to provide a clear definition of the term, and to then outline the details embedded in this definition. Essentially, the curriculum is the sum total of all aspects of the student's experiences as she or he goes through the learning process. Grant Wiggins and Jay McTighe, in their popular work on "learning by design" argue that:

> *curriculum* refers to the specific blueprint for learning that is derived from *desired results* – that is, content and performance standards (be they state-determined or locally developed). Curriculum takes content (from external standards and local goals) and shapes it into a plan for how to conduct effective and engaging teaching and learning. It is thus more than a list of topics and lists of key facts and skills (the "inputs"). It is a map for how to achieve the "outputs" of desired student performance, in which appropriate learning activities and assessments are suggested to make it more likely that students achieve the desired results.
>
> (Wiggins & McTighe, 2005, pp. 5–6)

Although this definition has a number of advantages when conceptualizing the curriculum within the formal and institutional context of the school, it is far too narrow to encompass all of the significant aspects of what students experience from a critical standpoint. Critiquing the fundamental assumptions of such a definition of curriculum, Peter McLaren (1989) has pointed out that critical pedagogues challenge the notion that schools are places where knowledge alone is passed on. In the case of foreign language education, this would include consideration how schools act as sites for sorting and empowering students based on some set or combination of sets of criteria, identifying elements of these criteria within planned curriculum and standards, and even challenging these criteria (see Arnowitz & Giroux, 1985, 1991). Further, as Joel Spring noted,

> Educational goals are a product of what people think schooling should do for the good of society. Consequently, they often reflect opinions and beliefs about how people should act and how society should be organized. Since there is wide variation in what people believe, educational goals often generate a great deal of debate.
>
> (Spring, 2011, p. 4)

In fact, the curriculum is an immensely complex and diverse matter, and one that can be understood in a number of quite different ways. Some of these ways of conceptualizing the curriculum (which can and do overlap) are discussed below.

The Planned and Unplanned Curricula

The most obvious and commonly used way in which the term curriculum is used is to refer to what can be thought of as the "planned" or "formal" curriculum. The planned curriculum is the "official" curriculum, in the sense that it is what the teacher and the school would claim to be a description of what is and should be occurring in the classroom. The planned curriculum will normally reflect the mission and vision of the school, as well as the goals and objectives of the particular subject area being taught. The planned curriculum is the explicit articulation of the content to be covered, as well as how that content is to be taught, and the ways in which the learning of the content will be assessed, both formatively and summatively. In the context of the world language classroom, the planned curriculum is often closely tied to the textbook used in the class. This is a very important point, since, as Allan Ornstein has observed,

> the most fundamental concern of schooling is curriculum. Students tend to view schooling largely as subjects or courses to be taken. Teachers and professors give much attention to adoption and revision of subject matter. Parents and community members frequently express concern about what schools are for and what they should teach. In short, all of these groups are attending to one thing: curriculum.
>
> (Ornstein, 1982, p. 404)

The "unplanned curriculum," in contrast to the planned curriculum, is basically everything else that takes place in the classroom: unintended and unplanned events, content, learning, and so on. The unplanned curriculum may be either positive or negative in nature. It is possible that students in a class might learn something very valuable about respecting other people, or about how to interact with others appropriately, or about how to politely and civilly disagree with others – all of which would be positive outcomes of the classroom experience, but none of which are likely to have been included in the formal, planned curriculum of the world language class. At the same time, there is considerable evidence about the teaching and learning of racism, sexism, ableism, and other kinds of bias in the classroom, none of which, one might wish to assume, is deliberate – but which is nevertheless an outcome of many educational experiences (see Jay, 2003; Ladson-Billings, 2003; Peters, 2015; Shaffer & Shevitz, 2001; Singer, 1995). To be sure, while we believe that a great deal of explicit bias in textbook and instructional materials in world language education has been eliminated in recent years, nevertheless many ideological and cultural biases do remain largely unexamined and unaddressed. As Susan Shaffer and Linda Shevitz have noted, "all aspects of the curriculum, including the 'evaded' curriculum, that which is not [explicitly] taught, can contain ... forms of bias that impede the learning and educational opportunities of all students" (Shaffer & Shevitz, 2001, p. 115).

The Hidden Curriculum

The phrase "the hidden curriculum" was first used by Philip Jackson in his 1968 book *Life in Classrooms*. Jackson described the hidden curriculum as follows:

> The crowds, the praise, and the power that combine to give a distinctive flavor to classroom life collectively form a hidden curriculum which each student (and teacher) must master if he [or she] is to make his [or her] way satisfactorily through the school. The demands created by these features of classroom life may be contrasted with the academic demands – the "official" curriculum, so to speak – to which educators traditionally have paid the most attention. As might be expected, the two curriculums are related to each other in several important ways.
>
> (Jackson, 1990, pp. 33–34)

Although a powerful insight, Jackson's conceptualization of the hidden curriculum was not tied to the political socialization and ideological aspects of public schooling, but rather to simply the non-academic aspects of schooling. Later scholars, however, extended the notion of the hidden curriculum in ways that emphasized such issues. Samuel Bowles and Herbert Gintis provided a critique of common views of the role of public schooling in the U.S. as agencies of social mobility, arguing that rather than encouraging upward mobility the schools reproduce existing social class structures for the vast majority of students, in part by sending messages to students about their intellectual abilities, personal traits, and appropriate educational and occupational choices (see Bowles & Gintis, 1976, 2002; Kentli, 2009). Jane Roland Martin suggested that the hidden curriculum can be seen in the social structure of the classroom, in the teacher's exercise of classroom authority, and in the rules that govern the relationship between the teacher and her or his students (Kentli, 2009; Martin, 1976). Writing in the context of the U.K., Paul Willis suggested that there are actually two hidden curricula – one that of the formal structures of the school, which determine in large part the reproduction of social class relations in society, but the other being constituted by the resistance of pupils to this process. Thus, on Willis's account, there is a far more complex dynamic with respect to social class reproduction and the role of the school in such reproduction (see Kentli, 2009; Willis, 1997). Finally, Henry Giroux has defined the hidden curriculum as the unstated norms, values and beliefs that area embedded in and transmitted to students through the underlying (and often unstated) rules that structure the routines and social relationships in the school and classroom (see Giroux, 1983, 1988; Kentli, 2009).

The Excluded Curriculum

In every society, there are many topics, perspectives, issues, ideas, and so on that are deliberately excluded from the curriculum. This is not, of course, an intrinsically bad thing – no curriculum in any discipline or field of study could possibly include all of the knowledge that exists in that discipline. *All* curricula involve making choices about what should and should not be included, and this is a perfectly legitimate aspect of the design and development of any curriculum. What is left out of the curriculum is called the "excluded curriculum," and almost by definition it is far larger than the planned, formal, overt curriculum. In the context of world language education, the excluded curriculum includes vocabulary and grammatical forms that are not considered to be essential for the student to master at a particular point in the curriculum. With respect to vocabulary, imagine that you are teaching a first-year course in French, German, Spanish or Russian. Table 9.1 contains a number of words that have been used thus far in this book. Which of these words would you consider to be appropriate vocabulary items for your beginner-level students?

Table 9.1 Selected Vocabulary

English	*French*	*German*	*Spanish*	*Russian*
assessment	évaluation	Bewertung	evaluación	оценка
bilingualism	bilinguisme	Zweisprachigkeit	bilingüismo	билингвизм
commentary	commentaire	Kommentar	comentario	комментарий
curriculum	programme d'études	Lehrplan	plan de estudios	учебный план
dynamic	dynamique	dynamisch	dinámico	динамический
ideology	idéologie	Ideologie	ideología	идеология
legitimate	légitime	Legitim	legítimo	законный
mythology	mythologie	Mythologie	mitología	мифология
observation	observation	Überwachung	observación	наблюдение
recursion	récursion	Rekursion	recursividad	рекурсия
stimulus	stimulus	Stimulus	estímulo	стимул

The chances are quite good that you would not decide to teach any of these words to your beginning-level students. This is not a matter of difficulty; almost all of these words, in most of the target languages, are actually cognates with their English equivalents, and so would be relatively easy for students to learn. The decision not to teach these vocabulary items is based on the very simple rationale that students are extremely unlikely to need any of them to meet their own, still basic, communicative needs. Excluding them from the formal curriculum is perfectly appropriate and reasonable. The same would be true of many grammatical features of the language. Almost without exception, we begin teaching students such grammatical features of the target language the present tense of verbs, singular and plural nouns, pronouns, gender (where appropriate), and so on. In an entry-level course, however, we would not teach such things as the imperfect subjunctive in Spanish, the *ne explétif* in French (as in the sentence, "*Ils sont plus nombreux que tu ne le crois*," "There are more of them than you think"), or provide a detailed explanation of verbs of motion in Russian.

There are other things that are sometimes excluded from the curriculum for less defensible reasons, however. The curriculum can be a source of considerable controversy, and it is not uncommon for topics and issues that might offend parents, politicians, religious figures, and so on, to be excluded from the curriculum. In some cases, such exclusion might not be particularly problematic, but in other cases, this can lead to what is essentially censorship in the curriculum. Such censorship is probably less common in world language education than in some other subject areas (such as social studies, literature, and so on), but it does nevertheless occur. The areas in which such censorship is most likely to occur are politics and ideological topics, sexual and lifestyle issues, religious matters, and similar areas in which there are significant ongoing debates in U.S. society. From the perspective of world language education, there is a problem here, since if we are trying to help our students to engage in communication about matters that are important to them, very often these matters include precisely the issues that are most controversial – issues of politics, sexuality and gender identity, and religion. Furthermore, insofar as we are committed to critical pedagogy, we are *assuming* that all education is political in nature, and so even if we wished to avoid many of these issues, it is not really possible to do so.

One valuable way to think about issues of the excluded curriculum and censorship is to distinguish between censorship and indoctrination. The key difference here is that while censorship involves decisions about the inclusion or exclusion of content, indoctrination is a far more serious matter. In his landmark study of indoctrination, I. A. Snook argued that "indoctrination is the teaching of any subject matter with the intention that it be believed regardless of the evidence," and further, that "indoctrination, so defined, is morally reprehensible" (Snook, 1972, p. 75).

Although Snook's fundamental concern is actually with the teaching of religion, his definition applies equally to other subjects. There is an important difference, in short, between teaching about a topic, and teaching about a topic in order that a particular belief is accepted by the student regardless of the evidence supporting or not supporting that belief. In the U.S. context, we often utilize this distinction in discussing "teaching religion" and "teaching about religion" – the former being unacceptable in a public school setting, while the latter being not only acceptable, but arguably necessary and even essential.[1]

The Historical Evolution of the World Language Curriculum in the United States

During the colonial era, schooling was for the most part restricted to a relatively small part of the population, and was far more common in New England than in the other colonies. For most children, schooling consisted of developing the basic skills of literacy, numeracy and acquiring religious knowledge – typically, the dominant Protestant denominational version of Christianity in each town or community. As early as the mid-17th century, schooling was mandated in parts of New England for all children. In the remainder of colonial America, schooling was less common and tended to develop later. In the South, the Planter élite provided tutors to educate their children, and the enslaved people upon whom the economy relied received no education. For the colonial élite generally, who often received a higher education either in a North American or British university, language skills were essential – principally, Latin, Classical Greek, and to some extent Hebrew (see Goldman, 2004). The rise of the Common Schools in the mid-19th century led to an institutionalization of schooling in most parts of the United States, and an expansion of the curriculum (Katz, 1968). It did not, however, include anything comparable to world language education – while there were a number of bilingual education programs for speakers of languages other than English (and especially German) (Kloss, 1998), second language instruction for native speakers of English was not included. Language study did take place, however, in secondary schools, where again the norm was for students to study Latin.

For secondary education in the United States, the development of the university may well be considered to have provided the origin of much of the standard or prescribed set of courses, or curriculum. The university, with its expectation of a classical curriculum that prepared students for college admission, was intended originally to have a more classical focus (see Brown, 1926; Monroe, 1940; Ornstein & Hunkins, 1993). Between 1850 and 1875, many universities added German to the list of world languages offered (called *foreign* at the time, of course), which brought the total number of languages to four (Ornstein & Hunkins, 1993). Between

1893 and 1895, the National Education Association's (NEA) "Committee of Ten" suggested that classical and modern languages were ideal as part of the standard high school curriculum. In 1918, the NEA Commission on the Reorganization of Secondary Education published the influential *Cardinal Principles of Secondary Education*, which marginalized world language education by suggesting it was appropriate for study in only part of the school-going population.

In short, for the vast majority of Americans the study of languages other than English has never been a significant component of the curriculum in the public school. The two important exceptions to this generalization have been the children (and especially the male children) of the social, political, intellectual and economic élite in American society, for whom language study has historically been a given, and heritage language speakers who have, in some times and places at least, been able to maintain their home languages in public school contexts (see Fishman, 2014). The contemporary lack of concern with and commitment to the learning of foreign languages is not an anomaly in our history; nor, unfortunately, is the resistance to languages other than English. Although concerns about languages other than English date back to the colonial era (Wiley, 1998, p. 215), perhaps the most serious challenges to our linguistic diversity took place during and shortly after World War I, when legal restrictions were placed on the teaching and learning of foreign languages (and most especially German) in a number of states (see Finkelman, 1996; Luebke, 1980; Pavlenko, 2003) – culminating in some cases with the public burning of books written in German.

Curricular Nullification

In the context of foreign language teaching, there has historically been an unfortunate tendency to confuse and conflate the curriculum with the textbook. This problem is not unique to foreign language teaching, but it seems to be more common in foreign language classes than in many other areas. There are a number of possible explanations for this tendency: institutional requirements that one follow the textbook, the ease of simply following the pre-determined course structure provided by a textbook, teacher insecurity about her or his own foreign language skills, and understandable (though perhaps somewhat inappropriate) assumptions about the knowledge, skills and competence of the creators and authors of foreign language textbooks. Taken together, all of these factors lead to what can be termed the "hegemony of the textbook," which refers to an unwillingness to question or challenge the textbook (see Ornstein, 1992, 1994). This is not meant to be an attack on textbooks *per se*; indeed, as Allan Ornstein has noted, there is much that is favorable about the use of textbooks:

> Good textbooks have many desirable characteristics. They are usually well-organized, coherent, unified, relatively up-to-date,

> accurate, and relatively unbiased. They have been scrutinized by scholars, educators, and minority groups. Their reading level and knowledge base match the developmental level of their intended audience. They are accompanied by teacher's manuals, test items, study guides, and activity guides. The textbook is an acceptable tool for instruction *as long as it is selected with care and is kept in proper perspective so that it is not viewed as the only source of knowledge, and it does not turn into the curriculum.*
>
> (Ornstein, 1994, p. 70, our emphasis)

The caveat added by Ornstein, though, is an extremely important one. Despite their utility, it is a serious error to conflate the textbook with the curriculum – a mistake that is often made in world language education contexts. Although it is clearly desirable for teachers to go beyond the textbook with respect to the curriculum, there is a process by which the critical pedagogue can challenge the hegemony of the textbook in a far more profound way than simply providing students with various kinds of supplementary materials. This process is called "curricular nullification," and it is analogous to the phenomenon of "jury nullification" in the United States, in which a jury chooses to ignore legal mandates in coming to a finding that they believe to be more just and appropriate (see Osborn, 2000, pp. 98–103). Curricular nullification refers to the teacher's ability to reject the set curriculum (whether this means the textbook or more formal and established institutional curricula), either to exclude certain features or units, or to include features or units that were absent in the original textbook or curriculum (that is, both additive and subtractive curricular nullification) (see Osborn, 2000, 2006; Reagan, 2016).

Additive Curricular Nullification

Additive curricular nullification in the world language classroom takes place quite often, especially as world language teachers add curricular content concerned with issues of culture. Such issues are typically the only non-linguistic and extra-linguistic ones that foreign language educators see as a core part of their teaching obligations, and active efforts are commonly made to integrate culture into the foreign language curriculum and classroom. There are a number of social, political, economic, cultural and historical themes that go well beyond those typically considered appropriate by world language educators that can be utilized in the context of the foreign language classroom to promote critical perspectives on issues of language and society (Osborn, 2006, p. 61). Among these themes are:

- personal and group identity;
- issues of conflict, struggle, and discrimination;

- socioeconomic class;
- ideology;
- hidden curricula;
- popular media (entertainment);
- other media (journalism, etc.);
- register and political/power relations;
- cultural hybridity;
- hegemony (linguistic, cultural, economic, political, etc.);
- issues of law and language;
- linguistic rights; and
- linguicism, resistance and marginalization.

It is precisely these themes, and others like them, that can contribute to the effective implementation of critical pedagogy in the world language classroom, and which provide guidance with respect to the kinds of curricular changes and modifications that might be required.

Additive curriculum nullification can also include discussions or even entire curricular units on such topics as language variation and language diversity, the linguistic hegemony of English and its impact on the particular language being studied, linguistic rights as human rights, assumptions about linguistic purity, ideas about "proper" language use, and language status, among others. For instance, additive curricular nullification might take place in a French course through the discussion of the differences between Parisian French and the French spoken in Montréal; in Spanish courses, going beyond the typical discussions of peninsular and Latin American Spanish to include other varieties, and especially local and non-standard varieties of the language would constitute such additive curricular nullification. There are also examples of phonological, lexical and grammatical variation that can be introduced in the foreign language class to encourage discussions on many of these topics.

Thus far, the examples of additive curricular nullification that have been offered here deal primarily with matters of sociolinguistics, issues of power and ideology, and so on, but there are also examples of additive curricular nullification that are related to phonology, the lexicon and the syntax of the target language. In Spanish classes, for instance, we almost universally teach students when and how to use *tú*, *usted*, and *ustedes*. *Vosotros* and *vosotras* are commonly but by no means universally taught, and so their inclusion or exclusion may be considered to be either an instance of negative curriculum nullification or positive curricular nullification. What is generally not taught, especially in beginning Spanish classes, is the *voseo* form (i.e., *vos*), in spite of its widespread use in a number of Latin American countries, and most notably in Argentina (see López, Franco & Yazan, 2019). The *voseo* form could very conceivably be added to the introduction of personal pronouns; to be sure, it may further complicate an already difficult concept for native speakers of English, but it also demonstrates the richness and diversity of Spanish.

Similarly, when we teach Spanish vocabulary, we often do so with a focus on Standard Spanish (or, more accurately, on a particular variety or set of varieties of Standard Spanish). To be sure, this is appropriate and valuable, but if one is teaching students in parts of the U.S. to speak Spanish, and is concerned with helping them to interact with the local *latino* community, then such words as *el broda* (the brother), *la norsa* (the nurse), *la troca* (the truck), *espelear* (to spell), *huachar* (to watch), and so on are likely, in some contexts, to prove at least as useful as their Standard Spanish equivalents.

One example of additive curricular nullification that we have discussed elsewhere is that which took place in the third term of a first-year high school Spanish class. The lesson used a text entitled "El otro 9/11" about the overthrow of the Allende régime in Chile in 2001, which was provided to the students as a handout in Spanish, and focused on reviewing the use of a number of different grammatical features that the students had already studied.

El otro 9/11

Cuando los americanos piensan en el 9/11 (11 de Septiembre del 2001), generalmente piensan en el ataque a las torres gemelas o *World Trade Center*. En el pasado, ya había existido otro importante 9/11 el cual ocurrió el 11 de Septiembre de 1973. Sucedió en Chile, cuando el Dr. Salvador Allende fue electo presidente en elecciones democráticas en 1970. El comenzó muchas reformas sociales y económicas. El 11 de septiembre de 1973 el presidente Allende y su gobierno fueron expulsados por un complot militar apoyado por la CIA de los Estados Unidos. Desde 1973 al 1990, el líder chileno fue Augusto Pinochet, quien encabezó una brutal dictadura en la cual 28,000 personas fueron torturadas y por lo menos 3,200 asesinadas, además de un gran número de personas desaparecidas.

English Translation

The Other 9/11

When Americans think about the date 9/11 (September 11, 2001), we usually think about the attack on the World Trade Center. There was already another important 9/11, though – September 11, 1973. In Chile, Dr. Salvador Allende was elected President in a democratic election in 1970. He began many social and economic reforms. On September 11, 1973 President Allende and his government were overthrown by a military coup supported by the United States CIA. From 1973 to 1990, Chile's leader was Augusto Pinochet, who headed a very brutal dictatorship in which 28,000 people were tortured, and at least 3,200 murders and disappearances took place.

Class Discussion

TEACHER: This reading is called "El otro 9/11." ¿Por qué? ¿Gustavo?

GUSTAVO: Chile … El presidente Allende, ¿sí?

TEACHER: Sí, pero … what *about* el presidente Allende? ¿Clase?

JUANITA: He was … well, his government was overthrown by a military coup.

TEACHER: Sí. ¿Cuando?

ROBERTO: Oh! 11 september 11 … umm … 1973.

TEACHER: El 11 de septembre, bueno.

SUSANNA: And Pinochet became Chile's new leader. And he was really bad, ¿de veras?

TEACHER: Pues, muchos personas en Chile lo creen. Pero, ¿por qué?

SUSANNA: The passage says that he tortured and killed people …

ROBERTO: And President Allende was killed.

TEACHER: Well, actually President Allende committed suicide during the coup. What about grammar … can you find some examples of noun/adjective agreement in the reading?

JUANITA: Sure. Las elecciones democráticas.

PEDRO: Y, muchas reformas sociales y económicas …

ROBERTO: Un complot militar, and los Estados Unidos, también.

TEACHER: Muy bien,clase. Y, ¿qué saben uds. sobre el verbo "piensan"?

JUANITA: Well, it comes from "pensar," so it's an *–ar* verb …

MARIA: Yeah, but it's one of those stem-changing verbs, because of the "*ie*."

JUANITA: And it's present tense, and goes with los americanos. That's … umm … third person plural, ¿sí?

TEACHER: Perfecto. Ahora, ¿hay algo aquí interesante?

JUANITA: Does it say that the United States … the CIA … supported the coup? That can't be true …

TEACHER: Pues, let's find out. Your homework is to go on-line and find out what you can about the 1973 coup in Chile. Let's find out if this reading is accurate, and what really happened.

As one can see in the class discussion, this passage provides numerous opportunities for reviewing a number of grammatical features of Spanish (gender, noun/adjective agreement, verbs – especially the preterite, as well as introducing a number of cognates), while at the same time providing very obvious and direct openings for in-depth discussions about politics and ideology in Latin America, and the role of the United States in recent Latin American history. Although we recognize that there are certainly some school settings where such texts would be problematic, the text is basically accurate and its claims demonstrably true.

Subtractive Curricular Nullification

Subtractive curricular nullification, on the other hand, basically occurs when mandated parts of the established curriculum are minimized or eliminated altogether by the teacher. Subtractive curricular nullification is less common in the foreign language context than in many other disciplines, since our curricula are generally articulated over a number of years, which means that removing material from the curriculum may present problems for both teachers and students in later years of language study. Nevertheless, subtractive curricular nullification does occur; we have already mentioned the case of the elimination of *vosotros/vosotras* in some Spanish courses and programs. Another example of curricular nullification that took place in French classrooms was the replacement of *la fin de semaine* with *le week-end*, a recognition that the lexical use in France had changed.

The Role of Interdisciplinary Units in the Critical Curriculum

We now turn our focus directly onto the concept of curricular integration with other subject areas. Connecting with other disciplines has, at least until recently, not been a particularly strong point of world language curricula and instruction, often because planners in the other core areas have failed to recognize the potential contributions our field can provide, and also because we ourselves have tended to focus on what can be done *within* the world language classroom with respect to disciplinary connections rather than looking for ways in which connections might be made between world language classes and other subject areas. As the latest state frameworks and national standards attest, however, interdisciplinary links have the potential to help students to create a powerful nexus among the issues that they study (see National Standards Collaborative Board, 2015; National Standards in Foreign Language Education Project, 1996, 2006). In fact, as world language education takes its much-coveted place among the core subjects offered in the schools, encouraging students to make these associations will prove invaluable for a number of reasons, some cognitive (such connections more accurately represent the reality of the nature of knowledge) and others pragmatic (connections to other subjects and disciplines help students to see the relevance of foreign language study).

During the past several decades, a growing number of educators working within and among the core content areas have advocated the development and implementation of interdisciplinary curricula as an important aspect of educational reform and renewal (see Lonning, DeFranco & Weinland, 1998; National Council of Teachers of Mathematics, 1991). An important aspect of the literature concerned with the interdisciplinary curriculum has been its emphasis on the hurdles faced by educators in integrating course content across disciplinary lines, which constitute a challenge of considerable scope and difficulty (Davison, Miller & Methany, 1995; Lonning & DeFranco, 1997). Within the field of world language education, as well, researchers and educators have looked for ways to effectively move beyond the traditional barriers of the classroom in terms of both pedagogy and instructional content (Biron, 1998; Gehlker, Gozzi & Zeller, 1999; Kaufman, Moss, & Osborn, 2003; Osborn, 1998a, 1998b, 2006, 2008; Overfield, 1997). These efforts reflect the values and articulated goals of the *Standards for Foreign Language Learning*:

> The conscious effort to connect the foreign language curriculum with other parts of students' academic lives opens doors to information and experiences which enrich the entire school and life experience. Those connections flow from other areas to the foreign language classroom and also originate in the foreign language classroom to add unique experiences and insights to the rest of the curriculum.
>
> (National Standards in Foreign Language Education Project, 1996, p. 49)

Contemporary educational thought in general tends to be decidedly supportive of interdiscplinary approaches to teaching and learning (see Shrum & Glisan, 2016), and we would certainly agree that the linking of foreign languages with content in language courses (and, indeed, across the whole curriculum) is certainly a worthwhile goal. However, desire alone is insufficient to direct and guide efforts of this type to successful fruition. A model for the initial planning stages of interdisciplinary curriculum development in and for world language courses is crucial. This is especially true because of the general difficulty involved in developing and implementing interdisciplinary curricula, as David Ackerman has stressed:

> While it unquestionably has high rhetorical appeal, curriculum integration presents daunting challenges to those who would like to see it more widely embraced as an alternative or counterpart to subject-based curriculum ... With its promise of unifying knowledge and modes of understanding, interdisciplinary education represents the pinnacle of curriculum development.
>
> (Ackerman, 1989, p. 37)

Heidi Jacobs has noted that, "in contrast to a discipline-field based view of knowledge, interdisciplinarity does not stress delineations but linkages" (Jacobs, 1989, p. 8). Ackerman has moved the interdisciplinary agenda forward by proffering intellectual and practical criteria to be considered as a "framework for teachers and curriculum developers deliberating over whether to adopt a curriculum integration approach for some portion of their instructional program" (Ackerman, 1989, p. 25). Perhaps most significant elements of Ackerman's framework are the concepts of *validity for*, *validity within*, and *validity beyond* the discipline (see also Lonning, DeFranco & Weinland, 1998, p. 315). Briefly summarized, these criteria require that an interdisciplinary theme or organizing center be important to relevant fields of study – that is, that they not be just a contrived connection. Further, the criteria must facilitate the learning of other concepts within the individual disciplines, and must give the student a "metaconceptual bonus" (Ackerman, 1989, p. 29; see also pp. 27–30). Within these parameters, however, one finds both the genesis of new ways of thinking about such units and about the limitations of current models for the foreign language classroom.

As Rob Lonning, Thomas DeFranco, and Tim Weinland have pointed out, the "selection of appropriate themes seems to be the key to providing instruction that is potentially more meaningful when taught in an interdisciplinary fashion than when the concepts are taught separately" (Lonning et al., 1998, p. 312). The model they propose for the integration of mathematics and science includes moving from standards and state frameworks, through a revision and evaluation process in selecting an applicable theme, to a refinement of activities that balance mathematics and science content. In an analogous fashion, units in the world language classroom can become interdisciplinary as they move from the usual textbook chapter topics to overarching and extendable curricular themes, especially insofar as such themes overlap and are tied to curricular content in other subject areas.

Yet, even as the newest standards challenge both traditional grammatical and even solely communicative approaches to world language education, curriculum planners may well find it perplexing to attempt to design an appropriate interdisciplinary theme for the world language class. A good place to see this problem is with the notion of "teaching culture." Simply put, the challenge is to determine which themes or topics can be included under the broad banner of traditional "culture," and how far and to what extent it is appropriate to deviate from time-honored categories when they seem too rigid, given new directions in the field. Understandably, Daniel Shanahan's (1998) contention that there are minimally five major approaches to the conception of culture with relevance for the world language classroom points to a lack of clarity about "culture" as the point of departure for non- or extra-linguistic course content in the foreign language classroom. Shanahan includes capital "C" culture and lowercase "c" culture, cultural studies which include political aspects, cross-cultural communicative facets, and an ecumenical cultural approach which focuses on the affective rather than the oppositional approaches of the primarily cognitive notions of culture.

The uncertainty about defining culture arises with good reason, since for both world language educators and others alike, the concept of culture is both a fuzzy and complex one. Judith Lessow-Hurley, for instance, has perceptively pointed out that, "Culture is something we all have but often find difficult to perceive. Culture, like language, is dynamic, changing to meet the needs of the people it serves. All cultures have coherent, shared systems of action and belief that allow people to function and survive" (Lessow-Hurley, 1996, p. 95). Goodman, on the other hand, relies on more traditional definitions of culture in asserting that culture is the "learned, socially-transmitted heritage of artifacts, knowledge, beliefs, values and normative expectations that provides the members of a particular society with the tools for coping with recurrent problems" (Goodman, 1992, p. 338). Though the definitions offered by many are not mutually exclusive, such a catch-all category is difficult to use in planning interdisciplinary units with other core curricula, even given the theoretical power and applicability of Ackerman's criteria (Ackerman, 1989) and Lonning, DeFranco, and Weinland's (1998) model for curriculum integration.

In practice, of course, it is quite difficult, if not impossible, to meaningfully separate the linguistic content of the world language course from its concomitant cultural components. As Claire Kramsch explains:

> One often reads in teachers' guidelines that language teaching consists of teaching the four skills [reading, writing, listening, and speaking] "plus culture." This dichotomy of language and culture is an entrenched feature of language teaching around the world. It is part of the linguistic heritage of the profession. Whether it is called (Fr.) *civilisation*, (G.) *Landeskunde*, or (Eng.) *culture*, culture is often seen as mere information conveyed by the language, not as a feature of language itself; cultural awareness becomes an educational objective in itself, separate from language. If however, language is seen as social practice, culture becomes the very core of language teaching. Cultural awareness must then be viewed both as enabling language proficiency and as being the outcome of reflection on language proficiency.
>
> (Kramsch, 1993, p. 8)

Osborn (2001) has stressed that cultural items included in the world language curriculum will be more similar to the home culture, the target culture, or both, and as a result critical interdisciplinary units will need to utilize themes and activities which include both connective validity and comparative integrity. Connective validity and comparative integrity imply that themes for interdisciplinary units possess features which simultaneously resonate as "authentic" with both members of the represented culture and experts in the field of study, thus achieving a balance among elements of disciplinary epistemology (see Reagan, 1999, 2002) and multicultural perspectives. Connective validity requires that any interdisciplinary unit includes the following aspects:

- a thoughtful integration of communicative aspects in the skills of reading, writing, listening, and speaking;
- a contextualization or subjectification of the domestic (or "home culture") perspective; and
- primary attention paid to the related global or local realities of pluralism, including any role played by language diversity. (Osborn 2001; Gerwin & Osborn, 2002)

An interdisciplinary unit focusing on defining who "we" are, and defining who "they" are, for example, might involve activities in the foreign language classroom, the social studies or history classroom, the English or language arts classroom, and the drama classroom. The integrated, interdisciplinary unit we suggest should focus on cultural identity themes that can be investigated through sources in the world language classroom, including documents, videos, audio recordings, and other media in relation to problem-posing. The world language teacher, utilizing the examples of commercials, cartoons, and advertisement or other, target language realia as communicative catalysts, then includes activities related to reading, writing, listening, or speaking in any combination. Though all of the activities need not specifically relate to the connections in each of the other classes, the point of connection should involve the acquisition of information in the target language as demonstrative of how we identify ourselves and portray dissimilar "Others." A unit should also include a concerted attempt to subjectify the "home" perspective. Henry Giroux (1997) refers to a "culture of positivism" which in the case of the world language classroom can lead students to understand, in error, that knowledge, including knowing one's identity is apolitical or beyond the influence of culture. The critical world language curriculum is built in cooperation with the other contributing disciplines to enable student understanding of the home perspective as one created from within a specific time and place framework (that is, that it is not *supra*historical), and to hear other voices that seek to challenge the dominant perspective with an often dissenting view. In this way, students grow to understand through the contextualization of the perspective that the identity being constructed in any narrative – literary, historical, linguistic, dramatic, or otherwise – represents a dominant ideology, not an unbiased fact.

Connective validity also suggests that a theme attends to the realities of global pluralism. If a theme does not relate to cultural diversity in some international or transnational way, then a connection to the world language classroom is likely contrived. The theme of defining who "we" are, defining who "they" are, however, most certainly attends to the realities of diversity both at home and abroad. In a related vein, Wong has attempted to raise warnings about the potential misuse of comparative approaches to literature:

> A key instructional means of eliciting insight being comparison and contrast, at every turn we need to decide what to compare a marginalized literature to, and to what end. If this is done from a fallacious assumption of one's impartiality, however well-intentioned, the purpose of broadening the curriculum, namely, to honor the articulation of previously suppressed subjectivities, will be seriously undermined.
> (Wong, 1993, p. 112)

A growing body of evidence suggests that cultural information as presented in classrooms is often culturally reductionist or misrepresentative (Brosh, 1997; Osborn, 1999, 2000; Reagan & Osborn, 1998; Wieczorek, 1994). Osborn (2001) contends that cross-cultural comparisons should be screened in an attempt to avoid defining cultural issues as cleanly dichotomous, including characteristics as follows:

- an *emic* voice in representing the cultural information;
- an absence of bifurcatious categorization; and
- an explicit articulation of multiple perspectives within the "home" culture.

The *emic* perspective is central to a unit theme or activity that possesses comparative integrity. If the classroom activities, discussions, or presentations attempt to act as paternalistic agent for representing a target cultural perspective, the derived depictions will unavoidably be both self-serving and reductionist. The avoidance of bifurcation, in relation to the unit we are proposing, implies that the teacher attempts to disclaim the use of "us" and "them" categories. Though seldom so blatant, discussions of the "American" versus "foreign" perspective present the same problem in the world language classroom. Such categories, obviously, trivialize the complexity of diversity as expressed in society and significantly call into question the ethical and educational value of any interdisciplinary unit. Further, by calling student attention to the multiple perspectives of who "we" are and who "they" are within both the home and target cultures, world language teachers can provide a dialectical understanding of cultural mediation for the students, and thus engage in the dialogical process advocated so compellingly by Paolo Freire (see Freire, 1973, 1974, 2002a, 2002b, 2002c, 2002d, 2018). Put simply, *no* issues related to identity are unidimensional, nor are they uncontested. Tensions and resistance exist in *all* cultural identity issues, and illuminating such facets for students is vitally important to the integrity of critical foreign language instruction.

Teaching Literature in World Language Education

The teaching of literature, whether in English courses or world language curricula, is often seen by both classroom teachers and others as a fairly difficult undertaking. As Jonathan Sell has noted,

> It is sometimes difficult for teachers and lecturers of literature to justify their professional existence, a difficulty that contributes in part to what literary scholar Elaine Showalter ... calls "the anxiety of teaching." It is therefore understandable that foreign and second language ... teachers and lecturers may sometimes find it even more difficult to justify the inclusion of literature in their lesson plans.
>
> (Sell, 2005, p. 86)

There is little doubt that Sell's observation about the challenges of including literature in the world language classroom is all too often true, in spite of the fact that one of the generally articulated goals for studying a language other than one's own is to be able to read and enjoy the literature produced in that language. To be sure, French literature, Spanish literature, German literature, Russian literature, and so on, can all be read in translation, and in reality this is how such literature is most often accessed by native speakers of English. This is understandable for a number of reasons; the two most significant are the level of fluency required in a particular language for such an undertaking, and the fact that most of us will never have access to the literature in more than a small number of languages. Relying on translations, however, also inevitably limits the extent to which one can appreciate the nuances of a particular text, and many foreign language educators would agree with the French proverb *traduire, c'est trahir* ("to translate is to betray"). The role and place of literature in the world language classroom, however, has been a matter of considerable debate (see Bredella & Delanoy, 1996; Brumfit & Carter, 1986; Collie & Slater, 1987; Lazar, 1993), especially with respect to elementary and intermediate level language courses, and this is a debate that has important implications for the implementation of critical pedagogy in the world language classroom.

There is an additional challenge in the teaching of literature – in any language – that must also be addressed, and that is the challenge presented by the existing canon in the language (see Altieri, 1983; Guillory, 1993; Joyce, 1987; Kolbas, 2001; Krupat, 1989; McCarthy, 1993; McDonald & Sanders, 2002; Pollock, 1999; Robinson, 1983; Shome, 1996). It is the canon that is arguably the single most important factor in determining which particular texts students will study in the world language class, and the canon is by no means the result of a neutral or objective process. Rather, the selection of works to be included in the canon – and, therefore, the determination of works *not* to be included in the canon – has considerable impact on the teaching of literature. In essence, it is the canon that determines which works in the target language are included in the curriculum, and which works are not included.

The teaching of literature in world language education courses is often claimed to serve a wide variety of purposes, not the least of which include:

- promoting cultural enrichment, understanding and awareness;
- providing models of "good" writing in the target language;
- offering students the opportunity to experience linguistic diversity in the target language;
- extending linguistic competence beyond the fundamentals typically covered in the classroom;
- providing authentic texts in the target language;
- giving students a memorable "archive" of texts (especially poetry and music);
- assisting learners to develop a sense for the rhythmic structures of the target language;
- motivating students by providing them with interesting, relevant and genuine linguistic input; and
- encouraging learners to develop skills of interpretation that will be useful in both the target language and the student's native language.

(Parkinson & Thomas, 2000, pp. 9–11)

These general benefits of the use of literature in the foreign language classroom are supplemented by more specific advantages with respect to the process of second language acquisition (see Nuessel, 2000, pp. 11–13). As Susan Bassnett and Peter Grundy have suggested, the benefits of teaching literature and the inclusion of literary texts in the world language classroom include:

- Literature is a part of a complete language learning experience.
- The language learner functions as a resource and the learner's stored experience and intuitive awareness may be utilized in the second-language acquisition process.
- "Creative writing" is the prerogative of any language learner and not just a select group of authors from a predetermined "canon." Writing should be taught as a basic part of the language curriculum. Writing is not simply analysis and paraphrase of someone else's work.
- Second-language methodology in the teaching of "foreign" literature must change. It must be more learner-centered, collaborative and communicative in its approach.
- Teachers who do not believe that literature is a part of the second-language curriculum fail to comprehend this rich cultural and linguistic resource.
- At this juncture, second-language instruction needs original and worthwhile uses of creative literature with a firm basis in linguistic principles and methodological rationales.

(Bassnett & Grundy, 1993, p. 1)

Beyond the key question of whether there is a place for the teaching of literature in the world language classroom, there are several related questions. As Sell has suggested, "the question that concerns [foreign language] teachers is what to do with literature and, perhaps more importantly, why do anything at all with it" (Sell, 2005, p. 87). In our view, perhaps the strongest reason for incorporating literature in the world language classroom is not included in most of the standard defenses for doing so – it is, rather, one grounded in critical perspectives on the reality of contemporary world language education. Specifically, we agree with the assertion that,

> Standard [foreign language] textbooks are fictions in a variety of ways. Not only do they tend to peddle a version of [the target language] which is abnormal in its normativeness, deviant in its purity, but they also use fictional storylines to introduce learners to various situations, points of grammar or lexical fields and often employ non-authentic recordings of actors with bogus accents for listening exercises. Apart from being fictive, this is all unconvincing and patronising and turns off the target learners .... Textbook topic contents are also often unreal in the sense of [being] irrelevant to the learners sitting in the classroom.
>
> (Sell, 2005, pp. 91–92)

In short, the inclusion of real, authentic literature in the target language – while admittedly often more difficult for students than the sanitized language presented in standard textbooks – can be both more defensible pedagogically and more compatible by far with the goals and objectives of critical pedagogy (see Block & Gray, 2018). At the same time, though, the use of authentic literature – especially that normally considered to be the canonical literature of the target language – poses its own quite serious challenges, a matter to which we now turn.

The Canon: Toward a Definition

The term "canon" is a complex one, with a number of different, albeit related, meanings. Etymologically from the Greek word κᾰνών, the historical uses of the term are largely religious in nature, referring to both the authoritative list of accepted parts of the *Bible* (both the Hebrew *Bible* and the *New Testament*[2]) and to any regulation or dogma decreed by a Church council (see Brueggemann, 2003; Halbertal, 1997; Sanders, 2005). This definition itself, though, points to some of the underlying problems with the concept of the canon and the identification of particular works as canonical (and others as non-canonical). The scriptural canon is the body of texts held by a particular religious community to be authoritative; indeed, for many religious communities, the scriptural canon is believed to be not merely authoritative but divinely inspired and protected or even literally true.[3] Furthermore, in the case of the Judeo-Christian tradition, different groups hold somewhat different views about what is and is not included in the biblical canon. Beyond the obvious difference that Christians accept the *New Testament* as a key part of Scripture while Jews do not, there are other differences as well. Although some scholars suggest that the Hebrew canon was relatively well-established by the 4th century BCE (or certainly before the 1st century BCE), the totality of the text was not completely finalized until the Masoretic text, which was compiled between the 7th and 10th centuries CE.[4] Then there are, for instance, the apocryphal books written between 200 BCE and 400 CE that are included by some, but not all, Christians in their versions of the *Old Testament*. Similarly, there are the deuterocanonical books and passages from the *Old Testament* that are considered to be fully canonical by the Roman Catholic Church, Eastern Orthodox Church, Oriental Orthodox Church, and Assyrian Church of the East, but which are seen as non-canonical by Protestants. Thus, even within the broad Christian tradition there are disagreements about precisely what constitutes canonical Scripture and what does not. It is important to note here that these disagreements about what is to be included in the scriptural canon are separate from other debates about how these texts are to be understood and interpreted, about their status as divinely inspired, and so on – problems of considerable significance theologically, of course, but also problems that do not arise, at least to the same extent, in the case of non-religious texts.

From these religious meanings, the term has expanded over time to refer to the generally accepted works in a literary tradition or discipline. When we talk about the "literary canon" in a language, we are basically talking about the collection of books, narratives, poems, and other kinds of texts in a particular language that have been deemed to be the "best" and most influential during a period of time or in a specific place. In other words, the canon is – by definition – both an evaluative and value-ascribing list that reflects the views, values, ideals, attitudes, ideologies, and so on, of the educated élite in a speech community. The canon does not develop on its own, nor is it the result of majority opinion, but is, rather, the product of a specific group in society with specific ends and goals in mind. As Jordan Bates has noted:

> The Western literary canon has historically been dictated by economically secure, traditionally educated, socially privileged white men ... Plus, literacy was historically the province of the privileged and so, the uneducated or minimally educated – which included some women but most laboring-class citizens, of both sexes, as well as children – were automatically excluded. The remnant of this class-based exclusionary thinking is visible in today's society in the disdain with which the cultural elite usually greet "popular" art like Harry Potter, graphic novels, country-western music, etc.
>
> (Bates, 2013)

It is worth stressing here that it is not only the evaluation of particular works that plays a role in determining whether or not a work is to be included in the canon; another important facet of the canon and debates about the canon historically is that the works of individuals in some groups (generally, historically marginalized groups) were far less likely to be included in the canon. As Gregory Rutledge has pointed out, for the most part efforts to delineate the contents of the canon "contained works by authors of a race, gender, social standing and perspective similar to the … canon-makers [themselves]" (quoted in Bates, 2013). This does not mean that there is not merit to the idea of the canon, but it does mean that it is important for us to recognize that it is a product of social construction that can not only be analyzed, but also one that can be critiqued and challenged, and, importantly, that can change and evolve over time.

The Western Literary Canon

A good place to begin our discussion of the Western literary canon is perhaps with the observation that there is not, and indeed has never been, any full or complete agreement about what should be considered to be included in the canon. At the same time, though, certain works are virtually always employed as illustrative examples of works that are definitively part of the canon – in the case of English (and, in fact, of the Western canon more generally), the example *par excellence* of this has been the collected work of Shakespeare. In fact, the Western canon is very much a work in progress, and has always been – it is in a process of evolution and change, with some works disappearing over time while others replace them. In the case of English, writers once considered canonical, such as William Blake and Matthew Arnold, have been largely replaced in the curriculum by texts produced by Ernest Hemmingway, Langston Hughes, and Toni Morrison, among others (see Lombardi, 2019). This is especially important when we take into account that for much of its history the Western literary canon was dominated primarily by white, educated, upper-class men, and was thus in no sense representative of Western culture, let alone humanity as a whole. In recent years, efforts have been made to expand the canon, to include both literature produced by historically marginalized and subaltern groups, and to incorporate and include non-Western works as worth study, examination and reflection (see Sargar, 2018).

Given the fact that the Western canon is not static or fixed, this does not mean that there are not examples of what works have been typically included in it. Table 9.2, which is based on the work of the American literary critic Harold Bloom and, in addition, is reflective to some extent of the Great Books curricula used at many U.S. universities,[5] provides some indications of the kinds of texts that are widely considered to be part of the canon, although it is certainly by no means exhaustive. Bloom divides

Table 9.2 Harold Bloom: The Western Literary Canon

The Theocratic Age (2000 BCE to 1321 CE)	
Main Traditions:	***Examples:***
The Ancient Near East	*Gilgamesh*, *The Book of the Dead*, the *Hebrew Bible* and the *New Testament*
Ancient India	*Mahabharata*
Ancient Greece	*Iliad* (Homer), *Odyssey* (Homer), and *Oedipus Rex* (Sophocles)
Ancient Rome	*Aeneid* (Virgil), *Metamorphoses* (Ovid)
The Middle Ages	*Confessions* (Saint Augustine)
The Aristocratic Age (1321 CE to 1832 CE)	
Major Bodies of Literature:	***Examples:***
Italy	*Divine Comedy* (Dante), *The Prince* (Machiavelli), *The Servant of Two Masters* (Carlo Goldoni)
France	*The Essays* (Montaigne), *The Misanthrope* (Molière), *Candide* (Voltaire)
Germany	*The Robbers* (Friedrich Schiller), *Faust* and *Italian Journey* (Goethe)
Spain	*Don Quixote* (Miguel de Cervantes), *The Trickster of Seville* (Tirso de Molina)
Portugal	*The Lusiads* (Luis de Camões)
Great Britain and Ireland	*Hamlet* (William Shakespeare), *Paradise Lost* (John Milton), *Gulliver's Travels* (Jonathan Swift)
The Democratic Age (1832 CE to 1900 CE)	
Country:	***Examples:***
Great Britain and Ireland	*Pride and Prejudice* (Jane Austen), *The Adventures of Oliver Twist* (Charles Dickens), *The Picture of Dorian Gray* (Oscar Wilde)
Italy	*The Betrothed* (Alessandro Manzoni), *The Adventures of Pinocchio* (Carlo Collodi)
France	*The Red and the Black* (Stendhal), *Madame Bovary* (Gustave Flaubert), *Les Misérables* (Victor Hugo)
Germany	*The Ring of the Nibelung* (Richard Wagner), *Children's and Household Tales* (Grimm Brothers), *Effi Briest* (Theodor Fontane)
Spain and Portugal	*Fortunata and Jacinta* (Benito Pérez Galdós), *La Regenta* (Leopoldo Alas)
Russia	*Crime and Punishment* (Dostoevsky), *War and Peace* (Leo Tolstoy), *The Seagull* (Anton Chekhov)
United States	*The Adventures of Huckleberry Finn* (Mark Twain), *Moby-Dick* (Herman Melville)

Table 9.1 (Cont.)

The Theocratic Age (2000 BCE to 1321 CE)	
The Chaotic Age (1900 CE to Present)	
Country:	***Examples:***
Great Britain and Ireland	*Ulysses* (James Joyce), *Mrs Dalloway* (Virginia Woolf), *The Waste Land* (T. S. Eliot)
Italy	*Six Characters in Search of an Author* (Luigi Pirandello), *Zeno's Conscience* (Italo Svevo)
France	*In Search of Lost Time* (Marcel Proust), *The Stranger* (Albert Camus), *Waiting for Godot* (Samuel Beckett)
Germany (and German-Speaking Central Europe)	*The Magic Mountain* (Thomas Mann), *The Castle* (Franz Kafka), *The Man Without Qualities* (Robert Musil)
Spain and Portugal	*Gypsy Ballads* (Federico Garcia Lorca), *The Book of Disquiet* (Fernando Pessoa)
Russia	*The Master and Margarita* (Mikhail Boulgakov), *The Gulag Archipelago* (Aleksandr Solzhenitsyn)
United States	*The Great Gatsby* (F. Scott Fitzgerald), *The Old Man and the Sea* (Ernest Hemingway)
Latin America	*Ficciones* (Jorge Luis Borges), *Canto General* (Pablo Neruda), *One Hundred Years of Solitude* (Gabriel Garcia Marquez)

the Western literary tradition into four ages: the Theocratic Age, the Aristocratic Age, the Democratic Age, and the Chaotic Age (Bloom, 1994).

Thus far, we have been discussing the Western literary canon as a whole, but in the context of the world language curriculum, it is the language-specific canon with which we need to be concerned. Bloom's model, of course, does include works from multiple linguistic traditions, but only a small number of such works from each language. In world language education, we are generally concerned with the canon of major works composed in the particular target language. Thus, although there are outstanding translations of Shakespeare available in Russian, these are not considered to be part of the Russian canon,[6] at least in the way that the works of Dostoevsky, Tolstoy, Pushkin, and so on are typically considered to be.

The Uses and Value of the Canon

Although it should be fairly obvious that we have serious concerns and reservations about the western canon, especially as it has been historically defined, there are nevertheless a number of valuable aspects to the canon that we need to be aware of. To some extent, the canon is useful for world language educators simply because it serves as a constant reminder that literature can be a valuable tool in the world language classroom, even at the elementary levels. Not only is literature useful for a variety of practical and pragmatic reasons, but it does have educational value. As we have suggested, although there are certainly problems with the ways in which the canon has been constructed, and with the decisions about the inclusion and exclusion of particular individuals and groups, not to mention with how the texts included in the canon are understood and interpreted, this does not mean that many of the works traditionally included in the canon are not of outstanding aesthetic character and value. Properly utilized in the world language classroom, many of these works can promote both critical understanding and concerns with issues of social justice in our students. In other words, the "canon controversy" can be effectively used in the classroom to help students develop critical perspectives on the study of world languages broadly understood.

Toward a Critique of the Canon

Apart from disagreements about the inclusion or exclusion of particular authors or works in the canon, beginning in the 1960s there were a host of criticisms and critiques of the canon – both of the Western canon in general, and of the canon in English in particular (see Bates, 2013; Guillory, 1993; Kolbas, 2001; McCarthy, 1993; Pollock, 1999; Robinson, 1983; Sargar, 2018; Shome, 1996). The central criticism in these critiques was that the canon had been determined by individuals from specific backgrounds (gender, race, class, education, and so on), and reflected not the "best" of literature but rather, only a relatively small subset of the literature in one or more languages. This criticism, in our view, was (and largely remains) a valid one. Although many – perhaps most – of the works in any particular canon are of extremely high quality, virtually every attempt at canonization *does* reflect the background and biases of those engaged in compiling the canon. To some extent, this is often the result of the lack of literary works by individuals from marginalized groups, but it is also an outcome of the ways in which canonical works are defined and determined. In addition, there are other non-western canons, both in English and the other commonly taught world languages and in other languages (see, for examples, Joyce, 1987; Kachru, 2005; Krupat, 1989). From the perspective of those committed to critical pedagogy, this creates a dilemma. On the one hand, we want our students to be familiar with the major recognized literary products in the target language – it would be inconceivable to imagine a credible advanced French curriculum that did not include at least some familiarity with such figures as Voltaire, Jean-Jacques Rousseau, Honoré de Balzac, Montesquieu, Alexandre Dumas, Victor Hugo, Gustav Flaubert, Albert Camus, Jean-Paul Sartre, Molière, and a host of others. At the same time, this is a list composed solely of white, largely upper-class males. At the very least, a more defensible conceptualization of the French canon would need to include such women as George Sand, Marguerite Yourcenar, Simone de Beauvoir, Madame de Lafayette, and the Cameroonian author Léonora Miano, as well as writers such as Kamel Daoud from Algeria, and the Senegalese authors Léopold Sédar Senghor and Birago Diop. Critical pedagogy would require not only that we expand the canon, but, in addition, that we engage in critical conversations about the existing works in the canon – the presence of sexism, racism, classism, and so on, in what are considered to be the "great" works in the canonical tradition.

These criticism of the canon might, we know, lead to questions about whether there ought even to be a canon. Although such questions are understandable, the fact of the matter is that a canon will inevitably exist, if for no other reason than a curriculum exists. The very existence of a curriculum – whether at the secondary level or the university level – establishes a canon of sorts, and insofar as curricula are similar across institutions, a canon *does* exist. The challenge that faces us is not to eliminate the canon, then, but to find ways in which the canon can be used effectively to promote the goals of critical pedagogy and social justice.

Revisiting the Canon: Critical Pedagogy and the Teaching of Literature

For the most part, the canon has been taken for granted as something of a given in world language education courses and programs. This is understandable, and there is certainly a valuable and important place for the traditional canon in such courses and programs – but there is also a different, far more critical, place for both the traditional canon and for alternatives and additions to that canon. One useful way to think about critical perspectives in the canon has been provided by Terry A. Osborn in his work on social justice in world language education (see Osborn, 2006). He has suggested that there are at least four important, perhaps essential, pillars in conceptualizing critical pedagogy in world language education: identity, social architecture, language choices, and activism. Each of these pillars can be utilized to assist students in asking key questions that will promote discussions and reflections about both personal and social matters that may, ultimately, lead to the emergence of critical perspectives. Examples of the questions in each of these pillars are:

Identity Questions about identity include not only those concerned with personal identity (Who am I? Who are we?), but also affiliation (Who are "we"? Who are "they"?), and thus lead to concerns with conflict, struggle, prejudice, bias and discrimination.

Social Architecture Questions about social architecture deal with what we believe, both individually and communally – including ideology, historical perspectives, the content of the hidden curriculum, media and entertainment, and certainly about language.

Language Choices Questions about language choice address not simply matters of manners and appropriateness, but also register, power relations, status, cultural differences, hybridity, and hegemony.

Activism Questions about activism are concerned, fundamentally, with issues of law and rights, although they also deal with matters of resistance and marginalization.

The questions related to each of these pillars can be incorporated into the teaching of any literary text or content, of course, but by expanding our understanding of the canon, we are likely to include works that facilitate such instruction in valuable ways.

Voices from the Field

One extremely positive development in world language education in the past few decades has been the commitment of many classroom teachers to critical pedagogy, and to the development of instructional materials that can be used effectively in the classroom to promote critical pedagogy and social justice concerns. Stacey Johnson (2018) has connected language learning to community-based global learning. She has developed an entire website/podcasts at https://weteachlang.com/ that is a priceless contribution to the field and pioneering in efforts to connect language educators. Columbia Gomez, a Spanish teacher from Austin, Texas, has offered teachers options at the elementary level, arguing that:

> *It's my responsibility as a Spanish teacher to step out of my comfort zone and find ways to bring Social Justice into my curriculum.* I decided this time to focus on immigration, something that I think is timely even if it's a charged topic (or because it's such a charged topic, I can't ignore it). With immigration as a current issue, and that unlikely to change for some time, I believe it is important for our students to understand why people come to this country, what their motivations are.
>
> (Gomez, 2018, our emphasis)

Mary Zampini and Joan Kerley (2013) address the other end of the educational spectrum – world language education at the tertiary level, with a focus on service learning that incorporates a Jesuit approach to social justice in world language education; David Smith (2009) tackles some of the same issues in university level world language education in the evangelical/Protestant traditions (see also Smith & Carvill, 2000). Florence Lojacono (2013) examines techniques of fostering social justice in a Web

2.0 environment, while Martha Bigelow (2016) suggested exploring social justice topics in world language education through a lens of pain. Dorie Conlon Perugini (2018) interviewed L. J. Randolph, Vice Chair of the Critical and Social Justice Approaches Special Interest Group (SIG) in the American Council on the Teaching of Foreign Languages – a SIG that was unimaginable when we wrote *The Foreign Language Educator in Society: Toward a Critical Pedagogy* – in a podcast in which he shares his own vision and practices in social justice-oriented language education. Cassandra Glynn and Pamela Wassell (2018) pose insightful questions as to who gets access to language education and how minoritized students are devalued, offering strategies to disrupt these historic trends. Stephanie Knouse (2018) conducted a mixed methods analysis of student attitudes toward the teaching of linguistic issues related to social justice offering suggestions as to how these can be incorporated (see also Knouse, Gupton & Abreu, 2015). Christy Rhodes and James Coda (2017) explored ways in which queer theory can be utilized to explore heteronormativity in the world language classroom, in a practice that has been referred to as "queering the world language classroom" (Paiz, 2019). Britta Meredith, Mareike Geyer, and Manuela Wagner (2018) document the use of fairy tales in beginning language classrooms as one avenue of introducing social justice topics. Karina Vázquez and Martha Wright (2018) developed an approach for partnering with museums in search for meaningful community dialogues on social justice. Begoña Caballero-García (2018) offers suggestions on using thematic units to move students from understanding the complexity of our linguistically diverse world to taking action based on their new insights.

Furthermore, the interest in this area continues to grow. In February 2019, the Illinois Council on the Teaching of Foreign Languages held a workshop facilitated by Michael Ayala on the topic of "Social Justice in the World Language Classroom," resulting in the awarding of professional development credits (Illinois Council on the Teaching of Foreign Languages, 2018). The 2019 Middlebury Institute of International Studies' Monterey Bay Foreign Language Education Symposium was dedicated to this same theme (Middlebury Institute of International Studies at Monterey, 2019), and the Center for Applied Research on Language Acquisition (CARLA), in collaboration with the American Association of Teachers of Spanish and Portuguese (AATSP) has offered various workshops on social justice in world language education (American Association of Teachers of Spanish and Portuguese, 2018). It is even possible now to take graduate courses or professional development asynchronously online treating these world language topics. What is perhaps most important to note here is that all of these efforts are but a small drop in the bucket; concerns with issues of critical pedagogy and social justice are now ubiquitous among the concerns of world language scholars and educators, if not universally found in world language classrooms.

Lourdes Ortega has perhaps best summed up the current situation in world language education when she noted that:

> We live in uncertain times .... In this uncertain and charged world scene, multilinguals are becoming more vulnerable than ever, particularly those who belong to marginalized communities, racially, economically, or otherwise .... The inequities multilinguals experience are inextricably related not just to language diversity but also to other socially constructed hierarchies of race and ethnicity, class and wealth, gender and sexual orientations, religion, and so on. Language-related inequities compound and are compounded by these other forms of oppression.
>
> (Ortega, 2018, pp. 1–3)

Indeed, the major change we have noted is that teaching for social justice as a part of a healthy language learning process is now a disciplinary imperative.

Conclusion

In the chapter, we have explored the themes of the curriculum and curricular practice in world language education in the United States. In our discussion of the world language curriculum, we distinguished among the planned curriculum, the unplanned curriculum, the hidden curriculum, and the excluded curriculum. We also discussed the nature of curricular nullification, and how both additive and subtractive curricular nullification can and do operate in the context of the public school. Last, we explored the concept of the literary canon, and discussed both its value and the challenges that it poses in world language education.

Questions for Reflection and Discussion

1. In this chapter, the authors distinguish among the formal curriculum, the hidden curriculum, and the excluded curriculum. In your own words, describe each of these, and provide an example from your own teaching or observations in world language classrooms.
2. What is additive curricular nullification? Can you provide examples of additive curricular nullification in a foreign language curriculum that are not presented in this chapter?
3. What is subtractive curricular nullification? Can you provide examples of subtractive curricular nullification in a foreign language curriculum that are not presented in this chapter?
4. How would you describe the tension that exists between most world language textbooks and the goals of critical pedagogy? How might this tension be utilized in the world language classroom?

5 What are the key works that would be found in the literary canon in the language that you intend to teach? Are there ways in which some of these works might be utilized to promote the development of critical perspectives in your students? To raise issues concerned with social justice?

Notes

1 Our focus here is on what takes place in the context of the public schools. Although there is a very broad, general consensus that it is inappropriate to teach religion in *public* schools, there are a number of other settings in which such instruction is perfectly appropriate. Private and parochial schools, Sunday school classes, and so on, are often concerned in large part (if not entirely) in teaching religion – that is, in inducting children into a specific religious tradition.

2 The labels given to the core scriptural texts in the Judeo-Christian tradition are actually somewhat problematic. What Christians refer to as the "*Old Testament*" includes a number of different Jewish texts: the *Torah* (תּוֹרָה) itself, which consists of the five "Books of Moses" (בְּרֵאשִׁית, שְׁמוֹת, וַיִּקְרָא, בְּמִדְבַּר, and דְּבָרִים; Genesis, Exodus, Leviticus, Numbers and Deuteronomy), the Prophets (נְבִיאִים, *Nevi'im*) and the Writings (כְּתוּבִים, *Ketuvim*). All of these texts taken together are called the *Tanakh* (תְּנַ"ךְ). For Jews, it is obviously misleading to talk about the *Tanakh* as the "*Old*" *Testament*, since they do not recognize the *New Testament*.

3 The status of scripture is a complex and controversial theological matter. For some believers, scripture is taken to be literally true – it comes directly from God, and should be understood in its exact and literal sense. This approach to reading the scripture is called biblical literalism. Others view the scripture as divinely inspired, but nevertheless a human product. This second approach to understanding scripture is commonly called the historical-critical method (see Friedman, 2019).

4 The Masoretic text is the Hebrew and Aramaic version of the *Tanakh* that was compiled, edited and codified between the 7th and 10th centuries CE, and which is considered authoritative for Rabbinic Judaism.

5 Great Books curricula are most strongly identified with Robert Hutchins, Mortimer Adler and Jacques Barzun, who, beginning in the 1920s and 1930s, sought to develop a broad university education grounded in the liberal arts tradition. The movement toward Great Books curricula was inspired by concerns about the increasing specialization and narrowing of the higher education experience for many students. Although no longer as significant as they once were, variations of the Great Books curricula continue to be used at many U.S. universities, including Boston College, Boston University, Columbia University, the University of Chicago, the University of Michigan, and the University of Notre Dame.

6 In fact, the impact of Russian translations of Shakespeare's works with respect to Russian literature, as well as the role of these translations on the Russian intelligentsia, have been the subject of considerable study (see Baer, 2006; Gibian, 1952; Kaganovich, 2014; Levin, 1993; Sukhanova, 2004; Vladimirovich, 2015; Zhatkin & Kruglova, 2015), as have been the various films of different Shakespearean plays (see Moore, 2012; Osborne, 1995).

References

Ackerman, D. (1989). Intellectual and practical criteria for successful curriculum integration. In H. Jacobs (Ed.), *Interdisciplinary curricula: Design and implementation* (pp. 25–38). Alexandria, VA: Association for Supervision and Curriculum Development.

Altieri, C. (1983). An idea and ideal of a literary canon. *Critical Inquiry*, 10(1): 37–60.

American Associate of Teachers of Spanish and Portuguese. (2018). CARLA Workshop: Teaching language through the lens of social justice. Downloaded from www.aatsp.org/events/EventDetails.aspx?id=1080346&hhSearchTerms=%22social+and+justice%22 on January 15, 2020.

Apple, M. (2006). Understanding and interrupting neoliberalism and neoconservatism in education. *Pedagogies: An International Journal*, 1(1): 21–26.

Arnowitz, S. & Giroux, H. (1985). *Education under siege: The conservative, liberal, and radical debate over schooling*. South Hadley, MA: Bergin and Garvey.

Arnowitz, S. & Giroux, H. (1991). *Postmodern education: Politics, culture, and social criticism*. Minneapolis, MN: University of Minnesota Press.

Baer, B. (2006). Literary translation and the construction of a Soviet intelligentsia. *The Massachusetts Review*, 47(3): 537–560.

Bassnett, S. & Grundy, P. (1993). *Language through literature: Creative language teaching through literature*. London: Longman.

Bates, J. (2013). Literary canons exclude works no matter how selective canon makers are. *The Daily Nebraskan* (April 25). Downloaded from www.dailynebraskan.com/culture/literary-canons-exclude-works-no-matter-how-selective-canon-makers/article_da83def2-ad43-11e2-b07a-0019bb30f31a.html on January 15, 2020.

Bigelow, M. (2016). Exploring social justice in world language education through the lens of pain. *The Modern Language Journal*, 100(2): 554–555.

Biron, C. (1998). Bringing the standards to life: Points of departure. *Foreign Language Annals*, 31(4): 584–594.

Block, D. & Gray, J. (2018). French language textbooks as ideologically imbued cultural artifacts: Political economy, neoliberalism and (self-)branding. In S. Coffey & U. Wingate (Eds.), *New directions for research in foreign language education* (pp. 115–131). New York: Routledge.

Bloom, H. (1994). *The Western canon: The books and school of the ages*. New York: Harcourt Brace & Co.

Bowles, S. & Gintis, H. (1976) *Schooling in capitalist America*. New York: Basic Books.

Bowles, S. & Gintis, H. (2002). *Schooling in capitalist America* revisited. *Sociology of Education*, 75(1): 1–18.

Bredella, L. & Delanoy, W. (Eds.). (1996). *Challenges of literary text in the foreign language classroom*. Tübingen: Gunter Narr Verlag.

Brosh, H. (1997). The sociocultural message of language textbooks: Arabic in the Israeli setting. *Foreign Language Annals*, 30(3): 311–326.

Brown, E. (1926). *The making of our middle schools: An account of the development of secondary education in America*. New York: Longman.

Brueggemann, W. (2003). *An introduction to the Old Testament: The canon and Christian imagination*. Louisville, KY: Westminster John Knox Press.

Brumfit, C. & Carter, R. (Eds.). (1986). *Literature and language teaching*. Oxford: Oxford University Press.

Caballero-García, B. (2018). Promoting social justice through 21st century skills: Thematic units in the language classroom. Downloaded from https://eric.ed.gov/?id=EJ1207916 on August 1, 2019.

Collie, J. & Slater, S. (1987). *Literature in the language classroom: A resource book of ideas and activities*. Cambridge: Cambridge University Press.

Davison, D., Miller, K. & Methany, D. (1995). What does integration of science and mathematics really mean? *School Science and Mathematics*, 95(5): 226–230.

Finkelman, P. (1996). German victims and American oppressors: The cultural background and legacy of Meyer v. Nebraska. In J. Wunder (Ed.), *Law and the Great Plains* (pp. 33–56). Westport, CT: Greenwood Press.

Fishman, J. (2014). Three hundred-plus-years of heritage language education in the United States. In T. Wiley, J. Peyton, D. Christian, S. Moore & Na Liu (Eds.), *Handbook of heritage, community, and Native American languages in the United States* (pp. 36–44). New York: Routledge, co-published with the Center for Applied Linguistics.

Freire, P. (1973). *Education for critical consciousness*. New York: Seabury.

Freire, P. (1974). *Pedagogy of the oppressed*. New York: Seabury. (Original publication 1968)

Freire, P. (2002a). *Cartas a quien pretende enseñar*. Buenos Aires: Siglo XXI Editores Argentina.

Freire, P. (2002b). *Pedagogía de la autonomía*. Buenos Aires: Siglo XXI Editores Argentina.

Freire, P. (2002c). *Pedagogía de la esperanza: Un reencuentro con la Pedagogía del oprimido*. Buenos Aires: Siglo XXI Editores Argentina.

Freire, P. (2002d). *Pedagogía del oprimido*. Buenos Aires: Siglo XXI Editores Argentina.

Freire, P. (2018). *Conscientização*. São Paulo: Cortez Editora.

Friedman, R. (2019). *Who wrote the Bible?* (2nd rev. ed.). New York: Simon & Shuster.

Gehlker, M., Gozzi, M. & Zeller, I. (1999). Teaching the Holocaust in the foreign language classroom. *Northeast Conference Review*, 46: 20–29.

Gerwin, D. & Osborn, T. A. (2002). Challenging the monovocal narrative: Interdisciplinary units in the foreign language classroom. In T. A. Osborn (Ed.), *The future of foreign language education in the United States* (pp. 77–91). Westport, CT: Bergin & Garvey.

Gibian, G. (1952). Shakespeare in Soviet Russia. *The Russian Review*, 11(1): 24–34.

Giroux, H. (1983). *Theory and resistance in education*. London: Heinemann.

Giroux, H. (1988). *Escola crítica e política cultural* (2nd ed.). São Paulo: Cortez Editora.

Giroux, H. (1997). *Pedagogy and the politics of hope: Theory, culture and schooling*. Boulder, CO: Westview Press.

Glynn, C. & Wassell, B. (2018). *Who gets to play?* Issues of access and social justice in world

language study in the US. *College of Education Faculty Scholarship*, 11: 18–32. Downloaded

from http://rdw.rowan.edu/education_facpub/11 on January 20, 2020.

Goldman, S. (2004). *God's sacred tongue: Hebrew and the American imagination*. Chapel Hill, NC: University of North Carolina Press.

Gomez, C. (2018). Social justice in an elementary Spanish class. Fun for Spanish teachers (July 9). Downloaded from https://funforspanishteachers.com/2018/07/social-justice-immigration-at-the-elementary-level/ on August 1, 2019.

Goodman, N. (1992). *Introduction to sociology*. New York: HarperPerennial.

Guillory, J. (1993). *Cultural capital: The problem of literary canon formation*. Chicago, IL: University of Chicago Press.

Halbertal, M. (1997). *People of the book: Canon, meaning, and authority*. Cambridge, MA: Harvard University Press.

Illinois Council on the Teaching of Foreign Languages (2018). ICTFL's WinterFest 2019: Interculturality and social justice. Downloaded from www.ictfl.org/winterfest.html on January 15, 2020.

Jackson, P. (1990). *Life in classrooms*. New York: Teachers College Press. (Original publication 1968)

Jacobs, H. (Ed.). (1989). *Interdisciplinary curricula: Design and implementation* (pp. 25–38). Alexandria, VA: Association for Supervision and Curriculum Development.

Jay, M. (2003). Critical race theory, multicultural education, and the hidden curriculum of hegemony. *Multicultural Perspectives*, 5(4): 3–9.

Johnson, S. (2018). Language education and community-based global learning. Downloaded from https://compact.org/weteachlang/ on August 1, 2019.

Joyce, J. (1987). The black canon: Reconstructing black American literary criticism. *New Literary History*, 18(2): 335–344.

Kachru, B. (2005). *Asian Englishes: Beyond the canon*. Hong Kong: Hong Kong University Press.

Kaganovich. B. (2014). A. A. Smirnov and Pasternak's translations of Shakespeare. *Russian Studies in Literature*, 50(3): 78–99.

Katz, M. (1968). *The irony of early school reform: Educational innovation in mid-nineteenth century Massachusetts*. New York: Teachers College Press.

Kaufman, D., Moss, D. & Osborn, T. A. (Eds.). (2003). *Beyond the boundaries: A transdisciplinary approach to learning and teaching*. Westport, CT: Greenwood.

Kentli, F. (2009). Comparison of hidden curriculum theories. *European Journal of Education*, 1(2): 83–88.

Kloss, H. (1998). *The American bilingual tradition: Theory and practice*. McHenry, IL: Center for Applied Linguistics and Delta Systems.

Knouse, S. (2018). High-impact practices in a hispanic linguistics course: Facilitating lessons about linguistic diversity and advocacy. Downloaded from https://eric.ed.gov/?id=EJ1207918 on August 1, 2019.

Knouse, S., Gupton, T. & Abreu, L. (2015). Teaching Hispanic linguistics: Strategies to engage learners. *Hispania*, 98(2): 319–332.

Kolbas, E. (2001). *Critical theory and the literary canon*. New York: Routledge.

Kramsch, C. (1993). *Context and culture in language teaching*. Oxford: Oxford University Press.

Krupat, A. (1989). *The voice in the margin: Native American literature and the canon*. Berkeley, CA: University of California Press.

Ladson-Billings, G. (Ed.). (2003). *Critical race theory perspectives on the social studies: The profession, policies, and curriculum*. Greenwich, CT: Information Age Publishing.

Lazar, G. (1993). *Literature and language teaching: A guide for teachers and trainers*. Cambridge: Cambridge University Press.

Lessow-Hurley, J. (1996). *The foundations of dual language instruction* (2nd ed.). White Plains, NY: Longman.

Levin, Y. (1993). Russian Shakespeare translations in the Romantic era. In D. Delabastita & L. D'hulst (Eds.), *European Shakespeares: Translating Shakespeare in the Romantic age* (pp. 75–90). Amsterdam: John Benjamins.

Lojacono, F. (2013). Foreign language acquisition: Fostering social justice and internalization within Web 2.0 environments. *Journal of Arts and Humanities*, 2(10): 45–55.

Lombardi, E. (2019). What is the canon in literature? Thought Co. (August 22). Downloaded from www.thoughtco.com/literary-devices-canon-740503 on January 10, 2020.

Lonning, R. & DeFranco, T. (1997). Integration of science and mathematics: A theoretical model. *School Science and Mathematics*, 97(4): 18–25.

Lonning, R., DeFranco, T. & Weinland, T. (1998). Development of theme-based, interdisciplinary, integrated curriculum: A theoretical model. *School Science and Mathematics*, 98(6): 312–318.

López, G., Franco, S. & Yazan, B. (2019). The exclusion of *vos* from the Spanish as a foreign language classroom: A critical examination through the lens of language management theory. *Critical Inquiry in Language Studies*, 16(4): 229–248.

Luebke, F. (1980). Legal restrictions of foreign languages in the Great Plains states, 1917–1923. In P. Schach (Ed.), *Languages in conflict: Linguistic acculturation on the Great Plains* (pp. 1–19). Lincoln, NE: University of Nebraska Press.

Martin, J. R. (1976). What should we do with a hidden curriculum when we find one? *Curriculum Inquiry*, 6(2): 135–151.

McCarthy, C. (1993). After the canon: Knowledge and ideological representation in the multicultural discourse on curriculum reform. In C. McCarthy & W. Crichlow (Eds.), *Race, identity, and representation in education* (pp. 289–305). New York: Routledge.

McDonald, L. & Sanders, J. (Eds.). (2002). *The canon debate*. Grand Rapids, MI: Baker Publishing.

McLaren, P. (1989). *Life in schools: An introduction to critical pedagogy in the foundations of education*. New York: Longman.

Meredith, B., Geyer, M. & Wagner, M. (2018). Social justice in beginning language instruction: Interpreting fairy tales. *Dimension*, 90–112. Downloaded from https://files.eric.ed.gov/fulltext/EJ1207922.pdf on August 1, 2019.

Middlebury Institute of International Studies at Monterey. (2019). Monterey Bay Foreign Language Education Symposium, "Social Justice in Language Education." (November 9). Downloaded from www.eventbrite.com/e/foreign-language-education-symposium-2019-fleds-tickets-63288940926 on August 1, 2019.

Monroe, P. (1940). *Founding of the American public school system: A history of education in the United States, from the early settlements to the close of the Civil War*. New York: Macmillan.

Moore, T. (2012). *Kozintsev's Shakespeare films: Russian political protest in Hamlet and King Lear*. Jefferson, NC: McFarland & Co.

National Council of Teachers of Mathematics. (1991). *Professional standards for teaching mathematics*. Reston, VA: Author.

National Standards Collaborative Board. (2015). *World-readiness standards for learning languages* (4th ed.). Alexandria, VA: Author.

National Standards in Foreign Language Education Project. (1996). *Standards for foreign language learning: Preparing for the 21st century*. Lawrence, KS: Allen Press.

National Standards in Foreign Language Education Project. (2006). *Standards for foreign language learning in the 21st century* (3rd ed.). Lawrence, KS: Allen Press.

Nuessel, F. (2000). *Linguistic approaches to hispanic literature*. New York: Legas.

Ornstein, A. (1982). Curriculum contrasts: A historical overview. *Phi Delta Kappan*, 63(6): 404–408.

Ornstein, A. (1992). The textbook curriculum. *Educational Horizons*, 70(4): 167–169.

Ornstein, A. (1994). The textbook-driven curriculum. *Peabody Journal of Education*, 69(3): 70–85.

Ornstein, A. & Hunkins, F. (1993). *Curriculum: Foundations, principles and issues* (2nd ed.). Boston: Allyn & Bacon.

Ortega, L. (2018). SLA in uncertain times: Disciplinary constraints, transdisciplinary hopes. *Working Papers in Educational Linguistics*, 33: 1–30.

Osborn, T. A. (1998a). Providing access: Foreign language learners and genre theory. *Foreign Language Annals*, 31(1): 40–47.

Osborn, T. A. (1998b). The concept of "foreignness" in U.S. secondary language curricula: A critical philosophical analysis. Unpublished Ph.D. dissertation, University of Connecticut, Storrs, Connecticut.

Osborn, T. A. (1999). Reflecting on foreignness: The challenges of a new millennium. *New York State Association of Foreign Language Teachers Annual Meeting Series*, 16: 21–24.

Osborn, T. A. (2000). *Critical reflection and the foreign language classroom*. Westport, CT: Bergin & Garvey.

Osborn, T. A. (2001). Making connections and comparisons: Integrating foreign language with other core curricula. *NECTFL Review*, 49(28): 30–33.

Osborn, T. A. (2006). *Teaching world languages for social justice: A sourcebook of principles and practices*. Mahwah, NJ: Lawrence Erlbaum Associates.

Osborn, T. A. (2008). Language learning as an interdisciplinary endeavor. In D. Moss, T. A. Osborn, & D. Kaufman (Eds.), *Interdisciplinary education in an age of assessment* (pp. 107–118). New York: Routledge.

Osborne, L. (1995). Filming Shakespeare in a cultural thaw: Soviet appropriations of Shakespearean treacheries in 1955–6. *Textual Practice*, 9(2): 325–347.

Overfield, D. (1997). From the margins to the mainstream: Foreign language education and community-based learning. *Foreign Language Annals*, 30(4): 485–491.

Paiz, J. (2019). Queering practice: LGBTQ + diversity and inclusion in English language teaching. *Journal of Language, Identity and Education*, 18(4): 266–275.

Parkinson, B. & Thomas, H. (2000). *Teaching literature in a second language*. Edinburgh: Edinburgh University Press.

Pavlenko, A. (2003). "Language of the enemy": Foreign language education and national identity. *International Journal of Bilingual Education and Bilingualism*, 6 (5): 313–331.

Perugini, D. (2018). We teach languages, Episode 82: Social justice and representation with L. J. Randolph. WTL Podcast Episodes (December 7). Downloaded from https://weteachlang.com/2018/12/07/ep-82-with-lj-randolph/ on August 1, 2019.

Peters, M. (2015). Why is my curriculum white? *Educational Philosophy and Theory*, 47(7): 641–646.

Pollock, G. (1999). *Differencing the canon: Feminist desire and the writing of art's histories*. New York: Routledge.

Reagan, T. (1999). Constructivist epistemology and second/foreign language pedagogy. *Foreign Language Annals*, 32(4): 413–425.

Reagan, T. (2002). "Knowing" and "learning" a foreign language: Epistemological reflections on classroom practice. In T. Osborn (Ed.), *The future of foreign language education in the United States* (pp. 45–61). Westport, CT: Bergin & Garvey.

Reagan, T. (2016). Language teachers in foreign territory: A call for a critical pedagogy-infused curriculum. In L. Cammarata, T. Osborn & D. Tedick (Eds,), *Content-based foreign language teaching: Curriculum and pedagogy for developing advanced thinking and literacy skills* (pp.173–191). New York: Routledge.

Reagan, T. & Osborn, T. A. (1998). Power, authority and domination in foreign language education: Toward an analysis of educational failure. *Educational Foundations*, 12(2): 45–62.

Rhodes, C. & Coda, J. (2017). It's not in the curriculum: Adult English language teachers and LGBT topics. *Adult Learning*, 28(3): 99–106.

Robinson, L. (1983). Treason our text: Feminist challenges to the literary canon. *Tulsa Studies in Women's Literature*, 2(1): 83–98.

Sanders, J. (2005). *Torah and canon* (2nd ed.). Eugene, OR: Cascade Books.

Sargar, S. (2018). *Aesthetics of subaltern literature: Protest in African American and Dalit autobiography*. Kampus Nagar, India: Shubham Publications.

Sell, J. (2005). Why teach literature in the foreign language classroom? *Encuentro: Revista de Investigación en la Clase de Lenguas*, 15: 86–93.

Shaffer, S. & Shevitz, L. (2001). She bakes and he builds: Gender bias in the curriculum. In H. Rousso & M. Wehmeyer (Eds.), *Double jeopardy: Addressing gender equity in special education* (pp. 115–131). Albany, NY: State University of New York Press.

Shanahan, D. (1998). Culture, culture and "culture" in foreign language teaching. *Foreign Language Annals* 31(2): 451–458.

Shome, R. (1996). Postcolonial interventions in the rhetorical canon: An "other" view. *Communication Theory*, 6(1): 40–59.

Shrum, J. & Glisan, E. (2016). *Teacher's handbook: Contextualized language instruction* (5th ed.). Boston: Cengage Learning.

Singer, A. (1995). Challenging gender bias through a transformative high school social studies curriculum. *Theory and Research in Social Education*, 23(3): 234–259.

Smith, D. (2009). *Learning from the stranger: Christian faith and cultural diversity*. Grand Rapids, MI: William B. Eerdmans.

Smith, D. & Carvill, B. (2000). *The gift of the stranger: Faith, hospitality, and foreign language learning*. Grand Rapids, MI: William B. Eerdmans.

Snook, I. A. (1972). *Indoctrination and education*. London: Routledge and Kegan Paul.

Spring, J. (2011). *American education* (15th ed.). New York: Routledge.

Sukhanova, E. (2004). *Voicing the distant: Shakespeare and Russian Modernist poetry*. Madison, NJ: Fairleigh Dickinson University Press.

Vázquez, K. & Wright, M. (2018). Making visible the invisible: Social justice and inclusion through the collaboration of museums and Spanish community-based learning projects. Downloaded from https://files.eric.ed.gov/fulltext/EJ1207917.pdf on August 1, 2019.

Vladimirovich, Z. (2015). Шекспирёвский канён в русскёй литературе на рубеже XVIII–XIX векёв [Shakespearean canon in the Russian literature at the turn of the 18th–19th centuries]. *Знание, пёнимание, умение*, 3: 374–386.

Wieczorek, J. (1994). The concept of "French" in foreign language texts. *Foreign Language Annals*, 27(4): 487–497.

Wiggins, G. & McTighe, J. (2005). *Understanding by design* (exp. 2nd ed.). Alexandria, VA: Association for Supervision and Curriculum Development.

Wiley, T. (1998). The imposition of World War I era English-only policies and the fate of German in North America. In T. Ricento & B. Burnaby (Eds.), *Language and politics in the United States and Canada: Myths and realities* (pp. 211–241). New York: Routledge.

Willis, P. (1997). *Learning to labour*. New York: Columbia University Press.

Wong, S. (1993). Promises, pitfalls, and principles of text selection in curricular diversification: The Asian-American case. In T. Perry & J. Fraser (Eds.), *Freedom's plow* (pp. 109–120). New York: Routledge.

Zampini, M. & Kerley, J. (2013). Social justice themes in the foreign language classroom. In M. Combs (Ed.), *Transforming ourselves, transforming the world: Justice in Jesuit higher education* (pp. 120–136). New York: Fordham University Press.

Zhatkin, D. & Kruglova, T. (2015). Shakespeare in Marina Tsvetaeva's eyes. *Mediterranean Journal of Social Sciences*, 6(5-S4): 509–517.

10 Critical Pedagogy, Social Justice, and National Standards

An Insurmountable Dilemma?

In this chapter, we turn to a discussion of national standards in world language education. The national standards movement has, since its inception, proven to be extremely controversial and divisive among educators, policy-makers, parents, and the general public. As Anne Lewis observed some 25 years ago,

> Whether lauded as a sign of progress or scorned as anathema, the notion of national standards for what students learn in public schools is the hottest item in educational reform today. It has provoked everything from federal laws promoting the development of sets of standards to fierce public policy debates ... But much of the turmoil surrounding standards stems from exaggerated claims by opponents and proponents. Beware of those who say that standards will "save" public education, but be equally skeptical of those who claim that standards will nationalize the curriculum. Neither group is right .... Nor is it true that national standards in education do not already exist. Researchers on curriculum and instruction have long pointed out that there is a sameness to what is taught in American public schools ... (1995, p. 744)

Lewis was correct in several ways. First, there is little question that the national standards movement has been, and continues to be, very divisive politically, ideologically and educationally in the United States. Second, much of the discourse surrounding the debate about national standards has been polemical, and further, has dichotomized both the positive and negative aspects of national standards to a far greater extent than is really reflective of the realities. Last, Lewis is correct in suggesting that the change brought about by the development and implementation of national standards is, to a significant extent, one of formalizing what already existed with respect to curricular commonalities in the United States.

The ACTFL *Standards* and the National Standards Movement

The ACTFL *Standards* were developed as part of the national standards movement, but in many ways they have been, and remain, tangential to the goals, objectives and concerns of the broader concern with national standards. This was made abundantly clear in President Bush's January 1990 "State of the Union" address, in which he identified six national performance goals for education to accomplish by 2000. This six performance goals were later codified in Public Law 103–227 (*Goals 2000: Educate America Act*):

- All children in America will start school ready to learn.
- The high school graduation rate will increase to at least 90 percent.
- American students will leave grades four, eight, and twelve having demonstrated competency in challenging subject matter, including English, mathematics, science, history, and geography; and every school in American will ensure that all students learn to use their minds well, so they may be prepared for responsible citizenship, further learning, and productive employment in our modern economy.
- U.S. students will be first in the world of science and mathematics achievement.
- Every adult American will be literate and will possess knowledge and skills necessary to compete in a global economy and exercise the rights and responsibilities of citizenship.
- Every school in America will be free of drugs and violence and will offer a disciplined environment conducive to learning. (Harnischfeger, 1995, p. 109)

Neither in President Bush's "State of the Union" address nor in *Goals 2000* was there any explicit mention of any language except English. Literacy is included, as are such subjects as English, history and geography – and, not surprisingly, the strongest focus is on science and mathematics. Unlike the earlier NDEA legislation, which had a similar concern with perceptions of the United States falling behind its competitors academically (and especially behind the Soviet Union, following *Sputnik*), *Goals 2000* appears to have presupposed the worldwide dominance of the English language. To be sure, *Goals 2000* does say that every adult American "will possess knowledge and skills necessary to compete in a global economy," but the lack of any direct mention of the need for the study of a language other than English suggests that world languages are simply not a part of the core curriculum. That is certainly not news to any world language educator in the United States; no state requires the study of a world language for all students, and only about 20% of all K-12 students in the U.S. actually study a world language.

This is, oddly enough, both bad news and good news. It is bad news because it demonstrates the on-going marginalization of world language education in the United States, and the extent to which the study of languages other than English is commonly seen as inappropriate for most students in the public schools. On the other hand, in subjects that are perceived to be "core" and of considerable importance, there have been increasing concerns with assessment and international comparisons of U.S. students and their counterparts in other countries. Such concerns are generally absent entirely in the case of world language education.

The ACTFL *Standards* and the "Five C's"

The ACTFL *Standards* were first published in 1996. Their development was funded under the auspices of the *Goals 2000: Educate America Act* (see Phillips & Abbott, 2011), and completed by, and with the support of, a broad base of world language educators in the United States. After fifteen years, the original standards were revised and the *World-Readiness Standards for Learning Languages* were promulgated. The ACTFL *Standards* resulted in changes not only in the curriculum itself, but also in textbooks, approaches to and concerns with assessment and evaluation, the preparation of world language teachers, and on-going teacher professional development (see Glisan, 2012; Lafayette, 1996; Magnan, 2008; Troyan, 2012; Wood, 2008).[1] A major concern among world language educators has been on finding ways in which the ACTFL *Standards* can be effectively integrated in the curriculum and manifested in other parts of world language education, and there has been considerable attention given over the past two decades to addressing these issues. For a variety of reasons, the ACTFL *Standards* have been considerably less controversial than those in most other subject areas. This is due in part because of the way in which the ACTFL *Standards* were developed, and also because of their overall quality. Perhaps as important, though, may be the fact that – unlike in many other subject areas – there is little external pressure to implement the ACTFL *Standards*, nor have there been any efforts at either the state or national levels to invest in assessment to measure their success.[2] This having been said, our concern with the ACTFL *Standards* is somewhat different from more common concerns; we wish to examine the *Standards* in a broader context, with a focus on the purposes and impacts of a standardized curriculum – along with the problems they create for critical approaches to language education.

At the outset of this discussion, we believe that it is important to recognize that there is a fundamental difference between curricular content structures and national standards in a specific content area. For instance, in a curriculum for a target language in which there are likely to be multiple instructors, sections, and so on, each individual teacher is not usually free to decide what to teach and what not to teach – in a beginning level Spanish or French course, for instance, there is a broad consensus that we teach certain grammatical features, vocabulary, and so on, and this is not only pragmatically good sense, but it is also perfectly reasonable and justifiable. In fact, such a unified approach is often absolutely necessary. Standards, however, take us far beyond curricular content structures – national standards, in fact, provide us with a definition of what constitutes functionally "official knowledge" (see Apple, 1993, 2014). Such an identification and delineation of official knowledge presents a number of extremely problematic challenges for a critically enlightened language classroom. National standards are, in fact, part of a larger neoliberal marketization strategy that also includes mandatory testing, performance-based employment practices, and accountability (see Apple, 2000; Moore, Kleinman, Hess & Frickel, 2011; Spring, 2014). The best way to frame our underlying concerns here is in a question: Are national standards and a critical pedagogy mutually exclusive? Our answer to this question may be somewhat surprising to some readers: we believe that a critical pedagogy of world language education can be reasonably consistent with national standards, even given the commodification and marketization of the *Standards* which characterizes the current milieu in world language education.

The ACTFL *Standards* do an admirable job of providing an overarching articulation of what the curriculum for any language would look like. We are particularly drawn to the underlying philosophical foundation upon which the ACTFL *Standards* rest:

> Language and communication are at the heart of the human experience. The United States must educate students who are linguistically and culturally equipped to communicate successfully in a pluralistic American society and abroad. This imperative envisions a future in which ALL students will develop and maintain proficiency in English and at least one other language, modern or classical. Children who come to school from non-English backgrounds should also have opportunities to develop further proficiencies in their first language.
>
> (American Council on the Teaching of Foreign Languages, 2015, emphasis in original)

As we have already suggested, there is no reason to doubt that this overarching goal is in principle achievable. At the same time, though, we would suggest that given the political, economic, cultural, social and linguistic situation in which we find ourselves in contemporary U.S. society, such a goal should be understood to be an aspirational one.

The fundamental organizing principle of the ACTFL *Standards* are the "Five C's": communication, cultures, connections, comparisons, and communities (see Lafayette, 1996; Phillips & Terry, 1999). Each of the "C's" refers to a broad, general objective, or goal, for students engaged in the study of any language:

- *Communication:* Students will be able to communicate effectively in more than one language in order to function in a variety of situations and for multiple purposes.
    - Interpersonal Communication
    - Interpretive Communication
    - Presentational Communication
- *Cultures:* Students will be able to interact with cultural competence and understanding.
    - Relating Cultural Practices to Perspectives
    - Relating Cultural Products to Perspectives
- *Connections:* Students will be able to connect with other disciplines and acquire information and diverse perspectives in order to use the language to function in academic and career-related situations.
    - Making Connections
    - Acquiring Information and Diverse Perspectives
- *Comparisons:* Students will develop insight into the nature of language and culture in order to interact with cultural competence.
    - Language Comparisons
    - Cultural Comparisons
- *Communities:* Students will be able to communicate and interact with cultural competence in order to participate in multilingual communities at home and around the world.
    - School and Global Communities
    - Lifelong Learning

(American Council on the Teaching of Foreign Languages, 2015)

Considerable attention has been given by researchers and world language educators, as well as the producers of textbooks and supplementary materials, with respect to how the ACTFL *Standards* can most effectively be implemented in practice in the world language education classroom (see, e.g., Blaz, 2013; O'Donnell, 2014; Schwartz, 2002). Although especially true in the cases of the more commonly taught languages, the implementation of the ACTFL *Standards* has also been the focus of teachers and researchers of many LCTLs, including Arabic (Allen & Allen, 1987), Chinese (Ke Peng, 2006), and Italian (Musumeci & Aski, 2010) – as well considerable concern to those teaching English as a second/foreign language in a variety of settings.

Sandy Cutshall wrote a series of essays, published in ACTFL's *The Language Educator*, addressing aspects of the classroom implementation of the ACTFL *Standards* (see Cutshall, 2012a, 2012b, 2012c, 2012d, 2012e). These essays, which have been widely cited, remain among the best discussions about what the ACTFL *Standards* ought to look like in real world practice. With respect to the first of the "Five C's," Communication, Cutshall has pointed out that:

> The National Standards present a very different approach to communication, even compared with the proficiency movement in the 1980s and early 1990s which preceded their development. While teachers have traditionally thought of communicating through the use of the four skills: reading, writing, speaking and listening, the *Standards* offer a new "Communicative Framework" consisting of three modes which place primary emphasis on the context and purpose of the communication.
>
> (Cutshall, 2012a, p. 34)

Further, the interpersonal, interpretive, and presentational modes weave cultural understanding through communicative acts. As a result, use of language is not viewed as merely an exchange of value-free information. Rather, values, and in particular cultural values are inextricably linked to Communication:

> Culture, as represented in the *Standards* is presented as the philosophical perspectives, the behavioral practices, and the products of a society. This "Cultural Framework" may sometimes be referred to as "3 Ps" and can be expressed through the image of a triangle with "Perspectives" at the top and "Products" and "Practices" forming the base, showing how the products and practices are derived …
>
> (Cutshall, 2012b, p. 32)

Teaching about Culture, in short, is not considered merely an "add-on" in a textbook chapter. Instead, it is fundamental to the process of effective communication – a point repeatedly emphasized in the literature addressing the ACTFL *Standards* (see Arens, 2010; Cutshall, 2012b; Jernigan & Moore, 1997; Musumeci & Aski, 2010).

Moving on to Connections, Cutshall makes a very broad claim, suggesting that:

> Connections can be made to all formal disciplines and school subjects, to emerging global themes and contemporary issues, or to virtually any information available in the target language and culture. They can be identified easily within the immersion context, but may also happen simply when an educator makes a commitment within his or her own classroom to focus on content using the language as a vehicle and not an end in itself.
>
> (Cutshall, 2012c, p. 35)

Though it could be argued that Connections could be stronger or weaker based on the organizing principles embedded both in the curriculum and in the dispositions of the classroom teacher, Cutshall's point is both well-founded and well-taken. Language learning *does* provide powerful opportunities for connections to other disciplines (see Osborn, 1998, 2002), although, as the research and literature suggests, it is sometimes difficult to implement this in practice.

The Comparisons standard suggests that students will develop insight into the nature of language and culture in order to facilitate interaction with others, presumably native speakers. They do so by using the language to explain and reflect on the nature of languages and cultures through a comparison of the "languages and cultures studied" and their own language and culture (see Cutshall, 2012d). In this area, critical examinations of the applications of the standard have suggested that this outcome is not particularly common – indeed, much of the time comparison can leads to a highlighting of the nature of the Other *as* Other, reinforcing the *foreignness agenda*, as Osborn (2000) has shown.

Finally, the Communities standard may be one of the more complex to implement, particularly as one contemplates the context in which world language learning generally occurs (see Allen & Dupuy, 2012; Weldon & Trautmann, 2003). Again, Cutshall argues that:

> The Communities Standards may be addressed through many activities, both within and beyond the school setting. These can include travel and study abroad; service learning projects; formal and informal interaction with native language speakers; visits to restaurants, ethnic festivals, or other locations where the target language is spoken or culture is celebrated; reading books and periodicals or listening to music in the target language; participating in sports or games from the target culture; and more.
>
> (Cutshall, 2012e, p. 33)

There is nothing intrinsically wrong with any of the five components of the ACTFL *Standards*; indeed, all are perfectly appropriate in the abstract, and one can certainly imagine how each might be utilized effectively not only in the teaching and learning of the target language, but also with respect to other content, including content that is more critical in nature. Nevertheless, we believe that the ACTFL *Standards* at the very least present challenges for critical pedagogy.

Toward a Critical Perspective on the ACTFL *Standards*

Although world language education, at least for the foreseeable future, will need to operate within a standards-driven environment, we must recognize that flexibility and sensitivity are preconditions for a social justice pedagogy. Freire reflects this sentiment as he cautions us against a simplistic view of cultural relations:

> From the linguistic point of view, if an illiterate is one who does not know how to read and write, a political illiterate … has a naïve outlook on social reality, which for this one is a given, that is, social reality is a *fait accompli* rather than something that's still in the making.
>
> (Freire, 1985, p. 103)

These are important conditions. The issues we address in social justice-oriented world language education cannot proceed from our own contemplation of what is important. We run the very real risk that we will move into a prescriptive list of social justice topics that fails to change with the sociocultural realities around us. If today the pressing issue for many is the issue of children at the U.S./Mexican border, for example, that is not to suggest that border crossing should *necessarily* become one of the "must haves" in any social justice approach. As William Ayers has commented:

> Teaching for social justice demands a dialectical stance: one eye firmly fixed on the students – Who are they? What are their hopes, dreams, and aspirations? Their passions and commitments? What skills, abilities, and capacities, does each one bring to the classroom? – and the other eye looking unblinkingly at the concentric circles of context – historical flow, cultural surround, economic reality. Teaching for social justice is teaching that arouses students, engages them in a quest to identify obstacles to their full humanity, to their freedom, and then to drive, to move against these obstacles. And so the fundamental message of the teacher for social justice is: You can change the world.
>
> (Ayers, 1998, p. xvii)

The national standards movement (and each content area's individual standards, including the ACTFL *Standards*) has had a number of positive outcomes, but it nevertheless also reflects a number of both practically and ideologically problematic assumptions and desired outcomes (see Ayers, 2010; Bohn & Sleeter, 2000; Hatch, 2002; Ohanian, 1999). Even more than this, though, is that in many ways the national standards movement has contributed to the further devaluing of the role of the teacher and of teacher knowledge. Indeed, the national standards movement is a direct contradiction of Henry Giroux's notion of "teachers as transformative intellectuals" (Giroux, 1985, 1988c, 1990). It also, of course, reinforces and strengthens the tensions between centralized and grassroots approaches to curriculum, assessment and accountability, further threatening any claim the schools might have to being truly democratic institutions. As Donaldo Macedo has commented,

> Far from the democratic education we claim to have, what we really have in place is a sophisticated colonial model of education designed primarily to train teachers in ways in which the intellectual

> dimension of teaching is often devalued. The major objective of a colonial education is to further de-skill teachers and students to walk unreflectively through a labyrinth of procedures and techniques. It follows, then, that what we have in place in the United States is not a system that encourages independent thought and critical thinking. On the contrary, our so-called democratic schools are based on an instrumental skills-banking approach that often prevents the development of the kind of thinking that enables one to "read the world" critically and to understand the reasons and linkages behind the facts.
> (Macedo, 2000, pp. 3–4)

Next, the national standards movement is grounded in a consumerist view of teaching and learning, and the ACTFL *Standards* reflect this.

We would also note here a specific concern with the ACTFL *Standards* that was raised by Sally Magnan, who insightfully noted that the "Five C's" are not organized in a neutral way, but rather, that they presuppose a potentially problematic power relationship among communication, culture, connections, comparisons and communities:

> Looking to Dell Hymes's portrayal of communicative competence and building on notions from sociocultural theory and the concept communities of practice, this paper questions this hierarchical ordering especially in terms of the primacy of Communication over Cultures and Communities. It is suggested that, of the five C's, Communities should be considered the most fundamental.
> (Magnan, 2008, p. 349)

Insofar as one is truly committed to critical pedagogy and social justice education, we would suggest that Magnan's point is especially well taken. This does not mean that the other C's are not important and valuable, but rather, that we have historically tended to overemphasize Communication over all other aspects of the world language curriculum and classroom.

Conclusion

Early in this chapter, we posed the question of whether national standards in general, and the ACTFL *Standards* in particular, can be manifested in ways that are compatible with – or at the very least, not completely incompatible with – the goals of critical approaches to teaching and learning, and to schooling concerned with social justice. There is no question that national standards in every content area present paradoxes and dilemmas for those committed to critical pedagogy. It may even be the case that critical pedagogy and national standards, especially as they have been articulated of late in the U.S., may be mutually exclusive in some subject matters. In the case of world language education, however, this is simply not the case. We believe that a critical pedagogy of world language education can be reasonably consistent with the ACTFL *Standards*, even given the commodification and marketization of the *Standards* which characterizes the current milieu in world language education. We recognize that this claim may be limited to world language education, but since our students are striving to learn a medium that will, we would hope, enable them to pursue even minimal communication with the disenfranchised second language speakers in our own context (and perhaps in other contexts), we are confident in this assertion.

At the same time, however, we think that it is important to take into account the broader and more general situation with respect to the national standards movement in the United States. In spite of the resources dedicated to the promotion and implementation of national standards in most curricular areas, Lawrence Stedman has argued that:

> The overall picture is a bleak one. In spite of a generation of effort, from *A Nation at Risk* and *Goals 2000* to state testing programs and No Child Left Behind (NCLB), there are few signs of improvement. Achievement has generally stagnated, especially at the high school level; most minority achievement gaps remain as large as they were in the late 1980s and early 1990s; and students still struggle in the major subjects … Class and race inequalities – and segregation – remain vast and vexing problems. Even in the two areas where the standards movement has apparently achieved some success – math achievement at the lower grades and academic enrollments in high school – there are grounds for skepticism. The gains were largely superficial, other forces such as teaching-to-the-test and social promotion were responsible, and serious deficiencies remain …. Beyond their failure to improve achievement, standards-based accountability systems have constricted curricula and warped school culture.
>
> (Stedman, 2011, p. 2)

With respect to the National Standards Movement writ large, we find Stedman's assertion compelling. The extent to which the ACTFL *Standards* have been more successful and effective is, of course, debatable, but there remains a strong case to be made for them as a significant exception to the general rule, at least in many ways.

Questions for Reflection and Discussion

1 The authors suggest that the six national performance goals identified in President Bush's "State of the Union" address in 1990 (and which were also reflected in *Goals 2000*) largely ignore world language education. Do you agree or disagree with them? To what extent, and in what ways, might the study of a world language be presupposed in one or more of the national performance goals?

2 How would you describe the tension between national standards and critical pedagogy in general? What about in the context of world language education?
3 Can you summarize, in your own words, the philosophical foundation upon which the ACTFL *Standards* are based? How does this philosophical foundation relate to both the traditional and alternative rationales for the study of world languages discussed in Chapter 4?
4 What do you believe the authors mean when they talk about "official knowledge" in national standards? How is such "official knowledge" related to (and perhaps reflected in) the curriculum?
5 Connections to other disciplines has a great deal of potential for world language education, but, as the authors suggest, such connections are sometimes difficult. Develop a proposal for a unit that might be taught as a collaborative effort between a world language teacher and a colleague teaching some other subject (e.g., history/social studies, English, etc.).

Notes

1 In the case of world language education, it is important to distinguish between the ACTFL *Standards* and the ACTFL *Oral Proficiency Interview* (OPI). The former, typically discussed as the "Five C's," provides curricular guidelines for the teaching of world languages. The ACTFL *OPI Guidelines*, on the other hand, are intended to provide a valid and reliable method for assessing how well an individual speakers a particular language in a 20 to 30 minute, one-on-one oral interview with a trained evaluator. In the case of the ACTFL *Oral Proficiency Interview*, the speaker's competence is evaluated using either the ACTFL *Proficiency Guidelines (Speaking)* or the *Inter-Agency Language Roundtable Skill Level Descriptors (Speaking)*. The ACTFL *Standards* and the ACTFL OPI are very different things, with very difference purposes and goals. Our focus in this chapter is solely on the former – the ACTFL *Standards*.
2 We want to stress here that we are not advocating the implementation of any sort of mandatory proficiency examination for world languages. Such examinations are already in place with respect to future world language educators, who are generally required to achieve a passing score on one of a number of different required examinations (including, but not limited to, the ACTFL *Oral Proficiency Interview* and ACTFL *Writing Proficiency Test*). Although we are deeply committed to ensuring that world language educators are well prepared and have a high degree of competence in the target language, we are not convinced that the current approach to evaluating future teachers' language proficiency is either effective or appropriate.

References

Allen, R. & Allen, R. (1987). The ACTFL Guidelines and Arabic. *Al-'Arabiyya*, 20(1/2): 43–49.

Allen, H. & Dupuy, B. (2012). Study abroad, foreign language use, and the communities standard. *Foreign Language Annals*, 45(4): 468–493.

American Council on the Teaching of Foreign Languages. (2015). Standards summary: World-Readiness Standards for Language Learning. Downloaded from www.actfl.org/publications/all/world-readiness-standards-learning-languages/standards-summary on January 15, 2020.

Apple, M. (1993). What post-modernists forget: Cultural capital and official knowledge. *Curriculum Studies*, 1(3): 301–316.

Apple, M. (2000). Between neoliberalism and neoconservatism: Education and conservatism in a global context. In N. Burbules & C. Torres (Eds.), *Globalization and education: Critical perspectives* (pp. 57–77). New York: Routledge.

Apple, M. (2014). *Official knowledge: Democratic education in a conservative age* (3rd ed.). New York: Routledge.

Arens, K. (2010). The field of culture: The Standards as a model for teaching culture. *The Modern Language Journal*, 94(2): 321–324.

Ayers, W. (1998). Popular education: Teaching for social justice. In W. Ayers, J. Hunt & T. Quinn (Eds.), *Teaching for social justice: A democracy and education reader* (pp. xvii–xxv). New York: Teachers College Press.

Ayers, W. (2010). The Standards fraud. In A. Canestrari & B. Marlowe (Eds.), *Educational foundations: An anthology of critical readings* (2nd ed.) (pp. 183–186). Los Angeles, CA: Sage.

Blaz, D. (2013). *Bringing the Standards for Foreign Language Learning to life*. New York: Routledge.

Bohn, A. & Sleeter, C. (2000). Multicultural education and the standards movement: A report from the field. *Phi Delta Kappan*, 82(2): 156–159.

Cutshall, S. (2012a). More than a decade of Standards: Integrating "Communication" in your language instruction. *The Language Educator*, 7(2): 34–39.

Cutshall, S. (2012b). More than a decade of Standards: Integrating "Cultures" in your language instruction. *The Language Educator*, 7(3): 32–37.

Cutshall, S. (2012c). More than a decade of Standards: Integrating "Connections" in your language instruction. *The Language Educator*, 7(4): 32–38.

Cutshall, S. (2012d). More than a decade of Standards: Integrating "Comparisons" in your language instruction. *The Language Educator*, 7(5): 32–37.

Cutshall, S. (2012e). More than a decade of Standards: Integrating "Communities" in your language instruction. *The Language Educator*, 7(6): 32–37.

Freire, P. (1985). *The politics of education: Culture, power and liberation*. Westport, CT: Bergin & Garvey.

Giroux, H. (1985). Teachers as transformative intellectuals. *Social Education*, 49(5): 376–379.

Giroux, H. (1988c). *Teachers as intellectuals: Toward a critical pedagogy of learning*. Westport, CT: Bergin & Garvey.

Giroux, H. (1990). Curriculum theory, textual authority, and the role of teachers as public intellectuals. *Journal of Curriculum and Supervision*, 5(4): 361–383.

Glisan, E. (2012). National Standards: Research into practice. *Language Teaching*, 45(4): 515–526.

Harnischfeger, A. (1995). Fad or reform? The standards movement in the United States. In W. Bos & R. Lehmann (Eds.), *Reflections on educational achievement: Papers in honour of T. Neville Postlethwaite to mark the occasion of his retirement from his Chair in comparative education at the University of Hamburg* (pp. 107–118). New York: Waxmann Verlag.

Hatch, J. (2002). Accountability shovedown: Resisting the standards movement in early childhood education. *Phi Delta Kappan*, 83(6): 457–462.

Jernigan, C. & Moore, Z. (1997). Teaching culture: A study in the Portuguese classroom. Implications for the National Standards. *Hispania*, 80(4): 829–841.

Ke Peng. (2016) Chinese as a foreign language in K-12 education. In J. Ruan, J. Zhang & C. Leung (Eds.), *Chinese language education in the United States* (pp. 123–140). New York: Springer.

Lafayette, R. (Ed.). (1996). *National standards: A catalyst for reform.* Lincolnwood, IL: National Textbook Co.

Lewis, A. (1995). An overview of the standards movement. *Phi Delta Kappan*, 76 (10): 744–750.

Macedo, D. (2000). Introduction. In N. Chomsky, *Chomsky on miseducation* (edited by D. Macedo) (pp. 1–14). Lanham, MD: Rowman & Littlefield.

Magnan, S. (2008). Reexamining the priorities of the national standards for foreign language education. *Language Teaching*, 41(3): 349–366.

Moore, K., Kleinman, D., Hess, D. & Frickel, S. (2011). Science and neoliberal globalization: A political sociological approach. *Theory and Society*, 40(5): 505–532.

Musumeci, D. & Aski, J. (2010). The integration of culture in Italian first year textbooks. *Italica*, 87(1): 21–36.

O'Donnell, M. (2014). Peer response with process-oriented, Standards-based writing for beginning-level, second language learners of Spanish. *Hispania*, 97(3): 413–429.

Ohanian, S. (1999). *One size fits few: The folly of educational standards.* Portsmouth, NH: Heinemann.

Osborn, T. A. (1998). Providing access: Foreign language learners and genre theory. *Foreign Language Annals*, 31(1): 40–47.

Osborn, T. A. (2000). *Critical reflection and the foreign language classroom.* Westport, CT: Bergin & Garvey.

Osborn, T. A. (Ed.). (2002). *The future of foreign language education in the United States.* Westport, CT: Bergin & Garvey.

Phillips, J. & Abbott, M. (2011). *A decade of foreign language standards: Impact, influence, and future directions.* Report of Grant Project # P017A080037, Title VII, International Research Studies, U.S. Department of Education to the American Council on the Teaching of Foreign Languages. Washington, DC: Author.

Phillips, J. & Terry, R. (Eds.). (1999). *Foreign language standards: Linking research, theories, and practices.* Lincolnwood, IL: National Textbook Co.

Schwartz, A. (2002). National standards and the diffusion of innovation: Language teaching in the United States. In S. Savignon (Ed.), *Interpreting communicative language teaching: Contexts and concerns in teacher education* (pp. 112–130). New Haven, CT: Yale University Press.

Spring, J. (2014). *Globalization of education: An introduction* (2nd ed.). New York: Routledge.

Stedman, L. (2011). Why the standards movement failed: An educational and political diagnosis of its failure and the implications for school reform. *Critical Education*, 2(1): 1–20.

Troyan, F. (2012). Standards for foreign language learning: Defining the constructs and researching the learner outcomes. *Foreign Language Annals*, 45(1): 118–140.

Weldon, A. & Trautmann, G. (2003). Spanish and service-learning: Pedagogy and praxis. *Hispania*, 86(3): 574–585.

Wood, P. (2008). Who is using the National Foreign Language Standards? *Foreign Language Annals*, 32(4): 435–440.

11 The Empire Strikes Back

Toward an Epilogue

We began this book by suggesting that world language educators need critical pedagogy, perhaps now more than ever. After exploring contemporary practice in world language education from a variety of different perspectives and through multiple lenses, we hope that you will agree with us. The real challenge that faces us as critical educators is not so much revamping the curriculum, rethinking how students are assessed, or changing our goals and objectives – although all of these things are both necessary and important. Nor, we would suggest, is our task merely to "speak truth to power," although that, too, is essential. Rather, we are increasingly faced with the job of simply *identifying* the truth, and the lies, and helping our students learn to do the same. Some twenty years ago, Donaldo Macedo could argue that, "Once intellectuals are adapted to the doctrinal system and rewarded by it, it becomes increasingly less difficult for them to live within a lie and ignore the true reality, even when faced with documented historical evidence" (Macedo, 2000, p. 174). Macedo was not wrong in his fundamental concern, but he could hardly have foreseen a time when truth mattered as little as it now does, when any media that one disagrees with can be dismissed as "fake media," and when "alternative facts" are taken to be every bit as credible as documented facts. Indeed, if there has ever been a need for critical pedagogy – not only in world language education, but throughout the curriculum – it is now.

What Do Two White Guys Know, Anyway?

Recent critical scholarship has made it increasingly clear that one's positionality has important and powerful impacts on how one constructs reality (see, for example, Applebaum, 2000, 2017; Brady & Kanpol, 2000; Howard, 1996; Larson & Ovando, 2001; McLaren & Muñoz, 2000; Sleeter & McLaren, 1995). Gender, race, ethnicity, language, and so on, are not merely *elements* or factors in how one sees the world, but rather, constitute the fundamental scaffolding within which and from which one organizes experience and knowledge. This makes it essential that an author identify and position herself or himself, so that readers will understand the social, cultural, economic and linguistic context in which her or his arguments and insights occur. We do not believe that there is any sort of deterministic connection between an individual's background and her or his beliefs, commitments and actions, but there is clearly a *relationship* that is relevant and which needs to be understood. We believe that such personal positioning is important, and, having presented a fairly complex set of arguments about contemporary world language education in the United States, now turn to a brief commentary on our own backgrounds. In our case, we are both White males, native speakers of two different varieties of American English, who have chosen to spend our lives studying and learning other languages and cultures. Although our strongest languages are German and Russian, between us we have also studied, albeit to varying degrees of proficiency, Afrikaans, American Sign Language, Anglo-Saxon, Danish, Dutch, Esperanto, French, Italian, Latin, Serbian, Spanish, Xhosa, and Zulu. We recognize that our understanding of the teaching and learning of world languages has been colored not only by race, ethnicity and gender, but also by our personal and professional interests in human language, as well as by our experiences in learning and living with other human languages and cultures. At the same time, though, we believe that while one's perspective is inevitably restricted by background and experience, this cannot be used as a justification for ignoring injustice and oppression. An important part of critical reflection is the need for us all to be aware of and sensitive to the many different kinds of oppression that surround us. As educators, we must not only be cognizant of oppression, but must use our teaching practice to challenge such oppression, and to help our students learn to do the same. In short, we are all faced with the rather daunting task identified by Christine Sleeter with respect to the preparation of future teachers:

> How … does one involve a class of male and female white students from mainly middle class backgrounds in a critique of various forms of oppression and at the same time help them to construct for themselves insights grounded in emancipation of *other people?*
>
> (Sleeter, 1995, p. 416, emphasis in original)

We hope that this book has made a contribution to this process.

Why This Book Should Not Have Been Written in English

Internationally, there are two major, and to some extent related, linguistic trends co-occurring at the present time. The first of these linguistic trends that is underway is the accelerating process of language endangerment and language extinction around the world. Today, there are probably somewhere between 6,500 and 7,000 languages spoken around the world. In 1992, the linguist Michael Krauss published a powerful article entitled

"The world's languages in crisis" in the journal *Language*. In that article, Krauss estimated that under the most optimistic circumstances, it is likely that in 150 years only 300 to 600 of these languages will still be spoken. In other words, while the endangerment of biodiversity in the world is (and should be) certainly of considerable concern, that of the linguistic world is far more serious. Since 1992, many linguists have attempted to deal with this challenge, both by drawing public attention to the situation and by working to revitalize threatened languages (see Evans, 2010; Fishman, 2001, 2006; Grenoble & Whaley, 1998; Hagège, 2000; Jones, 2015; Nettle & Romaine, 2000).

The other contemporary linguistic trend that is underway is the growing dominance and even hegemony of the English language. Advocates for English like to point out that English has replaced other *lingua francas* and become essentially *the* "global language" in the contemporary world. Although fewer than 500 million people speak English as their native language (still an impressively large number, of course), more than a billion people (at least) now speak it as a second or additional language. Braj Kachru has suggested that we should think about English around the world as falling into three concentric "circles": the inner circle, the outer circle, and the expanding circle (see Kachru, 1976, 1992a, 1992b).[1] The inner circle includes those countries in which English has a large community of native speakers and in which it is clearly the dominant language, such as the United States, the U.K., Canada, Australia, New Zealand, and so on. The inner circle is thus, in many senses, the "core" of the English-speaking world. The outer circle consists largely of countries which were colonized by English-speaking nations (primarily by the U.K. and the U.S.), and where English is widely used for formal and official purposes. Thus, government, education, the judicial system, and so on, typically operate largely or primarily in English, although the percentage of native speakers of English in the society is often relatively small. Examples of countries in the outer circle include India, Nigeria, and so on. Finally, the expanding circle includes countries where there is, for the most part, no historical connection to English-speaking colonial powers, but where significant numbers of people nevertheless study and learn English as a second or additional language. The expanding circle includes such countries as China, Brazil, Russia, and many others. David Crystal has suggested that it may be the case that the ratio of native speakers to second and additional language speakers of English may even have reached 1:3 (Crystal, 2003, p. 69) – which, apart from anything else, raises some very significant questions about the "ownership" of English (see Higgins, 2003; Kachru, 1988). Beyond this, though, English has become the dominant language of diplomacy,[2] of a good deal of popular culture,[3] of the media (both print and broadcast),[4] of the Internet,[5] of scholarship and academic publication[6] – even of air traffic control.[7] It is this growing hegemony of English that leads many native speakers of English to believe that there is no need for them to learn another language.

Both of these linguistic trends lead us to the belief that whatever action one can take – as an educator, as a scholar, and as a citizen – to preserve threatened languages is worth taking. Indeed, actions supporting any language *except* English are worth considering in any contexts in which this is possible. Unfortunately, the very nature of the problem – and especially of the hegemony of English – makes this difficult, as does the fact that many of the target audience for this book would not be able to read it if it were to have been written even in one of the world's other major languages – French, German, Russian, Spanish, or whatever. This is a great frustration to us, but one that we do not have a solution to.

Language Matters

Language, we believe, matters. Knowledge *of* language matters, as does knowledge *about* language. Attitudes and beliefs about language matter, as well. And yet, for the most part people in U.S. society are not only monolingual, but also know very little *about* language and linguistics. While a knowledge of mathematics or history, for instance, would be almost universally accepted as among the characteristics of an "educated person," the same cannot be said to be true for either knowledge *of* a second language or even for knowledge *about* language. As Suzette Haden Elgin has commented,

> It is all too easy to underestimate the power of language … because almost every human being knows and uses one or more languages, we have let that miracle be trivialized … We forget, or are unaware of, the power that language has over our minds and our lives; we use that power ourselves as casually as we use the electric power in our homes, with scarcely a thought given to its potential to help or harm. We make major decisions about language on the most flimsy and trivial – and often entirely mistaken – grounds.
>
> (Elgin, 2000, p. 239)

This is the case not only for the general public, but even for many of those who spend their lives teaching and learning languages. Such ignorance is not simply sad, either; it, too, makes a difference. As Terry A. Osborn has noted:

> if a student has a bad experience in high school biology, s/he may well not like science for the remainder of life … s/he may think that frogs are disgusting, insects appalling, and botanical studies quite boring. S/he may even think that biologists are strange individuals. But it is quite likely that the experience will not translate into some

> sociologically relevant bias. This assurance is much weaker if one has negative experiences in a foreign language class.
>
> (Osborn, 2000, p. 15)

Thus, the world language educator has an incredibly complex and daunting task. Traditionally, we have recognized that it is our job not only to teach students the linguistic basics of the target language, but also to provide them with an introduction to the cultures, literatures, and indeed, the worlds of the speakers of the target language. Our focus over the course of the 19th and 20th centuries has undergone a series of changes, moving first from a purely linguistic emphasis, as would be the case with a grammar-translation approach, to a teaching approach which included the "high culture" of the target language, to more recent efforts to present the many different cultures and literatures associated with the target language. We have also become increasingly concerned, of course, with ensuring that world language classes are more communicative in both nature and objectives. Although it would not be unreasonable for us to suggest that our job as world language educators is quite sufficiently complex already, the fact of the matter is that we *do* need to reconsider the functions and purposes of world language education for our students.

To be sure, world language educators have long pointed to the role of world language study in helping students to understand the grammar of their own language. All too few students come to us with any solid understanding of traditional grammatical terminology, for instance, and it is quite common to hear students and others assert that everything they know about formal English grammar they learned in a world language class. Such knowledge has considerable value, and should not be undervalued, although one might well suggest that students should have learned such things before they enter the world language classroom. However, it is clear that there is much about languages in general that educated persons should know and understand that goes far beyond such basic knowledge, and it is with this larger puzzle that we have been concerned here. In essence, what we have suggested is that the world language classroom is in many ways an ideal place for students to learn about what might be called the *metalinguistics* of human language in general, and of both their native language and the target language in particular.

The Metalinguistic Content of the World Language Classroom

What, then, is this "metalinguistic" content that students should learn? In recent years, a number of educational scholars have begun to articulate this metalinguistic knowledge base, both in terms of what students should learn and with respect to what classroom teachers (both teachers of language and others) need to know (see Andrews, 2001, 2006; Benesch, 2001; Byrnes, Kiger & Manning, 1997; Ovando, 2001; Pennycook, 2001;

Reagan, 1997; van Lier, 1995, 1996). Although a complete outline of such knowledge is neither possible nor appropriate here, it is useful for us to identify in general terms some of the core ideas and concepts that would have to be included in the articulation and implementation of such a metalinguistic knowledge base.

The different elements to be included in such a metalinguistic knowledge base are difficult to identify, in large part because they really include virtually all aspects of linguistics and applied linguistics, as well as elements drawn from anthropology, economics, geography, history, philosophy, political science, psychology, and sociology, among others. The interdisciplinary nature of the metalinguistic knowledge base also means that any attempt to conceptualize its distinctive elements will inevitably overlap in many ways. With this in mind, we believe that a reasonable summation of the metalinguistic knowledge base to which every student should be exposed can be divided into four broad categories: language and linguistics, language and society, language and politics, and language and education. More detailed and specific information is provided below.

- Language and linguistics:
  - the key components shared by all human languages;
  - the unique features of human language;
  - the nature and outcomes of language contact;
  - the nature and processes of language change;
  - the relationship among different languages;
  - the historical development of languages; and
  - the nature and implications of code switching and code mixing.
- Language and society:
  - language and communication;
  - individual bilingualism and multilingualism;
  - social bilingualism and multilingualism;
  - the "monolingual ideology" in U.S. society;
  - the social context of language use;
  - an awareness of the ecology of language(s);
  - the nature and extent of language diversity in different societies;
  - the economics of language;
  - language attitudes, biases and discrimination;
  - linguicism;
  - the nature and implications of linguistic variation; and
  - the relationship between language and culture.
- Language and politics:
  - ideology and language;
  - the relationship between language and power;

- issues of language standardization;
- issues of linguistic purism;
- language rights and language responsibilities;
- the nature and uses of language policy and language planning;
- linguistic imperialism; and
- critical language awareness.

- Language and education:
  - language differences versus language deficits;
  - language acquisition and language learning;
  - the purposes of language education; and
  - different kinds of L2 programs.
  - the development of individual literacy;
  - the emergence of mass or popular literacy;
  - the nature of literacy, and the concept of "multiple literacies"; and
  - the teaching of literature and the literary canon.

It should come as no surprise that we have included many of these topics in *World Language Education as Critical Pedagogy: The Promise of Social Justice.*

Problem Posing

Asking the right questions is among the most important and powerful activities that students can learn. A fundamental component of asking the right questions, of course, is in being able to pose the right questions, as Joan Wink has suggested:

> Problem posing brings interactive participation and critical inquiry into the existing curriculum and expands it to reflect the curriculum of the students' lives. The learning is not just grounded in the prepared syllabus, the established, prescribed curriculum. Problem posing opens the door to ask questions and seek answers, not only of the visible curriculum, but also of the hidden curriculum. Problem posing is very interested in the hidden curriculum, which is why many are uncomfortable with it. Problem posing causes people to ask questions many do not want to hear.
>
> (Wink, 2000, p. 61)

As Paolo Freire has noted,

> Problem-posing education does not and cannot serve the interests of the oppressor. No oppressive order could permit the oppressed to begin to question: Why? While only a revolutionary society can carry out this education in systematic terms, the revolutionary leaders need not take full power before they can employ the method. In the revolutionary process, the leaders cannot utilize the banking method as an

> interim measure, justified on grounds of expediency, with the intention of later behaving in a genuinely revolutionary fashion. They must be revolutionary – that is to say dialogical – from the outset.
>
> (Freire, 2000, p. 198)

Key points of problem posing in education are illuminated in this passage. Problem-posing will not serve the interests of the oppressor, since it constantly strives to answer the question, "Why?" Second, problem posing in world language education can be incrementally implemented. There is no need for current curricula to be rewritten from a problem-posing perspective. World language educators can implement critical curriculum pieces incrementally, beginning at any time. The dialogical or change-oriented focus of the classroom activities becomes a critical pedagogy immediately accessible to practitioners. Problem posing originates as a form of praxis the first day one uses it.

Problem posing in the world language classroom involves constructing units around questions, issues, concerns and puzzles related to language. Such units can and should have specific communicative outcomes in mind, and should of course be tied to the formal curriculum in appropriate ways. They should also, however, help students to begin to examine language, language use, and language attitudes (both their own and others') more critically. For instance, even in an introductory level class, one might explore advertisements, both in the U.S. media and in the foreign media. Among the issues that might be raised in such a unit are:

- How are different languages utilized in such advertisements?
- How are speakers of particular languages represented?
- What are the social, cultural, economic, political, and ideological messages that are conveyed in such advertisements?
- How are these messages consistent with or inconsistent with stereotypes found in different societies?
- What level of fluency would be required to understand world language texts in various advertisements?

It is essential to note that such questions will inevitably involve the incorporation of the skills of reading, writing, listening, and speaking in contextualized and communicative activities as students begin to explore the component parts of how these portrayals are made and what they mean. It is also, of course, significant to note that these same questions are the sort of questions that teachers themselves need to be asking about the entire curriculum that they teach.

Implications for World Language Pedagogy

Moving toward a critical pedagogy in the world language classroom will require fundamental changes not only to curriculum development, but also to the way we conceptualize what curriculum is. Themes of family, health, and weather or other vocabulary and grammatically-driven syllabi will give way to units built around the context in which language education takes place. This process of macrocontextualiztion in the foreign language classroom becomes a genesis for curricula, instruction, and evaluation that are sensitive to the issues of diversity, and optimistic in their regard for social justice.

Curriculum planners desiring to move toward interdisciplinary, thematic units can strengthen educational experiences for students by helping them break down some artificial disciplinary barriers imposed by contemporary educational practice. At the same time, however, reaching across disciplines can be approached from a carefully planned and thoughtful attempt to balance the exigencies of academic rigor and sensitivity to realities of cultural pluralism. The politics of school knowledge will continue to influence curricular decisions, and an awareness of the issues raised in developing cross-cultural understanding will empower developers to move forward in a most effective and ethical manner.

Teacher educators and teachers can begin to develop a critical awareness of instructional issues as well. *How* we present material related to cultural comparisons and academic connections is as important as *what* we choose to present in terms of achieving the goals of equipping students to live in an increasing diverse society. Language classes as part of the core curriculum will indeed be faced with challenges as we broaden our own horizons in addition to those of our students. Interdisciplinary thematic units can serve as a powerful tool for connections and comparisons as we fulfill the agenda set by the newest and most ambitious standards.

It is ironic that world language education appears to have come late to the realm of interdisciplinary unit development, as we noted in Chapter 9, since the world language field, unlike any other, is by its very nature concerned with bridging disciplines. The category "culture," in common use, has included strong components of studies of history, political science, food science, literature, economics, media studies, and so forth. Though collaborations with other disciplinary specialists within the academic setting may seem restricted, since the fluency required to discuss complex topics in the second language often eludes students, in reality the newest standards and mandates provide multiple opportunities for connections and comparisons in the second language classroom. The integration of world language education into the core will be enhanced as practitioners in the field become skilled in the development of integrated, interdisciplinary units including the language classroom in the core.

Praxis and World Language Education

As world language teachers employ critical reflection, curricular nullification, and other forms of activism in their classroom practice, the world language classroom moves from serving as a definer of deviance (that is, as we have seen, "foreignness") to, at least potentially, becoming an agency for both educational and social change. In other words, we begin to develop a *praxis* based on what Henry Giroux has called "critical multiculturalism":

> In opposition to a quaint liberalism, a critical multiculturalism means more than simply acknowledging differences in stereotypes; more fundamentally it means understanding, engaging, and transforming the diverse histories, cultural narratives, representations, and institutions that produce racism and other forms of discrimination … An insurgent multiculturalism takes as its starting point the question of what it means for educators and cultural workers to treat schools and other public institutions in which teachers, students, and others engage in daily acts of cultural translation and negotiation … Within this perspective, pedagogy is removed from its exclusive emphasis on management and is defined as a form of political leadership and ethical address.
>
> (Giroux, 1997, pp. 237–239)

At the core of such critical multiculturalism is the concept of discourse itself. As Peter McLaren and Henry Giroux have asserted in *Revolutionary Multiculturalism*:

> The excess of language alerts us to the ways in which discourse is inextricably tied not just to the proliferation of meanings, but also to the production of individual and social identities over time within conditions of inequality. As a political issue, language operates as a site of struggle among different groups who for various reasons police its borders, meanings, and orderings. Pedagogically, language provides the self-definitions upon which people act, negotiate various subject positions, and undertake a process of naming and renaming the relations between themselves, others, and the world. Educational theory is one of the discursive faces of literacy, pedagogy, and cultural politics. It is within theory and its concern with the prohibitions, exclusions, and policing of language along with its classification, ordering, and dissemination of discourse that knowledge becomes manifest, identities are formed and unformed, collective agents arise, and critical practice is offered the conditions in which to emerge. At the current moment of dominant educational practices, language is being mobilized within a populist authoritarian ideology that ties it to a tidy relation among national identity; culture, and literacy. As the cultural mask of hegemony, language is being mobilized to police the borders of an ideologically discursive divide that separates dominant from subordinate groups, whites from Blacks, and schools from the imperatives of democratic public life.
>
> (McLaren & Giroux, 1997, p. 16)

With this in mind, we would advocate world language classrooms themselves becoming sites where hegemonic ideologies are challenged, and emerge as places where students are liberated from oppressive cognitive, intellectual, and sociological constructs that have thus far been created or reinforced in the world language context. We thus seek to deter the psychological violence inflicted on oppressed segments of our society for which we, ourselves, as world language educators, can be held partially responsible. As Scott has explained:

> Another reaction that commonly occurs when a deviant label is applied is that within the community a feeling arises that "something ought to be done about him." Perhaps the most important fact about this reaction in our society is that almost all of the steps that are taken are directed solely at the deviant. Punishment, rehabilitation, therapy, coercion, and other common mechanisms of social control are things that are done to him, implying that the causes of deviance reside within the person to whom the label has been attached, and that the solutions to the problems that he presents can be achieved by doing something to him. This is a curious fact, particularly when we examine it against the background of social science research on deviance that so clearly points to the crucial role played by ordinary people in determining who is labeled a deviant and how a deviant behaves. This research suggests that none of the corrective measures that are taken can possibly succeed in the intended way unless they are directed at those who confer deviant labels as well as those to whom they are applied.
>
> (Scott, 1972, p. 15)

The critical pedagogy of foreign language education begins to apply those corrective measures to both oppressor and oppressed. The label of "foreign" language does indeed need to go, not in a shell game of political correctness, but as the outcome of a fundamental reordering of the conditions, the guiding principles and practices, and the social outcomes of foreign language education.

Toward a Critical Activism

Critical theories of education, though enlightening, often stop short of providing practical advice for the classroom teacher. The reason for this omission is likely multifaceted. In the first place, scholars often have not taught in the pre-university level for many years, if ever, and the practical considerations elude them – they have, in short, little or nothing to say. Second, critical advances do not always lend themselves well to practical advice, since the generalized assumptions one must make about a teacher's range of curricular and instructional options are unrealistic. And finally, the myriad of variables that enter into teaching make any formulaic assertions about a critical foreign language pedagogy either oversimplified, naive, or impossible. Nevertheless, there is a broad range of emancipatory avenues of educational reform available to practitioners, and such avenues must be the consideration that will become the litmus test of any critical pedagogy's ability to move from the margins to the mainstream in educational settings and dialogue.

How, then, can critical language educators proceed in the classroom? Certainly the curriculum writ large, as well as our objectives, classroom activities, assessment practices, and so on, cannot and should not be randomly and arbitrarily designed and implemented. There is, in short, clearly a need for an instructional plan which seeks to further the aims of what might be termed "emancipatory praxis." Arguing for a "holistic model" which incorporates and celebrates the social and cultural contexts of the schooling process, Joe Kincheloe, Patrick Slattery, and Shirley Steinberg point out that some view curriculum as:

> A process of understanding the self in relation to the world, not simply the concrete information students must memorize or master. Contemporary scholars analogize instruction to a personal journey, with the teacher as travel guide, advisor, author, wise mentor or philosopher more concerned with the growth, maturity, and empowerment of each student that with the information each student regurgitates on standardized tests. In this conception, evaluation becomes an authentic expression of each student's unique understanding and application of learning.
>
> (Kincheloe et al., 2000, p. 300)

Reflecting the process Osborn (2000, 2006) describes as "macro-contextualization," critical curriculum development in the world language classroom must proceed from the context of the world, the self in relation to the world, and the role of language and language education in the shaping of both-independent of and dependent upon the others.

Conclusion

In concluding both this chapter and the book, we believe that it is important to stress that we are *not* suggesting that world language educators cease to teach the target language, nor are we suggesting that such teaching is not merely worthwhile in its own right, but invaluable. We strongly believe that world language education can and should play a central role in every individual's education. What we are suggesting, though, is that as world language educators we need to continue our efforts to move beyond what might be called "technicist" concerns about the teaching of world languages. Debates and discussions about alternative teaching methodologies certainly have value, but we must also address the social, cultural, political and ideological contexts in which we teach, and in which languages are used.

Almost fifty years ago, Robert Bolgar, in addressing the decline in the study of Classics, wrote that:

> Two things emerge forcibly from any serious consideration of what one might call "the Latin problem." The first is that some considerable change in teaching method is inevitable if the subject is to survive. The second is that the majority of the profession – and particularly its older members – are bound to feel opposed to this change, which will demand great sacrifices on their part. We are faced, through no fault of our own, with a situation where our only alternative to hard work and hard thinking is to watch our subject dwindle till it disappears from the curriculum and leaves us stranded. The testing moment has arrived for classical studies. We must prove that they are fortifying, that they strengthen man's power to deal with the problems of life. We must prove their worth or see them perish.
>
> (Quoted in Sharwood Smith, 1977, p. 81)

The future of world language study in the United States is by no means as grim as was the future of Classics when this was written. Happily, Classicists have responded admirably to the changes about which Bolgar was concerned, and the study of the classical languages, and especially of Latin, is once again relatively popular. The challenge before us now is to advocate the study of world languages not only for the reasons that we historically offered, but to expand our efforts to include increasing student understanding and awareness of language, broadly conceived, as an outcome of the study of world languages. Language study, in short, must become a core element in the teaching of critical perspectives for life in a democratic society.

Questions for Reflection and Discussion

1. Explain, in your own words, what "problem posing" entails, and how this concept relates to teaching a foreign language. Can you give examples of student-based problem posing in the foreign language classroom?
2. When Osborn, in his discussion of the effects of high school teaching on students' life outcomes, notes that, in the case of biology, "the experience will not translate into some sociologically relevant bias" but further, that "this assurance is much weaker if one has negative experiences in a foreign language class," what does he mean? What does this point tell you about the significance of world language education as a component of a general education?

3 How can the world language educator assist her or his students in identifying their own unarticulated beliefs about language? Their own linguistic biases?
4 Do classroom world language teachers have a moral or ethical responsibility to the native speakers of the target language? If so, what is that responsibility?
5 What do you think that the authors mean when they refer to "technicist" issues in world language education? How does this concept fit with notions of "critical pedagogy" and "reflective practice" as you understand them?

Notes

1 Although Braj Kachru's "three circle" model has gained widespread acceptance, especially among TESOL and TEFL researchers, there are nevertheless a number of critiques of the model, as well as proposed changes and modifications (see, for example, Bruthiaux, 2003; Park & Wee, 2009; Tripathi, 1998). For our purposes here, however, the basic model is sufficient in its original form.
2 The shift from French to English as the most common language for diplomacy was primarily a 20th century phenomenon (see Brimelow, 1976; Finn, 2003; Northrup, 2013, pp. 110–114). Interestingly, in settings which claim to be bilingual or multilingual, such as both the United Nations and the European Union, English tends to predominate even (perhaps especially) in situations where non-native speakers are present (see Phillipson & Skutnabb-Kangas, 1996).
3 One especially powerful indicator of the power of English in popular culture is its use in advertisements and marketing (see Baumgardner, 2008; Bhatia, 2006; Gerritsen, Nicherson, Van Hooft, Van Meurs, Nedestigt, Starren & Crijns, 2007).
4 The dominance of English in the media is significant both in terms of the role of the English-language media and with respect to the impact of English-language media on the media in other languages (see, for example, Jiao Xue & Wenjing Zuo, 2013; McChesney, 2001).
5 Although there can be little doubt that the dominant language on the Internet is English (see Crystal, 2006; Cumming 1995; Northrup, 2013, pp. 140–141), there have been concerns about the implications of this dominance and efforts to challenge it (see Goggin & McLelland, 2009; Wolk, 2004). Further, although English is the dominant language, at the same time the Internet has, somewhat paradoxically perhaps, been something of a blessing for many smaller languages.
6 The language of academic publication in the sciences is especially strongly biased toward English, although to a lesser extent this is also true in the social sciences and humanities (see Ammon, 2001; Kirkpatrick, 2009; Northrup, 2013, pp. 148–157). This phenomenon has been extensively critiqued both in terms of its epistemological effects and with respect to its inherent unfairness, especially with respect to periphery scholars (see Canagarajah, 1996; Duszak & Lewkowicz, 2008; Lillis & Curry, 2006, 2013).
7 English is the only "official" language approved for use in air traffic control by the International Civil Aviation Organization. Pilots and air traffic controllers must communicate in either English or the local language, and in all cases English must be used if the pilot requests it (see Estival, Farris & Moleswoth, 2016; Wyss-Bühlmann, 2005). This has led to the development of what has been labeled "Air Traffic Control English," a specialized English that is

specifically intended to be used in the context of air traffic control situations. In spite of this requirement, there are nevertheless examples of mis-communication and misunderstandings due to linguistic differences between pilots and air traffic controllers (see, for instance, Jones, 2003; Tiewtrakul & Fletcher, 2010).

References

Ammon, E. (Ed.). (2001). *The dominance of English as a language of science: Effects on other languages and language communities*. Berlin: Mouton de Gruyter.

Andrews, L. (2001). *Linguistics for L2 teachers*. Mahwah, NJ: Lawrence Erlbaum Associates.

Andrews, L. (2006). *Language exploration and awareness: A resource book for teachers* (3rd ed.). Mahwah, NJ: Lawrence Erlbaum Associates.

Applebaum, B. (2000). Wanted: White, anti-racist identities. *Educational Foundations*, 14(4): 5–18.

Applebaum, B. (2017). Comforting discomfort as complicity: White fragility and the pursuit of invulnerability. *Hypatia: A Journal of Feminist Philosophy*, 32(4): 862–875.

Baumgardner, R. (2008). The use of English in advertising in Mexican print media. *Journal of Creative Communications*, 3(1): 23–48.

Benesch, S. (2001). *Critical English for academic purposes: Theory, politics, and practice*. Mahwah, NJ: Lawrence Erlbaum Associates.

Bhatia, T. (2006). World Englishes in global advertising. In B. Kachru, Y. Kachru & C. Nelson (Eds.), *The handbook of world Englishes* (pp. 601–642). Oxford: Blackwell.

Brady, J. & Kanpol, B. (2000). The role of critical multicultural education and feminist critical thought in teacher education: Putting theory into practice. *Educational Foundations*, 14(3): 39–50.

Brimelow, Lord. (1976). English as a language of diplomacy. *The Round Table: The Commonwealth Journal of International Affairs*, 66(261): 27–34.

Bruthiaux, P. (2003). Squaring the circles: Issues in modeling English worldwide. *International Journal of Applied Linguistics*, 13(2): 159–178.

Byrnes, D., Kiger, G. & Manning, M. (1997). Teachers' attitudes about language diversity. *Teaching and Teacher Education*, 13(6): 637–644.

Canagarajah, A. (1996). "Nondiscursive" requirements in academic publishing, material resources of periphery scholars, and the politics of knowledge production. *Written Communication*, 13(4): 435–472.

Crystal, D. (2003). *English as a global language* (2nd ed.). Cambridge: Cambridge University Press.

Crystal, D. (2006). *Language and the Internet* (2nd ed.). Cambridge: Cambridge University Press.

Cumming, J. (1995). The internet and the English language. *English Today*, 11(1): 3–8.

Duszak, A. & Lewkowicz, J. (2008). Publishing academic texts in English: A Polish perspective. *Journal of English for Academic Purposes*, 7(2): 108–120.

Elgin, S. (2000). *The language imperative*. Cambridge, MA: Perseus Books.

Estival, D., Farris, C. & Molesworth, B. (2016). *Aviation English: A lingua franca for pilots and air traffic controllers*. New York: Routledge.

Evans, N. (2010). *Dying words: Endangered languages and what they have to tell us*. Oxford: Wiley-Blackwell.

Finn, H. (2003). The case for cultural diplomacy: Engaging foreign audiences. *Foreign Affairs*, 82(6): 15–20.

Fishman, J. (2001). *Can threatened languages be saved? Reversing language shift, revisited: A 21st century perspective*. Bristol: Multilingual Matters.

Fishman, J. (2006). *Do not leave your language alone*. Mahwah, NJ: Lawrence Erlbaum Associates.

Freire, P. (2000). From *Pedagogy of the oppressed*. In R. Reed & T. Johnson (Eds.), *Philosophical documents in education* (2nd ed.) (pp. 188–198). New York: Longman. (Original work published 1972)

Gerritsen, M., Nicherson, C., Van Hooft, A., Van Meurs, F., Nedestigt, U., Starren & Crijns, R. (2007). English in product advertisements in Belgium, France, Germany, the Netherlands and Spain. *World Englishes*, 26(3): 291–315.

Giroux, H. (1997). *Pedagogy and the politics of hope: Theory, culture and schooling*. Boulder, CO: Westview Press.

Goggin, G. & McLelland, M. (Eds.). (2009). *Internationalizing internet studies: Beyond Anglophone paradigms*. New York: Routledge.

Grenoble, L. & Whaley, L. (Eds.). (1998). *Endangered languages: Current issues and future prospects*. Cambridge: Cambridge University Press.

Hagège, C. (2000). *Halte à la mort des langues*. Paris: Editions Odile Jacob.

Higgins, C. (2003). "Ownership" of English in the outer circle: An alternative to the NS-NNS dichotomy. *TESOL Quarterly*, 37(4): 615–644.

Howard, G. (1996). Whites in multicultural education: Rethinking our role. In J. Banks (Ed.), *Multicultural education, transformative knowledge, and action: Historical and contemporary perspectives* (pp. 323–334). New York: Teachers College Press.

Jiao Xue & Wenjing Zuo. (2013). English dominance and its influence on international communication. *Theory and Practice in Language Studies*, 3(12): 2262–2266.

Jones, M. (Ed.). (2015). *Policy and planning for endangered languages*. Cambridge: Cambridge University Press.

Jones, R. (2003). Miscommunication between pilots and air traffic control. *Language Problems and Language Planning*, 27(3): 233–248.

Kachru, B. (1976). Models of English for the third world: White man's linguistic burden or language pragmatics? *TESOL Quarterly*, 10(2): 221–230.

Kachru, B. (1988). The sacred cows of English. *English Today*, 4(4): 3–8.

Kachru, B. (Ed.). (1992a). *The other tongue: English across cultures* (2nd rev. ed.). Urbana, IL: University of Illinois Press.

Kachru, B. (1992b). World Englishes: Approaches, issues and resources. *Language Teaching*, 25(1): 1–14.

Kincheloe, J., Slattery, P. & Steinberg, S. (2000). *Contextualizing teaching: Introduction to education and educational foundations*. Upper Saddle River, NJ: Prentice Hall.

Kirkpatrick, A. (2009). English as the international language of scholarship: Implications for the dissemination of "local" knowledge. In F. Sharifian (Ed.), *English as an international language: Perspectives and pedagogical issues* (pp. 254–270). Bristol: Multilingual Matters.

Krauss, M. (1992). The world's languages in crisis. *Language*, 68(1): 4–10.

Larson, C. & Ovando, C. (2001). *The color of bureaucracy: The politics of equity in multicultural school communities*. Belmont, CA: Wadsworth.

Lillis, T. & Curry, M. (2006). Professional academic writing by multilingual scholars: Interactions with literacy brokers in the production of English-medium texts. *Written Communication*, 23(1): 3–35.

Lillis, T. & Curry, M. (2013). *Academic writing in a global context: The politics and practices of publishing in English*. New York: Routledge.

Macedo, D. (2000). Introduction. In N. Chomsky, *Chomsky on miseducation* (edited by D. Macedo) (pp. 1–14). Lanham, MD: Rowman & Littlefield.

McChesney, R. (2001). Global media, neoliberalism, and imperialism. *Monthly Review*, 52: 1–19.

McLaren, P. & Giroux, H. (1997). Writing from the margins: Geographies of identity, pedagogy, and power. In P. McLaren (Ed.), *Revolutionary Multiculturalism* (pp. 16–41). Boulder, CO: Westview Press.

McLaren, P. & Muñoz, J. (2000). Contesting whiteness: Critical perspectives on the struggle for social justice. In C. Ovando & P. McLaren (Eds.), *The politics of multiculturalism and bilingual education: Students and teachers caught in the cross fire* (pp. 23–49). Boston: McGraw-Hill.

Nettle, D. & Romaine, S. (2000). *Vanishing voices: The extinction of the world's languages*. Oxford: Oxford University Press.

Northrup, D. (2013). *How English became the global language*. New York: Palgrave Macmillan.

Osborn, T. A. (2000). *Critical reflection and the foreign language classroom*. Westport, CT: Bergin & Garvey.

Osborn, T. A. (2006). *Teaching world languages for social justice: A sourcebook of principles and practices*. Mahwah, NJ: Lawrence Erlbaum Associates.

Ovando, C. (2001). Language diversity and education. In J. Banks & C. Banks (Eds.), *Multicultural education: Issues and perspectives* (pp. 268–291). New York: Wiley.

Park, J. & Wee, L. (2009). The three circles redux: A market-theoretic perspective on world Englishes. *Applied Linguistics*, 30(3): 389–406.

Pennycook, A. (2001). *Critical applied linguistics: A critical introduction*. Mahwah, NJ: Lawrence Erlbaum Associates.

Phillipson, R. & Skutnabb-Kangas, T. (1996). English only worldwide or language ecology? *TESOL Quarterly*, 30(3): 429–452.

Reagan, T. (1997). The case for applied linguistics in teacher education. *Journal of Teacher Education*, 48(3): 185–195.

Scott, R. (1972). A proposed framework for analyzing deviance as a property of social order. In R. Scott & J. Douglas (Eds.), *Theoretical perspectives on deviance* (pp. 9–36). New York: Basic Books.

Sharwood Smith, J. E. (1977). *On teaching Classics*. London: Routledge & Kegan Paul.

Sleeter, C. (1995). Reflections on my use of multicultural and critical pedagogy when students are white. In C. Sleeter & P. McLaren (Eds.), *Multicultural education, critical pedagogy, and the politics of difference* (pp. 415–437). Albany, NY: State University of New York Press.

Sleeter, C. & McLaren, P. (Eds.) (1995). *Multicultural education, critical pedagogy, and the politics of difference*. Albany, NY: State University of New York Press.

Tiewtrakul, T. & Fletcher, S. (2010). The challenge of regional accents for aviation English language proficiency standards: A study of difficulties in understanding air traffic control-pilot communications. *Ergonomics*, 53(2): 229–239.

Tripathi, P. (1998). Redefining Kachru's "outer circle" of English. *English Today*, 14(4): 55–58.

van Lier, L. (1995). *Introducing language awareness*. London: Penguin English.

van Lier, L. (1996). *Interaction in the language curriculum: Awareness, autonomy and authenticity*. London: Longman.

Wink, J. (2000). *Critical pedagogy: Notes from the real world* (2nd ed.). New York: Longman.

Wolk, R. (2004). The effects of English language dominance on the Internet and the digital divide. Presented at the International Symposium on Technology and Society, June 17–19. Downloaded at https://ieeexplore.ieee.org/abstract/document/1314348/authors#authors on January 15, 2020.

Wyss-Bühlmann, E. (2005). *Variation and co-operative communication strategies in Air Traffic Control English*. Bern: Peter Lang.

Index

Page numbers in italics refer to figures. Page numbers in bold refer to tables. Page numbers followed by "n" refer to notes.